behavior analysis

Conference on

behavior analysis *in Education*
Areas of Research
and Application

Edited by

Eugene Ramp • *George Semb*
University of Kansas

PRENTICE-HALL, INC., ENGLEWOOD CLIFFS, NEW JERSEY

Library of Congress Cataloging in Publication Data

CONFERENCE ON BEHAVIORAL ANALYSIS IN EDUCATION, 4th,
    University of Kansas, 1973.
    Behavior   analysis, areas of research and applica-
tion.

    Bibliography: p.
    Includes index.
    1. Educational psychology—Congresses. I. Ramp,
Eugene, ed. II. Semb, George, ed. III. Title.
LB1055.C615 1975   370.15   74-30095
ISBN   0-13-074195-7

© **1975 by Prentice-Hall, Inc., Englewood Cliffs, New Jersey**

Printed in the United States of America

10 9 8 7 6 5 4 3 2 1

PRENTICE-HALL INTERNATIONAL, INC., *London*
PRENTICE-HALL OF AUSTRALIA, PTY. LTD., *Sydney*
PRENTICE-HALL OF CANADA, LTD., *Toronto*
PRENTICE-HALL OF INDIA PRIVATE LIMITED, *New Delhi*
PRENTICE-HALL OF JAPAN, INC., *Tokyo*

Table of Contents

Preface

Applied behavior analysis is a field that is expanding rapidly. It is expanding in terms of both the number of people now acknowledged to be applied behavior analysts, and the number of socially relevant programs that they offer the public. In the midst of such activity, it is difficult to present a comprehensive picture; and it is not the intention of this book to do so. Rather, it is our intention to present a composite picture of the field, very much as a photographer might do in attempting to capture the spirit and direction of a fast-moving event. One method of accomplishing this is to call together a carefully selected group of observers and participants, and ask them to present their current thoughts, programs, and educational research in the field of applied behavior analysis. The twenty-five papers that constitute this volume represent the thinking and the work of such a group.

The individuals who have contributed to this volume were part of a much larger group that met at the University of Kansas for the fourth consecutive year to participate in a conference on *Behavior Analysis in Education*. This conference is convened each year in the hope that it will provide the current research products of applied behavior analysis, and that it will serve participating researchers by providing a medium for the exchange of information describing the "state of the art" and its most immediate challenges. Publication of the conference proceedings is the vehicle by which this important information is made public. The conference was supported by the sale of previous conference proceedings (Ramp and Hopkins, 1971; and Semb, 1972). Similarly, all proceeds from the sale of this volume will be used to help support future conferences on *Behavior Analysis in Education*.

Acknowledgments

For their help in preparing the manuscript, in all of its many phases, the authors wish to thank Yvonne E. Miller and Kay Beehler. Their many suggestions and technical skills have greatly improved the content and the form of this manuscript. For her excellent clerical assistance, the authors also wish to thank Cheri Talley.

The authors express their gratitude to the members of the editorial review board for the *Fourth Annual Conference on Behavior Analysis in Education* for their help in selecting the twenty-five papers that appear in this volume from more than one hundred papers that were received. They are: David Born, Karen Busby, Don Bushell, Jr., Don Dorsey, Gil Hoffman, Bill Hopkins, Daniel Hursh, Brian Jacobson, Mike Kelly, Kathryn A. Kirigin, Doris Kolb, Judith LeBlanc, Tom Lovitt, Karen B. Maloney, Keith Miller, Bonnie Minkin, Neil Minkin, Elsie Pinkston, Todd Risley, Rich Saudargas, Jean Schumaker, John Scott, Susan Semb, Jim Sherman, Don Thomas, Lynn Weis, Jan Sheldon-Wildgen, and Montrose Wolf.

Finally, the authors thank Don Bushell, Jr. and the entire staff of his Behavior Analysis Program for making the *Fourth Annual Conference* possible; and also everyone who attended, for the very rewarding comments, suggestions, and discussions that took place.

part 1 / Questions,
Challenges,
and Thoughts

1 / Living Among the ABAS*— Retrospect and Prospect

Frances Degen Horowitz

Last year, Bill Hopkins, playing upon the identification of behavior analysts at Kansas as the Kansas Mafia, introduced me to this conference as the Godmother of the Kansas Mafia. I was so shocked at that introduction (for I had never really thought of myself in quite that light) that I could not comment upon it—either with wit or wisdom. But now, I think I should report to you. If Baer, Wolf, Risley, Sherman, Etzel, Hall, Hopkins, Miller, Green, LeBlanc, Semb, and Bushell constitute a Mafia-like group, I can tell you straightaway they are really quite a nice branch of the Mafia. For major underworld figures, they are really not a bad lot. As evidence, the invitation they extended me to speak to you today should suffice. For I have been, in one sense, a friend in court, but not a member of the inner circle. And as this friend in court, like the foreign anthropologist observing the comings and going of the society in which he or she is a guest, I have made a number of observations—which is easy enough to do,

* An expanding modern tribe.

especially if you don't have to worry about reliability. Thus, the title of this talk—"Living Among the Abas." As you might have guessed, "Abas" stands for Applied Behavior Analysts. The Abas can be conveniently described as an expanding modern tribe, born of and in the twentieth century, clothed by a jargon of their own, sheltered in the huts and houses of the American universities and other, fast-developing housing systems, held together by an *esprit de corps* characteristic of all evangelical movements, and fed and watered by a system of reinforcement that includes tokens, edibles, imbibables, and socials. It is a society whose economy is impregnable; inflation, devaluation, and recession are almost unknown; it is a society where a dedication to the values of honest and public reporting make intrigue, wire tapping, and pay-offs unnecessary; and it is a society that, by and large, generates helping behavior, concern for others, and abiding faith. It is not undeserving of a *Walden Two* medal. Lest, however, you reject such an uncritical and glowing account, let me assure you that the Abas are not without their stresses and strains, their periods of unhappiness, their episodes of annoyance, anger, or peevishness. But in terms of comparative, cultural anthropology, it must be said that, on balance, the Abas (at least the Kansas variety) have built a remarkably successful social order in a manner not unlike the early days of psychoanalysis, or the Gestalt movement, or the Iowa settlement of the Spence-Hullians. Whether they too will cull the land riding high upon its produce, only to deplete the tillable soil, remains an empirical question, for the historians to finally decide.

Analogies aside, however, I would like to share some of my serious observations with you who represent an important vanguard in the American scene. My assignment from the designers of this conference was to reflect upon the future in terms of what the field of applied behavior analysis ought to be doing in the next ten years, the issues to which it should address itself, and the projects it ought to generate. This is an extremely difficult task, for purveyors of futurism are easily vacuous and more often wrong. The hedge is, of course, that I was not asked to predict but to prescript—to say what ought to be. The danger in prescribing is presumption. How can I presume to tell you what ought to be? My only chance of evading such a position is to establish my own credentials in the hope that they will be ticket enough to your serious attention. And this is what I propose to do: first, to reflect upon some of the objections to applied behavior analysis, which from my point of view are invalid issues but which must be considered and answered; and second, to reflect upon what I consider some valid issues that must also be considered and answered, especially if the field is to progress.

Applied behavior analysis grew out of its parent—basic research in respondent and operant behavior. It bears some major resemblances to its progenitor, both in looks and spirit, and has inherited some of its major liabilities. These liabilities are more so for the child than the parent, because by its very nature of application applied behavior analysis cannot remain isolated from its problems; it cannot long survive the criticisms of its often uninformed but nevertheless powerful critics. Applied behavior analysis has made the necessary leap from the basic to the applied area that has eventually characterized every maturing science. But it is in that leap that the academic prejudice against "Skinnerianism" has become nonacademic. The prejudice involves a variety of rationales, depending upon the source or the issue of the moment. Partly because I am not, myself, an applied behavior analyst in the formal sense—though, I believe, ultimately we are all of such a breed—I sometimes find myself in other in-groups, present at discussions about those operant people, those nasty behaviorists, and similar pejoratives. After an appropriate interval, it is possible to quietly proclaim, "but you know, some of my best friends are Skinnerians," and to offer what defense I can in their and your, and basically my, behalf. Some of you might protest that extinction would be the best procedure to use in such a case; that argument, in the form of attention is a reinforcer for such comments. But, taking the long-term, developmentalist point of view: there are two reasons for participating in a "some-of-my-best-friends-are" discussion. The first is educational. I think there are some convincing points to be made in such discussions, and one should never shrink from opportunities to educate one's peers. The second is also educational, but the other way around. In arguments and discussions about applied behavior analysis, there are elements of real concern, fear, and valid criticism from which one can learn how to address some of these issues, and from which one can learn wherein lie some true questions and challenges that must be faced with honesty and objectivity. In that confrontation, I believe, lies the outline of the future "oughts" to which I was asked to address myself; in the successful resolution of some of the issues lie some of the significant advances for the field. Let me deal with these two aspects separately—those that involve matters for which there are valid replies, and those that involve matters that must be considered seriously if progress is to be made.

SOME ISSUES FOR WHICH VALID REPLIES ARE NOW AVAILABLE

There are at least four criticisms, comments, complaints, or cavils—depending upon your point of view—that appear and reappear in the liturgy of social seers. They involve the notions of mechanism, control, capitalism, and reinforcement—nee bribery. Interestingly, these issues have been leveled at behaviorism and behaviorists since the days of John B. Watson. But they have now become part of the popular culture, partly because of the success of applied behavior analysis. Thus, while neither the arguments nor their answers are new, they bear reiteration.

First, on the issue of mechanism, it is said that in aping the physical sciences, behaviorists see the human organism as a mechanistic unit—a *tabula rasa* in the beginning—to be writ upon with total impunity by any society or social system. Such a caricature of behaviorism claims that this mechanism ignores the dynamism of the human being, its creativity, its capacity for self-direction. How can you understand and appreciate human behavior if you ignore its complexity, its dynamic qualities, and the precious aspects of life, freedom, and individualism. This is a strange argument, for on the one hand it calls for "appreciation" that, though perhaps a by-product of science, is not science itself; and on the other hand it implies that the science is on the wrong track because there is something special about the human organism that calls for a special scientific approach. The response, it seems to me, is to challenge some of the basic assumptions that both the behaviorist and his critic must be employing in their every-day behavior. One of these assumptions is that people do not behave, from moment to moment, in a capricious manner. They behave with regularity and predictability. Teachers, parents, employers, the man or woman in the street, even psychologists, assume and act on such predictability—that behavior does not occur by chance in an unorganized fashion. When we talk about people behaving, we are talking about an ordered set of events about which there must be controlled and related elements. In fact, when children behave in a way that is funny or humorous to adults, that behavior often involves interesting violations of the expected, counted-upon patterns in the occurrence of behavior. People whose behavior is widely erratic are called sick. When one juxtaposes the complaining about mechanism against the assumptions that even the critic must make about human behavior, then the critic must be in the position of either denying that we all act as if behavior were lawful, or he must claim that there are special elements in behavior that are somehow different from unlawful elements. It is, of course, possible that at some levels of complex behavior, the laws that apply uniformly to other levels of behavior break down. But that is an empirical question that remains to be investigated. It seems to me that the valid answer to this position is that of an empiricist: True, at some levels the laws we are describing or discovering may not apply. There may be different or more encompassing laws—or, it is possible that chance and capriciousness obtain. But, at the present time we are concerned with understanding the laws and applying them to behavioral domains. And such applications are succeeding. When this success begins to break down, then maybe we will be at the juncture of complexity or capriciousness.

This line of discussion usually raises the second issue: control. "Control" is the element at which most of the criticism of *Beyond Freedom and Dignity* was directed, either because the readers saw the implications so clearly, or felt that Skinner ignored the implications by not discussing them. If behavior is lawful, then anyone utilizing the laws can control behavior and being controlled is supposedly inimical to free men. Therefore, if we are free, we cannot be controlled. I do not presume to explicate the issue that is so well discussed by Skinner, but it is important to answer the issue whenever it arises, not by suggesting that Skinner has provided a lengthy but reasonable response—because more often than not, the individual has read Skinner and has become fearful rather than persuaded —but by restating the obvious. It is not a question of if we discover the laws of behavior, *then* behavior will be controlled. If behavior is lawful, then, by definition, it is controlled, because law implies regularity, predictability, and orderliness. All behavior that operates within a lawful system is under control. It is not that we discover the law and then suddenly behavior is controlled or becomes controllable.

The issue is a semantic one, in part, but it is also more than that, for it must be resolved not by dismissing the objector as illogical or naive, but by persuading the individual that he or she must basically hold the same point of view as the behaviorist, and that since he or she is really a nice person such a point of view is not equivalent to being Machiavellian or an ogre. Behavior is a lawful phenomenon; it is controlled, but control is not necessarily bad just as lawful interactions are not necessarily bad. If one can proceed that far, then one can discuss what I believe is the real issue: that control is equated with exploitation. Because power is not evenly and mutually distributed within most societies, most people have come to see the concept of control in terms of one person or one group exploiting another. In the idealized sense, democracy is an attempt to distribute control so as to result in mutually beneficial outcomes that are as widespread as possible. Thus, one can suggest that it is not a matter of freedom versus control that must be discussed, but rather the relative distribution of control within and among peoples. And this raises the issue of the values held by a society that will determine the degree to which control mechanisms are concentrated or spread within a society—not whether they are present or absent—for by agreeing that behavior is not capricious, one must also agree that behavior is controlled, and the question becomes one of the conditions under which control operates.

There is, however, a valid concern in this semantic issue. If one fully understands how the laws of behavior operate, then it becomes possible for groups or individuals to systematically use such knowledge to gain and use power. Of course, looking at the history of humankind—both past and present—it is obvious that this is not a question about the future. Could we have a bloodier set of events than we in our own lifetimes have witnessed —in our relative state of ignorance about behavioral laws—if we were more knowledgeable? People who object to behaviorism because of the control that will become possible ignore the enormous amount of concentration of control in powerful groups that already exists. Assuming, however, that a full explication of behavioral laws would allow for very systematic control of behavior and development, one has two alternatives. The first is that we stop where we are now and refuse to discover any more about behavioral laws. This will leave us in our relative state of ignorance and knowledge. We opt for knowing no more than we know now in the fear that greater knowledge will lead to more evil uses of power than we have already known. The second alternative is that we continue our investigations, going to the fullest length possible to acquire knowledge. But, the utilization of full knowledge will depend upon the degree to which scientists and other citizens choose to apply the knowledge for good or evil purposes. The issue has become real rather than academic because people like you are showing that a technology can be applied and that results can be achieved. It is because of your success that the issue has become more pressing. We cannot afford to ignore the issue of control, but the valid and not the invalid aspects must be constantly analyzed not only for the sake of the critics but for the practitioners as well.

In the application of a behavioral technology—in the simple form in which it can now be applied—a third, more prosaic issue arises: capitalism. Only recently, I heard a major speaker at a national conference question the wisdom of using operant techniques in a classroom because, she said, token economies teach the child to buy and sell. To buy and sell is to teach the child to bargain and to make learning a capitalistic enterprise. Learning should be free, fun, and self-fulfilling. You should not have to bribe children to learn. In doing so, you put learning on a par with the commercial market place—and after all, life is not filled with immediate tokens and school should prepare one for life. It is hard, on hearing this line of reasoning, not to dismiss it as muddled thinking, but it is important to answer it seriously because it is a common and insidious line of reasoning. There are really several issues involved in it. The first is one of social responsibility. If children can learn in a classroom using operant procedures, then if one is to criticize operant technology on philosophical grounds and advocate its discontinuance, one ought to be prepared to offer in its place an equally or more effective set of procedures with evidence for the effectiveness of those procedures. Otherwise, one is saying, "Here is something that works, but I don't like it for philosophical reasons, so stop doing it—I don't have anything to substitute for it right now, but when I do I am sure it will be better and will not be philosophically objectionable." This is a socially irresponsible position, and it is ironic that only those people who have enjoyed the greatest benefits of an adequate education have the luxury of opposing educational techniques on theoretical grounds. But it is also true that people who see only token economies as the expression of the operant technology often have a very simplistic understanding of what is involved. Token economies are only one alternative among numerous procedures; the use of other subtler procedures is often more acceptable. But the major point is that whether one uses tokens or socials, one utilizes basically the same set of principles; it is the understanding and application of the principles that is significant. To object to operant procedures because they represent commercialism in the classroom is to simultaneously attribute a much more pervasive influence of a simple token system on one's larger economic philosophy and to display a lack of understanding about successful teaching. For as Don Bushell, Don Baer, and others consistently point out, good teachers have for eons applied and used the principles of behavior analysis. Good teaching, when practiced in its most artful and subtle form, is just as behavioristic as when practiced within the explicitness of a token economy or a point system.

The fourth and final objection often underlies the obvious discomfort of anti-Skinnerians and that is the objection to the notion of reinforcement itself. It is like one's shadow—something there is that doesn't love the bald description of human relations in terms of reinforcers. It strikes our more poetic and romantic colleagues as crude; it annoys our scientific and analytic peers as an oversimplification. The latter objection is quite valid. Reinforcement is only one of many variables in the behavioral domain— albeit a powerful one—and we will return to this issue shortly. The objection to reinforcement is one that reveals a common inclination to avoid analysis of human behavior: somehow, people think that if you analyze it you lose something. Somehow, to say that you laugh at my jokes and I smile at you and we are friends is more acceptable than to describe a relationship between two people as one that involves mutual reinforcement. Friendship is nice but mutual reinforcement is not. Only education and persistence will change this issue from one of objection to one of understanding. It is an important task. Uninformed, uneducated, and influential critics can stop programs, can influence lives, and can remove children from opportunities to learn. If the critics have reasonable and effective substitutions to offer, then the consumers of education—the parents—will have a choice among different kinds of programs, each with demonstrable benefit to their children. But if this is not the case, then it becomes the responsibility of those who can successfully educate children by utilizing behavior analysis techniques to take the time and make the effort that is necessary to discuss, argue, clarify, and convince—to make it clear that the issues of mechanism, control, capitalism, and reinforcement are not in their single or collective selves valid arguments against behaviorism or applied behavior analysis.

SOME VALID ISSUES

The argumentative positions of behaviorism and applied behavior analysis are now, however, invincible. But there are, I believe, legitimate concerns, the resolution of which may determine whether the field progresses or whether it becomes stuck at its present level of development. These issues can determine the oughts of future directions. However, there is a very fragile distinction that must be drawn by anyone who advocates where the field ought to go. In saying what must happen if the field is to progress, one must not simultaneously imply that the things now being done successfully should somehow be abandoned in the interest of progress. I and the others who have been asked to address themselves to the future will be making a variety of suggestions, some of which, if followed, will involve different lines of inquiry and eventually a change in the application of technology. But, it is important that the application of the current technology be continued at its present level until the technology can be improved. There is a danger in prophesiers saying, "Okay, you've demonstrated that token economies work, that reinforcement works, that social approval can be used—now what?" And by implication, so what? In labeling the successful application of the early stages of a technology as old hat, one endangers that successful application because it occurs within a supportive milieu, whose continued existence may be necessary for the technology. I suspect that built into the technology there are now important but unexplored components of the user reinforcement and maintenance system that can be abandoned in the quest for progress, but with their abandonment will come a lessening of the effective technology. The system of conferences, journals, publications, and status elements that behavior analysis teachers and researchers confer upon one another are probably important maintenance devices that can be disturbed and demolished by people denigrating the demonstration and redemonstration of the same principles over and over again. The first point I wish to make, therefore, is that prescriptions for progress that ignore the maintenance of the system that is now successful will ultimately mean regression. With this large qualification for the comments that follow, let us proceed to the issues I would like to discuss. The first concerns the relationship between applied work and basic research, and the second concerns the conceptualization of development.

Isolation may be functional for new ideas and new groups. You can avoid the punishment often accorded new ideas or fledgling attempts; in the privacy of the in-group you can be more effective critics of yourselves than others can. But there is a point at which the facilitating effects diminish and continued isolation becomes nonfunctional. Applied behavior analysis has solved some of the simpler problems of an applied technology and has made good use of the available basic knowledge. But basic knowledge is being greatly expanded, and applied behavior analysis is in danger of not having sufficient interchange with the basic research that has either occurred recently or is ongoing. If new information is not incorporated into the technology, then that technology may not become more sophisticated and it may not be applied in more specific and hopefully more effective ways.

A fully developed system of technology requires the combination of a basic understanding of the principles of the phenomenon with the principles of technology and with the development of delivery systems. Applied behavior analysis incorporates some of the principles of technology and is entering more and more into the field of the development of good delivery systems. But its application of technology will continue to be primarily to remedial problems or to relatively gross behaviors, unless it develops systems of keeping abreast of the basic research. A good case in point is the area of language development. There have been some excellent demonstrations in the use of reinforcement techniques combined with imitation training to show that the acquisition of language can be fostered in children who have not acquired language in the normal course of developmental experience. But the attempts to show that language acquisition, in fact, normally occurs within the same paradigm have been less successful, and the half-success, half-failure situation has led to an unbelievably fruitless controversy about the innate versus acquired aspects of language development. In the meantime, researchers have begun to show that the infant—whose production of speech has somewhat defied experimental analysis—may in fact be showing an orderly response to the language he or she hears—that for nine to twelve months the center of activity lies not in producing speech but in listening to language and developing a discriminative repertoire of receptive language skills. The grosser variables of contingencies and certain aspects of caretaker reinforcement may be less powerful during this period than some other variables in the acquisition of the discrimination of language from the receptive side. This is very exciting to infant researchers and may seem somewhat esoteric to applied behavior analysts. Yet, there is a closer nexus than might immediately seem apparent. If, in fact, natural language acquisition occurs in a series of related stages that involves, to some extent, a period of listening and discriminating experience with the sounds and organization of the language that the child is expected to acquire without any necessary contingent reinforcement for language production, then two possible situations obtain. If one were interested in preventing or insuring normal language development for young infants, and if one had control over the design of the infant's environment—such as in day-care or foster-care settings—then in the application of a technology to such environments one would want to attend to the elements that provide for sufficient receptive language development. This is a preventive or design aspect of applying technology to the normal environments of normal children. The second possible implication of this basic research work is that there may be a more efficient set of remediation procedures than are now employed, if one could determine whether or not language-deficient children are also deficient in receptive language in addition to their obvious deficiency in productive language. An assessment of receptive language in language-deficient children might need to attend to relatively subtle dimensions of receptive language, such as grammatical distinctions, because many language-deficient children can obviously respond to gross commands and "seem to understand." Yet, as the complexity and possible developmental sequences in receptive-language development are mapped, the assessment of receptive-language abilities will probably require a much less gross analysis than simple general signs of understanding. And receptive-language training might involve both the utilization of developmental sequences as well as some simultaneous productive expressive-language training. There is a possible gain to the whole enterprise of language remediation technology by keeping in close contact with basic research on receptive-language development.

There are numerous other examples, the catalogue of which I will not bore you. The point is that the application of behavior analysis and the development of a technology for shaping behavior and educating children may proceed faster and be more successful by increased contact with the relevant basic research on behavior development. Admittedly, there is much occurring in basic research that will likely lead to dead ends. Not everything that calls itself basic research is really expanding our knowledge base. Selectivity and acumen are necessary components in any attempt to attend more systematically to the ongoing basic research. But a point that Skinner (1972) has recently made regarding the need to reinforce good basic research is relevant. When I was a graduate student, we all accepted the sop that any and all basic research would ultimately contribute to improving this world. Today, fewer and fewer students are willing to buy that line. In the very valid rush toward relevancy, the status of basic research has suffered, and good students and some good researchers are steered toward applied work when both their talents and natural inclinations would more significantly contribute to the basic research field. In the long run, a reduction in good basic research will be detrimental to the applied field because the additional understanding that is needed in order to make the technology better will not be there.

As someone who is interested and involved in basic research, I also have a somewhat selfish reason for advocating closer ties between applied and basic work. Just as the applied field needs basic research, so the basic research needs the contact with applied problems. Basic research can easily become sterile and trivial; also, the reinforcement schedule in pay-offs can be very lean. The people working in the applied areas can help vitalize relevant basic research, and thus invest it with the excitement of the applied work in a very meaningful way. There is a symbiotic relationship to be built between the two kinds of enterprises that will enable students in centers that successfully develop such models to understand and use both approaches. There is more trial-and-error work in applied research than is necessary; there is more meandering in basic research than is necessary. The two in partnership could be mutually enhancing.

A second direction of applied behavior analysis that might prove fruitful is somewhat harder to communicate briefly, but I will try. It involves a fuller consideration of the developing human organism as a species with potential species-specific characteristics—the recognition of what may solve some problems in the development of good technologies. Probably the best way to speak of this is with respect to the issues in developmental psychology that the behaviorists have either ignored or regarded with suspicion. One such issue is the question of whether or not there are stages in development. Both Piaget and Freud based their entire developmental theories upon the existence of stages in development. What difference would it make to the behavior analyst if there were stages? A favorite problem that I pose to classes in Theories of Child Development is: Defend the proposition that the stimulus-response approach to response acquisition is compatible with the existence of stages as posited by Piaget in his accounting of the development of the child. In one sense, Piaget proposes a program of development and maintains basically that acquisition occurs under only one program. This is, of course, an empirical question, but it is possible that the efforts to develop good programmed materials might well be improved by taking into consideration the sequences of information processing that Piagetians have described; or it is possible that, as John Wright once suggested to me, by tracking developmental progressions as Piaget does, one could develop maximally effective programs. To state this as a possible experiment: Would you have better control over error rate in a program designed in accordance with Piagetian behavior sequences, compared to programs developed through experimenter and teacher trial-and-error methods? As to the question of errors themselves, a possible derivation from the Piagetian conception of the developmental process is that errors are maximally effective sources of information for children at certain points in development. Thus, as particular points in development, might relatively high error rates in fact produce better acquisition and retention, for brief periods of time, than major efforts to keep error rates low all the time? Research on children's cognitive development may well reveal some basic sequences in information processing strategies that could be potentially useful in the development of maximally effective sets of programmed materials.

Behavior analysts are notorious for ignoring the nature of the organism with which they are working. I have found that the hardest point to make in those "some-of-my-best-friends-are" discussions involves convincing people that Skinnerians are not simple-minded in regard to development; that there is no inherent reason why their system cannot eventually account for very complex and creative human behavior. But partly because of the resistance of behavior modifiers to speculate without data, and partly because of their tendency to avoid integrating their data with data gathered by non-behavior modifiers, the approach itself is dismissed as simplistic. This is obviously an unfair judgment. But with a little more care in qualification, a willingness to acknowledge the existence of the data of non–behavior modifiers, a greater recognition of the complexity of variables that are influencing human behavior, and with stated acknowledgements of possible biological parameters and the existence of developmental sequences, it will become more difficult to caricature the behaviorist —and with that, more communication to the benefit of the non-operant person as well as the applied behavior analyst. There is often too little recognition that in basic research on behavioral development, a lexicon of variables has been identified that appear to influence behavior. It remains to be seen which of these can be successfully and systematically employed in the development of an effective technology for affecting the development of children.

Sometimes I have the feeling that individuals approach applied behavior analyses either newborn or disillusioned. Both conditions predispose them to rapid and enthusiastic initiation into the society of Abas. As one who has enjoyed that society, learned from it, and grown in its company, I could hardly discourage new initiates. But, like all successful societies, extinction is always a possibility if there is not sufficient growth, adaptation, and change as the conditions warrant. Success is, of course, a major source of sustenance, but success can become stale and uninteresting if it is merely repetitive.

In sum, the practitioners of Applied Behavior Analysis can adequately deal with the typical objections to its enterprise. They are the same basic objections that have plagued behaviorism from its early days. For the most part they are straw men and relatively easy to answer—though an-

swered they need be. But there are other objections that will question
the ultimate expansion of applied behaviorism if that field does not develop
sufficient mechanisms to maintain contact with the expanding data base,
especially in the area of child development, or if it fails to recognize and
utilize information from new basic research findings, in the development
of more effective and elegant technologies.

It will be interesting to see if the conglomerate of new directions
suggested at this conference will, in aggregate, in fact identify the future
activity of the field and if, eventually, the progress prophesied will mate-
rialize. Should the Aba society become extinct, it would be a loss. In
what is sometimes a cheerless world, Abas have fun, are self-confident,
and are refreshingly dedicated. If a better social order results, we shall all
be its beneficiaries—and, thus, we cannot but afford to encourage the
gadflies and at the same time wish the enterprises of the Abas society all
possible success.

2 / In the Beginning, There Was the Response

Donald M. Baer

In the beginning, there was the response. And the behaviorist looked at the response and saw that it was good. At least it was real, and the behaviorist was weary of creativity. There had passed considerably more than six days, during which numerous psychologists had invented even more numerous souls, minds, instincts, feelings, drives, and mediating mechanisms, all to explain the response. But the behaviorist, who had started with the response because it was clearly there, began to explain the response with what was also clearly there, which was the external environment. And indeed, the response proved responsive to the external environment, indicating that the word was good, too. Therefore, another word was made to name those parts of the clearly-there external environment to which the response was responsive; and the new word was called stimulus. And together the two words were functional, and begat many new words, such that the land was filled with them. In the first generation were the reinforcers, positive and negative; and their children were called schedules. But the schedules were so numerous, and constantly coming and going, that *their* children were required to point out to onlookers which schedule was present at any given place or time; and so these children were called the discriminative stimuli. But then it occurred to the behaviorist that the schedules might be ordered into their times and places, by plan rather than by happenstance, and that their children, the discriminative stimuli, also might be ordered into the same plan, or forbidden from it, simply to see what the effects of doing so might be. The effects were wondrous: they existed; they were clear, powerful, and repetitive; and they hinted of eventual usefulness. But the effects were also mischievous: sometimes, they appeared only once, and then were never seen again. And at other times, they appeared not because of the schedules and discriminative stimuli that the behaviorist had noticed in the plan, but because of other schedules and discriminative stimuli that had come along with the first ones, probably to play, and had not been noticed. Playmates being what they are, these effects sometimes appeared in the same plan again, and sometimes did not. The behaviorist was often puzzled as to what conclusion might be drawn. But another generation was produced; its children were called the experimental designs, and they were the generation that made the rules according to which the schedules and the discriminative stimuli were ordered into plans to see what the effects of doing so might be. After the experimental designs came, the effects were still wondrous, but much less mischievous than they had been before; now they were said to have reliability. Therefore, the behaviorist was very pleased, and in explaining the response, began to respond according to one of the effects apparent in many of the plans: the behaviorist again and again did that which produced nonmischievous effects. It was clear that for the behaviorist, nonmischievous effects were positive reinforcers, and it was clear that the behaviorist, in explaining the response, had become a part of it. Indeed, it then seemed undoubtable that the behaviorist had always been a part of the response, even before beginning to explain it, and it was marveled that all this had come to pass despite the freedom and dignity with which the behaviorist had previously been afflicted.

The experimental designs were very fruitful; the effects produced after their generation were numerous. However, the effects were also extremely diverse. Some of them were weak, fragile children, healthy only when at play in university laboratories. Others could survive anywhere, but required a communal style of life; their clear existence became apparent only when they were amassed into large groups so that their average could be extracted from them. However, some of the effects produced after the generation of the experimental designs were strong and robust, singly or in groups. They could visit anyone, anywhere, even repeatedly, yet they always remained the same despite their travels and their repetitions.

These few effects were called the systematic replications, and they were said to have generality as well as reliability.

In the beginning, there was the response, and then there was the behaviorist; sometime after that, there was the federal funding agency. The federal funding agency, at first, was less interested in explaining the response than in proliferating those examples of it that were good. But, as there was widespread agreement that this could not be done until the response was explained, the federal funding agency temporarily devoted itself to the explanation of the response. In that the behaviorist had part of the explanation already in hand, the federal funding agency looked with favor upon the behaviorist. In that the federal funding agency was intelligent, bountiful, tolerant, and undemanding of any permanent, monogamous relationship, the behaviorist looked with favor upon the federal funding agency, and they were functional together. But they begat (to the surprise of the federal funding agency and the satisfaction of the behaviorist), not a proliferation of good responses, but rather a new generation of behaviorists. Of the new behaviorists, there were some whose most notable characteristic was their extreme approval of the systematic replication—the strong effect that was everywhere and always the same, no matter how often it was repeated. These new behaviorists were so reinforced by the systematic replications that they pursued them exclusively, using only those experimental designs that would selectively detect systematic replications robustly producing their maximal effects alone, repeatedly, anywhere. This selective concentration upon those designs led to the evolution of a new generation of designs, maximally suited for the purpose. In the hands of their advocates, these were called the experimental analyses, and we, their practitioners, became known as the behavior analysts. We behavior analysts were quantifiers, but we were also prone to integrate our quantifications into pictures of the response that nodded obediently to its controlling environment; these pictures were called graphs. The graphs often took the form shown in Figure 1-1; we relied upon them so thoroughly that they became not only our evidence but also our symbol; and, as symbols will, they took on a near-religious significance. Indeed, there was some belief that in this sign we would conquer.[1] Nevertheless, the graph also made it clear that an experimental analysis of the response had indeed been accomplished. For the baseline showed that the response could be measured, that it was stable over time, and that it might well be different than it was. The first experimental period, during which it was usual to see some schedule of positive or negative reinforcers applied to the response, perhaps with discriminative stimuli, demonstrated that the

---

[1] Exactly what would be conquered was left vague, perhaps because no one knew, perhaps so as not to alarm the beneficiary prematurely.

response not only might well be different than it was during baseline, but that indeed, it could be *made* different—promptly, markedly different—by the environmental manipulation used by the behavior analyst. The next periods were simply repetitions: a return to the conditions of baseline, followed by a resumption of the experimental techniques, during which the response likewise repeated its preceding cycles. Thus the response was analyzed: it had been shown that its occurrence could be a tight, simple function of the experimental techniques; the function was clear, it was extensive in its effects on the response, and it continued to be true upon repetition. Because the technique was turned on and off, it was called a reversal design. As explanations go, the one offered by the reversal design was not at all a bad one. In answer to the question, "How does this response work?" we could point out demonstrably that it worked like so (see Figure 1-1): Of course, it might also work in other ways; but, we would wait until we had seen the appropriate graphs before agreeing to any other way. And we would look at those graphs (if any ever came) to

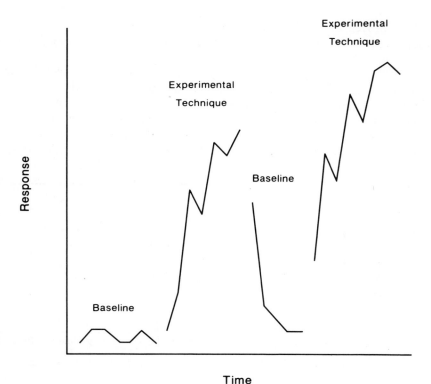

Figure 1-1

see if the response worked as thoroughly, as promptly, and as generally in any other way as it did in our way. Meanwhile, we would see if the response would work our way again, with some other subject, in some other setting, on some other day—to make sure that our way had as much generality as we thought it had (as it usually had). And we would try our way on any other response that came along, for the same reasons. Thereby, our research became somewhat repetitive, and critics often complained that our journals made dull reading. They were the same critics who earlier had denied that any responses of importance or interest actually worked through mere environmental contingencies. Later, apparently, they had conceded the point so thoroughly that they were not interested in examining the generality—or lack of it—with which environmental contingencies would control those interesting, important responses. Yet, generality was the most critical issue in that earlier dispute. No one doubted that the bar-pressings of rats and the key-peckings of pigeons could be controlled through such contingencies within the extremely specialized confines of the Skinner box. The issue was whether that constituted a model for all the responses of any organism in any setting. Fortunately, behavior analysts proved to be more concerned about generality than have the critics, and their journals still display primarily systematic replications, even unto the sign (Figure 1-1).

But, as overly relied upon symbols will, the sign attracted intense attention as a form, and fundamental questions were raised: must the systematic replication always show the sign? Reformation has occurred and been weathered, and now there is a second sign, one in which the baseline has become so multiple in its presence that it is never returned to, as shown in Figures 1-2, 1-3, and 1-4. In these systematic replications, the

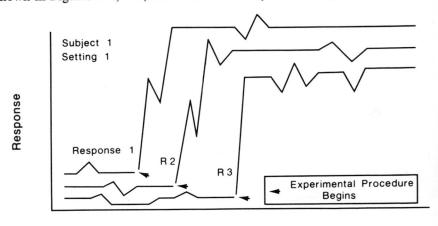

Figure 1-2

response may become many different responses of a given subject in a given setting, and the experimental contingencies are applied to each of these responses, but at different points in time, as shown in Figure 1-2. Alternatively, the response remains one, as does the subject, but the subject responds in many settings, and the experimental contingencies are applied to the response in each setting but at different points in time, as seen in Figure 1-3. Or, in yet another option, the response remains one and the setting remains one, but different subjects provide baselines of the response in that setting, and each subject undergoes the same experimental contingencies but at different points in time, as shown in Figure 1-4. That the multiple baseline lends itself to a trinity of variations will no doubt prove significant in itself, some day. What is already clear is that the multiple baseline is a variant of systematic replication, in that it displays powerful effects operating alone. Whether or not the effect is to be seen *repeatedly* is lost, in one way or another, across the trinity of forms. In the first case, different responses are emitted by a given subject in a given setting, and the same technique is applied sequentially to each of these responses (see Figure 1-2). No response is altered more than once in this design; thus, there is no assurance that the experimental technique would work again in the same way on any of those responses on a later occasion. What is clear is that the *technique* works repeatedly across a sample of different responses of a given subject. In the second case, a given subject emits the same response in a number of different settings, and the same technique is applied sequentially to the response in these settings (see Figure 1-3). In this case, the same response is altered repeatedly, but always in a different setting; thus, there is again no assurance that the response could be altered repeatedly by that technique in the same setting on a later occasion. Again, what is maximally clear is that the *technique* works repeatedly, no matter

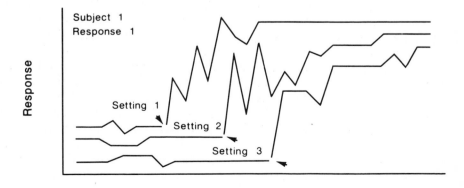

Figure 1-3

in what setting it is used. And, in the third case of the multiple-baseline trinity, it is a number of subjects who display the same response in the same setting, and are sequentially exposed to the same experimental technique (see Figure 1-4). So the same response is altered repeatedly by the

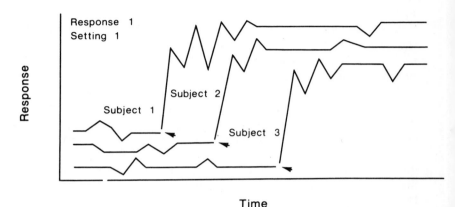

Figure 1-4

experimental technique, but always in a different subject; thus, there is no assurance that it could be altered again by the same technique in the same subject on a different occasion. As before, what is best established is that the *technique* works similarly on a given response in a given setting, no matter what subject may possess the response. Thus, consistently, multiple baseline is less an experimental analysis of the response than of the technique used to alter the response. In the reversal design, the response is made to work again and again; in the multiple-baseline designs, it is primarily the technique that works again and again, and the responses either work once each (if different responses are used) or else a single response works once each per setting or once each per subject. Repetitive working of the same response in the same subject or the same setting is not displayed. But, while repetitive working of the response is foregone, repetitive and diverse working of the experimental technique is maximized, as it would not be in the reversal design. Thus, the two techniques together produce a better range of systematic replications than either alone could, and if we are to conquer, it will be better done not in *this* sign but in *these* signs.

In the beginning, there was the response, then the behaviorist, then the federal funding agency, and then the behavior analyst and the systematic replication. But the behavior analyst, in pursuing the systematic replication, was seeking generality of the analysis. He sought it, finally, in a certain place, and thereby, with the help of the federal funding agency, generated yet another behaviorist: the applied behavior analyst. For the behavior analyst, all innocence and logic, had finally sought to test generality by analyzing those responses that were not only responses but were also social problems. Unless this were done, the systematic replications would have only restricted generality, and if their generality were restricted, it was necessary to know it immediately. For so many bar-presses, key-pecks, alley-runs, panel-pushes, chain-pulls, and switch-closings had been investigated and found to analyze similarly, that there was hardly any priority to trying another of them. Only the social problems were left; thus, their trial was mandatory.

Some of the behavior analysts now investigating social problems were seeking nothing more than generality in a truly acid test. Others, however, had craftily meant to solve the social problems all along; they had been pursuing systematic replications on responses that were less than social problems only because they obviously needed to tool up first. Consequently, when the first forays were made against the social problems, some behavior analysts took care to notify the federal funding agency. Sometimes, the federal funding agency was charmed: at last, it appeared, there might be a chance to proliferate good responses rather than merely further the explanation of responses in general. Sometimes, though, it appeared that the federal funding agency had been devoted to explanation for so long that it had forgotten that explanation was only the handmaiden to good response proliferation; in these sad cases, the federal funding agency explicitly turned away from the analysis of social problems, remarking that they constituted a particularly dirty arena in which to answer questions about the nature of the universe and the response. Fortunately, however, the federal funding agency very often remembered its original plan, and noting that the behavior analysts were now analyzing social problems, it functioned with them again, and so the applied behavior analysts were begotten.

Sometimes, a social problem was identical to a response. For example, some preschoolers lacked social skills for interacting with other children; some school children could not read; some adults had unfortunate sexual proclivities; and some campground users did not pick up litter when they saw it. In these cases, an applied behavior analysis was identical in form to an ordinary behavior analysis; in effect, it was just one more systematic replication, but this time on a response that had rather more social significance than had the previous responses similarly analyzed. Thus, the reversal and multiple-baseline designs were exactly adequate for the problem, and they were used. These analyses formed the first core of applied behavior analysis, and still do.

But other social problems did not seem to consist of a response, or if they did, it did not make good sense to attempt their analysis on that basis. Juvenile delinquency, for example, consisted of a few responses that were formally against the law and also very aversive to their victims and society. On the other hand, these responses also seemed to be the only ones with which the juvenile delinquents could gain the same reinforcers that non-delinquents gained by other, legal, socially desirable responses. But these other desirable responses did not appear to be within the repertoires of the delinquents. Thus, if their delinquent behaviors were directly suppressed, there might be no other way in which the delinquents could gain the neces-sary and socially approved reinforcers. If so, that would hardly constitute a very thorough solution of a social problem. Equally bad, the illegal re-sponses of the delinquents were extremely difficult to detect, so that an appropriate contingency that would suppress them could hardly be applied to them: the delinquents had learned to perform these responses at exactly the times and places that remedial contingencies would not be encountered. Thus, for both philosophical and technical reasons, it seemed that rather than to punish delinquent responses, it would be essential to modify some other responses instead: some responses that would allow the former de-linquents to gain the usual reinforcers in legal and socially approved ways, and, furthermore, responses with which there was some chance of actually applying a contingency often enough to accomplish a change. And indeed, exactly that approach has been pursued in recent years. Its most note-worthy aspect for the present discussion is that the approach consists of some analyses of responses that are not the problem, but presumably relate to the problem. Juvenile delinquents, for example, may undergo some systematic replications aimed not at delinquency responses but in-stead at housekeeping, grooming, polite and articulate speech, consistent hard work in school settings, and pleasant and cooperative interactions with their parents. In that case, their graph may resemble Figure 1-5, in which the multiple-baseline design has been used to demonstrate that the responses in question have been analyzed and altered as desired. But Figure 1-5 is an analysis of the responses, not necessarily of the problem. Conse-quently, some measure of the problem needs to be included. Figure 1-6 simply repeats the response analysis of Figure 1-5, but adds a hypothetical measure of delinquency taken both before and after the response analysis. (That measure, incidentally, is an extremely difficult one to collect. It may be a multiple measure composed of such things as arrest rates; severity of complaints, when they are made; ratings of cooperativeness and industry by teachers, parents, parole officers, and employers; steadiness of job tenure when placed; and so on. For this discussion, we may imagine that the measure can be made, putting aside its very real difficulties; it is how the measure is to be used, rather than how it is to be collected, that is at issue.) If Figure 1-6 is examined only for the delinquency measures it

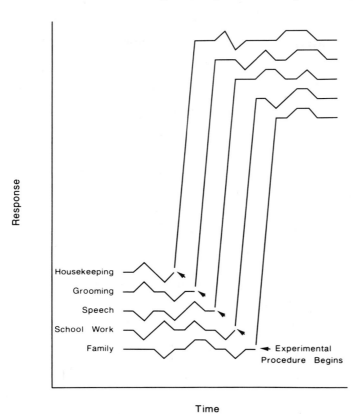

Figure 1-5

displays, then it is apparent that an alteration has been accomplished in delinquency, which suggests that the response analysis did indeed solve the problem; but it is also apparent that the two measures of delinquency do not constitute an *analysis* of delinquency—at least, not by the standards applied to the analysis of the five responses around which the delinquency measures were displayed. In fact, the two delinquency measures constitute the simplest A–B design, one in which there is not even replication within the A or B levels, let alone replication of their alternation. If the pre-measures were made repeatedly, and the post-measures were also made repeatedly, there would be replication within the A and B components of the design, and it would then be clear that there had been a change from the stably bad A condition to the stably good B condition. But whether that change had occurred *because* of the response analysis that occurred between A and B would still not be clear. It may be imagined that an

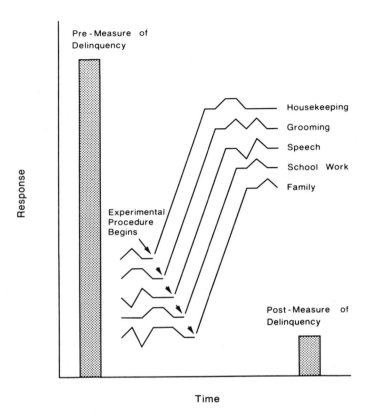

Figure 1-6

analysis of the delinquency measures, that is, of the problem, could be accomplished by making a reversal design of the delinquency measures. In imagination, it could be supposed that after several post-response analysis measures of delinquency had been made and found stably low, the five responses would then be lowered again to their baseline levels, to see if subsequent repeated measures of delinquency would now show a stable rise; and if they did, then, in imagination, the five responses could again be analyzed and increased to see if subsequent delinquency measures went down again and stayed down. If so, a complete reversal design would be in hand, as shown in Figure 1-7, and thereby the problem would have been analyzed in much the same way as the five responses had been. Indeed, the analysis of the five responses would have been shown to be the analysis of the problem. Such an analysis is a fantasy for many reasons, foremost amongst which are:

Delinquency   Measures

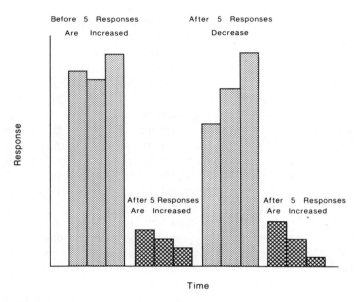

Figure 1-7

1. We cannot deliberately increase a problem such as juvenile delinquency, after what appears to be a successful elimination of it, and expect our society to credit our sanity.

2. The responses in question may not be so available for reduction, if they do, indeed, bring the previous delinquent into contact with better non-experimental reinforcement than experienced earlier.

3. There is a better design that will avoid both of the prior considerations.

If the experimental analysis of the five responses can be done on a *group* of delinquents, then as a group they may provide a pre-measure and a post-measure of delinquency, and in their numbers, these subjects will give those pre- and post-measures the replication—not across time, but across subjects—necessary to an evaluation of their usefulness as measures. More important, a second group of delinquents, comparable to the first, can be found, and they too can offer pre- and post-measures of delinquency. With the first group of delinquents, the five responses would be analyzed and increased. With the second group, they would not. If the five responses are, indeed, an analysis of the problem, then, in the first group there should result a clear decline in delinquency, while in the second group (for whom the five responses were not altered), no such change should be seen. That would constitute an analysis of the problem, in that it would have shown that where the five responses were altered, the problem was solved, but where the five responses were unchanged, so was the problem. Again, it could be concluded that the analysis of five responses was the the analysis of the problem. Furthermore, the applied behavior analyst conducting the study would not be considered insane, in that no attempt to reverse a solved delinquency problem would be proposed. Instead, the applied behavior analyst could now apply the same analysis of five responses to the group that had not yet had them altered, but had testified twice so far to their delinquency as a group. If, subsequent to the alteration of these five responses for the second group, the second group now showed a decreased delinquency score, as had the first group when their five responses were increased, then a replication of the problem analysis would result, one that constituted an obvious multiple baseline when graphed as in Figure 1-8.

The logic of this argument has been that the analysis of some problems is indirect: for these problems, there are certain responses that require analysis and change first. When they are changed, the problem will then be solved. It is not simply that the problem was not stated behaviorally, in terms of component responses. The problem, in fact, may consist of responses that may not be available for change, or that may be available but will not constitute a complete solution even if they are changed. Delinquency is a useful example: if stealing and property damage are reduced in delinquents, but no alternative skills exist in them for gaining the same reinforcers, then they can only become examples of no response; and, although we may no longer consider them a delinquency problem, we will surely find that they are now a welfare problem or a retardation problem. By contrast, if the desirable skills of gaining the relevant reinforcers are taught thoroughly enough, then no direct attack may be necessary on their stealing and destruction repertoires. Those undesirable responses may simply fall into disuse, displaced by the desirable (and more profitable) skills. To the extent that this logic is necessary, as behavior analysts seek generality and a better society through their analysis of social problems, then to that extent the logic of response analysis can also become the logic of problem analysis. The multiple-baseline, and perhaps the reversal design, can make their appearances, not only in the analysis of the responses involved in the problem, but also in the analysis of the problem itself, however it is measured. Clearly, there must be a measure of the problem if the utility of the indirect attack is ever to be validated. The moment that a measure of the problem comes into use, it thereby creates a need for as careful an experimental analysis of itself as

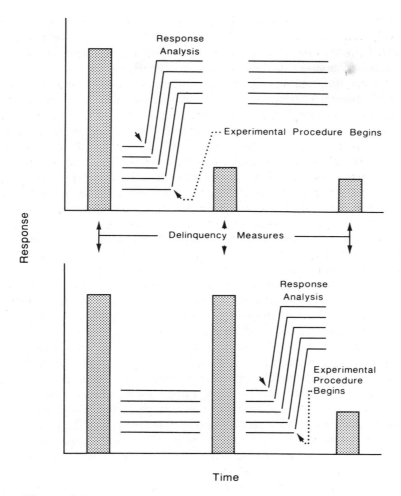

Figure 1-8

any response measure ever receives. The point is that the experimental analysis of a problem is a superordinate one—that is, it is an analysis based upon a subordinate analysis of the responses thought to underlie the problem. Thus, if we accept this challenge, our analysis efforts must increase exponentially; we are to analyze an analysis.

However, we may not accept the challenge to analyze the indirect problem as carefully as we do its subordinate responses. Elery Phillips, Dean Fixsen, Montrose Wolf and their colleagues have taken it up in their validation of the Achievement Place model; thereby, they have afforded this argument its most cogent example (and, as usual, have been ahead of the argument). But otherwise, the literature of applied behavior analysis is virtually empty of indirect problem analyses (though it probably contains several indirect problem *solutions*). This argument has been advanced as a recommendation not to let that state of affairs stand too long. Nevertheless, we may find that our society will not ask much more than the simple A–B of Figure 1-6 (plus some statements by the subjects of the program to the effect that they value it and are glad to be in it). However, what they may ask of Figure 1-6 is not analysis, but efficiency; and thereby, they may indicate for us the most laborious, but perhaps the most rewarding problem of all. In the indirect analysis of problems, some responses are nominated as the subordinate analysis. But which responses are the correct ones, or the best ones? Suppose that we find that juvenile delinquents who are taught housekeeping, grooming, speech, academic skills, and family cooperation skills improve dramatically on all useful measures of delinquency. We may well ask whether they would do even better if one more relevant response were added to the list; or, we may ask if they would not do just as well if one of the five responses were eliminated from the list. Thus, one student of the problem may suggest that the addition of a systematic training program in interpersonal negotiation, as increasingly used in behavioral approaches to marriage counseling, would yield even better results from the delinquents than are currently being gained. But another student may suggest that the present list of five responses not only is adequate, but is in fact too long by one, specifically, the family cooperation response, which is argued to be nothing but cosmetic. And so a further analysis has thereby been suggested: a comparative evaluation of the present list of five against the same list plus negotiation skills, and against the same list minus family cooperation skills. Such suggestions can be infinite in number. But some of them are likely to be important, in the sense that they contribute to efficiency. It is unlikely that we will become connoisseurs of every nuance of one list versus another, but efficiency is no small ingredient of socially significant analyses of behavior, and it seems inevitable that we will eventually make some comparative assays of a few different lists, at least until we have a list that solves the problem well enough. We may not need to know how to solve a problem optimally if we can solve it well enough. For in the beginning, there was the response, and that will always be with us; but at the end (now), there is the applied behavior analyst, and whether or not that mutant of the behavior analyst survives depends quite simply on how valuable the sport turns out to be. An orientation toward efficiency—toward some very good lists of responses, when the social problem turns out to be a case for indirect analysis—may be the one commandment.

3 / Positive and Negative Reinforcement, a Distinction That Is No Longer Necessary; or a Better Way to Talk About Bad Things

Jack Michael

THE DEVELOPMENT OF TECHNICAL TERMINOLOGY

Technical verbal practices evolve as a result of the behavior of specialists with respect to their subject matter and to one another. Ultimately, increased effectiveness of the verbal community is the primary determinant of such developments, but as in the case of biological evolution there are many nonfunctional factors that may exert a short-term effect, at least. The verbal behavior of a prestigious figure may be adopted and propagated because of his accomplishments in areas other than the one in which the term occurs. Verbal distinctions may be useful to a speaker for reasons other than his relationship with his scientific subject matter. For example, they may identify him as a member of a prestigious subgroup. More to the point, some terminological distinctions may be quite functional during the development of a field because of their relations to other concepts; and then, when these other concepts change, the distinction may persist in the repertoires of the individual scientists simply because the effort required to change is considerable and the reinforcement too delayed.

Though it is true that cultural evolution rather than social agreement seems to be the most important determinant of terminological developments, still we seem able to alter or hasten this evolutionary process to some extent by talking about our verbal practices. This is, of course, the essence of the areas called "philosophy of science" and "scientific methodology," and it is also the premise underlying my presentation to this conference. I hope to alter our current usage, or rather to hasten a change that seems already under way, by identifying some of the factors responsible for the original distinction between negative and positive reinforcement, and by suggesting why these factors are no longer relevant.

A BRIEF HISTORY OF THE DISTINCTION BETWEEN POSITIVE AND NEGATIVE REINFORCEMENT

A reasonable starting point for the experimental and applied analysis of behavior is B. F. Skinner's *The Behavior of Organisms* (1938). In the first chapter, Skinner discusses the need for a set of terms, and gives his reasons for not readily adopting popular terms.

> The important objection to the vernacular in the description of behavior is that many of its terms imply conceptual schemes. I do not mean that a science of behavior is to dispense with a conceptual scheme but that it must not take over without careful consideration the schemes which underlie popular speech. The vernacular is clumsy and obese; its terms overlap each other, draw unnecessary or unreal distinctions, and are far from being the most convenient in dealing with the data. They have the disadvantage of being historical products, introduced because of everyday convenience rather than that special kind of convenience characteristic of a simple scientific system. (p. 7)

Terminological developments involving reflexes and what Skinner called "respondent conditioning" had already taken place, and some of this terminology was applicable to the type of behavior that was affected by its consequences—Skinner's "operant behavior." The layman's terms for effective consequences were "reward" and "punishment," but these terms obviously suffered from some of the disadvantages mentioned by Skinner. "Reinforcement" was at that time widely used to refer to the unconditioned stimulus of respondent conditioning, for it "reinforced" or strengthened the relationship between the conditioned stimulus and the relevant response. This term, then, was a reasonable substitute for "reward" since the effect of a reward was to increase the future probability of the response in the particular situation, or to "strengthen" the response. But how should one refer to the other half of the consequence continuum, the "bad" things? "Punishment" seemed at that time to have some of the same disadvantages as "reward" and a substitute was obviously needed. Skinner's solution can be seen from the following passage (pp. 65–66 of *The Behavior of Organisms*), which introduced the topic of operant conditioning:

> The second type of conditioning, in which the reinforcing stimulus is correlated with a response, may be represented as follows:
>
> $$s.R^0 \rightarrow S^1.R^1$$
>
> where $s.R^0$ is some part of the unconditioned operant behavior of the organism and S^1 is again a reinforcing stimulus. The requirements for conditioning are some considerable strength of $S^1.R^1$ and the connection indicated by $\rightarrow$. The effect is a change in [$s.R^0$], which may be either an increase or, possibly, a decrease. In the present example of pressing a lever the strength may increase if S^1 is, for example, food, and it may decrease if it is, for example, a shock. There are thus two kinds of reinforcing stimuli—positive and negative. The cessation of a positive reinforcement acts as a negative, the cessation of a negative as a positive. Differences between the two types of conditioning will be summarized later. (1938, pp. 65-66) [A footnote after "shock" reads, "But see the section on negative reinforcement in this and the following chapter."]

In other words, "reward" and "punishment" were replaced by "positive reinforcement" and "negative reinforcement." This is quite clear from the above passage, and the equating of what we now call the punishment operation with negative reinforcement occurs consistently throughout Skinner's book. For example, in the description of the now famous "bar-slap" experiment Skinner says:

> The first experiment concerns the effect of negative reinforcement upon extinction. Extinction curves after periodic reinforcement with food were obtained from four rats. On the third day the slapper was connected for the first time at the end of twenty minutes, and all responses made during the rest of the hour and on the following day were negatively reinforced.

Although this terminological device successfully eliminates some of the disadvantages of the vernacular, it introduces a new clumsiness of its own, the ambivalence that results from two-word terms in which the two words are controlled by variables that are in some sense opposite or incompatible with each other. "Reinforce" is synonymous with "strengthen" in a number of usages; and although "negatively strengthen" as a synonym for "weaken" is not logically unreasonable, it is somewhat confusing, as would be such a term as "positively weaken." This ambivalence did not seem to cause much trouble in 1938, however, probably because Skinner's orientation was of interest only to specialists. A different version of this problem became more serious fifteen or twenty years later, when Skinner's revised approach (explained below) was being taught to college freshmen.

The substitution of "negative reinforcement" for "punishment" also left standing an increasingly serious problem inherent in both terms, the identification of an important independent variable by an operation that was of dubious behavioral effectiveness, or at least quite complex. Positive reinforcing stimuli were those whose occurrence increased the probability of the behavior that they followed—a simple and noncontroversial identifying operation. Negative reinforcing stimuli were those whose occurrence decreased the probability of the behavior that they followed, but by 1938 Skinner had evidence available that was not compatible with a simple interpretation of this effect. This consisted of the results of several experiments involving the presentation of a negative reinforcing stimulus contingent upon a lever-pressing response during extinction after fixed-interval positive reinforcement. The theoretical analysis is in terms of the later discarded concept of the reflex reserve, but even so, the implications of the results are quite clear.

> To sum up, the experiments on periodic negative conditioning show that any true reduction in reserve is at best temporary and that the emotional effect to be expected of such stimulation can adequately account for the temporary weakening of the reflex actually observed. (p. 157)

The next major landmark in the development of the field of behavior analysis was the publication in 1950 of *Principles of Psychology,* the highly influential introductory text of F. S. Keller and W. N. Schoenfeld. The line of experimentation begun by Skinner, which questioned the permanence of the weakening effect of negative reinforcing stimuli had been followed up by Estes (1944), whose work generally supported Skinner's earlier conclusions. Chapter three of the Keller and Schoenfeld text is called "Operant Conditioning," and near the end of it, in a section entitled "Positive and Negative Reinforcement," the concepts are introduced as follows:

> Thorndike, in his 1911 statement of the law of effect, spoke of the strengthening effect of "satisfaction" upon the bond between situation and response. Today, avoiding controversy about the nature of "satisfaction," we would say that the food he gave to his cats for opening a

problem-box door was *positively* reinforcing. On the observational level, this would mean exactly what Thorndike meant—that the effect of the food was to increase the frequency of the response that produced it. We know, too, that water, for a thirsty animal, would have had a similar effect. Food and water belong to a class of positive reinforcers.

This is not all that Thorndike said. He spoke also of the weakening effect of "discomfort" upon situation-response connections. Certain stimuli (electric shocks, loud sounds, strong lights, etc.) serve to *decrease* the frequency of responses in the wake of which they follow. Nowadays, we call them *negative* reinforcers, but they are not best defined in terms of their weakening function. By 1932, Thorndike himself argued that "rewards" and "punishments" are not opposed to each other in the manner implied by his earlier formulation; and we shall offer evidence, in the next chapter, to show that the weakening effect of negatively reinforcing stimuli is not permanent.

Another, and probably a better, way of handling the matter is to define *positive* reinforcers as those stimuli which strengthen responses when *presented* (e.g., food strengthens bar-pressing or loop-pulling behavior), and *negative* reinforcers as those which strengthen when they are *removed.* (p. 61)

The evidence presented in their next chapter consisted of the results of Skinner's earlier experiments, plus the findings of Estes.

The impermanence of the weakening effect of a negative reinforcing stimulus that is being referred to by Skinner and by Keller and Schoenfeld requires further explanation. It was, of course, recognized that the strengthening effects of positive reinforcement were temporary, in the sense that the occurrence of the previously reinforced response without its reinforcement—the operation referred to as "extinction"—would result in a decrease in the response frequency. It was not expected that the weakening effects of negative reinforcement would be any more permanent in this sense: when the response occurred without being followed by the negative reinforcer, the effects of the negative reinforcement would "wear off." But the weakening effects of negative reinforcers showed an additional type of impermanence, which was not thought to characterize the strengthening effects of positive reinforcers. Keller and Schoenfeld describe the critical finding as follows:

> Estes found that when bar-pressing was punished in the usual way during a short period of extinction, and this was followed by a two-hour period in which the rat was left in the response chamber, *with no bar present and no further punishment,* the effect of the shock was almost entirely absent when the bar was re-introduced and extinction was resumed. Leaving the rat in the chamber without the bar led to a nearly complete dissipation of the emotional upset caused by the shock. Except for a small depression at the start, the final extinction curve was in no discernible way different from that provided by animals that had never been shocked." (p. 109)

In other words, the weakening effect of a negative reinforcer on a response could be eliminated in some other way than by the occurrence of the response without the consequence. This form of impermanence, furthermore, was seen (by Skinner and by Keller and Schoenfeld) to have important practical implications, suggesting that the widespread use of negative reinforcement to eliminate behavior was a practice of questionable value.

To return to the issue of terminology: as can be seen from the excerpt above, Keller and Schoenfeld were by 1950 much more willing to use the term "punishment" than Skinner had been in 1938. In one instance (probably because of the introductory nature of their text) they even seemed to prefer "punishment" to "negative reinforcement": they relabeled two of Skinner's figures "The effect of punishment" which he had called "The effect of negative reinforcement" (Figures 28 and 29 of the Keller and Schoenfeld text, on pp. 107 and 108; Figures 45 and 47 of Skinner's *Behavior of Organisms,* pp. 152 and 154).

In his own introductory textbook, *Science and Human Behavior* (1953), Skinner completely reversed part of his previous usage. In a section titled "What events are reinforcing?" he distinguishes between the two types of reinforcement as follows:

> Events which are found to be reinforcing are of two sorts. Some reinforcements consist of *presenting* stimuli, of adding something—for example, food, water, sexual contact—to the situation. These we call *positive* reinforcers. Others consist of *removing* something—for example, a loud noise, a very bright light, extreme cold or heat, or electric shock—from the situation. These we call *negative* reinforcers. In both cases the effect of reinforcement is the same—the probability of response is increased. (p. 73)

The relationship of these events to punishment is described in a later section, immediately after the reality of the supposed direct weakening effect of punishment has been called into question.

> We must first define punishment without presupposing any effect. This may appear to be difficult. In defining a reinforcing stimulus we could avoid specifying physical characteristics by appealing to the effect upon the strength of the behavior. If a punishing consequence is also defined without reference to its physical characteristics and if there is no comparable effect to use as a touchstone, what course is open to us? The answer is as follows. We first define a positive reinforcer as any stimulus the *presentation* of which strengthens the behavior upon which it is made contingent. We define a negative reinforcer (an aversive stimulus) as any stimulus the *withdrawal* of which strengthens behavior. Both are reinforcers in the literal sense of reinforcing or strengthening a response. Insofar as scientific definition corresponds to lay usage, they are both "rewards." In solving the problem of punishment we simply ask: What

is the effect of *withdrawing a positive* reinforcer or *presenting* a *negative?* An example of the former would be taking candy from a baby; an example of the latter, spanking a baby. (pp. 184–85)

As used in behavioral analysis, the term "stimulus" seems most often to refer to a static stimulus condition: a stimulus change is usually indicated by "stimulus onset" or some such expression. There is some ambiguity with this usage, but this is usually not serious because of the additional information provided by the context. However, in attempting to define the various terms relating to effective behavioral consequences any ambiguity of this sort can easily lead to more serious confusion. For this reason, in the sections below I shall generally use the somewhat cumbersome, but unambiguous "static stimulus condition" and "stimulus change."

What Skinner proposes in the passages cited above is that we designate a stimulus change that strengthens behavior as "reinforce*ment.*" When the change can be described as presentation, this change should be called "positive reinforce*ment":* when it can be described as withdrawal (or removal or termination), the change should be called "negative reinforce*ment.*"

It is convenient at this point for us to note that to describe any form of change, we must at least describe the static condition existing before the change and the static condition existing after the change. For greater precision, it is also usually necessary to describe the time required for the former to be replaced by the latter, and to describe any intermediate conditions. A change *consists* of nothing more than the fact that a pre-change condition is replaced by a post-change condition, in a certain temporal manner and with certain intermediate conditions. (This, of course, ignores the problems of a continuum, where the language of mathematics becomes essential.)

What Skinner proposes for the term "reinforc*er,*" then, is that it should refer to a static stimulus condition of those stimulus changes that function as reinforce*ment.* When the stimulus change is positive reinforcement—that is, when the change can be identified as a presentation— then the static *post*-change condition should be called a positive reinforc*er.* When the stimulus change is a removal, and thus negative reinforce*ment,* the static *pre*-change condition should be called a negative reinforc*er.* Punishment is also a stimulus change; it consists of the reversal of those changes that we have found to be reinforcements. The essence of Skinner's new approach, then, is that "negative reinforcement" is now applied to stimulus changes that strengthen the behavior preceding them, whereas it previously referred to the same changes, but in the opposite direction. Although the distinction between "reinforcer" and "reinforcement" was not explicitly made earlier, "reinforcer" generally referred then to the static pre-change conditions (negative reinforcer) or post-change conditions (positive reinforcer), as it does also in the new usage.

For a while in the late 1950s or early 1960s, about half of the students of behavioral analysis were learning basic concepts from the Keller and Schoenfeld text, and the other half from Skinner's *Science and Human Behavior,* a situation that generated considerable confusion with respect to the critical term "negative reinforcement." The confusion was especially keen when both texts were used in the same course. But in 1961 the programmed text by J. G. Holland and B. F. Skinner, *The Analysis of Behavior,* was published. It naturally continued the terminological practices that Skinner had introduced in the 1953 book, and began to replace Keller and Schoenfeld as an introductory text, thus tipping the balance in favor of Skinner's new definition of negative reinforcement. The critical frames appear in Set 9 (beginning on p. 53) and Set 37 (beginning on p. 245) of the programmed text. The situation regarding this terminological issue has remained relatively stable since the mid 1960s, and for the adherent of Skinner's approach, since 1953.

WHAT IS WRONG WITH THE PRESENT USAGE

"Negative reinforcement" with its opposite implications is a source of considerable confusion. Since 1953 there must have been thousands of man-hours spent in the attempt to prevent the learner of behavioral terminology from equating this stimulus change with punishment, the change made in the opposite direction. It appears that Skinner's earlier usage, even though it is ambiguous its own way, is more compatible with our other verbal practices than the revised usage. The common-sense opposition, reward and punishment, is probably responsible for a similar usage involving the technical terms: if reward is positive reinforcement, isn't it reasonable that punishment should be negative reinforcement? Because this usage is so natural, one might be tempted to suggest a return to the older meaning of negative reinforcement as a solution to the problem, but we have no way of knowing at this time how common the other type of error would then become. The earlier usage was not really tested on unselected college freshman, elementary school teachers, hospital attendants, and so on. It is quite possible that if we returned to the earlier usage, we would spend thousands of man-hours trying to prevent the interpretation of negative reinforcement as a strengthening stimulus change, since in all other usages in our language reinforcements certainly strengthen.

The attempt to clarify the issue by requiring a sharp distinction between "reinfor*cer*" and "reinforce*ment*" is probably hindered by the fact that in most other occurrences of these suffixes our reactions to the two terms, at least the evaluative component of those reactions, are quite similar. In the case of "negative reinforcer" and "negative reinforcement," they must be quite the opposite of one another: even though we generally dislike negative reinforcers, we should always welcome negative reinforcement; of course, we would not welcome the presentation of the negative reinforcer—a form of punishment—but once it has been presented, we certainly "enjoy" its removal. This situation constitutes another uphill struggle against long-standing patterns of verbal behavior, and probably causes more difficulty than it cures.

"Aversive stimulus" as a synonym for "negative reinforcer" (see p. 36, above) has some advantages in terms of ordinary language usage, but synonymy is not generally desirable in the case of technical terms. If we go to considerable trouble to restrict the usage of one term, why complicate the issue with a different term, which must be controlled by exactly the same carefully specified conditions? With such synonyms there is always the possibility of subtle drifts in usage, which result in the necessity for further specification and in the proliferation of unnecessary distinctions.

Another difficulty with current usage is that the critical distinction between positive and negative reinforcement depends upon our being able to distinguish stimulus changes that are presentations from those that are removals or withdrawals; the latter terms are not very satisfactory descriptions of changes. In much vernacular usage, the circumstances in which we have a tendency to say "present" certainly seem to differ from those in which we say "remove," but some of these differences are irrelevant to a science of behavior, and there are a number of circumstances where the distinction is not easily made.

In much common-sense usage, "present" and "remove" may serve primarily to identify the nature of the variables controlling the person who performs an action rather than the nature of the change itself. A presenter makes a display or an exhibit, for which he is held responsible or for which he may receive praise. He offers something for consideration or as a gift, in which case he may turn it over to the receiver and no longer have it in his possession. "Removal" is more neutral, but sometimes has overtones of disapproval, as in a dismissal from office, or when used as a euphemism for "assassinate." A science of behaving organisms, however, must be written in terms of the relations between behavioral changes and environmental changes: the motives or responsibilities or attitudes of the person who effects the environmental changes are generally not relevant; if they are, they should be described as additional aspects of the behaving organism's environment.

From the point of view of the behaving organism, in other words, presentations and removals are both simply types of environmental changes. If they differ, the difference must not be based upon the variables controlling the person who causes the change. (One must, of course, make a tentative exception to this statement when considering the field of social psychology, but the trend in behavioral social psychologies has been to reduce such social factors to the same kinds of environmental events that affect the various individual organisms behaving with respect to one another.) So, when do we appropriately refer to an environmental change as a presentation and when do we refer to it as a removal? We cannot, here, rely on common-sense usage because it is so seldom neutral with respect to the motives of the person producing the change. We must actually look at our own behavior as scientists, since "present a stimulus" is not really ordinary usage. As indicated earlier, all changes involve at least a static pre-change condition and a static post-change condition. We seem to use "present" when we wish to implicate the post-change condition as the one most relevant to behavior, or the most in need of specification. We use "remove" when the pre-change condition is the most significant condition. Similarly (but not exactly), we use "present" when the characteristics of the pre-change condition can be taken for granted and "remove" when the post-change conditions can be taken for granted. When we say that we present a food pellet to a rat, the listener can always assume that the pre-change condition is one in which no food is available. We could say that we remove the "no-food" condition, but then the behaviorally important aspect of the change would remain to be described. When we say that we terminate a fifty-volt electric shock, the subsequent "no-shock" condition can generally do without further description; but if it were described alone, little information would be provided.

In other words, it appears that "present" and "remove" are abbreviations that can sometimes replace a more complete description of both the pre-change and post-change conditions. The abbreviation is usually possible in the case of unconditioned reinforcements, though even here it must always be possible to infer the characteristics of both pre- and post-change conditions if we are to imply behavioral significance. Note that to describe a pre-change condition as "a fifty-volt shock" is of no help in understanding the behavioral effect of the change. A change from fifty volts to one hundred volts will certainly not strengthen the response that precedes the change; a change from fifty to twenty volts probably will, but not as much as a change from fifty volts to zero volts.

WHY DO WE BOTHER?

As we apply behavioral analysis to more and more complex human situations, we find it increasingly difficult to distinguish between presenting and removing, or we find an increasing number of situations that seem to involve both. A fairly common response to this situation is to avoid making the distinction, to simply refer to the relevant environmental change as "reinforcement," without attempting to determine whether a positive reinforcer is being presented or a negative one removed. One might well ask, then, why we bother making the distinction even in those cases where it can easily be made.

One possibility is that although both positive and negative reinforcement strengthen behavior, the strengthening effects are in some important way different from one another. Perhaps they have different temporal properties, or different relations with other independent variables. Perhaps it is easier to develop discriminations using one rather than the other. It is quite true that the various environmental changes that function as reinforcement each have unique properties that one must know about in order to predict or control behavior effectively. However, these properties seem just as relevant to the distinctions among the various kinds of positive reinforcements as to those between positive and negative reinforcement. It is quite clear that for someone to replicate some particular behavioral manipulation, it is not much more helpful to know that it involved negative reinforcement than to know, simply, that it involved reinforcement: the details must still be provided, and without them the situation remains quite unclear.

Another possibility is that the two kinds of reinforcement involve different underlying physiological structures or processes—the posterior versus the anterior nuclei of the hypothalamus, for example. By maintaining the distinction between the two types of reinforcement at this time, we may thus facilitate future links between physiological and behavioral research and theory. However, in view of the general troublesomeness of this particular distinction, the pace of developments within the field of physiology, and our past efforts to develop behavioral terminology on the basis of supposed or real physiological entities, this is not a very attractive strategy.

Still another possibility is that by maintaining this distinction, we can more effectively warn behavior controllers against the use of an undesirable technique. "Use positive rather than negative reinforcement." But if the distinction is quite difficult to make in many cases of human behavior, the warning will not be easy to follow; and it is an empirical question at the present time whether such a warning is reasonable—a question that many feel has not been answered. Furthermore, to maintain a distinction at the level of basic science because of its possible social implications seems a risky practice, and one that is usually avoided in other sciences when possible.

None of the reasons given above seems sufficient to justify making the distinction between the two kinds of reinforcement. However, I would like to suggest another, more important function that this distinction serves. The layman frequently finds it necessary to identify an environmental event or condition as one that he doesn't like, one that he attempts to escape or avoid. He may refer to such an event as "bad" (without the moral implications of this term), "undesirable," "unfavorable," and so on, and he also may use "punishment" as a contrast with "reward." A science of behavior also needs a way of identifying such events. "Punishment" was unacceptable as a technical term, at first for the same reason that "reward" could not be used—there were too many other implications besides the simple effect of such events upon the operant behavior that preceded their occurrence. "Negative reinforcement" was a satisfactory replacement and retained the convenient sense of contrast with "positive reinforcement," the replacement for "reward."

The permanence of the effect of "bad" things on the behavior that *preceded* their occurrence, however, began to be brought into question almost as soon as this technical term for such things appeared. The results of Skinner's "bar-slap" experiments and the later experiments by Estes using electric shock suggested that any apparent weakening effect of negative reinforcement (in its early sense) was not really the weakening of the operant that preceded the negative reinforcement, but rather the strengthening of behavior that was incompatible with that operant—the "competing-response" interpretation. This being the case, it seemed much safer to identify this important type of environmental change in terms of the strengthening effect that resulted when the change occurred in the opposite direction (when the negative reinforcer was removed), an effect that is essentially uncontroversial. And as long as this removal is the critical operational definition, we might as well call *it* negative reinforcement, the essence of Skinner's 1953 revision.

So, even if the strengthening effects of the two kinds of reinforcement are identical in all respects, we need to make the distinction in order to have a name for the bad things in our world: we can call the static conditions whose presence we escape or avoid "negative reinforcers." But what do we call environmental changes that we do not like? Apparently, there is a strong tendency to call them "negative reinforcement," even though this is erroneous according to current usage, in which "negative reinforcement" refers to changes in the direction that we *do* like. We can and should call bad changes "punishment," remembering that this term is defined as a reversal of a reinforcing change. It is awkard, however, to identify an event in terms of the behavioral effects of the reversal of the event, both because reversal is not always a clearly identifiable operation, and because such usage seems, as Azrin and Holz suggest (1966, p. 382), to require prior demonstration of the strengthening effect of such reversal.

THE SOLUTION

The important dates in the development of this terminological problem were 1938, when Skinner's *Behavior of Organisms* was published; 1950, Keller and Schoenfeld's *Principles of Psychology;* 1953, Skinner's *Science and Human Behavior;* and 1961, Holland and Skinner's *The Analysis of Behavior*. Now we can add another date, which signifies the beginning of the end to the problem: 1966, when N. H. Azrin and W. C. Holz summarized the results of over five years of operant research on punishment in their chapter in Honig's *Operant Behavior: Areas of Research and Application*. In a series of ingenious and thorough experiments, Azrin and his colleagues disentangled the complexities that had marred earlier research in this field. They avoided the complexities resulting from the dependence of the effects of grid-shock punishment (used in most previous research) upon the particular topography of the animal's behavior, by using as a punishing stimulus electric shock delivered through electrodes implanted in the fleshy tail region of the pigeon. They also concentrated on the effects of a punishing stimulus change on behavior that continued to receive reinforcement, a strategy that eliminated the confounding of the weakening effect of such a stimulus change with its novelty effect and its effect as a discriminative stimulus. (This particular confounding rendered several of the earlier experiments by Skinner and by Estes essentially uninterpretable.) Their research also had the advantage of the availability of all of the improvements in operant instrumentation and all of the various procedural and conceptual refinements that had occurred during the approximately twelve very productive years since the work of Estes had been reported.

The general result of this new evidence is to discredit the results that were thought to be incompatible with the interpretation that punishment directly weakens the response that precedes it. The new information does not necessarily invalidate the more complex competing-response theory, but renders it unnecessary, and thus less attractive than the simpler interpretation. In addition, this body of research clarifies a number of procedural and conceptual problems that had been interfering with our understanding of the effect of punishment.

The majority of the experiments summarized by Azrin and Holz in the chapter in the 1966 text were reported originally in the *Journal of the Experimental Analysis of Behavior,* from 1959 to 1965. If the general conclusions summarized in 1966 had had any major weaknesses they would probably have been reported in subsequent issues of this journal, for this is where most of the research originating from the "Skinnerian" or "experimental analysis of behavior" orientation appears. A survey of the volumes of his journal that have been published since 1966 (volumes 10 through 19) failed to reveal any refutation of any of the major conclusions bearing on this interpretation of the weakening effect of punishment, and revealed a number of reports supporting and extending the generality of this interpretation. Either the basic researchers have been quite content to drop Skinner's competing-responses interpretation, or they have been unable to bring any experimental evidence to bear favorably on that interpretation, or they have been unable to question the more direct interpretation supported by Azrin's work.

So, the solution to our terminological problem is to refer to the good things as reinforcers and reinforcement, and the bad things as punishers and punishment. One set of terms is operationally tied to a strengthening effect and the other to a weakening effect. The distinction between two types of reinforcement, based in turn upon the distinction between presentation and removal, can be simply dropped. This does not prevent us from observing the generalization that environmental changes that have one type of effect on behavior will often have the opposite effect when the direction of the change is reversed. Furthermore, the distinction between reinforc*er* and reinforce*ment* and that between punish*er* and punish*ment* can generally be ignored, or simply left to ordinary verbal usage to determine, because the consequences of erroneously saying "punishment" when "punisher" is actually correct are of little significance. Finally, "aversive stimulus" can also be dropped as a technical term, since it is an unnecessary synonym for "punisher" or "punishment," depending upon whether it refers to a static stimulus condition or a change.

My final point is a form of testimonial. My involvement in the field of behavior analysis consists mainly of teaching and public speaking, in both the basic and the applied areas. The arguments set forth above convinced me about six years ago to stop making the distinction between negative and positive reinforcement and to refer to the bad things as punishers and punishment. I can report that I have been able to get by quite nicely without the terms that were dropped, and I have encountered no previously hidden implications that must be salvaged by compensatory shifts in the usage of other critical terms.[1]

---

[1] Since this material was first presented there seems to be an increasing usage among behavioral psychologists of the expressions "positive consequence" and "negative consequence," especially when presenting their work to non-professional audiences. "Negative consequence" is a useful euphemism in those circumstances where "punishment" might be misunderstood and as a result disapproved of; but even so, this approach may be a satisfactory way out of our present terminological difficulties.

4 / Toward Experimental Living, Phase II: "Have You Ever Heard of a Man Named Frazier, Sir?"

Roger Ulrich

The nature of my topic here today at Lawrence, Kansas, the world's center of applied behavior analysis, is closely related to the nature of the invitation that I received. Gene Ramp, who just gave me that beautiful introduction, called me and said that there would be a number of invited addresses at this year's conference; he asked if I would come and more or less "rap" with everybody, telling what I'm doing at this particular time. I, of course, feel honored that the conference organizers would think that a group such as all of you would give a damn. But I accepted and here I am. Perhaps the real reason for my being here is that a lot of younger colleagues, such as Gene Ramp, have over the years drifted to Kansas to finish their Ph.D. So I have some lobbyists here. Gene was one of the group of seniors and graduate students that I met in 1965 when I went to Western Michigan University as head of the psychology department. Gene has the distinction, in my memory, of having done some very innovative research at Indian Lake Elementary School in Vicksburg, Michigan, subsequently published in the

Journal of Applied Behavior Analysis. Also, he persuaded a number of people at Indian Lake to enthusiastically accept males who had long hair. In 1965, long hair and beards weren't the rage in the country surrounding small Michigan towns. Gene went to Indian Lake and soon generated many positive relationships between himself and the teachers. During the time that he worked very closely with the teachers, his sideburns and his hair slowly got longer. At the end of two years, the teachers at Indian Lake, without even realizing it, had living among them a bearded, long-haired "freak" whom they really liked.

Another thing that burns Gene into my memory is that he got me a part in one of the Malotts' early slide shows. Dick and Kay were presenting a paper at the Psychonomic Science convention. (As you all realize by now, "paper" is an inadequate description of anything put together by the Malotts.) Anyway, they were about to break up the Psychonomic Science people with a "far-out" data presentation session on stimulus control. People around the Behavior Research Lab realized that I was one of the better pigeon imitators in the world, so when the script called for various pigeon sounds I received a late-night call, rushed to the taping session, cooed several times, and proudly walked away, having once again discharged my responsibilities as a departmental head.

TOWARD EXPERIMENTAL LIVING, PHASE I; PLUS POEMS

The talk today is entitled in part, "Toward Experimental Living, Phase II." Phase I of the same title is contained in a report published recently as a *Behavior Modification Monograph* (Ulrich, 1973). It is a summary of some of the things that happened when the group of people that I am associated with in the Kalamazoo area started to establish an experimental community. I started writing that first report over a year and a half ago, accelerated by a request from the conference organizers that I present it in October, 1972 at the First International Conference on Behavior Modification in Minneapolis. They asked for a copy of the manuscript before the conference and I tried to oblige by sending a paper entitled, "Toward Experimental Living: A Report on the Lake Village Experimental Living Project in Kalamazoo, Michigan Plus Selected Poems." I said at the time and would like to repeat here that there is no way one person can take credit for a project such as the one described here, and that if the paper weren't a personal account it would be co-authored by a number of people: Galen Alessi, Marilyn Arnett, Syd Dulaney, Carmen Hren, Rob Hren, Alex

Luvall, Dorathy Marine, Kay Mueller, Bob Pierce, Jim Scherrer, Rick Spates, Sue Stiener, Darwin Stier, Paul Surratt, Sharon Surratt, Marshall Wolfe, Sue Wolfe, and Carole Ulrich. Near the beginning of the unrevised version of the paper I talked about having read *Walden Two* (Skinner, 1948) in the early fifties. I admitted that although I found it interesting, it didn't immediately strike me as being either a literary classic or absolute truth. Following this was a little poem that read:

> What we know of tomorrow's
> Reality from yesterday's stories
> Is oftentimes looking back nothing stuff
> When tomorrow is now.

I went on to say that *Walden Two* did become more meaningful to me after 1958, when I began graduate school at Southern Illinois University. There I met Guru Goldiamond, who insisted I reread the book.

At SIU I not only acquired a profound respect for B. F. Skinner, I learned some other things as well. I studied statistics:

> S.D. in stat
> Ain't the same for a rat
> Though both may prevail,
> By wiggling a tail.

I studied personality theory:

> Isn't that nice?
> You graduate student,
> You future Ph.D.
> Sitting there cramming Freud
>   When you'd rather be
> Doing almost anything else.
> Isn't that nice?
> You gutless mis-wired robot
> Ticky, ticky, ticky sonofabitch
> With no tellamtogofuckit
>   button.

I read Charles Sherrington:

> Take two rats that are dirty,
> One named Mike and one named Gertie.
> If the reflex you elicit
> Kinsey did not solicit
> A doctor you'll be before thirty.

I did some research, and learned about the realities of writing a dissertation:

> So what if you've ruined your vision,
> And lost all power of decision,
> Put down that knife,
> Don't take your life,
> You need only one more revision.

Most importantly, at SIU I became acquainted with the strategies of the experimental laboratory and found words for some of the attitudes that had been within me for a long time but had remained unexpressed. The attitudes were those of science and the experimental analysis of behavior. I found that behavior analysis worked very well in the laboratory, and over the years it began to seem reasonable as a way of life.

I then talked about becoming a departmental head after leaving SIU, first at Illinois Wesleyan University and later at Western. When I left SIU, I was working at the Behavior Research Laboratory at Anna State Hospital. My colleagues, Nate Azrin, Bill Holz, Don Hake, and Ron Hutchinson, sent me off with these words of wisdom:

> You've studied all day, and even in bed,
> Just to prove that you were well read.
> Now forget what you've learned,
> Let your books all be burned,
> For now you're a departmental head.

That gives you some idea of the nature of the paper, which eventually described how in 1971 several of us tried to figure out how to program another phase of our experiment in life, that of living together.

In brief, the organizers returned the paper, saying that the style was not exactly what they had in mind. The paper didn't fit with the rest of the proceedings. Could I make some changes? I said yes, and in the best tradition of my style of life, I passed it on to Kay Mueller, with whom I had worked closely for the past eight years analyzing what's been done in the areas of behavior modification and the experimental analysis of social behavior. Kay and I subsequently spent much time modifying the original manuscript and resubmitted it to the Minneapolis group, who still felt it didn't fit. Finally, as I said earlier, it was published as a *Behavior Modification Monograph*.

THE FRAZIER EXPERIMENT

The experience with the first experimental living paper caused me to do a lot of thinking about what I was doing in relation to my current research interests. People kept asking me for data of the type that appears in the *Journal of Applied Behavior Analysis.* They asked what kind of experimental design we had for the research at Lake Village. The package I presented wasn't neat; I hadn't planned, then done, then reported. In some ways I wasn't feeling good. I was Roger Ulrich deviating again from an accepted formula and, to be honest, at times I felt guilty and out-of-bounds. But I had fought feelings of guilt before, while pursuing a behavioral pattern that was right, at least for me.

The approach to data collection that I have followed I relate closely to the point pressed by Rogers on Professor Burris in Skinner's *Walden Two:*

> "Why don't we just start all over again the right way?" Rogers continued with great difficulty, almost in anguish, as if he were being forced to accuse me of some egregious shortcoming.
>
> "Some of us feel that we can eventually find the answer in teaching and research." I said defensively.
>
> "In research, maybe," said Rogers quickly. "In teaching, no. It's all right to stir people up, get them interested. That's better than nothing. But in the long run you're only passing the buck—if you see what I mean, sir." He stopped in embarrassment.
>
> "For heaven's sake, don't apologize," I said. "You can't hurt me there. That's not my Achilles' heel."
>
> "What I mean is, you've got to do the job yourself if it's ever going to be done. Not just whip somebody else up to it. Maybe in your research you are getting close to the answer. I wouldn't know."
>
> I demurred. "I'm afraid the answer is still a long way off."
>
> "Well, that's what I mean, sir. It's a job for research, but not the kind you can do in a university, or in a laboratory anywhere. I mean you've got to experiment, and experiment with your own life! Not just sit back —not just sit back in an ivory tower somewhere—as if your own life weren't all mixed up in it." He stopped again. Perhaps this *was* my Achilles' heel.
>
> I missed my chance to give him a reassuring word. I was thinking of Frazier and of how remarkably well his ideas had survived transportation. A professional theory occurred to me: perhaps this was the test of the goodness of an idea, of its internal consistency. But Rogers' noise broke through.
>
> "Have you ever heard of a man named Frazier, sir?" (pp. 4–5).

That was the most important lesson I learned from *Walden Two:* to experiment with life, to look at life as an experiment, for that's exactly what it is. Very seldom, when we're on the fringe of discovery, do we really know what to do. In spite of all the knowledge we have gained from the experimental analysis of behavior, we must still, in all our applied settings, make guesses daily as to what behavior will produce the desired result.

We're always trying new things and "trying new things" is a good definition of "experiment."

My dad taught me a very important thing when I was young: Don't be afraid of new things. Seek them out. Try something for a while until you get a feel for it (a baseline, though he never called it that). Then try something different and compare that with how you felt before and after you did the different thing. Some different things feel so good that you do them again. Some different things feel so bad that you don't do them again.

You can't always articulate in advance how you will collect, analyze, and report your findings. If you try, more often than not, the experiment will never get off the ground. In the beginning, an attempted experimental analysis will necessarily be different from what it will later become. For the most part, I see the experimental community movement as still in the building-the-laboratory stage, and much of what I have reported and will be reporting for a while will relate more to the facts of construction than to anything else. In 1966, I presented a paper entitled "The Experimental Analysis of Behavior as a Systematic Approach to Teaching Psychology." It sketched what we ought to do in building a department of psychology that adhered to the methods and results of behavior analysis. A few years later, I was able to quantify some of the results (Ulrich, 1972). In fact, I've run quite a few experiments that I jumped into first and sorted out and reported later. There was the experiment of being the head of a psychology department, first at a small midwestern Methodist institution and later at a large state institution. I've also experimented with a situation that can be called an "attempted coup," in which I was the "coupee." There were experiments in the public schools (Ulrich, Wolf, and Bluhm, 1968). There was an early education project that followed children from birth to eleven years of age (Ulrich, Louisell, and Wolf, 1971; Ulrich, Alessi, and Wolf, 1971). Before I began those experiments, I wasn't sure what kinds of data I would encounter, let alone how to quantify them. But in every instance, the result was data. I might add that had I known in advance what some of those data would be, I would have greatly limited my involvement, and the products of my involvement would also have been limited. The naïveté of the experimenter as well as that of the subject can be truly important.

When I was a graduate student at SIU, I was carefully programmed to believe that research is not something you enter into with a fixed idea of what you expect to find. You may have to convince certain members of your graduate committee that you had a hypothesis that you have been systematically testing in the laboratory and that now you are presenting the results of what you have tried. Most people involved in the experimental analysis of behavior have especially stressed paying close attention to the accidents of the laboratory: look out for the behavior you don't expect; watch for apparatus failures and see what they produce. I have watched the results of accidents in experiments run in psychology departments, in public schools, in state hospitals, in homes for the retarded, in job corps programs, and also in the Learning Village. In many instances I didn't realize that what I had was a multiple baseline, in which, at different times, one variable or another would change. Because I didn't know beforehand what would happen, I wasn't always ready with my observers, microswitches, response definitions, and reliability checks.

Incidentally, all of these experiments fall into the category Mont Wolf has called second-level research, or program evaluation (Goodall, 1973). In setting up and evaluating a program, detailed studies of the behavior of participants are not necessarily conducted. Rather, the results of previous detailed studies are applied. Results reflect the overall effectiveness of the program: an increase in publications and grant money raised by faculty and students in a psychology department; a decrease in referrals to mental health personnel in a public school; the academic achievement of students in an experimental school. As Wolf points out, years elapse between the inception of a program and the appearance of such results. During those years, funding is difficult to obtain and credibility is stretched because the project hasn't produced data. The more "far-out" a project, the worse the problem.

So anyone who wants to run a Frazier experiment will probably not have the luxury of sitting back in an air-conditioned office and planning a sophisticated research design. Rather, he will be busy dealing with contractors and government agencies and bootstrapping money. Years later he may produce some noteworthy data. But the delay in reinforcement is long.

BECOMING A SUBJECT

The problem of running a tight experimental design becomes many times more acute when the subject of your research is your entire life and the lives of others. You can't sit down and say, "First I'll decide on sleeping arrangements; I'll compare these three types of arrangements and take these data using this design; in six months' time I'll be able to think about eating; then in two years or so, we'll be able to start cleaning up after ourselves;" and so forth. If it's your life you're experimenting with, you don't have all that much to say about when you stop and start different phases and what you emphasize or what you neglect. You *are* the experiment and you've got to keep it alive.

In the lab the experimenter tries to be a dictator. He tries to achieve total control, changing individual variables at his discretion. When we ran an experiment or started a program in a hospital ward or a classroom, most often we also decided what to study and how to study it. Occasionally, we would consult with the subjects, but we never gave them complete freedom to decide what behaviors would be studied and how. Some of our greatest difficulties at Lake Village have been in the area of decision making, particularly in regard to whose goals should be adopted. We have had problems deciding when and if snowmobiles should be used and cigarettes smoked. As yet, I can't imagine similar decisions being made about what and whose behavior we should study, who should study whose behavior, how it should be studied, and what manipulations should be performed in a live-in situation where everyone is at once experimenter and subject. Perhaps some day, agreement will be more likely, but we'll need a different system than we have now.

Most people will resist becoming subjects, and behavior modifiers are no exceptions. *Psychology Today* recently published an article about "behavior shapers" (Goodall, 1972) that told of what has occurred in the world of behavior modification. Many of the people you have heard at this conference, and other people with whom you've studied or worked, were cited in that paper. To all readers of that article and to all individuals who are thinking about hiring any one of us as consultants, I would warn that many of the world's behavior shapers still cannot get their own children to pick up and put away their own shoes.

All my life, I have left things lying around and forgotten where I put them in much the same way that I observe Tommy, Traci, and Kristen Ulrich leave things around and forget where they put them. Nevertheless, I have not yet been totally successful in imparting to my youngest daughter that socks really don't belong on the kitchen table. And this malady is not unique to my daughter, though she is scolded in a way behavior shapers seldom experience. Last evening, I arrived with Steve Louisell at the Kansas City International Airport and waited patiently for my friend Keith Miller to pick us up. When he finally arrived, we all went to the parking lot, and from there to Lawrence. Keith had earlier assured us that he had plenty of room for taking people to Lawrence, because he had a station wagon. When we were in the parking lot, however, we began to look for a blue Volkswagen "bug." Both Steve and I helped in the search, lugging our bags around the parking lot, until we remembered Keith had said something about a station wagon. Keith thought for a while, then proclaimed that we were right, he did have a station wagon. Sometime later, we found a large brown State of Kansas station wagon parked far away from the supposed resting place of the blue Volkswagen. We all laughed heartily and left. When you are little, you forget where you put your shoes; when you are big, you forget where you put your car.

The level of behavior control that people are willing or able to achieve in themselves and their loved ones is far lower than the level they achieve in experimental subjects. Although we impose control on "others" such as squirrel monkeys or school children, we are not ready to control our own children, much less ourselves. Recently, I attended a conference at Stockton College in New Jersey where we discussed aggression. Ken Moyer was describing some of the recent research that used brain stimulation and lesions to control aggression, along the lines suggested by the work of Heath, Delgado, and others. During the course of his talk, I wondered to what extent the people who implant electrodes in the brains of others would be interested in undergoing the operation themselves. We are all, at times, very aggressive and would prefer to avoid some of the unpleasant emotions and consequences associated with these episodes. No doubt, the objects of our aggression also would prefer us to control ourselves. How many of the people in this audience would be willing to experience the drug therapy that has been administered in a number of hospitals? Better yet, how many of you would be willing to put yourselves under the strict contingencies of the worlds we engineer: the hospital wards, homes for the retarded, classrooms, and so forth? In-seat behavior may be good for somebody else, but not necessarily for ourselves. I, for one, don't like to sit very long in one spot—I never did and teachers had problems with me in that respect.

Steven, a religious communard, described behavior control at Twin Oaks after visiting there:

> The lawn-clipping sheep of *Walden Two* stay neatly within their electrically fenced boundaries. At Twin Oaks the pigs root up the back yard after knocking down the electric fence, starting a minor brushfire in the process. In *Walden Two* the children are taught self-control by receiving a lollipop reinforcer for *not* eating the powder-sugar coated lollipop that has been dangling on a string around their necks. At Twin Oaks the members were trying to get in the habit of picking up after themselves by setting aside a little money each day for orange juice if the dining room tables were clean. Melba, the house manager, was going to keep track, but kept forgetting. After a month of observation Melba gave up but served orange juice anyway, and we loved it.
>
> The community opts for the more natural, less self-conscious means of shaping the behavior of incoming members. Nobody likes to feel manipulated. And most people do not like to feel they are manipulating others. Strong community norms have developed in this regard. (1971, p. 11)

As soon as the experimenter himself becomes a subject, certain methodologies become far less practical and far less attractive.

WHY YOU SHOULD BECOME A SUBJECT;
OR, WHY SHOULD YOU BECOME A SUBJECT?

The solution, traditionally, has been to maintain the apparent dichotomy between experimenter and subject. It makes life easier (at least for the experimenter), but I wonder if it doesn't ignore some important data. Earlier, I mentioned Iz Goldiamond, who is responsible in many ways for some of the direction that my life has taken. A couple of years ago Iz was in a terrible car accident that left him paralyzed and unable to walk. Recently, at a conference at Northwestern University, he presented a paper entitled "Coping and Adaptive Behaviors of the Disabled." He started that paper by saying:

> In these days when only women are supposed to write about women's problems and blacks about blacks', I come with an unfair advantage over others who write about disabilty—I am writing from a wheel chair. In these days when authority is legitimized only through personal experience, I present impeccable credentials. (p. 1)

In 1967, I attended a conference at Harvard that I'll talk more about later. At that conference Sanford Unger showed some films of interviews with people who had taken LSD. At that time I knew very little about the subject and was skeptical about effects from drugs. I surmised that the behavior of the patients was all a product of their conditioning. Nevertheless, I had to admit to myself that I really didn't know. After talking with some of the people who administered LSD to their patients, I discovered that they didn't know either, for they hadn't tried it. I concluded that the only way to understand what happens with patients who take LSD would be to take LSD myself. As a result, I did take LSD and immediately became aware of the fact that it was certainly not simply a placebo effect—something that many other people had known for a long time, and had talked about in a literature to which I had not been introduced. Somewhere in the middle of my first trip I had, among other revelations, a fantastic urge to phone Doug Anger and Ron Hutchinson and explain to them how important it was that we enter another research area.

After that first experience, I experimented again and again. My experimentation brought me in closer contact with the drug culture: I read its literature, talked with its people, and continued to experiment, not only with LSD, but with all of the drugs that were beginning to become a central social issue. I must admit that the investigation was not conducted purely for the data but often simply because I found it fun and interesting, which is, of course, why people should do research. Once, years later, I experimented with a combination of mainlining cocaine and simultaneously taking a heavy dose of LSD. I would describe that experiment as an apparatus failure or accident. It was certainly nothing for which I had a well-thought-out hypothesis. I did, however, have the most unforgettable experience of my life; it included the irrevocable knowledge that I had somehow stepped into an eternity of internal experience. I began to move more and more swiftly through all the information that was ever available to me through my total genetic and cultural evolution. Everything that I had ever experienced whizzed by me until I was going so fast and understanding so much that the whole system broke down and I found myself faced with the revelation that some of those things I had learned in my youth were true, that there was indeed a heaven and a hell and I had landed in the wrong place. That was the reality at the moment and there was no arguing against it. It was a fact. My history, the cocaine, the LSD, and my dinner then combined to make my stomach growl. My senses had been conditioned to magnify, and that growl represented all the growling that had ever occurred in the history of all living organisms. The needle pricks in my arms where I had injected the cocaine were accentuated to the extent that I felt I had hold of grids attached additively to all of the Grason-Stadtler shock generators that had ever been built, that I had been plugged into every power source in the universe. I was in pain. Once again, had I known ahead of time what I was going to experience, I would have declined stepping into the experimental chamber.

But, apparently, nothing lasts forever and at some point I mercifully died, which again I understood as a fact against which there was no argument. I remember very well the feeling: Oh, so this is what it is like. I felt a little bad about the fact that people were going to find me with needles and all the other paraphernalia, but I more or less believed that they would understand that Roger was just trying something new again. After all, he was educated in the tradition of the experimental analysis of behavior, wasn't he? Sometime later I discovered that although I had died, I was again back among the living, a testimonial to rebirth. I guess I had what some people call a bad trip, but I refuse to look at it that way because in the end a thing is neither a good nor a bad trip, but is just there to be looked at and described in whatever way one can best describe it. Or, if you will, it becomes data! Today, I have a much more profound understanding of drugs than I did in 1967, and I am in a much better position to talk about drugs and to articulate their dangers than are some of the individuals who make up drug abuse panels or who lecture children who know more about drugs than do the lecturers.

In his paper on disability, Iz Goldiamond described as a phony a newspaper reporter who attempted to understand "us" by spending almost a week at the Rehabilitation Institute, much of it in a wheel chair, and who ignored most of the patients. I suggest that that sentiment might be present in many of the individuals whom we have visited, not only as reporters but also as manipulators of alien behavior. However, I have not noted any great reluctance on the part of many of us to comment on areas of behavior with which we have had little experience.

Earlier, I touched on a conference I attended in 1967 at Harvard University on behavior control technologies. The conference was part of a program sponsored by IBM to inquire into the effects of technological change on the character of society and into the reciprocal effects of social progress on the pace and direction of scientific and technological development. Thanks to IBM, seventeen scholars gathered at Harvard for a one-day interchange of ideas that was later described in the book *Human Aspects of Biomedical Innovation* (Mendelsohn, Swazey, and Taviss, 1971). Conference participants were drawn from a wide range of disciplines: psychology, psychiatry, biophysics, physiology, demography, history of science, history of philosophy, political science, and law. Prior to the conference, working papers were prepared by Jose Delgado, Sanford Unger, and myself. Delgado of course talked about controlling behavior through brain stimulation, Sanford Unger talked about research with LSD, and I talked about conditioning. It was an extremely far-sighted conference; it touched on many of the issues that will confront us in the next few years. Topics discussed included the fact that deliberate control is aversive, the old issue of freedom, the squelching of creativity, the selection of goals, and the legal controls needed to cope with these new technologies.

At the conference, I spoke on how behavioral scientists should get out of the laboratory and apply their findings to human situations. E. G. Mesthene, who was Director of the Harvard Program on Science and Technology, replied that the social consequences of behavior research should not be left in the hands of scientists alone. He said,

> So long as the scientist stays in the test tube, there is still an interference with nature, but very few people really are going to deny him the right to do anything he wants in the test tube. But as soon as he starts exploding nuclear bombs in the atmosphere or trying to gain control of the local school system, then it seems to me that the society begins to have a stake in what is done initially for scientific purposes. As soon as the consequences become other than just scientific, you raise questions of the structure of attitudes and social controls within which the enterprise of science can be conducted. (pp. 125–26)

I agree that scientists should not necessarily rule the world and that controls are essential. However, the fact is that the situation does not change much whether we are in or out of the laboratory. We do affect an experiment by participating in it. We are members of the total research team, both the subject and the experimenter, and there is nothing we can do about it.

I, as many of you, have often pointed out that no one is exempt from the laws of behavior. We try to pretend that we are the experimenters and that we are in control, but what is really happening? The government gives us money to study positive reinforcement and then uses our results to train soldiers to go to Indochina and kill people more effectively (Holland, in press.) I recently testified for the American Civil Liberties Union in a complaint brought by the National Prison Project against the Federal Penitentiary Treatment Facility in Springfield, Missouri. Some prisoners, especially politically oriented ones, would not adjust to prison life. They were sent to Springfield for treatment in a "behavior modification" project directed by a man trained at one of our better centers for producing behavior modifiers. The project began by depriving the prisoners of many of the rights they had already earned in another setting. The idea was to use these rights as reinforcers.

I myself set up an early education program that was supposed to train people to work with disadvantaged populations; these people were to use behavior modification to give children that might grow up illiterate and unable to cope with the world the chance to acquire the skills that would help them survive and even change the environment in which they would live. Money is scarce now, and the people we have trained are going to work in schools for children whose parents have much more money. We have trained, at government expense, superior day-care workers for people who could afford superior child care all along. Before the civil war we owned slaves. Now we rent them for a while and sometimes train them to become behavior modifiers.

You can't pretend that by establishing yourself as an experimenter you have exempted yourself from being a subject. If you set up an experiment in which you impose a program on people who have very little to say about what happens to them, you can't expect your results to be applicable to a situation in which no one has that kind of power. When you set up an experiment in this way, you have traded one kind of subject-hood for another.

DATA

Many of you are probably thinking, but if we give up the objectivity of the experimenter and the reliability of his data, if we let in subjectivity and attend to data that can't as yet be quantified or observed by more than one person, we will be giving up our unique position as an island of science in a sea of speculation; we will be back where we started from; we won't know what's True and what's False. But we must remember that it's we who define data and it's we who have had histories of reinforcement that taught us that one type of data is interesting and another isn't. If we get so inextricably tied up in looking at only one kind of experiment, I think we begin to lose the essence of what it was that got us all started. We have made a lot of gains by paying a great deal of attention to quantifiable data. We've attached numbers to events and we've been able to run reversals and multiple baselines. With this strategy we've been able to see correlations (which are so consistent that we call them functional relationships) between what we believe to be independent variables and dependent variables. The fact remains, however, that there are many different kinds of data and functional relationships.

Years after my father, Ralph "Slim" Ulrich, taught me to try new things, Izzy Goldiamond taught me that Y is a function of X given a constant K. For those of us in behavior analysis, this means that we can describe the functional relationship between certain behaviors (X) and certain environmental events (Y) if we can hold all other relevant variables constant. Thus, by doing a great many experiments in which different behaviors are studied, different environmental events programmed, and other relevant factors held constant, we felt that eventually we could perhaps describe the relationship between all behavior and all environmental events. In one sense, we were moving toward a goal that included the possibility of explaining all behavior. The success of this approach led to some excess, in that we at times became overly evangelistic. At least I did. It was as if we had found a new religion. The entire universe was accessible and easily packaged. We used Science to explain everything just like some Christians use God. The same rules that applied in our little black boxes in the laboratory would work in schools, in our homes, and in many other places. When they did seem to work, we simply became further hooked. Our methodology was right and we could solve problems almost anyplace they existed. Unfortunately, we forgot now and then that our success in applied settings was related to the degree that we could identify and control the relevant variables of our equation, $Y = f(X)$ given K. Also, we seemed, at times, to forget that our original success at discovery was related to our willingness to try to look at things in different ways.

We sometimes criticized other approaches to human experience because of their limitations, just as other people have criticized us for our approach. We say introspection is no good because the data aren't reliable or quantifiable. We ban from existence the kind of data that is reported by a mystic or by a person who has taken a psychedelic drug. However, we very rarely look at the limitations of our own way of knowing and generalizing from our experiments. We talk as if our findings pertain to all behavior, when we are really only looking at behavior under the narrow conditions we create in the laboratory. We think we can dispose of all those variables we lump into K, but different "K" variables at different values may produce vastly different functional relationships between X and Y. We would have to describe those changes, and we aren't prepared, either technologically or mathematically, to do so. So we observe the relationships we *can* look at and pretend that we are explaining all those other relationships we can't look at.

When a person says, "I've experienced some behavior that I don't think 'science' can account for at this time," we criticize his methodology. But how good is our methodology? There is some consistency in our results, so we must be doing some things right. But there is also consistency among people who report psychic experiences. We say we don't know what nonscientists study or how they study it. But are we all that sure of what we're studying? Our measurement techniques are crude at best; they simplify and change the behavior we're studying. Suppose we become much more proficient scientifically, that our measurement techniques become more sophisticated, that we handle much more complex situations. Even then there will probably be limits to what we can understand. Izzy once scolded me for asking, "Why?" He said we can never really understand "why" because there'll always be another time we can ask "why" again. He was attacking Aristotelian logic for trying to solve the problems of the universe. He sided with Galileo and the physicists who told us just to ask "how" and not be concerned with "why." And he was right: science will never be able to tell us why and I'm now convinced it will never be able to satisfy us completely as to how.

The subject matter of physics is far more straightforward than the subject matter of psychology. Physics has developed to a high level of sophistication. Psychology, to develop to a comparable level, will require even greater ingenuity and insight. As physics became more and more sophisticated, it began to discover limitations on its ability to depict the world. As the laws of physics were extended to microscopic systems such as atoms, the construction of new mathematical machinery became necessary. A consequence of this new mathematical machinery was the so-called Heisenberg uncertainty principle. It states that the scientist cannot know exactly and simultaneously two conjugate properties of a particle—its speed and position, for example. Psychology will certainly encounter similar limitations.

In attempting to apply the results of the laboratory to complex social situations, I have experienced an analog of the Heisenberg uncertainty principle. Some reasonably reliable functional relationships have been found within the restricted conditions of the laboratory. These relationships can be extrapolated to settings in which we have considerable control over the environment of other human beings. Our results in these settings have not been as clear-cut as in the laboratory, but they have been sufficient to influence profoundly fields such as education and mental health. When I first thought of moving to an experimental community, I expected to experience a similar sort of extrapolation. However, when you move from a controlled, authoritarian situation in which you study one behavior, to a flexible situation in which you must deal with a whole variety of behaviors, the situation becomes so complex that it strikes me as almost impossible to handle by the models and techniques we have so far relied on. I could of course, choose some aspect of the situation that is amenable to experimental analysis. I could submit to the *Journal of Applied Behavior Analysis* a paper on how various contingencies affected the number of dishes washed or the number of gallons of gas consumed. There would be nothing wrong with doing those studies. But as a representation of what's really occurring they would be grossly inadequate. And, right now, I don't know what I would do to make them adequate.

When my barbaric ancestors found Christianity they thought they had the answer to everything. But they didn't, so among some of their sons and daughters Christianity was gradually replaced by Science. Scientists began to act as if they had the answer to everything. But they didn't. Some day another religion will rise and replace Science. Perhaps the only religion that's safe is the one that honors change—and for me science and its methodology still does that.

One weapon in the verbal armory against behavior analysis is the story of the man who was looking for a lost key under a street lamp. A passer-by, noticing his lack of success, asked him if he was sure he had dropped it there. The man replied, "No, but this is the only place I can see." Although we pretend to look only under the street light, and even pretend that it lights the world, we often grope about on our hands and knees hoping to find something in the dark. When we do find something, we quickly shine a light on it and claim we knew it was there all along. Some data we can't, as yet, quantify. But we need those data to understand others that we can quantify. If we only go where we feel safe, we may be insuring our own ignorance.

Let me point out that I still think contingencies do affect the world and that, when possible, the strictest rules of science should be followed. Science is still my favorite religion. At Lake Village we have tried some things that we perhaps would not have tried had we not known what we do about behavior. But working within complex institutions and societies is a difficult thing. I believe that we will never be able to describe communities and governments by using only the type of experiment that will now be accepted by our better-known journals. Perhaps all the events that occur in a community could be translated into *JABA*-type data, but no one will ever take all that data and present those figures. With the budget we now have, we won't even come close. New techniques will be needed for studying new types of endeavors, and traditional behavior modification research will have its place. Some day we hope that the community at Lake Village will be running so smoothly that we'll be able to sit back and ask, "What was it we did that makes things work?" or say "If we change this, we now know that something else will change because of it." We might be able to market our system in a way similar to some of the gadgets and systems we have marketed as a result of other applied behavior analysis efforts. We may even find that some variation improves things, so that life becomes comfortable—and when that happens, if it ever does, for some it will be the signal to move once again into another setting to await patiently the next accident.

And that is the experiment as we see it. I simply don't know the answer at this time, and perhaps I never will, but I feel I have a better chance of discovering some now-hidden secrets by actually going into situations myself than I would were I to confine myself to one kind of data. The more efforts we make—regardless of how varied—in trying to discover how complex human interactions evolve, the better.

5 / Following Up on the Behavior Analysis Model: Results After Ten Years of Early Intervention with Institutionalized, Mentally Retarded Children

Stephen I. Sulzbacher · *John D. Kidder*

Early in 1962, a group of researchers under the overall direction of Sidney Bijou established one of the first elementary level, special education classrooms to employ exclusively the behavior analysis model (Birnbrauer, Bijou, Wolf, and Kidder, 1965). This demonstration classroom was sponsored by the White River School District, the Rainier School for the mentally retarded, and the University of Washington, through grants from the National Institute of Mental Health. The published reports of the research done in this classroom during the early 1960s are now standard references on programmed instruction (Greene, 1966; Bijou, Birnbrauer, Kidder, and Tague, 1966) and classroom management (Birnbrauer, Wolf, Kidder and Tague, 1965.) In 1965, the music (and the grant support) stopped and the researchers from the University of Washington found themselves sitting in chairs at the Universities of Arizona, Illinois, Kansas, and North Carolina. The teachers in the Programmed Learning Classroom remained at Rainier School, however, and the classroom continued to be run without grant support. The classroom is in operation today and has influenced nearly all of the other educational programs at Rainier School.

During its eleven years of operation, the Programmed Learning Classroom at Rainier has served approximately one hundred institutionalized mentally retarded children on a full- or part-time basis. The present report documents what happened to these children and how their experience under the behavior analysis model improved their prognosis and materially enriched their lives.

PROCEDURES IN THE PROGRAMMED LEARNING CLASSROOM (PLC)

Although some important changes have occurred in the classroom procedures and educational curriculum employed in PLC, many of the fundamental features of the classroom have remained unaltered. During the days of grant support, research assistants did much of the scoring and tutoring of children in the classroom. Currently, the children score nearly all of their own work (with periodic probes by the teacher) and know where to go to get their next assignment. When a new child (or visitor) comes to the classroom, he is assigned to one of the students for orientation. Parts of the curriculum that require one-to-one teaching were originally administered by the teachers, but currently are almost exclusively administered by students who have completed those sections of the curriculum. The curricular materials are systematically filed so that each child can, and does, prepare each day's lesson plan before he leaves on the previous afternoon. The children receive marks for successfully completing their work; whereas these were often originally exchanged for trinkets or candy, it is currently more common for the children to save them for larger, long-range treats such as field trips and parties. Misbehavior in the classroom is no longer handled by a warning followed by time-out. This contingency was abandoned five years ago, and misbehavior is now uniformly extinguished by the other students in the class. New students, usually referred to PLC because of their disruptive classroom behavior, quickly adjust to the fact that there is no peer support for deviant behavior, and teacher-applied punishment is rarely needed.

Table 1-1 gives the ages and IQs of the children who entered PLC between 1962 and 1965 as reported by Bijou, Birnbrauer, Kidder, and Tague (1966). It can be seen that these children had intelligence scores that place them in the trainable or educable range. They were selected from among the residents at Rainier School who had been unable to profit from other clasroom placements, mostly because of severe behavior problems.

Table 1-1   *Chronological Age and Peabody (PPVT) Mental Age and IQ * of the Children Grouped According to the Year They Entered the Project*

	RANGE	MEAN
	1962–63	
	N = 8	
CA	9–4 to 14–9	12–1
MA	4–5 to 9–6	7–2
IQ	44–66	59
	1963–64	
	N = 9	
CA	8–7 to 12–0	10–4
MA	4–10 to 10–6	7–0
IQ	56–87	66
	1964–65	
	N = 10	
CA	8–10 to 11–4	10–2
MA	3–8 to 9–8	6–8
IQ	39–93	65

* Two scores were from the Wechsler Intelligence Test for Children.

Some had, in fact, been previously excluded from school. These characteristics are also typical of the children who entered PLC after 1965.

RESULTS AND DISCUSSION

Data on current school or job placement and living situation of all students who attended PLC full-time for at least one year were obtained from school records, and are summarized in Table 1-2. These 52 children represent about half the number of children who have been served in PLC; the others were either part-time students, or were referred for specific classroom behavior training and returned to other school situations when that behavior problem was remedied in a short period of time. If a child is still at Rainier School and not attending PLC or another program oriented toward community placement, he could be considered a "failure." Table 1-2 lists two such cases who attended PLC for only one year and one other child who was a student for four years. The remaining 13 children still at Rainier School show every indication of ultimately moving out of the institution and into the community. Table 1-3 summarizes in somewhat greater detail the current status of the PLC students who have attended for two or more years. These case summaries document the fact that PLC

Table 1-2 *Summary of Current Job, School and Living Situation for PLC Students who Attended for at Least One Year between 1962 and 1973*

		NOW LIVING IN COMMUNITY					DIS-CHARGED (RECORDS UNAVAILABLE)	STILL AT RAINIER SCHOOL			
YEARS OF ATTENDANCE AT PLC	N	Fully Employed	Sheltered Work Situation	Attending High School	Attending College and Working	Not in School and Not Working		Enrolled in PLC	Enrolled in Community Oriented Pre-voc. Program	Others	DISABLED OR DECEASED
6–8 years	10	—	2	2	1	—	1	3	—	—	1
4–5 years	6	1	3	—	—	1	—	—	—	1	1
2–3 years	8	2	—	3	—	—	—	2	—	2	—
1 year	28	4	4	4	2	—	4	2	6	2	—
Total N = 52											

Table 1-3 *Current Status of PLC Students who Attended for Two or More Years*

YEARS OF ATTENDANCE AT PLC	N	CURRENT SITUATION
6–8 years	10	Three are still enrolled in PLC; live at Rainier School; are also enrolled in driver's training; and it is expected they will leave Rainier for successful community placement.
		Two live in group homes: one is employed as a busboy and attends a Junior College; the other attends a regular high school (limited program) and plays varsity football.
		Two have been returned to their parents' homes and are employed in sheltered work situations.
		One lives in a limited-care boarding home and is in an on-the-job training program.
		One was discharged and is living in another state (no further records available).
		One is deceased.
4–5 years	6	Three returned to their parents' homes and are employed in sheltered workshops.
		One lives independently, drives his own car, and is a city employee in a small town.
		One lives in a group home and did some work in a sheltered situation, but is now unemployed.
		One has been moved to a lower-level hall at Rainier; even though she has made academic progress at PLC, it is not likely that she will leave the institution.
2–3 years	8	Two are still enrolled in PLC; one lives at Rainier School, and the other at home in a nearby community; both are expected to eventually have successful community placement.
		Three live with parents or foster parents and attend regular or special classes at local high schools.
		Two are in independent living situations, manage their own affairs, and are fully employed.
		One is hospitalized with a degenerative nerve disease.

students were able to successfully apply the results of their classroom training; even the three children we have defined as "failures" were able to demonstrate considerable reading and arithmetic skill gains as a result of their experience at PLC.

At the time the PLC project was begun, Greene compiled a list of

60 "cohorts," who were from the same residence halls as the children chosen for PLC and therefore similar in intelligence, behavioral characteristics, and prognosis to the PLC group. They were not a matched control group, and after Greene left Rainier School, the cohort list was forgotten and filed in a drawer of old testing records. The present authors "discovered" the list in the course of preparing this report and found that 30 of the "cohorts" were subsequently enrolled in PLC. However, records of the remaining 30 were used as a comparison group to assess the long-term effects of PLC placements. These data are presented in Table 1-4.

Table 1-4 *Comparisons of PLC Students with Matched Cohorts on Selected Indices of Subsequent Success*

	PLC (n = 52)	COHORT (n = 30)
Percentage who are currently productively engaged (working or in school)	91.5	76.6
Percentage living in community	68.5	66.7
Percentage who live independently and are fully employed	13	10
Percentage who failed on placement and were returned to institution	1.8	13.3
Percentage who have committed legal offenses	0	6.6

Overall, 91.5 percent of the PLC group were judged to be productively engaged (work or school) versus only 76.6 percent of the cohorts. The likelihood of leaving the institution was apparently unaffected by PLC treatment. However, the State of Washington has enacted legislation to drastically reduce the number of institutional residents by funding group homes and smaller community-care facilities. This is, of course, a highly desirable situation, and has resulted in community placement for some residents who might not otherwise have had that opportunity, but it also contributes to such statistics as the 23.3 percent of the cohorts on placement, but not working or receiving schooling.

Similarly, the data show that PLC alumni are considerably less likely to be returned to the institution after being placed in the community (none of the PLC group have had trouble with the law, whereas two cohorts have been arrested, one several times for theft and the other for a serious drug offense). More PLC people than cohorts attend public schools, and a slightly greater percentage are fully independent and employed. An analysis of the types of jobs held by this latter group is perhaps the best index of what differentiates the PLC from the cohort group: typically, those who have been in PLC are given greater responsibility, and reports from job supervisors at Rainier School and in the community characterize the PLC group as more trustworthy and reliable. All of the cohorts presently fully employed in the community have the same kind of job: washing and cleaning cars for auto dealers. The PLC group includes a telephone company clerk, a sanitation man, and a supervisor of peers in group homes and in training programs at Rainier School. It should be noted, however, that all of the children who attended PLC also benefited from numerous other educational experiences at Rainier School, and the credit for their ultimate success rests also with other White River School District teachers and Rainier School staff, as does the success of many cohorts. Similarly, many of the PLC teaching and classroom management tactics have been incorporated, by other teachers, into the curriculum of classes attended by cohorts. In fact, the behavioral curriculum developed largely from the PLC model is now in use throughout the school. Portions of the PLC curriculum have been published as the Edmark programs.

ILLUSTRATIVE CASES

Hugh was the subject of one of the early reports of the Programmed Learning Classroom research (Birnbrauer, Bijou, Wolf, and Kidder, 1965.) Hugh had already made considerable progress at the time that article was written, and was also very popular with his classmates and with all of us who have worked in PLC. We were all greatly saddened, therefore, when Hughie died accidentally in 1969. At that time, his class time at PLC had been reduced as he had worked his way up from janitor to assistant janitorial supervisor, a position where he supervised other resident apprentices. In addition, Hugh had become something of an entrepreneur in that he offered a variety of services to others in his residence hall in exchange for the marked pages they had earned at the Programmed Learning Classroom. He apparently set up a mini-classroom in the hall, where he tutored his fellows in exchange for marks.

Another of Hugh's classmates, Lee, attended PLC for four years. Lee came from an extremely disruptive home, and two of his brothers had been placed in institutions. However, Lee now lives on his own in the small town nearby, where he drives his own car, is employed by the municipal government, and earns a salary greater than some of the teacher aides who taught him at PLC.

A third case, Dale, attended PLC for seven years and is now living at home with his parents in a nearby community. He commutes to Rainier School where he attends a high school class for two hours a day. Dale is learning to drive a car, and is also taking a course in home economics that is designed to teach independent living. He also has a job in the kitchen at Rainier School, where he supervises some of the other apprentices working in the kitchen. Lee and Dale have both voted in recent elections.

In spite of the typically pessimistic prognoses that characterized all of PLC's students before they were enrolled, the cases discussed are illustrative of a generally successful group of alumni. Three are attending community colleges, many have made a successful transition to high schools in community settings, and virtually all of them have functional reading, writing, and arithmetic skills. They are graduates of a classroom that, for the past eight years, has been run by one teacher and a part-time aide, with no facilities or money beyond those available to any other special education classroom in public schools.

CONCLUSIONS

Although the primary emphasis at the Programmed Learning Classroom had been to teach the fundamental academic skills of reading, writing, and arithmetic, proficiency in these skills does not appear to be the most important factor in the subsequent success of the students. On the basis of the anecdotal evidence gathered from the students and their parents, employers, and case workers, other factors seemed more closely related to the success of these retarded individuals:

1. PLC graduates were consistently reliable and responsible in the execution of assigned tasks. It is likely that this characteristic was learned at PLC, where students are required to plan and correct their own daily work and to remain on task while in the classroom.

2. Conversational skills of the PLC group are relatively sophisticated. PLC teachers have a conversation period every morning and socially reinforce the use of a varied vocabulary and complex sentence structure, and the choice of socially appropriate topics.

3. The PLC students seem to have a more varied repertoire of social skills than the cohorts, and these skills appear in the appropriate social context.

If the above speculations prove to be valid, it would appear that programs devised specifically to teach these social skills might be of more benefit to retarded individuals, when compared to the usefulness of reading and arithmetic skills, though the latter obviously cannot be omitted either.

part 2 / Programs

6 / A Behavioral System for Group Living

L. Keith Miller · Richard Feallock

The search for the Good Life is probably as old as man. Over the centuries intellectuals have speculated on the different ways it could be achieved. One frequent type of speculation certainly goes back as far as Plato's *Republic*. Plato's dreams were echoed in Augustine's *City of God,* More's *Utopia,* and Bellamy's *Looking Backard*. None of these works ever led to a serious attempt to built a community fashioned after their description.

We wish to thank the many individuals who have helped us to develop this program. Prominent among these are Hal Weaver and Steve Fawcett, who helped design the initial system. Thanks go to Drs. Donald Baer, Dean Fixen, Don Bushell, Judith LeBlanc, Bill Hopkins, Dave Born, John Wright, Don Green, and Elery Phillips for their many helpful discussions about the project and this write-up. Particular thanks go to Dr. Mont Wolf for sharing with us so many helpful ideas that derived from Achievement Place. And the Project probably would have failed long ago without the special help and unflagging encouragement of Dr. Jim Sherman.

Over the last 150 years another approach to the Good Life was made by many activists who started experimental communities. A description of many of these communities was provided by Charles Nordhoff (1875). It is clear from his description that these communities were not successful ventures in Utopian living. They were racked with dissent and organizational problems, and sooner or later all of them folded or drastically changed their character.

What seems to have been lacking in all of these attempts is a science of behavior capable of engineering the desired behavioral and cultural changes. In reading descriptions of past attempts at experimental living, one is struck by the frequency with which behavioral problems are mentioned. Many people didn't do their share of the work, others weren't thrifty enough, tools and equipment were ruined, people were argumentative or cruel, and so on. The procedures that were used to control these problems included social ostracism, expulsion, and mutual criticism. Apparently, these techniques were not sufficient to solve the problems, which recurred and, reportedly, led to the dissolution of the experimental communities. Thus, some systematic techniques for increasing the occurrence of socially desirable behaviors and decreasing the occurrence of socially undesirable behaviors seem to be needed to create a successful Utopia. In short, what seems to have been missing in all of the attempts at creating a better community is a science of behavior—a set of techniques for engineering the desired behavioral and cultural changes in the members of the community.

B. F. Skinner, in his Utopian novel *Walden Two,* speculated on what a community based on such a science of behavior might be like. Such a science has clearly emerged since Skinner wrote *Walden Two*—the science of applied behavior analysis—and it has been used to engineer total living environments. For example, the pioneering work of Ayllon and Azrin (1968) with token economies was undertaken in a group living environment.

Ayllon and Azrin worked with a group of about 45 institutionalized "mental patients" in a state mental hospital. This group, though made up of so-called "abnormal" individuals, had many of the same problems that any community of "normals" would have. They lived together 24 hours a day. The socially desirable behaviors that Ayllon and Azrin selected to work with included behaviors that would be desirable in any group-living environment. They sought to increase such behaviors as cleaning hallways and bathrooms, serving and clearing meals, washing dishes, and caring for one's own area. As these problems are common to any group-living situation, it can be argued that the technology developed by Ayllon and Azrin is relevant to experimental communities. This possibility has been described in *The Last Whole Earth Catalogue* (Bray, 1971).

Of course, a hospital setting like the one Ayllon and Azrin worked in is clearly quite different from a voluntary community of "normal" adults. A major difference is that the people in a hospital environment are not free to leave and do not have the well-developed behavioral repertoires that might permit them to change or modify the system. Thus, issues such as who is going to specify the behavioral goals of the group, the contingencies of reinforcement to be used, and other issues of self-government do not arise. In other words, the basic issue of gaining the consent of the governed does not usually arise in such a setting.

A major step in the direction of dealing with issues of "self-government" has been taken by the pioneering work of Fixsen, Phillips, and Wolf (1973) with juvenile delinquents. These researchers have developed Achievement Place—a "family-style" rehabilitation center for youth in trouble. Their system uses behavioral techniques, including a token economy. However, they are dealing with young adults with well-developed—in fact, overdeveloped—repertoires that clearly would permit them to change or modify the system. Furthermore, the "family-style" center is relatively open in that the youths go to school every day and stay at Achievement Place at night. Thus, it is fairly easy for the youth to run away. This means that these researchers not only had to develop a system for involving the youth in some form of self-government, they also had to keep the system on a relatively pleasant basis. Thus, the work of Achievement Place is clearly another major step toward working with normal adults in a voluntary living arrangement.

The experiment that we will describe in the following pages takes another step toward developing a behavioral technology for a voluntary community of adults. The description will be divided into two parts. First, we will describe the "worksharing system": how the basic work of the house is managed. Second, we will describe the "self-government system": how the members of the Project govern themselves.

WORKSHARING

The Physical Environment

The experimental living project is housed in a large three-story frame house with two wings connected by an area that serves as a lounge. There are 29 private sleeping-study rooms, which are assigned primarily to single occupants, though occasionally two individuals share the same room. (See Figure 2-1.)

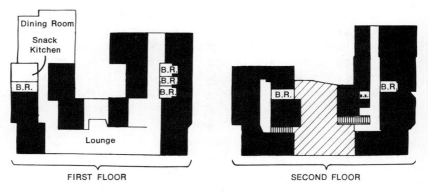

Figure 2-1 *House floor plan.*

The common areas of the house include hallways, bathrooms, storage areas, the lounge, a dining-meeting room, and a small snack kitchen. A large institutional-size kitchen is used to prepare the evening meal and is located in the basement of one wing. A game room and a shop are also in that basement.

The house, though old, is in reasonable condition. The floors are generally level, the walls are solid and intact, and the roof is sound. Few complaints have been made about noise being conducted through the walls or ceilings. Such features as plumbing, furnaces, window fittings, and electrical wiring are in as reasonable condition as can be expected of a 50-year-old house.

The house was purchased in 1969 for about $35,000 and is owned by a nonprofit corporation called the University of Kansas Student Housing Association. This is a totally independent corporation having as its board of directors a largely behavioral-oriented faculty group, as well as several local residents.

Who Lives There

The membership of the house consists of young adults who are enrolled as students at the University of Kansas. They range in age from 18 to 28. At any given time, roughly half of the members are male and half female. The members' fields of study include business, psychology, behavior modification, social work, chemistry, and the fine arts. Though most of the members are from Kansas and Missouri, some come from as far away as New York and California and, usually, several are from other countries. Overall, the members seem to represent a fairly random cross-section of the university population.

Becoming a Member

Before detailing the worksharing and self-government systems, we will provide an overview of the agreements that an entering member makes. This agreement is in two parts: a legal "tenant contract" and a quasi-legal "behavioral contract." Together, these documents define a starting point for the new member.

The legal contract specifies three things: first, the date and amount of the room and board payments; second, the consequences of not meeting the payments (first a fine and then eviction); and third, agreement by the members to abide by a behavioral contract (the *Member's Handbook*). The behavioral contract specifies the current operating rules of the community plus a set of rules by which members can change those rules. This contract is 80 pages long and provides the basis for both the self-government and the worksharing systems.

In addition to these two contracts, incoming members are required to post a $25 damage deposit, which helps ensure that they will leave their room clean and undamaged when they move. Also, they are required to post a $40 bond that ensures that they will live up to the terms of the behavioral contract (Mann, 1972; Stuart, 1970).

The Worksharing System

The worksharing system is designed to specify in behavioral terms the common chores of group living, to provide a mechanism for determining whether or not the chores have been done, and to provide a consequence system for maintaining these behaviors. The common chores have been subdivided into three subsystems: the cleaning system, the food program, and the repair program. Altogether, there are about 100 jobs occurring once a week that are specified by these three subsystems. A list containing these jobs is posted each Thursday, and members are asked to sign up for any assortment of jobs for the next week. They have complete flexibility as to how they select these jobs. They might sign up for only food preparation jobs. Or they might sign up for jobs in the early evening. Or they might sign up for jobs that all occur on a specific day. Thus, they can arrange their array of jobs in many ways because of the flexibility of the system. Each job is inspected according to a set of publicly available criteria. Each job is defined in terms of 5 to 15 measurable criteria. A trained member of the house does the inspection once a day. Members earn credits for their work, according to a simple point system. This system is more fully described in the sections below.

The Credit System

The credit system is a token economy that is used to reward each member. Each of the approximately 100 weekly jobs in the system is assigned a credit value, which is based on the length of time that the job should normally take and the desirability of the job. Credits are assigned at a base rate of 15 per hour to each job. Jobs that are not readily signed up for at that rate are assigned more credits. Thus, cooking, a popular job that takes two hours, is assigned 30 credits. Cleaning the grease from the oven, a very unpopular job that takes about one hour, is assigned 30 credits.

Each member can use up to 100 credits per week as a rent reduction. Each credit is worth ten cents, so the members can earn a rent reduction of up to $10 a week and maximum of $40 per month.

If a member earns more than 100 credits in a week, the surplus is put into a savings account. If a member earns less than 100 credits in a week, he can draw on those savings, if he has any. He is also permitted to borrow credits from a friend if the friend has savings. If the member earns less than 100 credits, and doesn't have any savings or a friend with savings, then he loses part of his potential rent reduction (at the rate of ten cents per unearned credit). Since the average rent and board without the reduction is $100, the member who maintains his work can earn an average of a $40 rent reduction so that room and board totals an average of $60 per month. This system means that a member is given a strong positive consequence for doing his share of the work.

The actual functioning of the credit system reveals its flexibility. Only 51 percent of the members earn 100 or more credits during an average week. The other 49 percent of the time they earn less. Specifically, 37 percent of the time they use savings accrued during prior weeks to make up their full 100 credits; 7 percent of the time they borrow credits from another member of the house who has accrued savings. And only 5 percent of the time does the average member end up not earning his full $10 rent reduction. Furthermore, this latter figure seems to be falling so that the full rent deduction is earned virtually all of the time by the members. Thus, the system is flexible enough so that a member needn't earn his full credits every week, as long as he has saved credits in the past or has a friend who has saved credits and will lend some to him. The result is that all the work is done, without the system being inflexible.

There is one more important contingency in the worksharing system. We found that members with savings would sometimes sign up for a job, such as cooking, and then fail to do it because the missed points could be covered out of their savings. This meant that others had to do these persons' work at the last minute and that such things as the evening meal might be late.

To avoid this problem, any job that is signed up for but not done at all results in a fine of $2. This has virtually eliminated failure to do jobs.

The Cleaning System

The goal of the cleaning system is to keep the common areas of the house clean and neat. The areas thus maintained are the bathrooms, the hallways, five common rooms, and the outside areas around the house. Maintaining these areas involves such chores as vacuuming, sweeping, mopping, scrubbing, emptying wastebaskets, and picking up trash.

The organization of this system requires a coordinator (who signs up for the job) to maintain the equipment and supplies required to do the jobs. Once a week, this coordinator checks the four storage areas, one located in each part of the building, to determine whether or not any additional materials should be purchased (or repaired). If so, he purchases the needed materials and places them in the appropriate storage area.

The coordinator is a key component in the cleaning system. By having a coordinator, the ordinary day-to-day jobs of cleaning can be routinely carried out by the housemembers who sign up for the jobs during a particular week. However, the coordinator's failure to do his job makes it impossible for others to do their jobs; because of this added responsibility, the coordinators are required to sign contracts specifying their duties in some detail and providing for special consequences if these duties are not completed.

The day-to-day cleaning jobs are defined by means of a behavioral checklist. Each job is broken down into 5 to 15 component parts, each of which is inspected to determine whether or not the job has been done. Between 50 and 150 cleaning components are inspected each day. (More details about the inspection system will be found on p. 83.)

Figure 2-2 shows the results of the daily inspection of cleaning jobs for the first three months. An average of about 95 percent of the components of all the cleaning jobs were judged "satisfactory" over the first 60 weeks of the program. These daily inspections ranged from about 70 percent satisfactory to 100 percent satisfactory. This level of cleanliness has been maintained for an additional 12 months since these data were taken.

Single-subject experiments, to be more fully reported below, have been conducted in which the functionality of the credits, inspections, and rent reductions were evaluated. The percentage of cleaning behavior decreased markedly with the elimination of any one of these components. Thus, there is evidence that credits, inspections, and rent reductions are all functional in maintaining cleaning behavior.

Figure 2-3 shows the mean ratings of 20 members of the house in

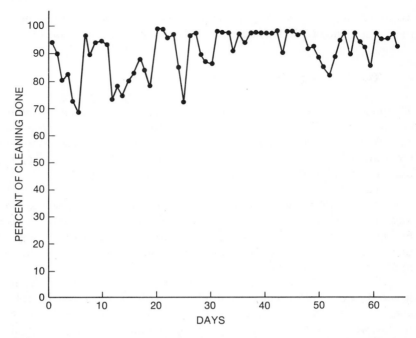

Figure 2-2 *Percentage of cleaning jobs done during the first 65 days of the program.*

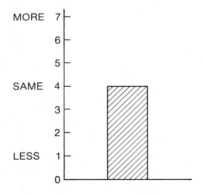

Figure 2-3 *Mean rating of response to the question, "How clean is the house kept, compared to a dormitory?"*

response to the question, "How clean is the house kept, compared to a dormitory?" The average rating on a 7-point scale was 4.1, which indicates that they considered it to be about the same cleanliness. It was our concern that the house be maintained at about that level of cleanliness, but not so clean that it approximated a hospital or a similar environment that might make members uncomfortable. In response to another question, all members rated the cleanliness of the public areas as "about right," as opposed to "too clean" or "too dirty."

The results of direct observation, when combined with the rating data, suggest that the worksharing system produced and maintained a level of cleanliness that was comfortable for the members of the house.

The Food Program

The goal of the food program is to provide inexpensive but tasty meals six nights a week. This system is not completely specified at this time, but basically it consists of a preplanned menu, cooks, servers, dishwashers, kitchen cleaners, inventory clerks, and food buyers.

The most important element of the food program is probably the preplanned menu. Members of the house have developed a menu covering about three months of meals. Detailed recipes for each dish specified in these meals have been developed. They are placed where the cooks can use them for each day's cooking, and a buying guide specifying how much of what items are needed for each month's menu has been developed.

The system works in the following way. A menu coordinator (who signs up for the job) places the menu for the day plus the associated recipes in the kitchen each morning. Then another person checks the pantry to determine if each required item is present in sufficient quantity. These items are put in a convenient place for the cooks. If any items are missing, the menu coordinator purchases them prior to the preparation of the meal. Then at 4:00 P.M. each day, the two members who signed up for cooking begin preparing the meal. A server sets the table for each member and brings the meal to the table. After dinner, the table is cleared, leftover food is stored, the dishes are washed, and the kitchen is cleaned and dishes are put away. Once a week, someone checks the menu for perishable items that will be required for the next week's meals and purchases them. Once a month, a pantry inventory is compared to the buying list to determine what food must be purchased. These items are purchased wholesale.

Thus, the food program consists of an interlocking set of jobs designed to cover the whole process from determining what should be purchased to washing dishes. The preplanned menu is an important component to the system as it eliminates the requirement that a dietitian be a member of the house (or be hired) to plan meals. However, the system is flexible enough so that any house member may suggest menus if he also provides detailed recipes. Such substitutions are voted on by the members.

Figure 2-4 shows the percentage of food program jobs that were done

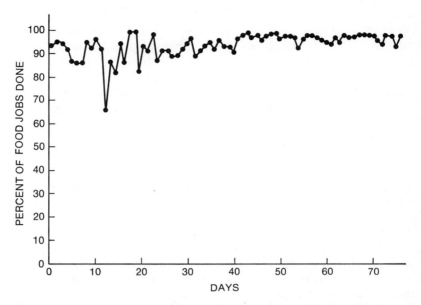

Figure 2-4 *Percentage of food jobs done during the first 75 days of the program.*

in the first three months after a reliable method of observing such jobs was introduced. The average percentage of jobs done during that period of time was about 95 percent. Because a disruption of the food program would have very serious consequences for the house, no experiments have been conducted to determine the functionality of the system. However, as Figure 2-4 shows, the required behaviors have been maintained at a rather high level and have been maintained for an additional six months since these data were taken.

Figure 2-5 shows the results of asking members of the house, "How good is the food, considering the price, compared to a dormitory?" On a 7-point scale the members of the house rated the food an average of 6.2 (the highest rating of any component of the program). The combined results of direct observation and the members' ratings suggest that the behavior specified by the food program produced food that is very satisfactory to the residents.

The Repair Program

The goal of this program is to repair, maintain, and improve the basic physical structure of the house. This includes repairing broken windows and doors, fixing plumbing problems, building improvements such as

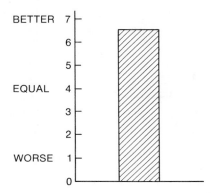

Figure 2-5 *Mean rating of response to the question, "How good is the food, considering the price, compared to a dormitory?"*

closets, and painting a portion of the house. If most of this work is done by members of the house, then outsiders do not have to be hired and rent money can be saved.

The repair program relies very heavily on a coordinator who is skilled in handyman-type jobs. It is his job to identify problems in the house and to specify by means of a detailed checklist how the jobs are to be done. These jobs are then posted, and after someone signs up and completes a repair job, the coordinator uses the checklist to inspect the job to determine whether or not it has been done properly. Currently, these job specifications are being accumulated so that eventually a file of the most common 100 repair jobs can be created. Standard job descriptions will then be carefully specified and will include detailed inspection criteria. The next step will be to develop an in-house training program to teach handyman skills to most house members.

At this time we do not have reliable observations as to the percentage or amount of repair work done on a weekly basis.

Figure 2-6 shows the reaction of members to the question, "How rapidly are repairs made here, compared to a dormitory?" The average rating on a 7-point scale was 3.9 This indicates that members felt that repairs were made about as rapidly in the house without professional help as they are made in a dormitory, and suggests an adequate level of satisfaction with the repair program.

The Inspection System

The goal of the inspection system is to have a simple, inexpensive technique for determining whether or not the members of the house have satisfactorily completed the jobs for which they signed up. We wanted to make the

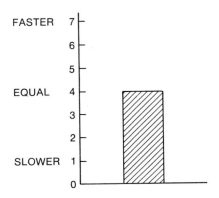

Figure 2-6 *Mean rating of response to the question, "How rapidly are repairs made here, compared to a dormitory?"*

observational system reliable, yet simple enough to be implemented by members of the house. Thus, the system becomes a technique for evaluating the daily work of each member of the Project.

The inspection system relies on the use of an extensive checklist. The length of the checklist varies according to the day of the week and the jobs available on that day. The overall checklist varies in length between 200 and 400 items. The inspections occur between 8:00 P.M. and 9:00 P.M. each day, and are usually completed in about 30 minutes.

The inspectors (who sign up for the job) are under contract to finish the inspection by 9:00 P.M. or lose some of their points. The reason for this rule is that previously, members of the house with work to complete prior to inspection often asked the inspectors to give them special exceptions for such things as dates, late studying, and so on. As a result of these requests, the job of inspector frequently lasted from 8:00 P.M. to as late as 1:00 A.M. This made the job very undesirable, and we had trouble getting people to sign up for it.

The members who want to be an inspector must go through a training program in which a trained inspector shows them how to conduct the observations: what to inspect, what criteria to use, and what exceptions to make. This is done by examining and discussing each component to be inspected. Later, the instructor and trainee inspect independently until they attain an agreement of 90 percent or higher. At that point, the member is considered trained and can then sign up for the job and earn credits.

Reliability is routinely checked on the average of once a week. A student not living at the house is hired to inspect the house according to a predetermined random schedule. This inspector begins after the time that the regular inspector has completed his or her inspection. Then, the two

independent observations are checked for agreement and a reliability coefficient is computed.

Figure 2-7 shows the results of the reliability computations for the
first 60 weeks that the program was in operation: the reliability was almost
always over 90 percent, and the average for the entire period was 94
percent. This suggests that this method of observation consistently produces a high level of agreement between independent observers.

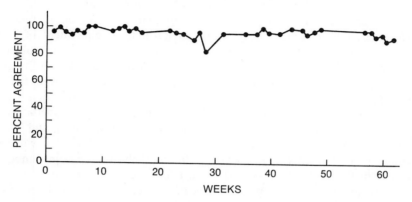

Figure 2-7 *Percentage of agreement between outside observer and*
inspector.

We are currently preparing a worksharing manual that specifies each
job, how to do it, and how to inspect it. It is our goal to make this manual
a self-contained program for training inspectors. This would eliminate the
need for personal training and make it possible to export the system to
other groups desiring to implement it. It may even improve still further
the reliability of the observational system.

SELF-GOVERNMENT

The aim of the self-government system is to develop a truly democratic
system of participatory government. Thus, we have sought to turn the
government of the program over to the residents of the house. This has
been in the process of development for over one year.

When the program was initiated, it was not democratic. That is, we
set up a behavioral system without consulting with the residents (because
they had not yet moved in). We tried to anticipate what target behaviors
would be important and what type of consequence system would maintain
those behaviors. This system was imposed on the people who moved into

the house. Furthermore, we did not initially have any provision for residents to make any input to this system.

The system that originally was instituted was the worksharing system discussed above. Our goal was to develop a system for sharing the work, and, according to our analysis, the reasons that other experiments in living (particularly local "communes") failed was that they did not have an effective system for sharing the work. Therefore, we focused on developing such a system, and we succeeded in doing so. During the first three months of our program the work was effectively shared by all house members. However, this may have been the behavior-analysis equivalent of having the trains run on time. The residents complained, rebelled, and lobbied for a voice in the system. The apparent satisfaction of residents with the group living program was very low. The house was clean and well fed, but unhappy.

In the spring of 1972 we wrote an 80-page handbook spelling out a system in which the residents could make their own rules and change old rules. At the same time, we anticipated the possibility that with such control, the residents might vote out the worksharing or some important aspect of it. Therefore, to guard against this, we started teaching a course in behavior analysis so that residents might better understand the system and change it in behaviorally-oriented ways.

Finally, as residents took over the rule-making, they requested a voice in the expenditure of their money. In the winter of 1972 we developed a financial system that could be run by members of the house. The rest of this section will describe three subsystems of self-government: the governing system, the finance system, and the education system.

The Governing System

The governing system is based upon the *Handbook*. Everyone agrees by contract to abide by the *Handbook* when he moves in. The *Handbook* provides an initial agreement as to the rules that each potential resident agrees to when he moves into the house. However, it also provides a set of rules for changing those rules. It is, thus, somewhat like the body of law that a legislative body develops, plus a constitution that governs the way in which that body can make or change rules.

The rules for making or changing rules are simple. They specify who is a member, what constitutes a quorum (75 percent of the members), and what majorities must exist to make or change rules. A 75 percent majority is required to change an existing rule. This requirement is designed to make the rules system a bit more stable, so that rules will only be changed when there is substantial consensus among the members that it should be changed. All decision making occurs at a weekly meeting that is open to the entire house membership. Typically, these meetings are conducted for about an hour. Each member who attends is paid 15 credits (toward his 100-credit weekly requirement). Figure 2-8 shows the percentage of mem-

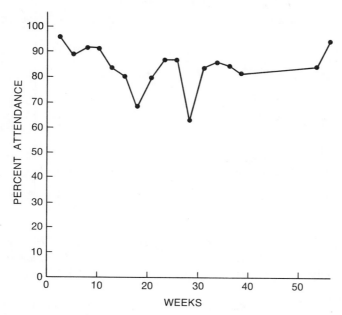

Figure 2-8   *Percentage of members attending weekly meetings.*

bers attending meetings that they are paid 15 credits for attending. As shown in the figure, attendance averaged 83 percent.

Figure 2-9 shows the rating by house members of the number of

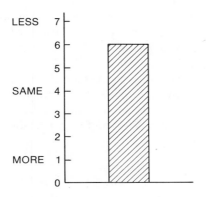

Figure 2-9   *Mean rating of response to the question, "How many undesirable rules are there, compared to a dormitory?"*

unnecessary rules in the Project, compared to the number in a dormitory. As you can see, the average rating is about 5.7 on a 7-point scale. This indicates that on the average, the members state that there are fewer unnecessary rules in the Experimental Living Project.

Figure 2-10 shows the rating by house members of the amount of

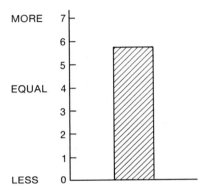

Figure 2-10   *Mean rating of response to the question, "How much influence do you have in determining important aspects of the house, compared to a dormitory?"*

influence they feel that they each have over decisions in the Project, compared to how much they have in a dormitory. Again, the ratings of the Project are quite high: about 5.7 on a 7-point scale, with no member of the house rating the dormitory as a setting in which they have more influence (a rating less than 4). This indicates that all members of the Experimental Living Project believe that they have a good deal of influence in making and changing rules.

From a purely personal point of view, it was unpleasant for us to visit the house before the system of self-government was instituted. We knew that there would be some kind of a hassle over issues of control. However, since the self-governing system was instituted, it has been a pleasure to visit the house. The system is stable and responsibly managed by the participants. We certainly do not feel that this outcome is automatic. It is probably necessary to have a reasonable set of initial rules and a reasonable procedure for changing those rules. We also found that the control of money was important.

The Finance System

The goal of the finance system is to turn over the management of the rent money to members of the house. There are four major components of this system: a system of bookkeeping, a training procedure for the bookkeeper, a procedure for auditing the expenditures, and a budget. The major problems of developing such a system consist of how to gain voluntary compliance with expenditure of money for the long- and short-term good of the community, how to prevent misuse of the money, and how to prevent a member of the house from misusing power arising from involvement in this system.

We have tried to decrease the power of our treasurer primarily in three ways. First, the treasurer receives less than half of his 100 weekly credits from his job. He is required to earn the other half in the food, cleaning, or repair programs. This prevents the treasurer from becoming an "elite" member who does not have to share in the common tasks of the group.

Second, the job of treasurer has been carefully analyzed in behavioral terms, and a training program has been established in which any member of the house can learn the job in several hours. We now have five members of the house who are trained as treasurer, in addition to the treasurer. This means that there are a number of other people in the house who know what the treasurer is supposed to do and who can check on him relatively easily. This step may help to prevent the treasurer from using his expertise and knowledge to obtain more power than others. Furthermore, the treasurer is required to give a detailed report of house finances at weekly meetings.

Third, we have a system of auditing the books. This system involves a "Comptroller" whose job it is to keep the documentary evidence of expenditures and to develop a set of books parallel to those kept by the treasurer. Thus, our first check on the treasurer is provided by these parallel records. In addition to the Comptroller, we have an auditor. The auditor comes into the house once a month (this can be reduced as the system is perfected) to check the treasurer's and the Comptroller's books. The use of such an auditor provides assurance that the treasurer is not misusing funds.

In addition to limiting the power of the treasurer, we have attempted to develop a system in which long-term needs of the community will be protected. What we had observed in the past was that the group living in the house at any given time frequently voiced a desire to strip the treasury of any "surplus" money. Yet money must be put aside for future needs. For example, there are periods of the year when the house is not totally rented—particularly during the summer and between semesters. At these times less money is being paid by members than is needed. Since it did not seem fair to raise rentals during such periods some advance saving of money was required. However, we found that current members who were planning on moving out before such a period tended to argue against such savings, often maintaining that it wasn't their problem. Money must also be saved against major repairs to the house. For example, last fall we spent over $1,500 for a major electrical rewiring job.

The expenditure of money is now governed by a budget. The budget allocates monies to different categories of expenditures on a monthly accumulating basis. Table 2-1 shows our last budget. The treasurer is

Table 2-1 *1972–73 Budget*

CATEGORY	MONTHLY ALLOCATION	MINIMUM BALANCE
Utilities	300	500
Small Repairs	70	150
Major Repairs	120	1500
Cleaning Supplies	60	25
Equipment	25	100
Insurance and Taxes	120	300
Loan Repayment	250	0
Miscellaneous	25	25
Reserves	50	400
Food	*	200
House Improvements	**	0
Totals	1020***	3200

* All food payments
** All income in excess of $1020 (except food payments)
*** Plus house improvements and food payments

provided with a detailed list of expenditures that might arise and how these are to be classified. He is then bound by contract not to overspend any budget, under penalty of a fine that he must pay himself. This budget means that every member of the group contributes through their rent payment to a budget that is regarded by us as "fair" to all present and future members of the group.

The budget includes $50 a month for "reserves," which are to be used any month that the minimum $1,020 in rent is not paid because of low tenancy. Further, the budget includes $120 a month for major repairs whenever they occur. And, finally, $250 is put aside each month to repay the nonprofit corporation for money that it spent to purchase the house. This will be used to purchase additional houses so that the system can grow.

Furthermore, if more than $1,020 is paid in a month, the surplus is placed in a special category labeled "house improvements." This money can be used at the discretion of the group for any improvements in the house; any such action is decided by vote. So far, a piano has been bought from these funds and a recreational room has been made available.

As an incentive to not spend money in a category just because it exists, any net surplus in the categories over the "minimum" listed in the budget that exists at the end of a fiscal year is transferred to "house improvements," to be used at the discretion of the house. Furthermore, the allocation for that category is then automatically changed for the next year, based on this experience.

Our results to date suggest that this system of jobs and budgeting rules has manifested very responsible money management in the group. Figure 2-11 shows the extent to which members feel their rent is spent

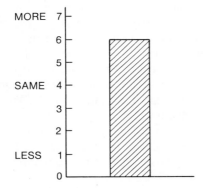

Figure 2-11   *Mean rating of response to the question, "To what extent is the rent money you pay spent in ways that benefit you, compared to a dormitory?"*

in ways that benefit them, compared to a dormitory. As you can see, the members give the system a high rating of 5.9 on a 7-point scale.

The Educational System

The goal of the educational system is to develop a behavioral culture that will encourage the use of behavioral approaches to group problems. In its broadest sense, the educational system includes the initial reading of the handbook as well as the training programs for specialized jobs (such as treasurer, chairman, and so forth).

More specifically, the education involves taking an introductory course in behavior analysis. Each member that enrolls in the course signs a contract agreeing to a specific timetable for completing the course. They are then paid at the rate of 15 credits per lesson completed (with a total of 26 lessons in the text). Each student is provided with a copy of the text. They study a lesson on their own, and when ready they attend a specific "class time," during which they may ask their "proctor" questions about the lesson. They may then take a 10-item quiz, which the proctor grades. If they answer 8 or more correctly, they are eligible to proceed to the next lesson; if they answer fewer than 8 correctly, they are required to complete some written homework and to take another form of the quiz until they pass at the 80 percent level. The proctors in the course are other members of the house who have previously taken the course, and are paid 50 credits per week for this duty.

The course uses the text *Introduction to Everyday Behavior Analysis* by Miller (1975). This text is designed to generalize behavioral principles to everyday behavioral situations involving normal adults. A new teaching procedure called "concept programming" is used (Miller and Weaver, 1974). Briefly it consists of three parts. First, each lesson provides a definition of a basic concept and a brief description of how to use it, including examples. Second, the student is given 20 hypothetical behavioral examples that in fact may or may not be examples of the concept; the student must decide. They are given hints in the form of leading questions for the first 10 examples, but these are eliminated for the last 10 examples. These examples require the student to actively use the definition presented in the lesson and to discriminate one concept from other closely related concepts. Finally, after completing the examples, the student is given a "self-quiz" that functions like a study guide. The questions that they will be given to test their grasp of the lesson are drawn from the self-quiz. Research has shown that students mastering this program can correctly answer novel questions on a "generalization post-test" at the 75 percent level, compared to pre-test scores of about 15 percent.

Figure 2-12 shows the effect of credit assignments on the rate at which members work through the lessons. When they receive credits, they complete about two lessons a week. When they don't receive credits, they

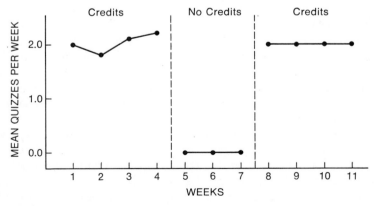

Figure 2-12   *Mean number of quizzes worked per week, per person.*

complete no lessons in a week. Thus, the use of credits appears to be necessary to maintain progress through the course.

Casual observation suggests that basic behavioral concepts are increasingly used by members of the house to propose solutions to behavioral problems. Furthermore, there seem to be fewer attempts to change the worksharing and self-governing systems in idealistic, nonbehavioral ways. Thus, such an educational system may be crucial to the maintenance of the behavioral system that has been implemented in the house and appears to create not only the consent of the governed, but their active participation in government.

SUMMARY

The Experimental Living Project has developed behavioral systems for defining and consequating behaviors in two areas that are probably important to most living groups. The first area concerns the behaviors that are necessary to maintain the basic physical aspects of the living situation: cleaning, food preparation, and physical repairs. Behavioral systems in this area have been developed by defining the behaviors, allocating them to individuals on a weekly sign-up basis, inspecting the results of the work so that these individuals may be held accountable for their work, and implementing a credit system based on rent reductions to maintain the behaviors. The major components of this system have been subjected to single-subject experimental analysis to determine their functionality. In a report to be published elsewhere, evidence will be reported indicating that the inspections, credit assignments, and rent reductions are all functional for maintaining these behaviors.

The second area concerns the behaviors that are necessary for self-government: government, finances, and education. Behaviors in these areas are defined, allocated, inspected, and consequated, as with the basic maintenance behaviors. However, these behaviors are considerably more complex. Looked at behaviorally, they tend to involve discrimination and concept formation, both of which Applied Behavior Analysis has somewhat less experience with than the simpler responses involved in the area of maintenance. To date, our data in the area of self-government suggests that the members of the group rate the governmental and financial systems quite highly.

One question asked by many people is whether or not residents of the house "like" living there. In answering this question, we have taken two different approaches. First, in an attempt to approach the question in a behavioral way, we computed the average number of months that the members residing in the house at the beginning of each month had been there.[1] Figure 2-13 shows that the average length of stay has increased

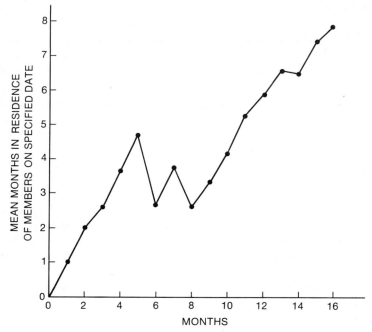

Figure 2-13   *Mean months in residence, by months.*

from a necessarily very low value to almost eight months at the last point of computation. Thus, members are staying with the Project for a period of time paralleling the nine-month school year. Perhaps even more important is that the average stay has gradually increased.

Our second approach to determining whether or not members "like" staying in the house has been simply to ask them. Figure 2-14 shows that the members rate their overall enjoyment of living in the house, as compared to living in a dorm, at an average of 5.7. Furthermore, 18 of the 20 respondents rated the Project as *more* desirable than living in a dormitory. Though verbal rating data is seldom used in behaviorally-oriented projects, it provides some evidence that if someone were to visit the Project, the residents would likely report that they enjoy living there.

These results suggest that the behavioral system produces an enjoyable environment in which people live for moderate periods of time. Thus, it

[1] Specifically, we made a list of all members living in the house at the beginning of each month. We then examined the records to determine how many months they had resided there, as of that month. Their length of residence at that date was then averaged across all members on that month's list.

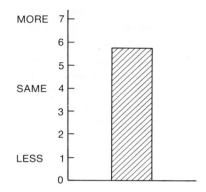

Figure 2-14 *Mean rating of response to the question, "Overall, how much do you enjoy living here, compared to a dormitory?"*

seems reasonable to conclude at this stage that we have demonstrated the feasibility of developing a behavioral system that produces a satisfactory group living situation.

Our speculations about what constitutes the critical elements in this system focus on seven components. First, we have specified a set of basic maintenance behaviors necessary to keep the house clean and repaired and the members fed. Second, the members' work is inspected to determine whether or not it is done. Third, a practical set of consequences based on rent reduction appears capable of maintaining these basic behaviors. Fourth, the members read and sign a fairly detailed statement, contained in the *Handbook,* specifying how the system is to be run. Fifth, they put up a bond of $40 to help insure that they will abide by the rules of the *Handbook.* Sixth, the members are provided with a means for changing the system. Seventh, the members are taught enough about behavioral methods so that they can change the system in ways that are likely to work. All of these features of the system seem to us to be important in making it an effective living environment.

We are currently extending the system in several ways. First, we are developing a detailed training method to teach the residents to produce and maintain what Don Whaley calls a "positive verbal community." The most important aspect of such a verbal community from our point of view is that members engage in frequent positive interactions with one another (praise, statements of interest, and so on) and minimize negative interactions. We hope to develop a method of training based on role playing and feedback that is similar to procedures now being developed by the research group. If this endeavor is successful, we feel that we will have solved the last major problem in producing a virtually Utopian living situation.

Finally, we are in the process of writing detailed manuals and training procedures so that we will have full specifications of how the system works. Our first step will be to use this set of specifications to replicate the present system with a similar group. Hopefully, we could then train other groups so that they could also start such a program. Our second step will probably be to extend the system to an adult group involving families and children. If we are fortunate enough to move even part way along that path, a real, functioning, specifiable, *Walden Two* may not be too far off!

7 / Specialized Day Care as a Psychiatric Outpatient Service

Todd Risley · *Thomas Sajwaj* · *Larry Doke*
Stewart Agras

PREFACE

The papers by Todd Risley, Thomas Sajwaj, Larry Doke, and Stewart
Agras in this reading present a markedly different intervention strategy for
working with behavior-problem children—that of specialized day care.
They argue that although the technology for remediating children's problems is reasonably well established, the technology for establishing and
maintaining necessary levels of parental and teacher cooperation is very
poorly developed. Until the training technology for recalcitrant parents and
teachers progresses to the point where the child in need can be speedily
served, an alternate intervention strategy that affords the child immediate
relief is necessary.

The initial paper, by Todd Risley, introduces these arguments by noting that parental training implies surveillance in the home and, as such, may be unacceptable to parents of those children most in need of service. As an alternative, he notes the wide acceptance of day care and its possibilities as an intervention strategy. The second paper, by Larry Doke and Thomas Sajwaj, describes such a therapeutic day-care program for older preschool children. The program is an integral part of a psychiatric outpatient child clinic yet is community-based, with one center being operated in very close conjunction with the local Head Start program. Such a close integration of psychiatry, day care, and behavior modification is certainly unique. The third paper, by Thomas Sajwaj and Larry Doke, describes a therapeutic day-care program for high-risk infants. In particular, this paper presents the serious difficulties of parental involvement and argues for a more careful balancing of children's needs and parental rights. The last paper, by Stewart Agras, emphasizes sometimes neglected issues in providing outpatient services to children. He notes that applied behavior analysis is in an excellent position to provide cost-effectiveness data, the data on which the future of the field will depend. Agras introduces the novel notion of basing service programs on surveys of specific behaviors of social interest, not on diffuse categories such as emotional disturbance or retardation. He also introduces the touchy issue of community involvement in setting treatment priorities.

Overall, these authors seem to be urging applied behavior analysis to adjust its tactics and strategies more closely to the present structure of society, and to research those service delivery systems that are most compatible with that structure—such as day care.

DAY CARE AS A STRATEGY IN
SOCIAL INTERVENTION *

Applied behavioral research with children appears to be concerned increasingly with entire social systems that produce and maintain behavioral change. Tactics for teaching specific behaviors have been superseded by strategies for altering social systems. Residential institutions, public schools, and the family have been the social systems most probed by behavioral research.

For nonacademic problems of noninstitutionalized children, home intervention and parent training have been assumed to be the only possible routes to durable behavioral change. However, for all but a few problems

---

* This section of Reading 7 was written by Todd R. Risley.

and a select few parents, home intervention and parent training have been the despair of behavioral researchers. It is usually much easier to modify the child's behavior than to try to change his parents.

Furthermore, a pervasive change in parents' behavior toward a child in the home requires pervasive feedback to the parent. Feedback implies surveillance. The pervasive surveillance necessary to effect durable and general change in the child's behavior through home intervention is acceptable to only the most desperate parents. The assertion that home intervention and parent training could be instituted nationally to solve the massive social problems of children of poor, uneducated, dispirited, and unconcerned parents (cf. Risley, 1968) is absurd in this perspective. In light of the prevailing xenophobia of minority groups, a national program— even the most altruistic—that required big brother to *really* be watching in the home would achieve nothing but revolution.

Fortunately, another social system, newly important on the national scene, provides an alternate method of dealing with the nonacademic problems of noninstitutionalized children. Day-care centers, both government-sponsored and proprietary, are beginning to take responsibility for many of our children during most of their waking hours. When children spend less time in the home, the parents' abilities to sustain effective child-rearing practices become less important. Furthermore, many parents are eager to avail themselves of the child-rearing services of day-care programs. They will gladly leave to the day-care staff the primary responsibility for rearing their child—even when the staff does not wish that responsibility. Thus, day care may be a particularly appropriate method of achieving pervasive behavioral benefits for children—especially children of disorganized families—inasmuch as direct family intervention is particularly inappropriate in our society.

To realize the potential of the day-care setting for massive therapeutic and educational impact on children, we must conduct our research so as to make explicit what is now usually implicit in good programs for young children. We must empirically examine how activities are organized, how materials are selected and presented, and how facilities are designed, so that children are better served in group-care situations. We must establish additional goals for applied research that relate specifically to living environments and child-rearing practices for groups of children.

The importance of day care as a route to social intervention is suggested in the following papers. These represent a concerted attempt to approach familiar clinical problems through the unfamiliar route of day care. That route may lead applied behavioral efforts out of the morass of family intervention and into a productive effort to change children's behavior through well-organized day-care programs.

COMMUNITY-BASED DAY CARE INTERVENTION
FOR OLDER PRESCHOOLERS WITH BEHAVIOR PROBLEMS *

Traditionally, outpatient services to problem children have consisted of weekly visits to a professional therapist who intervenes either directly, through play therapy or discussions with the child, or indirectly, through advice to parents or consultation with the child's teacher. The latter strategy, indirect intervention, has been more compatible with behavioral approaches to the treatment of childhood disorders. The major argument supporting this strategy is that parents and teachers are the proper therapeutic agents, since they are with the child most of his waking day. Behavior therapists have found this strategy to be both effective and efficient, if close cooperation is obtained from parents and teachers. However, problems arise when parents and teachers either refuse to cooperate or cannot implement a systematic program because they lack many basic requisite skills or because they are faced with competing demands. For example, many mothers of preschoolers cannot carry out intensive programs for their children because they must work outside the home during most of the day. Other parents admit that their children are having problems, but sometimes refuse to implement suggestions for dealing with the problems.

The same observations apply to many caregivers in community daycare and preschool programs. Persons working in community programs for preschoolers cannot always be relied upon to cooperate with instructions for managing children's behavior problems. Ten local preschool teachers were asked to fill out the Behavior Problem Checklist (Quay and Peterson, 1967) for five children who were selected at random from each class. Each teacher was told that her checklist would be collected the next day. Because these teachers often have contact with matters related to psychological services, it is unlikely that they considered this request unusual. However, only four of the ten teachers completed the checklist. Seven out of nine other teachers did complete the checklist, basing their answers on children who scored low on standardized tests and who were designated by professionals as probably having other difficulties. However, only one out of these seven teachers followed through with the

* This section of Reading 7 was written by Larry Doke and Thomas Sajwaj. Components of work presented in this paper were supported by the Mississippi State Department of Public Welfare, the Avery Fund for Research in the Behavioral Sciences, and the Department of Psychiatry of the University of Mississippi Medical Center. Reprints are available from Larry Doke, Children and Youth Services, Moccasin Bend Psychiatric Hospital, Moccasin Bend Road, Chattanooga, Tenn. 37405.

suggested intervention procedures, even though they had agreed to try them and had stated that they understood what was to be done. In short, many caregivers have stated that they would like to do something to help, but just do not have time to go through the long ordeal of finding a way to correct the child's difficulty. Compounding this problem is the fact that very little is known about motivating initially uncooperative teachers and parents in existing programs.

This dilemma points to the need for an outpatient-service delivery system for preschool children whose caregivers or parents will not or cannot cooperate. This paper describes such a system in the form of two specialized community-based day-care centers for three- to six-year-old preschoolers who are presenting behavior problems. This day-care model is called simply "The Children's Program," to avoid the misleading connotations of words such as "treatment," "psychiatric," and "behavior-disordered." The particular techniques that are found to be effective are by no means unusual. Good caregivers and parents have probably been using them effectively for years. However, one goal of The Children's Program is to document these techniques reliably enough to permit their being recommended to subprofessional personnel. In this way the present day-care technology may be expanded to include intervention for children with problems, as well as for normal children.

Although The Children's Program probably promotes many educational goals, and although the program operates in a therapeutic setting, it has been found that using these terms ("education" and "therapy") in descriptions of the program too often incorrectly implies objectives that are strictly academic or services that are only extended to "sick" or "crazy" children. To avoid such confusion, the general objectives of The Children's Program are stated as follows:

1. to eliminate behavior problems that prevent the child from profiting from regular preschool experiences
2. to train the child in nonacademic and some preacademic skills that will enable the child to function better in other settings, now and later
3. to systematically document effective intervention techniques in a form that will permit their transfer to other child-care workers and parents
4. to place children whose problems are resolved in appropriate, existing child-care programs, while continuing follow-up assistance to personnel in these other settings.

Locations

Of the four day-care centers that compose The Children's Program, Jones Center and Fondren Center both serve older preschool children. Each of these centers is located in the community and is served by city bus lines. Jones Center lies in the heart of an all-black neighborhood in a building that houses numerous other community-service programs, including Head Start classes for 300 children. Fondren Center is located adjacent to an all-black neighborhood in a church that frequently sponsors community enrichment programs and service projects. Approximately 17 children are enrolled in each of these centers. Both facilities comply with local, state, and federal health and safety requirements for group day care.

Types of Children Served

The Children's Program serves poverty children who are presently excluded, or are likely to be excluded, from existing group-care programs. Candidates with reported behavior problems are given priority. At Jones and Fondren Centers these problems cover a broad spectrum, ranging from failure to comply with adults' instructions, shyness, and irritability to self-destructive behavior, psychotically withdrawn behavior, and violent tantrums. Between these extremes fall children with moderate behavior problems and skill deficiencies that vary in severity. Brothers and sisters of these children are also served at the parents' request.

Children at Jones and Fondren Centers are roughly between the ages of three and six. Criteria for admission to the program are largely behavioral. Younger children who are toilet trained and are using language and self-help skills may be assigned to either center, especially if their physical development will permit them to interact safely with older children. At the other extreme, children up to the age of eight may also be admitted, particularly if they do not qualify for special services in the public schools and do not pose a physical threat to smaller children.

Screening

Children are screened for the program in one of two ways. Some children are enrolled after having been seen in the outpatient child clinic of the Department of Psychiatry of the University of Mississippi Medical Center. The decision to enroll these children is typically made because of the teacher's or parents' failure to record problems or to carry out simple home interventions.

Other children are screened in their homes, preschool classrooms, or day-care centers if one of these agencies so requests. If such children can be readily served in their present settings, close assistance is given to parents and caregivers in planning intervention and then monitoring its effects. On the other hand, children whose current caregivers or parents fail to follow instructions are referred to one of the day-care centers of The Children's Program.

Admission is usually completed in one meeting with the child's parents. Paper work includes completing an outpatient admission form and background information form, documentating immunization, and signing forms that grant permission for day-care services, transportation, physical exams, and publication of behavioral records. Within two weeks of each child's admission, a detailed family history and casework plan is prepared. The child then begins to attend a center only after his present caregiver and another representative of his current program have agreed in writing to plans for placement in The Children's Program.

Referrals to The Children's Program have come from numerous sources, including local physicians, State Board of Health nurses, Head Start, county welfare caseworkers, and the Department of Pediatrics at the University Medical Center. Head Start, with its large enrollment of poverty-level, older preschoolers has been a major source of referrals for the Jones and Fondren Centers.

Staff

Personnel in each day-care facility consists of a supervisor and a caregiver, who plan and implement daily developmental activities. In addition, a child-care technician collects and summarizes records of each child's progress toward developmental objectives. Hence, staff-child ratios in both Centers comply with those established by federal day-care regulations. About one day per week, psychologists and psychology interns help design intervention procedures for specific problems and modeling techniques for caregivers.

CENTER ROUTINES

Activities

The Children's Program currently transports 85 percent of the children it serves. Hours for the children at the Centers are from 8:00 A.M. to 4:00 P.M. The daily schedules at both Centers feature: (1) *formal, adult-led activities* meant to train children to attend to the caregiver and to provide correct responses to questions about the material that the caregiver presents; (2) *informal, free-play activities* designed to promote language usage, appropriate social interaction, active and flexible use of materials, gross and fine motor coordination, and compliance with rules and impromptu instructions; and (3) *toileting, eating, dressing, and grooming periods* for the purpose of developing or maintaining these self-help skills.

Both programs also provide hot lunches and snacks that meet state and federal nutritional standards for day care and that probably surpass the nutritional value of meals served in the children's homes. Also scheduled, in compliance with licensing requirements, are outdoor exercise periods and a one-hour nap after lunch.

Many of the children at the Centers present behavior problems that occur at low frequencies under normal conditions. For this reason, specific events that occasion higher probabilities of misbehavior are identified. Waiting periods are a good example. Such activities may then be deliberately scheduled as periods for recording and treating specific problems. For example, one child intermittently threw violent temper tantrums when given instructions. Instead of waiting for these tantrums to occur, a period of the day was designated as a time for the caregivers to issue very frequent group and individual commands. These arrangements served to increase the efficiency of both measurement and treatment operations.

Service Evaluation

Procedures for evaluating services at the Centers conform to specific group and individual objectives. Some of these procedures are outlined in the following paragraphs.

A group objective that is common to both centers requires maximal child involvement in planned activities and minimal wasted time. To evaluate each Center's progress toward this goal, full-day group participation profiles are obtained at regular intervals: closely spaced spot-checks are made throughout the day on the number of children participating in planned activities (Doke and Risley, 1971). The daily participation profiles that result from these records enable staff at both centers to identify problem periods in their daily routines. Steps may then be taken to remedy significant planning or implementation deficiencies.

Another common group objective is for children to develop some basic preacademic skills. Evaluation of this objective consists of individual, weekly, ten-minute assessments of color discriminations, counting, number and letter naming, right–left and up–down discriminations, and other skills that caregivers may specify as preacademic training objectives. Records are also kept on various nonacademic behaviors of the children, such as physical appearance, table manners, dressing and toileting skills, and language usage.

Objectives for individual children vary significantly. Problems seen in some children include temper tantrums, aggressive actions, hyperactivity, thumb sucking, withdrawn behavior, crying and screaming, inappropriate toy play, autistic mannerisms, talking out of turn and other disruptive behaviors, pulling away from caregivers, inappropriate sex role identification, and cursing. Deficiencies have been noted in toileting and dressing skills, self-feeding, language usage, eye contact with teachers, smiling, motor coordination, and other preacademic behaviors.

When such problems as these are observed, they are listed by the staff on a form that is reviewed at weekly staff meetings. The problems of each child remain on this problem sheet until they are resolved. The day-care staff then specify methods for quantifying and dealing with each problem. Successful interventions in the first six months at the Jones and Fondren Centers have included numerous behavioral techniques that others have already documented: *time-out* contingent upon tantrums, aggressive behavior, cursing, and noncompliance; *contingent snacks and privileges* for attending to caregivers, appropriate play, proper toileting and dressing, smiling, prolonged attention to tasks, and increasingly complex motor behaviors; *differential attention procedures* for hyperactive behavior, talking out of turn, sex-appropriate play, mildly disruptive behavior, and crying; *overcorrection* for certain autistic mannerisms; *access to day-care materials* contingent upon correct language usage and preacademic requirements; and a combination of *shaping and fading* for self-dressing, appropriate play, and self-feeding.

After effective techniques have been established and the child's problems have been resolved at the Center, the child's parents and a caregiver from the program to which the child will be transferred are invited to observe demonstrations of the intervention procedures and to practice implementing them with the child or with other children in one of the day-care centers. Children with other special problems (articulation, hearing, and so forth) are usually transferred to existing community agencies that are best equipped to serve their needs.

Because many behavior problems respond rapidly to systematic intervention techniques, a continuous turnover in enrollment occurs at both centers. Although Jones and Fondren Centers are geared to serve a total of only 30 to 35 children at a given time, it is anticipated that a continuous turnover in children will permit 50 to 100 children to be served in these centers over a year's time.

Organizational Difficulties

This description of The Children's Program model for serving preschoolers with problems would be incomplete without mention of some of the difficulties encountered in starting the program. Some of these problems may be common to other programs that must justify their existence through service to the community. Before any services could be started, employment interviews had to be held; staff had to be hired and oriented; space for the Centers had to be located; equipment had to be ordered and delivered; food services and transportation had to be arranged; community referral sources had to be contacted; local, state, and federal licensing regulations had to be met; children had to be screened; records systems had to be developed; and personnel policies had to be specified. Completion of these tasks was seriously impeded by fluctuating federal regulations, by university red tape, by low-quality construction of available buildings, by zoning and leasing requirements, and by a two-month funding freeze that began in the third month of operation. All of the tasks were completed, however, within nine months, and the program operated at full capacity for the last three months of the first funding year.

Projected Activities

In addition to the local service objectives at Jones and Fondren Centers, more work is needed to supplement existing day-care and preschool technologies with efficient and well-documented procedures for serving problem children. Techniques that are effective are described in the following paragraphs in a form that will permit their implementation by regular day-care personnel.

Much attention is being directed toward identifying the behavioral effects of what has been referred to as "impersonal" aspects of group care (LeLaurin and Risley, 1972; Doke and Risley, 1972). Risley and his colleagues have led in this type of research by documenting the effects of different methods for assigning caretaker responsibilities, different activity schedules, methods for changing activities, physical arrangements, and materials inventories. Other organizational components, such as staff-to-child ratios, staff screening procedures, space requirements, child orientation methods, and family admission requirements, still await experimental analysis.

The following preliminary study illustrates this area of program development. Caregivers at Jones and Fondren Centers reported that different types of activities, "formal" versus "informal" activities, seemed to be having different effects on the children's behavior. A formal activity is characterized by a requirement that all children in the group remain within a specified area and watch the caregiver or another child who is displaying materials, telling a story, giving a lesson, illustrating a recording narrative, or leading a song. The formal activity is essentially led by an adult.

Children in formal activities are considered to be involved if they are looking at the activity leader, responding to a question, participating in unison (reciting, singing, and so on), or going through motions that accompany a group song or recitation. The only materials that the children can manipulate during formal activities are those that must be used simultaneously and uniformly by all children. In contrast, informal developmental activities feature settings in which children may request different materials, at any time, for a wide variety of uses. When the caregiver in an informal activity is not distributing materials, he moves among the children and interacts with them one at a time. Interactions between the caregivers and children that are appropriate to developmental or educational goals thus proceed informally as the children use and exchange materials.

For three mornings at the centers the activity schedule shown in Table 2-2 was in effect. This schedule featured alternating formal and in-

Table 2-2 *Morning Activity Schedule at Jones Center* *

TIME	TYPE OF DEVELOPMENTAL ACTIVITY	
9:30–9:45	Informal	(blocks and cars area)
9:45–10:00	Formal	nursery rhymes
10:00–10:15	Informal	(housekeeping area)
10:15–10:30	Formal	language lesson
10:30–10:45	Informal	(manipulative area)
10:45–11:00	Formal	story

* Note that "formal" and "informal" activities alternate every fifteen minutes.

formal activities. Throughout each activity, a technician recorded children's participation or non participation by spot-checking a different child every ten seconds. These records were found to be highly reliable. Results for the three days showed changes in child involvement that were a function of the type of activity. Figure 2-15 shows reductions in child participation for formal activities that followed each informal activity.

This pattern of higher levels of involvement in informal activities was seen in all but three of the eleven children, as shown in Figure 2-16. Open bars in this figure show the percentage of time that each child was involved in the informal activities. Closed bars show levels of involvement in the formal activities. The differences in activity involvement were not seen for Child 2, Child 3, and Child 10. However, it should be noted that none of these children showed significantly higher levels of involvement in the formal activities. A further observation was that misconduct was more likely to occur during formal than during informal activities.

Figure 2-17 presents a later one-day replication of the main effects

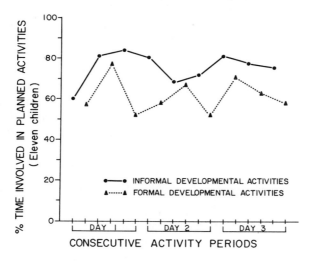

Figure 2-15 *Percentages of time children were involved in planned activities across the six morning activities for three days. Circles indicate levels of group involvement in the informal activities. Triangles indicate levels of group involvement in the formal activities that followed each of the informal activities.*

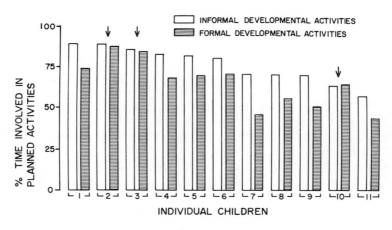

MDN. RELIABILITY = .94 (RANGE - .77 - 1.00)
EACH BAR SUMMARIZES DATA FROM 30-50 SPOTCHECKS (MDN.= 43)

Figure 2-16 *Percentages of time individual children were involved in the informal (open bars) and in the formal (shaded bars) activities. Data were summarized across activities and across the three days of the study.*

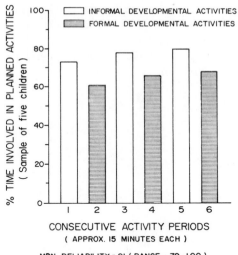

Figure 2-17 *Percentages of time children were involved in the formal and informal activities that alternated every fifteen minutes for one morning period. Only five children in the group were sampled, in order to increase the number of spot-checks per child within each activity period.*

for five children. As before, higher levels of participation were obtained for informal activities (the open bars in Figure 2-17). This was true for each of the five children sampled. Presently, efforts are being made to demonstrate these effects more convincingly and to identify their limiting parameters.

Hence, the research activities at the Centers are not restricted to studies of contingency management and stimulus control. Systematic changes in some of the more global, impersonal aspects of day-care organization show evidence of having significant, reliable, and cost-free effects on children's behavior. Furthermore, these impersonal variables can usually be modified by caregivers who have had very little *formal* training.

Future work will also include the collection of "diagnostic baselines." Presently, the staff at Jones and Fondren Centers identify problems for individual children, then begin baseline measures. Figure 2-18 shows baselines on Julie and Omar shortly after they entered Jones Center. Even though no intervention was deliberately introduced for these children, their hyperactivity (squirming) was observed to decrease in occurrence over a period of time. At this point, it is difficult to determine which dimensions of the program were responsible for these gradual improvements. However, the fact that these patterns have appeared numerous times with many children suggests that measurement must begin before children enter the program. Only then can the changes shown in Figure 2-18 be described as improvements upon their behavior in other settings. If these are genuine improvements, then an identification of specific differences between these other settings and The Children's Program is in order.

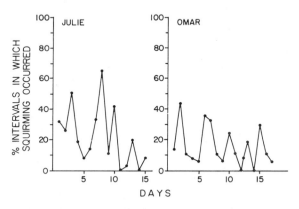

Figure 2-18 *Percentage of ten-second intervals in which hyperactive movements (squirming) occurred for two preschool children. These data were obtained from the time that each child entered the day-care program. No deliberate "treatment" was introduced.*

A third direction for continued activity pertains to the training of new caregivers. From the inception of the program, the paucity of procedures for training persons who respond neither to our instructions alone nor to intervention techniques that are modeled for them has been all too obvious. This observation suggests experimental analyses of various admissions requirements or service commitments from parents and community programs that request help. These program dimensions may be modified systematically, while monitoring the cooperation of other caregivers and the efficiency with which each child's problems are resolved.

Finally further research must focus on cost analyses of the out-patient model provided at Jones and Fondren. Based on a yearly patient load of only 34 children, not allowing for a turnover in children, the estimated costs of service at the Centers is approximately $200 per month per child. This figure is slightly higher than the estimated cost of $160 per month per child in regular Head Start classes and local costs of from $60 to $150 per month per child for private *unspecialized* day care. However, the most reinforcing data are anticipated in cost-effectiveness comparisons to traditional private outpatient clinics. At the going rate of $35 per hour, costs for only three hours of traditional office treatment would cover more than 80 hours of service at Jones or Fondren. When enough data are available to allow cost analyses in combination with intervention *effects,* the benefits of The Children's Program model for older behaviorally-handicapped preschoolers promise to be even more dramatic.

CLINICAL INTERVENTION WITH INFANTS: PARENTAL VERSUS DAY-CARE STRATEGIES *

This paper will make two major points: (1) any delivery system for behavioral techniques that depends heavily on parents as the prime therapeutic agents is not viable on an extensive basis at this time; and (2) in lieu of parents, child behavioral problems are best attacked through a day-care strategy.

The problems of choosing an effective and practical intervention strategy become paramount in a psychiatric outpatient clinic for children. The starting point for its operations is the referral, typically by a social agency, of a child who is currently experiencing or will potentially experience some type of behavioral difficulties. The clinic's goal, then, is the rectification of specific difficulties of individual children. Typically, an extremely wide range of children are referred to a child clinic; these children represent a very broad spectrum of behavioral problems, diverse socioeconomic backgrounds, widely differing familial and parental characteristics, and highly variable histories. Infants, from 2 to 30 months, from poverty families constitute an important subgroup being referred to the child outpatient clinic of the Department of Psychiatry of the University of Mississippi Medical Center. These referrals come primarily from the county welfare department and the High Risk Infant Clinic of the Medical Center's Department of Pediatrics. The difficulties experienced by these infants fall roughly into three categories: (1) specific behavior problems, such as eating and sleeping difficulties and excessive crying; (2) general neglect and lack of stimulation; and (3) failure to thrive. Failure to thrive involves severe physical and development delay (for example, weight below the third percentile) and marked lack of appropriate responsiveness, with no evidence of causal organic disease. There are signs of deprivation and familial disorganization (Barbero and Shaheen, 1967). Treatment tech-

* This section of Reading 7 was written by Thomas Sajwaj and Larry Doke. Material contained in this paper was supported in part by funds made available by the Mississippi State Department of Public Welfare, the Avery Fund for Research in the Behavioral Sciences, and the Department of Psychiatry of the University of Mississippi Medical Center. Reprints are available from Thomas Sajwaj, North Mississippi Retardation Center, P.O. Box 967, Oxford, 38655.

niques for these three categories of infant problems are fairly straight-forward. Specific behavior problems can be attacked through the use of behavior modification tactics, notably the manipulations of the consequences of the problem behavior (Etzel and Gewirtz, 1967). The cognitive and intellectual effects of impoverished environments has been shown to be offset, at least to some extent, by providing a more stimulating and diverse environment (Karnes, Teska, Hodgkins, and Badger, 1970). Failure-to-thrive infants respond very well to high levels of noncontingent attention and adequate care. Weight gains of up to 40 percent of pretreatment weight within two weeks have been reported (Talbot and Howell, 1971). Nutrition is also a factor, but apparently one of secondary importance.

Parents as Agents of Intervention

The critical problem for the outpatient clinic, however, is not one of finding promising treatment tactics, but one of finding ways to implement these tactics. One obvious and attractive possibility is to utilize parents. The earliest behavioral work (Wahler, Winkel, Peterson, and Morrison, 1965) clearly demonstrated that parents could effectively use techniques of behavior modification with their children. Wahler (1969), among others, has extended the successful use of parents as behavior modifiers to the analysis of infant behavior. The Karnes Program at the University of Illinois has demonstrated that poverty parents, often a difficult group with which to work, could be successfully trained to provide their infants with a richer and more stimulating environment (Karnes *et al.,* 1970). Poverty mothers have also been successfully counseled to provide the mothering and love necessary to reverse the failure-to-thrive syndrome (Elmer, 1960).

However, difficulties in the use of parents as therapeutic agents have been reported in the literature (Tharp and Wetzel, 1969; Salzinger, Feldman, and Portnoy, 1970; Sajwaj, in press). For example, Elmer (1960) reported that the desired level of maternal cooperation needed in order to cope with failure-to-thrive infants was obtained in only two of five cases. Hospitalization or foster-home placement had to be sought in lieu of parental involvement for the other three infants. In the child outpatient clinic of the Department of Psychiatry of the University of Mississippi Medical Center, it is apparent that many parents, probably the majority, are unwilling or unable to provide the degree of cooperation necessary to obtain significant clinical improvement with behavioral techniques. Many parents are actively opposed to therapeutic involvement, and others adopt a "garage" attitude similar to the attitude they have when they take their car to the shop to be repaired: "Fix my child; I'll be back later; Don't bother me until you're done." Other parents' repeated attempts to help their child have extended over several years, with transient or no success; by that time, their involvement with their child is extinguished, or nearly so. Many other parents are quite willing to work seriously with their children. However, the degree of their cooperation is often seriously limited by competing domestic demands, chaotic household conditions, educational limitations, or cultural obstacles. These difficulties cut across social-class lines and are experienced with poverty, working, and middle-class parents.

The degree of cooperation that can be expected from parents is illustrated by several requests made to the mothers of infants in the child outpatient clinic last year. At parent meetings called early in the year to discuss the program and the progress of the children, only 13 percent of the mothers were present. Mothers of infants were asked to send diapers or training pants for the day-care program. Only 7 of 16 mothers complied. Mothers were also asked to send at least one bottle of formula for their child. Of 11 mothers, only 4 sent usable formula. Overall, of the 16 mothers of infants in the program at that time, the staff considered only 9 of the mothers to be dependable in any way. Of these 9, 2 were temporary foster mothers. All of the families served were receiving aid-to-dependent children welfare support and 50 percent of the mothers worked or attended school. There was no male reliably present in 81 percent of the homes. These difficulties in eliciting cooperation are similar to those encountered by the University's public health nurses in working with similar families. Note that these tasks required only minimal parental effort. What can be the fate of a comprehensive behavioral program that calls upon these mothers to observe and obtain reliable frequency counts of their infant's behavior and that requires these mothers to respond to different classes of infant behavior in very prescribed ways—ways that may directly contradict the mothers' entire history?

How can these difficulties be reconciled with the successes reported by Karnes *et al.* (1970) and others in working with poverty mothers? The critical difference appears to be in the nature of the sample of children and families involved in these successful programs. Most researchers are interested in demonstrating the full potential of their treatment techniques or their enrichment program. Hence, the prescribed procedures must be properly implemented, which, in turn, necessitates a fairly high level of parental cooperation. Karnes *et al.* (1970), for example, do not report how many families were approached in order to find 20 cooperative mothers. This number was probably substantial, for they reported that they encountered considerable skepticism on initial contact. Further, of the 20 cooperative mothers selected, 25 percent terminated by the end of the second year. Salzinger, Feldman, and Portnoy (1960) found that only 4 of 15 families completely carried out a behavioral program for their retarded children. In his analysis of infant-mother interaction, Wahler (1969) initially contacted 25 mothers; only two agreed to participate, and one of them terminated before completing the project. Many workers in applied behavioral areas admit freely that the parents with whom they are most successful constitute a biased sample of the general population of parents. Other workers admit difficulties indirectly by elaborating on diverse techniques aimed at increasing parental cooperation (Hess, Bloch, Costello, Knowles, and Largay, undated; Karnes and Fehrbach, 1972).

Unfortunately, an outpatient clinic for children does not have the luxury of selecting its children on the basis of parental characteristics. Its children are selected by some community agency on the basis of each child's need. Although the clinic's treatment techniques may be 100 percent effective, it must still cope with the very difficult problem of delivering the techniques once the child has been identified as possibly having difficulties. Consequently, any failure to meet the child's needs must be counted as a failure of the delivery system of the clinic. If the clinic requires the mother to bring the child to the clinic for an initial evaluation and if the mother misses the appointment because she feels that her child has no problem, then the clinic must count this case as a failure. If the clinic requests the mother to praise her negativistic four-year-old for compliance and if the mother fails to carry out this instruction because her other three children have chicken pox, then this case must be counted as a failure. If the clinic requires daily 30-minute training sessions with mother and child interacting and if the mother does not attend because of a lack of reliable transportation, then the clinic must count this case as a failure. Problems of delivery systems are certainly not new. Knowlton (1967) noted the failure of a psychotherapy-based nursery-school program for autistic children because of transportation and administrative difficulties. The treatment of alcoholism and homosexuality based on respondent conditioning has been continually plagued by substantial dropout rates due, in part, to the aversive stimuli often employed. Behavioral techniques for children with problems are at a serious disadvantage in comparison to psychotherapy techniques, because a far greater reliance on the parents is necessary for their implementation. Certainly, the greater the effort required for a desired outcome, the less likely that outcome becomes.

Earladeen Badger, from her experience with the Karnes Program (Badger, 1971, p. 169), writes, "I am convinced, however, that even the most apathetic mothers can be spurred to activity in the interest of their children—with patience and conviction on the part of those who would bring this about." This is probably true, and remediation through parents is most assuredly preferred. Certainly, a technology that can teach pigeons to play ping-pong should be able to develop reliable instruction following in mothers—given enough time and environmental control. However, it is clear that the present technology for developing and insuring parental cooperation is poorly developed. The behavioral technology for working with children is far ahead of the technology for working with parents. Until this latter technology is more viable, parental work will be, as Badger emphasizes, a matter of time, patience, and flexibility. However, the most serious questions are whether or not the child in need will be able to afford the time, and whether or not society will allow the environmental control necessary to develop adequate parental cooperation. Certainly, clinicians cannot allow the child's suffering to continue or his development to lag further behind while parental cooperation is being built. To keep the child from paying for the necessary time, an interim intervention strategy is necessary.

Day Care As An Intervention Strategy

Assuming that there is a significant number of infants who need assistance but whose parents are unwilling or unable to implement behavioral techniques, placement of the infant in a day-care program has several attractive possibilities as an intervention strategy. First, treatment can be implemented for about 40 hours a week, which is a very significant portion of an infant's time. This amount of time allows accurate diagnoses to be made and permits evaluation of specific intervention techniques for specific infants. Second, treatment is administered primarily by the caregiver staff, minimizing costly involvement by doctoral-level staff. Third, groups of infants can be treated simultaneously, thereby increasing the number of infants served. Fourth, the day-care environment is flexible enough to allow a heterogeneous grouping of types of infant difficulties. Fifth, more careful supervision of medical and nutritional problems, serious problem areas in poverty infants, can be provided. Sixth, parents need be involved only to the extent of allowing their infant to be brought to the day-care center. Seventh, reasonable levels of funding from local, state, and federal programs are likely in the foreseeable future. Eighth, since many day-care programs will probably be established in the near future, a specialized intervention program can potentially be inserted into these programs, allowing great numbers of infants to be served.

Overall, a day-care strategy provides a setting in which environmental alterations for diagnostic and therapeutic purposes may be pursued without extensive reliance on parents and without disregarding needy infants because of parental difficulties. Thus, day care allows the child's needs to be met while parental cooperation is being established. If parents are cooperative initially, then the day-care center becomes an ideal setting for "on-the-job" training in child care and therapeutic procedures.

Carry-over to the Home

There is little argument that infant behavior problems can be successfully treated in well-operated, appropriately supervised day-care programs, foster homes, or hospital wards (Richmond, Eddy, and Green, 1958; Elmer, 1960; Lang and Melamed, 1969; Barbero and Shaheen, 1967). The critical issue is whether or not this improvement carries over to the home. It seems to be reasonably well accepted that improvement in a given setting obtained through the use of behavioral techniques will not always be accompanied by improvement in settings where the techniques are not in use. Certainly, the relevant research literature might lead one to expect strong situational discriminations. However, well-controlled analyses of generalization in applied settings are few.

Several considerations pertain to carry-over effects. First, some direct carry-over of skills learned in the day-care centers to the home should occur without deliberate attempts to promote generalization. The extent and range of the carry-over and, hence, its significance must be carefully determined. Certainly, some of the behaviors developed in the centers will elicit naturally occurring reinforcers in the home. Newly developed behavior that allows the infant to explore and to seek stimulation in the centers will be functional when the infant explores his home environment. In other instances, the parent may not be willing or able to provide the effort and time necessary to develop a new skill in the infant. However, they may well be pleased to see the child return home with the skill and may welcome the skill with contingent approval. There are clinical case reports in the pediatrics literature of failure-to-thrive infants who maintain and continue to accelerate development after hospital discharge, even though little effort is made to rectify the home situation (Barbero and Shaheen, 1967). Second, if carry-over does not occur naturally, generalization may be promoted deliberately by training across adults and situations. Specific desirable behaviors and skills that might be reinforced at home can be developed in the day-care center, even though these behaviors might not ordinarily be appropriate in the day-care program. The explicit development of a wide-ranging imitative repertoire is an example. Last, suppose a specific behavior is established in the day-care center and no carry-over to the home appears. Later, the parents are taught to establish the behavior at home. It may well be that there will be a more rapid acquisition of the behavior with less effort when the parents make this attempt. Thus, carry-over to the home may not appear concurrent with day-care, but may save effort at a later time. Difficulties would then be minimized for the parents, and their efforts might be more rapidly reinforced. Consequently, parental cooperation should improve.

Suppose, though, that none of these carry-over effects occur, and suppose that the parents completely refuse to cooperate beyond consenting to allowing their infant to participate in the day-care program. The strategy in this instance would be to accept the lack of improvement at home and to concentrate heavily on preparing the child as much as possible for typical types of day-care or nursery programs. When sufficient progress has been made in the therapeutic day-care program, the child would not be simply discharged. Instead, he would be transferred to a regular day-care program with follow-up consultation provided in that program to maintain the child's progress. The child would be transferred eventually to other nursery and preschool programs until he starts elementary school. The result would be that the child would have obtained the preacademic, social, and emotional benefits provided by the regular programs, even though his difficulties might persist in his home situation.

Description of the Infant Center's Operations

The outpatient child clinic of the Department of Psychiatry of the University of Mississippi Medical Center has established a day-care center for infants and a center for toddler-age children. The infant center serves 12 infants from 2 to about 18 months of age. The toddler center serves 8 children from about 18 to 30 months of age. The toddler center is newer and is not described in this paper.

The first problem in the development of the infant center was the design of a physical environment and caregiver routines that allow appropriate care of the basic needs common to all infants, that is flexible enough to be easily modified to fit a particular infant's needs, and that provides a high level of stimulation to the infants. These characterstics are found in the infant day-care model developed by Todd Risley at the University of Kansas. As a whole, this model specifies a technology of infant day care that includes the physical design, equipment and materials, and staff duties sufficient to provide quality care to infants from normal home environments (Cataldo and Risley, in press-a). Specifically, this model proposes an "open center" design for infant care (Cataldo and Risley, 1972a; 1972b) and an efficient procedure for assigning staff according to specific areas of responsibility rather than specific groups of children (LeLaurin and Risley, 1972; Risley and Cataldo, in press-b). This model for infant day care provides a basic structure to which can be added specialized components of child-care practices and curriculum to meet the needs of particular infant populations.

The therapeutic infant day-care intervention system has applied the basic day-care model of Risley to the "high-risk" infant population of

Mississippi. Each infant is always in one of four areas located within a single room. Movement from one area to another is very easy for the staff, and staff and infants are always within sight of one another. Infants are in their cribs only when asleep, and are removed as soon as they awake. Infants spend about 25 percent of the day in their cribs. The diapering area is located between the sleep and play areas, and all supplies needed for diapering are kept there, making it possible for staff to diaper an infant in less than two minutes. The feeding area, located immediately next to the play area, likewise contains all the supplies and materials necessary to feed the babies. Infants spend about 60 percent of their days in the play area, a large section of carpeted floor surrounded by low barriers. The area is divided into two sections, one each for mobile and immobile babies. The low barriers allow the staff easy access to the babies for care and play purposes.

The center has three staff members who are rotated hourly through the main functions of diapering, feeding, and caring for the sleep and play areas. Staff routinely record time and other facets of care in a given area, allowing a monitoring of any infant's day. The reliability of staff recording of these data is over 90 percent. A full-time child-care worker routinely records data on specific child behaviors and on the quality and degree of staff-infant interactions.

The center began with 3 babies. It was hardly surprising that the one-to-one infant-staff ratio afforded quality care. However, as the census was increased to 12 babies, there was some concern that the quality of care would decline—that is, that the number of diapers changed per infant would drop; that crib time would increase, thereby reducing infants' access to toys and other infants and their interactions with adults; or that play-area time, when most of the child's stimulation should be occurring, would be reduced. Rough indexes of care were kept during the five-week period over which the number of babies was increased to 10. Figure 2-19 shows the average number of diapers changed per infant per four hours as a function of the number of babies present. No tendency to decrease was observed for this index. Instead, an increase in the number of changed diapers occurred for several babies. Each baby had his diaper changed, on the average, every 75 minutes. Other available indexes of care were not adversely affected. The census has since been increased to 12 babies, resulting in a four-to-one ratio with no decrement in these indexes. This physical arrangement of the center, together with the function-based division of staff responsibility, will probably allow five-to-one and perhaps six-to-one infant-staff ratios without serious decrements in amount or quality of care. Such demonstrations are not the intent of this program, however. Rather, the data merely demonstrates that the staff continued to do its job even though 12 babies were enrolled.

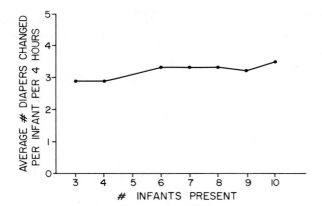

Figure 2-19 *The average number of diapers changed per infant per four hours as a function of differing numbers of babies present in the day-care center.*

With the staff having established their basic routines and procedures, the next and most critical phase of the center's development was the insertion of therapeutic tactics into these basic routines. Practices found effective in stimulating cognitive and intellectual growth (such as the techniques developed by the Karnes Program) and techniques established in behavior modification (such as differential reinforcement) are tailored and suitably modified so that they can be routinely administered to all the infants while their basic care needs are being met. For example, the diapering area not only is the place where the baby receives a fresh diaper, it also provides a setting for language and social development. Similarly, the play area becomes the locus of mini-programs designed to increase motor development, object manipulation, smiling, and so on. The advantages of such a combination of therapy and routine care are:

1. A great deal of therapy is possible without burdening the staff with extra distinct therapeutic tasks.
2. All infants, regardless of specific problems, are exposed to mini-programs designed to foster their overall development.
3. Costly involvement by Ph.D. staff is limited to general staff supervision and to the development of extraordinary tactics when the basic therapeutic routines fail.

Three cases illustrate the program. Charles was an 11-month-old boy who was almost completely unresponsive to his environment and who exhibited little gross motor behavior. Overall, his behavior was similar to that described as anaclitic depression (Spitz and Wolf, 1946). Within two weeks of attendance Charles changed dramatically. He rapidly became responsive to the caregivers and to objects. His motor development also accelerated. Routine care and stimulation procedures were used; no special programs were designed for him.

Eve was a very pronounced example of failure to thrive. Although she was 15 months old, her Vineland and Denver Developmental Scales placed her at about the 6-month level. Her weight was below the third percentile. The staff has taught her to walk and has obtained other gains in motor and physical development. Language development, however, has shown little improvement.

Lynn, a 10-month-old girl, refused all food except milk that was given her in a bottle in her crib. As with all babies, Lynn was placed in a high chair or infant seat and offered cereal, fruit, and vegetables with a spoon. Milk was offered in a cup. After five minutes of refusal, she was returned to the play area. All crying was ignored. Feeding attempts were made hourly, and her weight was carefully watched. She began accepting food within a week.

Problem Areas

Day care as an intervention strategy for infants does have several liabilities. First, work with poverty families necessitates provisions for reliable transportation to and from the center. Unfortunately, transportation is not only costly but is also a major administrative headache. Second, absence is a problem in some cases. In a six-week period in March and April, 1973, the overall absence rate for the infant program was 13 percent, with individual baby's absences ranging from zero to 34 percent. Absence not only reduces the impact of the program on the infant but also results in a waste of staff time and center resources. Third, infant illness has consumed a very significant portion of staff time. Day care provides the infants with responsible supervision for long periods and allows many heretofore unnoticed medical problems to be detected. The day-care staff has been responsible for uncovering at least one moderate to severe medical problem in virtually every infant. Seeing that the parent obtains appropriate medical care has constituted a major staff effort. Fourth, and most important, it is apparent that for many of the babies the day-care staff has assumed care functions that a poverty family cannot adequately provide. Food consumption by the babies is high, and serious nutritional imbalances in the home diet are obvious. All of the babies are bathed daily because it is obvious that their mothers do not do this. Clothing must also be provided, which many of the families cannot provide adequately.

All of these factors increase costs. Next year, [1973–1974] the projected cost per child per month for the overall program, including the research costs, will be about $260—exclusive of transportation costs, which will add about $18 per child per month. This cost is well above private infant day-care costs, which are about $100 per infant per month in the Jackson, Mississippi area. These higher costs result in part from the professional nature of the staff, the inclusion of research and evaluation components, increased subsistence costs of food and clothing, and the development of a meaningful curriculum.

IMPLICATIONS

The pursuit of day care as a clinical intervention strategy will most certainly encounter some resistance. It will appear to many that this approach abandons parents. Opposition should be expected from the fields of social work, child development, and law, all of which have a strong prejudice in favor of parents. This bias is seen in the fact that children have precious few legal rights in comparison to their parents. The process of taking a child from his parents requires almost an act of God, regardless of the psychological well-being of the child. The day-care experience will force us into greater contact with the total needs of children and will provide data that will hopefully prompt a greater recognition of the child's right to love and care.

SOME CLINICAL ISSUES IN A
PSYCHIATRIC OUTPATIENT PROGRAM FOR CHILDREN *

The function of a children's therapeutic program in a setting such as a general hospital is to provide service to all comers. Of late, this has often included the responsibility for providing services to a geographically defined area, or "catchment" area as the current jargon has it. An applied behavior analytic program in such a setting must assume these broad service responsibilities or it will fail.

Traditional children's services in the general hospital have been based on the child guidance model (Silberstein, 1969) that was developed during the first half of this century. In classic form, a diagnostic team headed by a child psychiatrist and including a psychologist and social worker evaluated the problem and recommended treatment. Roles were well defined: the psychologist used testing methods, the social worker focused on social and family problems, and the psychiatrist concentrated on biologic and intra-

* This section of Reading 7 was written by W. Stewart Agras, M.D.

psychic problems. The treatment approach most frequently used was individual psychotherapy. The rationale was that behavior problems were caused by intrapsychic conflicts and that the positive affective relationship that developed between therapist and child would transfer to other relationships, notably to those between the child and his parents. Psychotherapy became the highest status occupation within the child clinic, and psychologists and social workers also became psychotherapists, blurring the original well-defined roles. As Silberstein (1969) notes, this treatment approach would be acceptable if the great bulk of children that apply to the child clinic could gain the greatest benefit from psychotherapy, but unfortunately such is not the case. Moreover, there is very little evidence to suggest that psychotherapy applied to children is beneficial (Levitt, 1963). Often, this relative lack of success spurred psychotherapists to more heroic effects that involved significantly lengthened treatment time for individual cases. Fewer and fewer children, selected according to increasingly narrowed criteria, were treated.

To prevent such distortions, a therapeutic system must be guided in setting treatment priorities by the accuracy of the feedback concerning the effectiveness of prior performance. To do this, the population to be served must be defined. An epidemiologic approach is necessary that examines a representative subsample of the population to determine what the behavior problems are and what their relative rate of occurrence is. From such figures, a therapeutic program can be evaluated in terms of its success in reaching all of the population to be served and, if the population is not reached, whether or not active case finding or outreach to special populations is required. Although the frequency of some rather broadly defined entities, such as mental retardation in various populations, is known, there are no studies that have used behavioral measures to give objectively arrived at prevalence figures. For the moment, the practitioners of both traditional and behavior analytic programs aimed at the general population of child behavior disorders must admit that they simply do not know whether or not they are meeting that population's needs.

A second method of determining priorities and performance depends on the cost of providing services. Figures for fifteen traditional child treatment units for the year 1965–66 show that only 36 percent of the children referred to the clinics were treated (an example of the growing selectiveness of such programs). In the 15 clinics, 302 staff members completed the treatment of 1,049 children, or 3.5 children per year per professional staff member. If one takes the average improvement rate of 64 percent and applies it to these clinics, then there were 2.2 children improved per staff member per year (Minuchin, 1969). This amounts to a conservative estimate of $5,000 per improved child. Even then, services to the child younger than three years were almost completely neglected (Silberstein,

1969). These figures reflect the expense and inefficiency of the one-to-one therapeutic relationship. By providing a therapeutic environment for several hours a day within a day-care program, the cost per child treated can be significantly reduced. The behavior analytic method should be able to provide more sophisticated cost analyses. The problem behaviors of each child are measured continuously, and the time taken to resolve each type of behavior problem is known. Thus, it should be possible to cost the treatment for each individual problem and to accurately predict the treatment cost for any child having a cluster of problems. Given the limited resources of any program, priorities based on frequency should be modified by priorities based on cost.

Finally, priorities must in part be set by the community being served, for different communities have different values. How one obtains this kind of feedback from a large and varied community is not clear, but attention needs to be given to potential mechanisms. Perhaps a multi-centered, community-based treatment system can more easily relate to its own smaller community than the larger unitary center.

What has been described thus far would lead to a precise specification of aims, and a simple comparison of results and aims should lead to a corrective experience. Still another issue confronts the therapeutic system: the permanence of results. Todd Risley's doubts concerning the possibilities of working with all but a select few families are well taken. Thus, a concerted effort must be made to provide therapeutic environments that will supplement the family who cannot cope with their child. Obviously, day care and the schools are one such system, and a therapeutic day-care system must logically follow its treated clients into the nontherapeutic day-care centers, the schools, and other organizations such as Youth Courts, to modify those environments in order to maintain maximal benefits. Thus, the applied behavior analytic program must, of necessity, establish co-operative working relationships with a variety of different agencies, substituting systems of care and social environmental modification for the more traditional one-to-one therapeutic or consultation relationships. Research in the future will have to be concerned with various administrative arrangements and relationships as they affect the behavior of children within the program, both in the short and the long run.

8 / A Computerized System for Selecting Responsive Teaching Studies, Catalogued Along Twenty-Eight Important Dimensions

Richard G. Fox · *Rodney E. Copeland*
Jasper W. Harris · *Herbert J. Rieth*
R. Vance Hall

Since 1967, R. Vance Hall and the personnel at Juniper Gardens Children's Project have been teaching a course in responsive teaching. In this class, teachers, parents, and others interested in managing behavior learn to do the following:

1. Record behavior reliably
2. Graph data
3. Apply behavioral procedures, including the use of consequences available in homes and public schools.

The studies presented here were supported in part by the following research and training grants: NICHHD grant (HD 03144-06); BEH grant (OEG 0-72-0253); OE grant [OEG 7-72-0006(509)], Project N. 16090, University of Kansas. The authors also express their appreciation to Betty Smith, Pearl Watson, Deloris Rabon, and Alva Beasley for their assistance in preparing this manuscript.

124

4. Verify scientifically whether or not changes are a function of these procedures by using reversal, multiple baseline, and changing criterion designs.

As one of the requirements for credit in this course, the participants are asked to carry out a behavior modification project in their classroom or home (see Hall and Copeland, 1971; and Hall, Ayala, Copeland, Cossairt, Freeman, and Harris, 1971, description of the Responsive Teaching Model.) To date, nearly one thousand studies have been completed, encompassing a wide range of behavioral problems. Over 60 of these studies have been published (e.g., Hall, Fox, Willard, Goldsmith, Emerson, Owen, Davis, and Porchia, 1971; Hall, Cristler, Carnston, and Tucker, 1970; Hall, Axelrod, Tyler, Grief, Jones, and Roberston, 1972; Hall, Axelrod, Foundopolous, Shellman, Campbell, and Cranston, 1971.)

Many of these studies have investigated problems of paramount educational and social interest while maintaining highly rigorous scientific standards. They also represent a potentially useful resource for practitioners of responsive teaching. For example, if an elementary school teacher were interested in developing a program to improve word recognition skills in a student whose reading achievement was low, he might draw upon the studies completed by the participants of the responsive teaching course for ideas and supportive data. The problem here becomes how to retrieve these studies more rapidly than by sorting the files manually, a procedure that is no longer feasible because of the increasingly greater number of studies now available.

This paper describes how computer science can be exploited. A retrieval program written in Fortran IV was developed by the first author. The program operates as follows. First, each study is abstracted by the author on a preprinted key-punch form that, in addition to recording information about the author, categorizes the study along 28 dimensions. (See Figure 2-20). The author finds the appropriate code from a booklet (Fox, 1973) and enters it in the blanks on the abstract form for each of these categories. At a later time, group leaders (or teaching assistants) compare these data with the actual write-up of the study to insure the reliability of the author's report. The abstract form typically provides such information as the following: number of subjects, population, age, setting, dependent variables, independent variables, results, and other information (including profession of the experimenter, nature of reliability and post-check procedures, type of design, baseline and graph, whether more than one treatment was employed before a change was effected, publication status, whether the study includes any fabricated data [with the approval of the instructor, for studies that are impossible to complete before the end of the course], whether the study represents a potential new contribution to behavioral technology, and quality of the research.)

Responsive Teaching Computer Program
Study Abstract/Keypunch Form

Serno _____ Author _____
            4   Last   First   Middle   26

Address   _____   Phone _____
City, State   _____   Zip _____
Group Leader _____   Date _____

1. Study Number   └─┘
                  27

2. Number   └──┘
           28

3. Population   └──┘   _____
           31

4. Age   └──┘   _____
           33

5. Setting   └──┘   _____
           35

6. Target
    Behavior   #1   └──┘   _____
                     37

                 #2   └──┘   _____
                     39

                 #3   └──┘
                     41

7. Measurement
    Technique   #1   └─┘   _____
                     43

                 #2   └─┘   _____
                     44

                 #3   └─┘   _____
                     45

8. Treatment   #1   └──┘   _____
                     46

                 #2   └──┘   _____
                     48

                 #3   └──┘   _____
                     50

9. Procedure   #1   └──┘   _____
                     52

                 #2   └──┘   _____
                     54

                 #3   └──┘   _____
                     56

10. Results   └─┘   _____
           58

11. Experimenter   └──┘   _____
           59

12. Design	⌞__⌟		
	61	18. More than 1	
13. Reliability	⌞__⌟	Treatment	⌞__⌟
	63		68
14. Post Checks	⌞__⌟	19. Fabricated Data	⌞__⌟
	64		69
15. Quality	⌞__⌟	20. Special Interest	⌞__⌟
	65		70
16. Baseline	⌞__⌟	21. Publication Status	⌞__⌟
	67		71
17. Graph	⌞__⌟	22. Other	⌞__⌟
	68		72

Figure 2-20   *Study-abstract key-punch form for retrieval program.*

Second, the data on the abstract forms are then key-punched on cards, one for each study. These cards form the source deck upon which a disc file on the IBM 1130 is built. This not only saves core storage in the computer but also protects the file from loss or destruction.

Third, when studies must be identified along certain dimensions, a find card is punched. This card contains the values of the specific studies to be found. The data representing each of the studies is compared to the values on the find card, and if they match, the name(s) of the authors are printed out. The user can then read the write-ups of these studies to more closely inspect the categories of interest (for example, studies done in the home, studies using prompts in combination with reinforcement, or studies having post-checks).

The following study-abstract key-punch form is that for the first responsive teaching study to be presented. As can be seen in Figure 2-21, this form serves several functions. It provides a biographical record of each author, in case further contacts must be made after the end of the responsive teaching course. This is often necessary if an attempt is made to publish the research. It provides, at a glance, a literal description of the important characteristics of each study. And, as stated before, it provides the specific codes to be key-punched on the computer cards, one representing each study.

The studies that follow were selected from among those available in the responsive teaching computer file. The subject populations range from a three-year-old boy in Experiment 12 to five classes of high school physical education students in Experiment 3. Many subjects were enrolled in regular classrooms, inasmuch as the responsive teaching program is designed to help regular teachers deal with social and academic behavior problems; placing pupils in special classes was avoided. Several subjects were identified as exceptional, however, and were placed in special class-

Responsive Teaching Computer Program
Study Abstract/Keypunch Form

Serno <u>0 0 5 1</u> Author <u>B a u m s t i m l e r   N o r m a</u>
         4   Last   First   Middle   26

Address   <u>204 Wall St.</u>   Phone <u>621-1721</u>
City, State   <u>Kansas City, Kansas</u>   Zip   <u>66101</u>
Group Leader <u>Betty Smith</u>   Date   <u>Fall 1972</u>

1. Study Number		<u>1</u> 27	
2. Number		<u>0, 0, 1</u> 28	
3. Population		<u>0, 1</u> 31	*Underachievers*
4. Age		<u>0, 5</u> 33	*8th grade*
5. Setting		<u>0, 8</u> 35	*School*
6. Target Behavior	#1	<u>5, 1</u> 37	*Completed math problems*
	#2	<u>0, 0</u> 39	
	#3	<u>0, 0</u> 41	
7. Measurement Technique	#1	<u>3</u> 43	*Permanent products*
	#2	<u>0</u> 44	
	#3	<u>0</u> 45	
8. Treatment	#1	<u>4, 2</u> 46	*Teacher praise*
	#2	<u>3, 5</u> 48	*Privileges*
	#3	<u>0, 0</u> 50	
9. Procedure	#1	<u>0, 7</u> 52	*Extinction*
	#2	<u>1, 8</u> 54	*Reinforcement*
	#3	<u>0, 0</u> 56	
10. Results		<u>2</u> 58	
11. Experimenter		<u>1, 5</u> 59	*Teacher*

12. Design	_0_ _3_	*Reversal*	
13. Reliability	61 _4_	18. More than 1 Treatment	_1_
14. Post Checks	63 _2_	19. Fabricated Data	68 _1_
15. Quality	64 _3_	20. Special Interest	69 _9_
16. Baseline	65 _1_	21. Publication Status	70 _9_
17. Graph	67 _1_	22. Other	71 _0_
	68		72

Figure 2-21   *Example of a responsive teaching study that has been abstracted on the Study-abstract key-punch form.*

rooms. As reported in Experiment 6, the data indicate that these special pupils, such as the boy in Experiment 11, were as amenable to systematic teaching as was the youngster enrolled in a regular class.

The target behaviors in the studies were both social and academic. Though several studies were concerned with such disruptive behaviors as being tardy (Experiment 3), talk-outs (Experiment 11), and out-of-seat behavior (Experiment 9) several others focused on academic behaviors, such as increasing the number of correct answers to problems (Experiment 1) or increasing the percentage of assignments completed (Experiments 6 and 13).

Most of the experiments were conducted in regular or special classrooms located in either urban, low socioeconomic area schools, or middle- to upper-middle-class suburban area schools. Experiment 9 was conducted in a special education class in Panama City, Panama. This study was one of several generated as a result of a responsive teaching workshop held at the National Panamanian Institute of Special Education in August, 1972. The final study (Experiment 12) is presented as an example of the numerous experiments being conducted in the home by parents trained in responsive teaching procedures.

The studies encompass a wide range of recording and experimental procedures. Though most of these procedures involved the presentation of reinforcers contingent on the occurrence of appropriate behavior, examples of the use of extinction (Experiments 1, 7, and 11) and punishment (Experiments 3, 5, and 12) were also included. In two of the studies (Experiments 7 and 9) more than one procedure was implemented before a successful change in behavior was effected.

In every study, an attempt was made to assess the reliability of observation by having a second observer make a simultaneous but independent record of the target behaviors. In addition, each study employed either a reversal or a multiple-baseline design to demonstrate a functional relationship between the procedures used and a change in behavior. The original write-ups of the experiments that follow were submitted by the first author of each experiment and included an introduction, detailed explanations of observation, recording and reliability procedures, as well as a more complete description of the various conditions of the study, and a more extensive discussion. In the interests of space, however, the studies were abbreviated to their present form.

The first author listed on each experiment that follows is the person who carried out the research. The second author is the person who acted as the group leader and consultant in conducting the study. The name of the presenter is identified in a footnote to the title of the experiment. All of the presenters are either master's or doctoral students in the departments of Special Education or Human Development at the University of Kansas, and have helped teach the responsive teaching course for teachers and parents.

We hope that the studies presented below will indicate the range and dimensions of the studies included in the Computer Retrieval program. Similarly, we hope that the fact that over one thousand studies have been generated in a variety of settings will support the premise that it is feasible for most teachers and parents to use an applied behavior analysis approach when working with children. If this is accomplished, more studies describing effective procedures for dealing with the total spectrum of populations and behaviors will become available. With its broad parameters, the retrieval system described herein makes it possible for those using the service to quickly identify the studies that will satisfy their particular interest. This, in turn, makes it possible for the user to retrieve and utilize these studies; ordinarily, they would be stored and would, for all intents and purposes, remain inaccessible.

EXPERIMENT 1: EFFECTS OF TEACHER ATTENTION AND PRIVILEGES ON THE ACADEMIC BEHAVIOR OF AN EIGHTH GRADE GIRL *

Subject and Setting

Etta was an eighth grade student in a suburban junior high school. She was a member of an independent study class designated for underachievers. Each student was working at his own rate and was required to show what

* By Norma Baumstimler and Ersaline Porchia.

he had completed each day. Etta had to be prompted to open her book and begin working. Occasionally, she would become disruptive. The teacher's typical response was a verbal reprimand.

Behavior Measured

The teacher counted the number of math problems Etta completed during a 50-minute work period. If a problem had several components, each component was counted as a problem. Etta was informed that the teacher was counting, and that a reliable student would be used to determine the reliability of her count. The agreement between the records of the teacher and those of the student (computed by dividing the smaller score by the larger, and multiplying by 100) was 99 percent for all conditions.

Experimental Procedures and Results

Baseline₁

The mean number of math problems Etta worked during this 14-day baseline period was 2.0. (See Figure 2-22.)

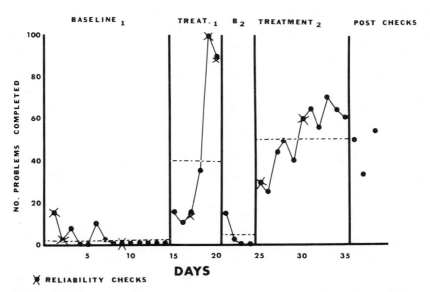

Figure 2-22 *Number of math problems completed by an eighth grade underachieving student, during baseline, treatment (teacher attention and contingent privileges), and post-check conditions.*

Treatment$_1$

The teacher ignored disruptive behavior and praised Etta when she worked on her math assignment. In addition, Etta was told that she could go to the rest room and get a drink if she completed 10 problems. On the second day, the criterion for leaving the room was raised to 15 problems. After the second day, there was no criterion for leaving the room. These conditions produced an increase in the number of problems worked for this phase to a mean of 42.

Baseline$_2$

Baseline conditions were reinstated and the level of responding immediately declined to a mean of 4.0.

Treatment$_2$

When the reinforcement procedures were reinstated, the behavior returned to a mean of more than 50 problems.

Discussion

Many of the endeavors of behavior management in the classroom have dealt with decreasing the occurrence of disruptive behavior. Instead of tackling the disruption problem directly, this teacher decided to arrange for the student to come in contact with reinforcement through the curriculum. Although the teacher did not objectively measure disruptive behavior, she observed informally that Etta was less disruptive and displayed a more positive and cooperative attitude.

EXPERIMENT 2: REDUCTION OF THE NUMBER OF TALK-OUTS BY A THIRD GRADE BOY *

Population and Setting

David was a nine-year-old boy in a third grade classroom. Test scores indicated that David was above average intellectually, even though he was not doing well academically. The teacher observed that David made disruptive noises and frequently talked out in class during lessons. We believed that if David's behavior could be changed, it would benefit him as well as the rest of the class.

* By Sharon Metcalfe and Marjorie Walker.

Behavior Measured

Talking out was defined as any verbal utterance by David that was directed to the teacher, to classmates, or to himself. The teacher observed David for 20 minutes during a reading period and counted the number of times he talked out. Reliability procedures were conducted in each of the four conditions of the experiment by having a team teacher independently record the number of talk-outs during the same 20-minute period. The larger recorded frequency was divided into the smaller, and the result was multiplied by 100 to obtain an index of reliability. Reliability on the four checks ranged from 80 to 100 percent, with a mean of 95 percent.

Experimental Procedures and Results

Baseline₁

During a 6-day baseline condition, talk-outs were recorded, but no new program was introduced to reduce their frequency. During this condition David averaged 34 talk-outs per 20-minute period. (See Figure 2-23.)

Treatment₁

During treatment, David received extra attention from the teacher in the form of smiles, pats on the back, and verbal approval when he

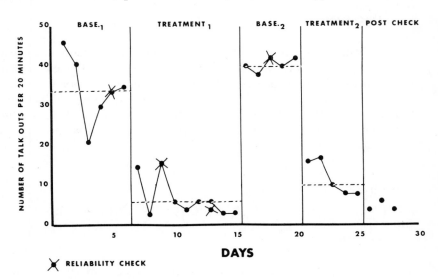

Figure 2-23 *Number of talk-outs by a third grade boy during baseline treatment (teacher attention and privileges contingent on quiet study behavior) and post-check conditions.*

exhibited quiet study behavior. David was also allowed to choose special privileges if he talked out 5 times or less during the 20-minute session. The privileges included being a line leader, being first out to recess, being the teacher's helper, or sitting next to her. A drastic reduction in the number of talk-outs was observed during this condition. The median number of talk-outs was 6, with a range of 16 to 4.

Baseline$_2$

On day 16 of the study, David was told that he was doing fine, and that he no longer needed extra attention or privileges. During this 5-day period David's median rate of talk-outs was 40, with a range of 38 to 42.

Treatment$_2$

On day 21, David was told that he could choose a special privilege if he reduced his talk-outs to 5 or less. The teacher once again began to give him attention contingent on quiet study behavior. During this phase, the median number of talk-outs during reading was 10.

Post-Checks

Post-checks were taken on three occasions following day 25 of the study, and David's rate of talk-outs remained low.

Discussion

This study demonstrated that a teacher-implemented procedure was effective in reducing one child's rate of inappropriate talk-outs. The consequences delivered for low rates of talk-outs and quiet study behavior were natural to the classroom and did not require unusual added responsibilities on the teacher's part. It should be noted, also, that during the final treatment condition, David did not come in contact with the special privileges, although he did receive praise for not talking out.

EXPERIMENT 3: MODIFYING ATTENDANCE IN BOYS' PHYSICAL EDUCATION CLASSES *

Subjects and Setting

The subjects in this study were all high school boys. There were 31 juniors and seniors in hour 1, 29 sophomores in hour 2, 34 freshmen in hour 3,

* By Len Mohlman, Linda Wade, and Mary Collins.

34 freshmen in hour 4, and 37 freshmen in hour 5. All of the classes were conducted at Bishop Miege High School, a private parochial school in northeastern Johnson County, Kansas.

Behavior Measured

This study was designed to increase the on-time behavior of all boys attending physical education classes in hours 1 through 5. A student teacher and a student observer made reliability checks in all conditions throughout the study, and reliability was found to be 100 percent.

Experimental Procedures and Results

Baseline

A multiple baseline design was used to measure the effect of the procedures on on-time behavior of the five respective classes. Prior to any manipulation, baseline records of the number of boys on time for class was taken in all five classes. Baseline conditions were in effect 10 days for the hour 1 class, 14 days for the hour 2 class, 18 days for the hour 3 class, 22 days for the hour 4 class, and 26 days for the hour 5 class. During baseline conditions, the median number of boys on time to class was 18.5 for hour 1, 11 for hour 2, 22.5 for hour 3, 25 for hour 4, and 23 for hour 5. (See Figure 2-24.)

Contingent Exercise

At the end of the class period on the tenth day of the study, the boys in the hour 1 physical education class were told that if all class members came to class on time, they would have to repeat an exercise (consisting of rigorous calisthenics) only 10 times instead of the usual 25. However, if one person was late, the entire class would have to repeat that exercise 50 times. There was a sharp increase in on-time behavior for class members in hour 1. Because of the rapid increase in on-time behavior by the students, this procedure was successively introduced to the other classes every fourth class day.

The median number of boys on time during the contingent exercise condition rose from 18.5 to 28 in hour 1, 11 to 28 in hour 2, 22.5 to 33 in hour 3, 25 to 34 in hour 4, and 23 to 36 in hour 5. Subsequent post-checks showed that the behavior was being maintained at a level equal to or surpassing that achieved at the formal conclusion of the experiment.

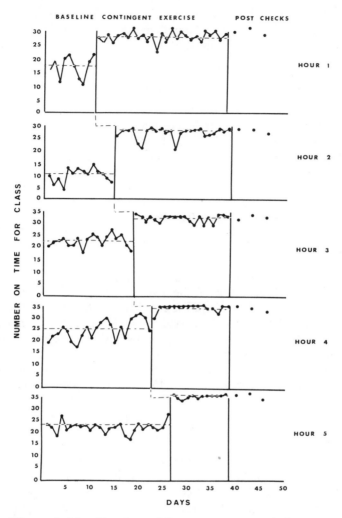

Figure 2-24 *Number of boys on time to daily senior high school physical education classes during hours one to five under baseline, contingent exercise, and post-check conditions.*

Discussion

This study illustrates the effects of introducing a treatment procedure that contained both reinforcing and punishing operations. However, it is not clear which aspect of treatment controlled the behavior: being late resulted in an increased number of calisthenics, but on-time behavior meant that fewer calisthenics had to be performed and more time could be spent on recreational games.

EXPERIMENT 4: THE EFFECTS OF A REINFORCEMENT PACKAGE ON THE COMPLETION OF SEATWORK READING ASSIGNMENTS *

Subjects and Setting

Richard was a seven-year-old boy in the second grade at a public elementary school. Although he was of average intelligence and posed no unusual discipline problems, he often did not complete his seatwork reading assignments. The assigned seatwork reading questions were read and answered orally in a daily reading group. The students were then required to return to their seats and to write on work sheets the answers to the questions about the reading material.

Behavior Measured

Each day, four work sheets from Richard's basal reading series were assigned. A completed assignment was defined as one that had no incorrect or incomplete answers. The teacher, acting as observer and experimenter, checked and recorded the number of completed assignments. Reliability was checked during each condition by a reliable student and was found to be 100 percent on all occasions.

Experimental Procedures and Results

Baseline$_1$

A baseline was obtained over a five-day period. The mean number of completed assignments was found to be .8. (See Figure 2-25.)

Reinforcement$_1$

Richard was told that each day in which he completed his daily seatwork assignment, he would receive a dot-to-dot picture, a special activity period, and the opportunity to move his "rocket ship" to the location of

* By Susan Heidrich and Barbara Terry.

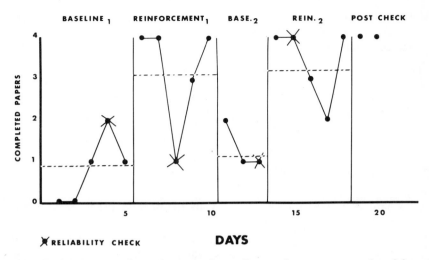

Figure 2-25 *Number of seatwork reading assignments completed by a second grade student during baseline, reinforcement (access to activities and "very good" chart, contingent upon completing assignments), and post-check conditions.*

"very good" on the classroom bulletin board. During this condition, the number of assignments that Richard completed increased significantly to a mean of 3.2.

Baseline₂

When the reinforcement procedure was discontinued, the level of the behavior decreased to a mean of 1.3.

Reinforcement₂

The reinforcement package was again instituted, contingent on completed assignments, with a subsequent increase of the mean to 3.0.

Post-Checks

Over the next ten days, two post-checks revealed that Richard was continuing to complete his assignments at a satisfactory rate.

Discussion

Here, the teacher used a number of readily available consequences in an educational setting to change the academic performance of an underachieving student. Because she identified a number of probable reinforcers and introduced them in a package, one cannot be certain which was responsible for the change. It should be noted that the teacher felt the work to be within the capabilities of the student, and, therefore, that the procedure merely brought the behavior under instructional control. Furthermore, it would seem that the treatment procedure could be easily implemented by others because the dependent measure, assignment completion, is one that most teachers consider routine, and because the reinforcers are available in most classrooms.

EXPERIMENT 5: EFFECTS OF A TOKEN SYSTEM ON INCREASING THE USE OF A HEARING AID AND GLASSES BY TWO SECOND GRADE STUDENTS *

Subjects and Setting

Two second grade students in a regular classroom were the subjects of this study. David had poor vision, and in the two months preceding the study, had not worn his glasses once. Greg was hard of hearing, and rarely wore his hearing aid.

Behavior Measured

The teacher used a time sampling procedure to measure the behavior. She measured whether Greg was wearing his hearing aid, and whether David was wearing his glasses. Four observations were taken throughout the day, and a recording sheet with four squares for each child was marked by the teacher. Reliability checks were made by two classmates of the subjects, and were found to agree 100 percent.

Experimental Procedures and Results

Baseline₁

A record of the pretreatment levels of the behaviors of each subject was obtained. David did not wear his glasses, and Greg wore his hearing aid only one out of the eight days of baseline.

Slips₁

The experimental procedure was introduced to the subjects on a staggered schedule. Initially, David received five slips of paper each day

* By Robert Harms, Jeane Crowder, Ersaline Porchia, and Jill Brake.

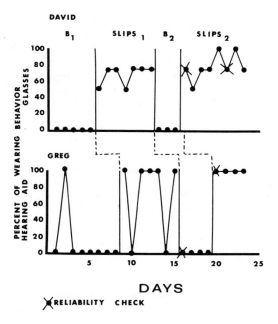

Figure 2-26 *Percentage of hearing-aid- and glasses-wearing behaviors of two second grade students during baseline and slips (tokens backed by special activities contingent upon wearing behavior) conditions.*

and was told that the teacher would check periodically to see if he was wearing his glasses. If he was not, the teacher would remove one slip. On Friday, the remaining slips were exchanged for the opportunity to engage in special activities. Greg was introduced to the treatment three days after David. David's mean rate of glasses-wearing went from zero during baseline to 68 percent in the slips₁ condition. Greg's wearing of his hearing aid increased from 12.5 to 71 percent.

Baseline₂

Baseline conditions were reinstated, again on a staggered schedule. During this condition, the teacher told the subjects that he was too busy to work with the slips. The level of the behavior during this reversal condition dropped to zero for both subjects.

Slips₂

Following this reversal, the slips condition was reinstated with a subsequent increase in wearing behavior by both students.

Discussion

This study showed that the contingent removal of slips, backed by special activities, could function to change the behavior of two youngsters regarding the use of glasses and a hearing aid. It is not clear whether the change was due to the feedback, prompting, or consequential properties of the procedure, or to a combination of these components. What should be emphasized is that the teacher could conveniently measure and record these important behaviors, and with a minimum expenditure of time and energy, change them for the better. The investigation incorporated aspects of the reversal and multiple-baseline designs. The multiple-baseline design employed was novel in that the same treatment was applied to two different behaviors across subjects.

EXPERIMENT 6: THE EFFECTS OF CONTINGENT RECOGNITION ON COMPLETED ASSIGNMENTS *

Subjects and Setting

Miles was a ten-year-old sixth grade boy from a middle socioeconomic suburban neighborhood. He had scored within the 130–135 IQ range on all tests administered to him through the school testing program. He also exhibited a high verbal interest in academic subjects. If, for instance, a science project was discussed, Miles contributed significantly to the discussion. However, once a project was started, his part was generally left undone. Likewise, Miles attempted seatwork in arithmetic or English only when coerced by the teacher. Miles' parents reported that he exhibited similar behavior patterns at home: he showed great verbal enthusiasm toward an endeavor until that endeavor required some action other than talk on his part.

Behavior Measured

A measure was taken of the rate at which Miles completed seatwork and homework assignments in all academic subjects. This was accomplished by assigning a value of one to each required answer within an assignment,

* By M. D. Saunders and Linda Wade.

regardless of whether it was objective or essay in nature. The percentage of work done correctly was figured and graphed to the nearest tenth percent on a daily basis. To insure that the measure was reliable, another teacher graded the papers independently. This was done for each day's assignments, and agreement between the two graders was always 100 percent.

Experimental Procedures and Results

Baseline₁

During a ten-day baseline period in which Miles was either encouraged to do better or berated for his lack of work, he completed assignments at a level of 13 percent. (See Figure 2-27.)

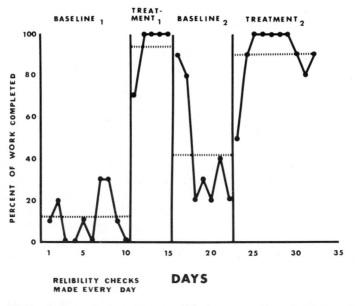

Figure 2-27 *Percentage of assignments completed by a sixth grade boy during baseline and treatment (posting on board papers of first student finished) conditions.*

Treatment₁

Following baseline, a treatment procedure was introduced. Miles was proud of the fact that he "caught on" to new concepts quicker than most of the others in the class. The authors decided that this feature of Miles' personality could be capitalized upon. The teacher announced at the beginning of the week that the person who first completed the work correctly would have the privilege of putting his or her work on the board as a key by which the others could correct their papers. Miles responded to this announcement as the teacher suspected he might. He finished the first assignment of the day before anyone else, and his answer was entirely correct. His work was therefore transferred to the board as a model for the other students. The teacher also commended him before the class. He failed to complete the next two assignments of the day, and his closest intellectual rival, a girl for whom he held no great love, won the honors. For the rest of this five-day experimental period, Miles finished his work at a 100 percent rate and also completed his work before his rival, so that he generally won the honor of having his assignment put on the board. His mean rate of completed work was 94 percent. This represented an 82 percent increase over baseline conditions.

Baseline$_2$

The teacher then declared Miles champion of the class and announced that the second person done would put his work on the board as a model. During this procedure, Miles' rate of completing assignments decreased to a mean of 42 percent.

Treatment$_2$

After seven days in the reversal phase, the original treatment conditions were reinstated: the first person to finish his work correctly was allowed to place his answers on the board for the others to use in correcting their papers. In this second ten-day treatment condition, Miles generally won the honors and finished assignments correctly at a 90 percent rate. This represented a 48 percent increase over the previous procedure.

Discussion

In this study, a teacher successfully created an environment that brought about increased academic response in one student. Although the treatment procedure was applied to the entire class, no measures were taken with the other children. The data collected were permanent products, and daily reliability checks were made to ensure accurate measurement. The design, though not technically a reversal, yielded evidence that the treatment procedure was controlling the behavior. Of primary significance was the creative application of operant procedures by the teacher. Providing consequences, however, is a difficult task and demands creative strategy-building by teachers.

EXPERIMENT 7: THE EFFECTS OF REINFORCEMENT AND PUNISHMENT ON THE OUT-OF-SEAT BEHAVIOR OF A FIRST GRADE GIRL *

Subject and Setting

The subject was Suzette, one of 23 students in a first grade classroom in a low- to lower-middle-income socioeconomic area. Suzette had been labeled a brain-injured child by a pediatric neurologist, and her injury reportedly manifested itself in motor hyperactivity, such as being out of her seat, walking around the room, talking out, disturbing others, and so forth. The subject was under a doctor's care and was required to take daily doses of mysoline and diantin, which were supposed to help lessen the degree of her hyperactivity. The subject, however, still exhibited the same inappropriate behaviors listed above. For this reason, an applied behavior analysis strategy was instituted.

Behavior Measured

The teacher used a 1-minute-interval recording technique to record the level of out-of-seat occurrences by the subject during a 30-minute period. Out-of-seat behavior was recorded during the interval if at any time Suzette's posterior was not touching the chair for more than three consecutive seconds. Out-of-seat behavior did not include the time Suzette was out of her chair with teacher permission. Reliability during all conditions was measured by the school nurse. The percentage of agreement was computed by dividing the number of agreements by the number of agreements plus disagreements, and on multiplying by 100. The mean agreement for the entire study was 93 percent.

Experimental Procedures and Results

Baseline₁

A baseline was obtained over a five-day period for 30 minutes of observation per day. During this period, the classroom teacher taught a

* By Colleen Dixon and Pat Bergmann.

math lesson to the entire class. The mean percent of intervals in which Suzette exhibited out-of-seat behavior was 68 percent. On the last day of baseline, Suzette's percentage of out-of-seat behavior was down. Reportedly, this was due to overmedication, which tended to make her drowsy. (See Figure 2-28.)

OUT OF SEAT BEHAVIOR OF A FIRST GRADE GIRL

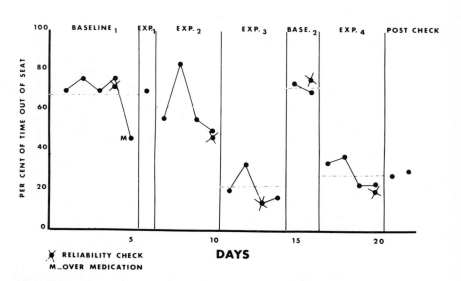

Figure 2-28 *Daily occurrences of out-of-seat behavior of a first grade girl during thirty-minute observation periods, under baseline₁, experiment₁ (praise for in-seat behavior), experiment₂ (smiling face for in-seat behavior), experiment₃ (candy for in-seat, swat for out-of-seat), baseline₂, experiment₄ (same as experiment₃), and post-check conditions.*

Experimental Condition₁

Since Suzette responded fairly well to verbal praise, during this condition she was verbally praised every time the teacher looked at her and found her in her seat. The result was out-of-seat behavior 70 percent of the time on the first day.

Experimental Condition₂

This was not a decrease, so a second condition was instituted the following day. During this condition, Suzette received praise plus a smiling face on a square of paper when she remembered to remain in her seat for one minute. Out-of-seat behavior was ignored as much as possible. She was told ahead of time to try to collect as many smiling faces as possible during the 30-minute session. The mean percent of out-of-seat behavior during this condition was 62 percent. On the tenth day of the study, Suzette was found to be out of her seat 53 percent of the time.

Experimental Condition₃

Since, in the teacher's opinion, the behavior was still not at a desirable level, a third procedure was instituted: the subject received a jelly bean plus praise immediately following in-seat behavior of one consecutive minute. In addition, she received a swat on her posterior whenever she was out of her seat. This procedure resulted in a rapid decrease in out-of-seat behavior to a mean level recorded at 21 percent. Punishment was administered only three times during this Condition.

Baseline₂

During a two-day reversal procedure, Suzette's out-of-seat behavior increased to a mean of 72 percent.

Experimental Condition₄

When the conditions of experimental condition₃ were reinstated, the mean percent of out-of-seat behavior decreased to 29 percent.

Post-Checks

Post-checks were made on days 27 and 33 of the experiment; they showed out-of-seat behavior to be at the levels of 27 percent and 30 percent, respectively.

Discussion

This study demonstrated that out-of-seat behavior, even though attributed to a physiological condition, could be decreased by applying systematic reinforcement combined with a minimal amount of mild punishment. The teacher reported that as a result of the procedure, an environment more conducive to learning for both Suzette and her classmates was established.

EXPERIMENT 8: THE EFFECTS OF A CLASSROOM GAME ON THE PERCENTAGE OF COMPLETED MATH ASSIGNMENTS IN THREE FIFTH GRADE CLASSROOMS *

Population and Setting

The subjects were three classes of fifth grade students at Apache School in the Shawnee Mission School District of Kansas City. Each of the three classes of 26 students met daily for 45 minutes, and, unless a test was given, an assignment was made. The assignments were due the following day at the beginning of class. Several students in each class did not finish their assignments.

Behavior Measured

In each class, a student was selected to record the number of students that completed their daily assignments. The student grader did this by having each pupil in the class show the previous day's work to him at the opening of the class period. The grader then recorded on a wall chart a star for completed work, a zero for incomplete work, and "ab" for students absent that day. The daily percentage of completed math papers was then computed for each class. Reliability checks on the student grader's work were conducted periodically by the teacher, who collected math papers and recorded the scores in her grade book. Reliability was 100 percent for each of the checks made. From one to five checks were made during each experimental phase in each classroom.

Experimental Procedures

Baseline₁

For ten consecutive days, baseline measures were recorded for each class to determine the rate at which they were completing math assignments. Care was taken not to mention the experimental procedures or to comment on class performance, though class performance was charted. The range of completed assignments for the three rooms was from 72 percent to 92 percent, with the means for the three classes being 81.7 percent, 77.7 percent, and 88.6 percent. The data for class 2, which are representative of the other two classes, are presented in Figure 2-29.

* By Marion J. Howe, Ace Cossairt, and Cynthia Winstead.

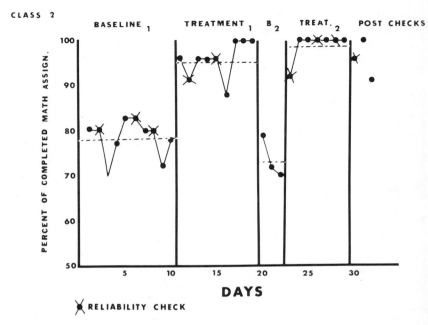

Figure 2-29 *Percentage of completed math assignments for 26 fifth grade students during baseline₁, treatment₁ (participation in classroom game contingent on completion), baseline₂, treatment₂ (reinstatement of treatment₁), and post-check conditions.*

Treatment₁

During the treatment phase, the children were told that those who had their previous day's math assignment ready at the beginning of the math period could play an indoor game called "Mum" for five minutes at the end of the period. "Mum" is a simple game in which a ball is tossed and the player who does not catch it is out. No one is permitted to talk during the game, hence the name "Mum." This treatment condition resulted in increases in all three classes in the percentage of completed math assignments. The daily range across the classes was from 100 percent to 88 percent, with the means within the classes being 98.6 percent, 95.9 percent, and 99.3 percent.

Baseline₂

For the purpose of scientific verification, a reversal procedure was instituted on the 21st day of the experiment. The teacher told the classes that there would be no time devoted to the game. The results for the three-day reversal procedure were as follows: the daily range across the three rooms was from 100 percent to 70 percent, with the means in the three classes being 85.3 percent, 73.6 percent, and 93.3 percent.

Treatment₂

In the final treatment condition, the teacher changed the individual contingency to a group contingency. The class had to show a 100-percent completion rate for the day in order to play "Mum" for five minutes. This resulted in a range across classes from 92 percent to 100 percent, with the means in the three classes being 99.8 percent, 98.8 percent, and 98.8 percent.

Post Checks

Three post-checks revealed a decrease in the completion rate.

Discussion

This study involved three fifth grade classes with a total of 78 children. Because the measurement procedures were conducted primarily by students, the teacher was not required to devote an unusual amount of time to gathering the data. The classroom game was easily administered and fit naturally into the school setting. The data indicated that both the individual and group consequences were effective.

EXPERIMENT 9: MODIFICATION OF INTERRUPTIVE CLASSROOM BEHAVIOR IN A TEN-YEAR-OLD BOY BY USE OF A TOKEN ECONOMY *

Population and Setting

Jaime was a boy in a classroom for the "educable" retarded at the Special Habilitation Institute of the Republic of Panama. His chronological age was 10 years, 10 months, and he was described as a very pleasant and friendly child. The classroom teacher was weary of Jaime's constant inter-

* By Consuelo M. Barrios and Francisco Alvarado.

ruptions, which consisted of out-of-seat behavior, destruction of his work, talk-outs, laughing at his peers, repeating the teacher's verbalizations, hitting peers, and constantly making noises with his school supplies. The teacher had already seated him apart from the children with whom he fought most frequently.

Behavior Measured

An interruption was defined as when Jaime talked out without permission, either to the teacher or his peers, or when he left his chair. Each behavior that had been classified as an interruption was recorded by the classroom teacher. The observation sessions were held daily from 11:00 to 11:30 A.M.

Experimental Procedures and Results

Baseline$_1$

During baseline, the interruptions averaged 10. (See Figure 2-30.) Two teachers recorded the child's behavior independently and obtained 93 percent reliability.

Tokens for Noninterruptive Behavior$_1$

Starting on day 4, Jaime was told he would receive a token on a 5-minute interval schedule if he did not interrupt the class during the preceding 5 minutes. After the class, the tokens could be exchanged for money, one penny for each token he had earned. It was explained that at the end of a week he could have 30 cents. Under these conditions, the number of interruptions decreased during the first session. The following day Jaime was absent, and on day 2 the number of interruptions increased. The following days they decreased. In conjunction with the token economy, the teacher occasionally praised Jaime when she observed appropriate behaviors. The mean number of interruptions was 4 during this condition.

Baseline$_2$

On day 9, tokens were suspended; the child was assigned work and no contingencies were applied. This produced an increase in the child's interruptive behavior to a mean of 5.8 percent.

MODIFICATION OF INTERRUPTIVE CLASSROOM BEHAVIOR
IN A TEN YEAR OLD BOY BY USE OF A TOKEN ECONOMY

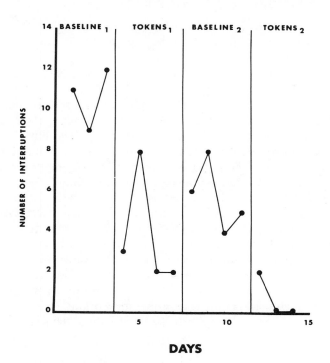

DAYS

Figure 2-30   *Number of interruptive behaviors of a ten-year-old boy during baseline and token (tokens backed by pennies contingent on noninterruptive behavior) conditions.*

Tokens for Noninterruptive Behavior₂

On day 14, the child was again told he would receive tokens if he did not interrupt the class; the behavior again decreased, to a mean of .6 percent.

Discussion

This study demonstrated that the utilization of a very simple token economy with money as a backup effectively reduced the rate of a child's interruptions. It was observed that after Jaime's interruptions decreased, his peers were friendlier, his work improved and the teacher felt better. A reversal demonstrated the causality of the procedure used.

EXPERIMENT 10: INCREASING THE PERCENTAGE OF COMPLETED WORK FOR A FIRST GRADE CHILD IN AN AFTERNOON LANGUAGE ARTS CLASS *

Population and Setting

The subject of this study was a six-year-old boy from a low socioeconomic area elementary school in Kansas City, Kansas. As a kindergartner, the subject was so disruptive with his talk-out, bizarre noises, and out-of-seat behavior that he was dismissed from the kindergarten classroom during the first semester and referred to the guidance center for a two-month period. At the guidance center, he worked on materials on a one-to-one basis with the staff, and according to the records received, his behavior improved. During the second semester, the subject returned to the kindergarten classroom with few occurrences of disruptive behaviors. During this study, the subject was in a first grade classroom whose students were participating in an intensive learning program. In this classroom, there were two teachers and approximately 22 students who spent two hours each day in reading and language arts activities. The activity schedule was so arranged that during language arts class, each teacher was responsible for working with a group of only 5 to 7 students in an effort to provide them with a "concentrated" learning session.

Behavior Measured

The behavior measured was the percentage of work completed during the afternoon language arts activities. The subject usually completed his morning language arts assignment without comment. However, by afternoon, he did very little work and remarked continually that he had too much to do and that the work was too difficult. A direct measurement procedure was used to record the data. A school consultant made a reliability check every day on the percentage of papers completed, and agreement was always 100 percent. Correctness of responses was not a concern in this investigation.

Experimental Procedures and Results

Baseline₁

During Baseline₁, the percentage of work completed varied from zero to 100 percent. Baseline conditions were in effect for 10 days and yielded a mean of 50.5 percent. (See Figure 2-31.)

* By Ernestine Massey and Cynthia Montgomery.

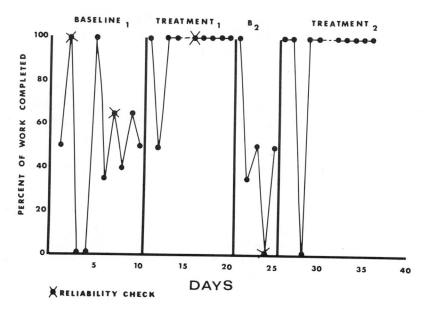

Figure 2-31 *Percentage of work completed during language arts period by a first grade boy during baseline and treatment (praise, candy, and showing work to principal contingent on completion of assignments) conditions.*

Treatment₁

Treatment began on day 11. The teacher showed the child a box of penny candy. She told him that for each day he completed his afternoon language arts assignment he could choose a piece of candy from the candy box. In addition to the piece of candy and praise from the teacher, the teacher took the child to the principal's office to "show off" completed assignments. On one occasion, when the teacher was called to the telephone, the subject thought she had forgotten him and he cried and tore up his paper. That was the only day his percentage dropped below 100 percent during treatment. During the 10 days of treatment₁, the mean of papers completed was 94.4 percent.

Baseline₂

During baseline₂, the teacher discontinued the reinforcement procedure and told the child that he was doing so well that she was no longer going to provide candy for him or tell the principal when he completed afternoon language arts assignments. On the first day of this reversal, his percentage of completed assignments was 100 percent. That was the only time during baseline$_2$, however, that the child completed his work. The mean for baseline$_2$ was 39.1 percent.

Treatment$_2$

After 6 days, the teacher reinstated the reinforcement condition. Again, assignments returned to a 100 percent completion rate, with the exception of day 27.

Discussion

This study does not provide us with information as to which consequence brought about the increase in completed assignments. It does demonstrate, however, that the treatment used was successful. The teacher was also concerned with the accuracy of the work completed, and planned to shift the consequences to increase accuracy as well as assignment completion.

EXPERIMENT 11: EFFECTS OF TOKENS ON ATTENDING BEHAVIOR [*]

Population and Setting

Billy, age 8 years, 10 months, was in a class for the trainable mentally retarded at a small semiprivate school in Kansas. He was in a class with 9 other students. The main concern in the class was to develop appropriate oral responses as well as other aspects of language development. During a 49-minute class, Billy was constantly talking out. Many of the talk-outs were unrelated to lesson content.

Behavior Measured and Reliability

An observer recorded the number of inappropriate talk-outs during a 35-minute class. During the study, a simultaneous record was made by an independent observer. The agreement between observers was 87 percent. Talk-outs were defined as inappropriate verbalizations not related to the topic being discussed. Interruptions were also considered talk-outs if the teacher was speaking or listening to another child.

[*] By Joe Meyers and Mary Hupka.

Experimental Procedures and Results

Baseline

During a 4-day baseline period, the number of talk-outs ranged from 14 to 21. The mean number of talk-outs was 17. (See Figure 2-32.)

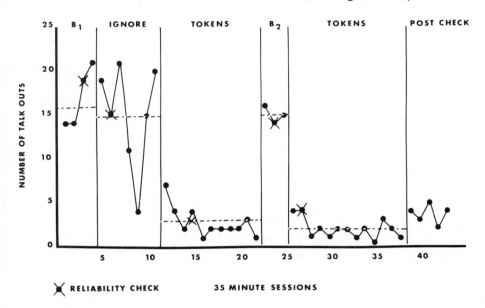

Figure 2-32 *Number of talk-outs by an eight-year-old boy in a TMR class during baseline, ignore (teacher ignoring talk-out behavior), tokens (backed by M & Ms contingent on hand raising for permission to talk), and post-check conditions.*

Ignore

At the end of the baseline period, Billy's talk-outs were ignored and he received verbal praise during the times he was properly attending. During this period, Billy's talk-outs varied from 4 to 21 with a mean rate of 15. Because there was little success with this ignoring procedure, a token economy was initiated.

Tokens

The first day that tokens were used, the entire class was told that they would receive a color chip when they raised their hands before responding. For every five-color chip they received, they were awarded one M & M candy. On the first day of this condition, Billy's talk-outs dropped to 8 and eventually they dropped to 1; the mean rate of talk-outs was 2.8 per 35-minute session.

Baseline₂

A three-day reversal study was conducted with the token system being withdrawn. Billy's talk-outs ranged from 15 to 17, with a mean rate of 16.

Tokens₂

When the token system was reinstated, Billy's talk-outs ranged from 4 to zero, with a mean rate of 1.9.

Post-Check

Five post-checks revealed a very slight increase in talk-outs.

Discussion

This study was conducted to improve the learning situation for the class as a whole. The study was easily conducted without making any major adjustments in the normal classroom routine. The teacher felt that when the token system was started, she improved her teaching by being more alert in giving positive reinforcement. The study had an effect on the whole class: the behavior of the entire class improved to the degree that slower students began to volunteer responses in order to receive the color chips. During baseline₂, the class was quite upset that they were not receiving tokens. Numerous inappropriate behaviors appeared, such as talk-outs, being out of seats, and lack of interest in the lesson. As soon as the tokens were reinstated, the majority of these behaviors disappeared.

EXPERIMENT 12: REDUCING DISOBEDIENCE IN A THREE-YEAR-OLD BOY THROUGH THE USE OF A TOKEN ECONOMY AND TIME-OUT PROCEDURE *

Population and Setting

The subject of this study was Robbie, a three-year-old boy of average height and weight without any physical problems. Robbie displayed a variety of inappropriate behaviors both at home and in other settings, the most

* By Marilyn Clark.

frequent of which included hyperactiveness, tantrums, and disobedience to his parents. Examples of Robbie's behavior included emptying a box of soap into the washing machine, running away from the assigned play area, playing in his mother's oil paints, and leaving his bed at naptime.

Behavior Measured

The mother wore a wrist counter to secure an event record of the disobedience. This behavior was defined as doing something after being told not to do it. At least once during each phase of the study, simultaneous observations were made by Robbie's father for the purpose of checking reliability; agreement ranged from 92 percent to 100 percent.

Experimental Procedure and Results

Baseline₁

During baseline, Robbie's frequency of disobedience ranged from 6 to 16 times per day, with a mean of 11. (See Figure 2-33.)

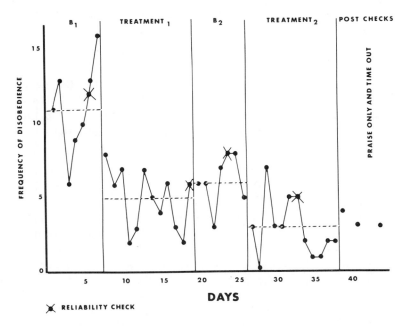

Figure 2-33 *Frequency of disobedience by a three-year-old during baseline, treatment (tokens backed by food and activities) and post-check conditions.*

Time Out and Tokens$_1$

Beginning on the ninth day, Robbie's mother explained to him that he would earn a chip each time he did what he was asked to do, that he could put his chips into a special container, and that later he could buy a cupcake, Popsicle, the use of a new set of paints, or an extra bath with his chips. Initially, each of these cost two chips, and later, three chips. Whenever Robbie disobeyed, he was placed in a time-out area for five minutes. Under these conditions, disobedience ranged from 2 to 8 with a mean of 5.

Baseline$_2$

On day 20, Robbie was told that his mother was busy and that they would not play the token game. She did not use the time-out room when Robbie disobeyed. Disobedience increased, though not to the level of Baseline$_1$. The mean during Baseline$_2$ was 6.

Time Out and Tokens$_2$

When the parents reinstated the token game and the time out area, the range of disobedience was from zero to 7, with a mean of 3. On day 6 of this condition, the cost of a special event was increased from two to three tokens.

Post-Checks

Post-checks were made at one-week intervals over the next three weeks. Three days prior to the first post-check, the use of chips was discontinued. Parent praise for obeying and time out for disobeying maintained a low level of disobedience. Special treats were not used during the remainder of the study.

Discussion

This study is interesting because it deals with a behavior that is a problem in many homes and schools. The parents reported that prior to the study, they had become so frustrated in trying to make Robbie mind that they had considered requesting medication for their son. After learning new management techniques, they expressed a delight in day-to-day living with their son.

part 3 / Research
in Training

9 | Training Teaching-Parents: An Evaluation of Workshop Training Procedures

Kathryn A. Kirigin · Hector E. Ayala
Curtis J. Braukmann · Willie G. Brown
Neil Minkin · Elery L. Phillips
Dean L. Fixsen · Montrose M. Wolf

The development of training programs designed to teach the principles and procedures of behavior modification to professionals, paraprofessionals, and parents is currently receiving the attention of many applied behavior analysts. This development largely reflects a widespread need to provide solutions to some long-term social problems. The scope of the development is underscored by the 1971 Banff conference, which was devoted entirely to papers concerning strategies for implementing behavioral programs in school and clinical settings (Clark, Evans, and Hamerlynck, 1972). The

This investigation was partially sponsored by PHS Training Grant HD #00183 from the National Institute of Child Health and Human Development to the Kansas Center for Research in Mental Retardation and Human Development, and by grant MH20030 from the National Institute of Mental Health (Center for Studies of Crime and Delinquency) to the Kansas University Bureau of Child Research.

161

papers presented at that conference made three important points: 1) there is a growing need for training programs to produce effective agents of behavior change; 2) in applying behavior modification procedures, training programs should focus on specific skill development; and 3) training programs should be evaluated systematically in order to establish the most effective and efficient training procedures.

For the past two years, the Achievement Place research project has been developing a training program designed to provide couples with sufficient skills and knowledge to implement community-based, family-style, group home-treatment programs based on the Achievement Place Teaching-Family Model. The couples who operate teaching-family homes are called teaching-parents. Each set of teaching-parents lives in a large home with six to eight delinquent, dependent-neglected, emotionally disturbed, or mildly retarded adolescents. They are the sole staff of the program and are responsible for redirecting the lives of the youths by teaching them more acceptable behavior patterns at home, in school, and in the community. To accomplish these goals, the teaching-parents must work closely with the youths' parents and teachers, with the local juvenile court and department of welfare, and with a community board of directors that is responsible for establishing policy and financial guidelines for the home. For a more detailed account of the Teaching-Family model, see *The Teaching-Family Handbook* (Phillips, Phillips, Fixsen, and Wolf, 1974).

The training program has evolved from one that emphasized academic skill development (primarily reading and attending lectures about the principles of behavior modification) to one that stresses practical skill development and practice in applying the modification procedures. The present training program consists of a five-part sequence that is completed in one year.

1. An initial five-day, fifty-hour workshop held at Kansas University to provide the basic knowledge of the program and the skills needed to implement the procedures.

2. A three-month practicum period with frequent consultation with the training staff, which begins when the trainees begin to operate their own treatment programs.

3. At the end of the three-month practicum, the training staff evaluates each trainee's program. The evaluation consists of sending questionnaires to the juvenile court, department of welfare, school personnel, board of directors, and the youths' parents to ask their opinions about the program's effectiveness in correcting the youths' problems and about the cooperation of the teaching-parents. In addition, a professional evaluator makes an on-site visit to rate the teaching skills of the teaching-parents, to evaluate the general social behaviors of the youths, and to give the youths a questionnaire asking them to evaluate the fairness, concern, and effectiveness of the teaching-parents and other dimensions of the program. We have found this to be an economical means of

evaluating a program, one which provides the teaching-parents with valuable feedback from the important individuals and agencies in the community.

4. The next nine months of training include a second five-day workshop at Kansas University, followed by continued consultation with the training staff and additional program evaluations at six and nine months, if necessary, to provide the trainees with specific feedback about the strengths and weaknesses of their program. With such feedback, the trainees can make any necessary corrections.

5. After the trainees' program has been operating for twelve months, the first annual program evaluation will be conducted to determine the certification of the trainees as teaching-parents.

The present training program has been operating for less than one year, and we are just beginning to isolate and define some of the important skills that are characteristic of successful teaching-parents. Past research with the treatment program has demonstrated that teaching-parents can modify a number of behavior problems if they make effective use of the token economy (Phillips, 1968; Phillips, Phillips, Fixsen, and Wolf, 1971). Points, backed up by privileges that are naturally available within the treatment setting, have proved to be effective in motivating the youths to increase several appropriate behaviors and to decrease several inappropriate behaviors. However, we have found that point consequences alone are often insufficient to teach the youths alternative appropriate behaviors if those behaviors are absent from their repertoire. To teach these behaviors, the teaching-parents must be able to provide the necessary instructions and corrective feedback that will enable the youth to acquire the new skills. We have found that teaching-parents can reduce inappropriate behaviors most effectively by combining the token economy with effective *teaching* of appropriate alternative behaviors.

By observing the behavior of successful teaching-parents as they correct problem behaviors, we have identified several teaching behaviors that seem to be important. Typically, the successful teaching-parents begin most interactions in a pleasant way by smiling, by giving recognition of accomplishment and statements of approval, or by positive physical contact. They then define the problem for the youth; they provide a rationale for engaging in a more appropriate alternative behavior; they describe and, if necessary, model the appropriate behaviors; they break down the more complex behaviors into small teachable components; they provide the youth with many opportunities to practice the new behavior according to an acceptable criterion; and they give social feedback and points to the youth for his cooperation in learning the new skill.

Presently we are closely analyzing our training program as a means of teaching teaching-parent trainees these seemingly important teaching-interaction skills. Thus far, we have identified and defined eight behavioral components that appear to be consistently involved in teaching interactions. In order to teach the interaction sequence to the trainees, we begin with the simplest components and gradually add the others until the entire interaction is mastered. What follows is a description of the training procedure. For each of the components, a behavioral description is provided, a rationale for its inclusion in the teaching interaction is presented, and an example of the use of the component is included. The examples that accompany the descriptions of the components illustrate how the teaching interaction might be used to correct a problem social behavior by teaching the appropriate social skill. In the situation below, one of the youths ignored guests as they were leaving the home. To begin the teaching-interaction, the teaching-parent typically calls the youth aside.

TEACHING-INTERACTION COMPONENTS

1. INITIAL PRAISE. The onset of the teaching seqence is usually signaled by the delivery of a statement of praise or an approving comment. The praise is typically brief and descriptive, and is an indication to the youth that the teaching-parent recognizes and approves of some aspect of the youth's behavior. This is important because it helps begin the interaction on a positive, pleasant basis. Initial praise often includes approving words such as "nice," "good," or "appreciate." An example of a statement of initial praise would be:

> "Say Harold, I appreciate the way you showed George and Marge around the house and talked with them while they were visiting."

2. DESCRIPTION OF INAPPROPRIATE BEHAVIOR. If the interaction involves correcting an inappropriate or an undesirable behavior displayed by the youth, it is important to specify those behaviors to the youth in terms that are clear and descriptive. Although the youth's misbehaviors may often lead to disruption of the household routine or may even embarrass the teaching-parent, it is important that the teaching-parent be able to maintain composure when teaching. The inappropriate behaviors should be described as physical observable events, in a manner that is nonconfronting and nonaversive. For example, after providing initial praise, the teaching-parent might describe the behavior problem by saying:

> "Harold, I'd like to talk with you about your behavior when George and Marge were leaving. Now when they said 'Good-bye' to you, you didn't look over at them, or stand up, or say anything to indicate that you'd even heard them. You just kept watching television."

3. RATIONALE. After the problem has been described, or in any interaction that involves teaching a new behavior, it is important to provide the youth with a valid reason or rationale for learning the behavior you wish to teach him. These rationales typically include some statement of why the present behavior is unacceptable or an indication of the consequences of a more appropriate, alternative behavior. Rationales are a very important component of the teaching interaction because they help identify for the youth the possible natural consequences of particular behaviors. Rationales, if repeated frequently enough, can also help teach the youth to use those same rationales when asked to explain his actions. To continue with our example, the teaching-parent provides a rationale to the youth for learning some new social skills:

> "Harold, we want our guests to feel that they are welcome visitors. Now, they'll probably feel more welcome if you would acknowledge them when they say good-bye and say something to let them know you were glad that they visited."

4. DESCRIPTION OF THE APPROPRIATE BEHAVIOR. The teaching-parent must be able to tell the youth the specific behaviors that are appropriate in the situation. In many cases, the teaching-parent will need to break down complex behaviors, such as academic or maintenance tasks, into more simple, teachable components. In teaching a new behavior, it may be necessary for the teaching-parent to demonstrate or model the desired behaviors as he or she is describing them. Such demonstrations seem to enhance the verbal description and help minimize possible misinterpretation of the behavior that is required of the youth. For example:

> *Teaching-Parent:* "Now Harold, when a guest says good-bye to you, I'd like you to stop whatever you're doing, stand up, look at the guests, give them a smile, and say good-bye. You might also want to thank them for coming or maybe ask them to come back some time. Now let's pretend that you're the guest who's leaving, and I'm you watching television. Now, can you remember what the first step is after the guests say good-bye?"
>
> *Harold:* "You're supposed to stand up and look at them."
>
> *Teaching-Parent:* "That's right. Now, say goodbye to me as though you were leaving and I'll show you what I'd like you to do. Ok, ready?"
>
> *Harold:* "Good-bye. Nice to see you."
>
> *Teaching-Parent:* (models the appropriate behavior) "Notice that the first thing I did was to stand up and look at you. Did you notice the big smile? Then I said good-bye and asked you to come back some time? Now you see how it works?"

5. POINT CONSEQUENCES.   In the teaching interaction the teaching-parent should specify the number of points that the youth can earn or lose by engaging in the appropriate or inappropriate behavior. Points will provide the youth with some immediate and tangible consequences for his behavior. In addition, they can provide an important incentive to the youth for learning an alternative or new behavior. For example:

> "Harold, I'll give you 1000 points if you can remember to use all of the steps I've just shown you when a guest is leaving."

6. REQUEST FOR ACKNOWLEDGMENT.   Requests for acknowledgment involve brief questions or probes from the teaching-parent, which require some form of verbal feedback from the youth. During the interaction it is important for the teaching-parent to have the youth make some type of a response to the instructions being provided. In cases where the youth lacks simple acknowledgment skills, it will be necessary for the teaching-parents to teach appropriate acknowledgment behavior. Acknowledgments typically consist of one- or two-word statements from the youth such as "uh-huh," "yes," "no," "all right," "OK," or a similar response. When the youth provides such acknowledgments in response to questions from the teaching-parent, the teaching-parent has some indication that the youth is attending. Acknowledgment is most important in maintaining a positive social interaction between the teaching-parent and the youth, and in maintaining the teaching-parents' instructional behavior. Teaching-parents (as well as natural parents and teachers) seem to be very averse to interacting with an unresponsive, "passive-aggressive" youth. Thus, appropriate acknowledgment is an important interaction skill for the youth to learn. One way to provide opportunities for acknowledgment in an interaction is to periodically pose questions about the instructions that have been given. Requests for acknowledgment are typically phrased in the form of a question such as:

> "Do you understand what you are supposed to do when visitors say good-bye? Do you know why it's important to act that way?"

7. PRACTICE AND FEEDBACK.   At some point in the teaching-interaction, usually after the description and/or demonstration of the appropriate behavior has been provided, it is important to allow the youth to practice the behavior being taught. It is important because it allows the teaching-parent to determine whether the youth has mastered the skill. As the youth practices the behavior, the teaching-parent should provide immediate feedback and additional instructions until the youth achieves the desired performance.

Teaching-Parent: "All right Harold, let's see if you can do it. Now I'll pretend I'm the guest who's leaving and I'll say good-bye to you. Ready? OK. Good-bye Harold. It sure was nice seeing you again."

Harold: (Stands up, looks at teaching-parent) "Good-bye. Come back again some time."

Teaching-Parent: "Good, Harold, you stood up and looked over here at me. The good-bye was nice, and you included a very nice follow-up in asking me to come back, but you forgot to smile. Let's try it once more, and let's see if you can remember to include a nice big smile. OK?"

8. FINAL PRAISE. When the youth masters the desired behavior to criterion performance, it is important for the teaching-parent to commend his accomplishments and provide enthusiastic praise. It ends the interaction on a positive note, and will perhaps facilitate future teaching interactions with the youth. The final praise is most typically accompanied by the delivery of points. By presenting points simultaneous with praise and other forms of social approval as a consequence of learning, the teaching-parent can begin to strengthen the youth's social behavior. Final praise along with the points can also help increase the likelihood that the youth will use the new skills he has learned in future situations. In closing the teaching interaction, the teaching-parent should try to encourage the youth to do this. As an example of final praise, the teaching-parent might say:

"Great job, Harold. I appreciate your cooperation in learning these new behaviors. Give yourself 1000 points. Now if you can remember to do all those things the next time a guest leaves, I'll give you another 1000. Fair enough? Great."

Because of the newness of the training program, we have only recently begun to evaluate the effectiveness of the procedures for training teaching-parents to carry out these components. The present study was conducted in order to assess the effectiveness of the initial training workshop in developing the trainees' teaching skills, which we believed to be one of the most critical sets of skills that had to be taught to them.

METHOD

Subjects and Setting

The subjects for the study were six couples. All were in their 20s or early 30s, and at least one member of each couple held a college degree in one of the behavioral sciences. All had applied to the teaching-parent training program.

Four of the six couples attended the initial five-day workshop for teaching-parents. Prior to the workshop, they received a packet of materials consisting of *The Teaching-Family Handbook*—which offers a detailed description of the program—a study guide to facilitate reading the *Handbook,* and a copy of the *Achievement Place Novel.* They were asked to read the materials and to complete the study guide questions before coming to the workshop.

The two couples who did not participate in the workshop received copies of *The Teaching-Family Handbook* and study guide. One couple had completed the accompanying study guide; the other couple had frequently visited a Teaching-Family home. Neither couple received any formal training during the time the workshop was conducted.

Testing

Prior to the onset of the workshop, midway through it, and immediately following it, each of the twelve subjects was tested to obtain a performance measure of his or her teaching skills. The tests consisted of five role-playing situations involving interactions between a teaching-parent and a "youth." The situations included greeting an adult, a good report from school, cleaning a table, swearing and arguing, and fighting. In each situation, a graduate student played the role of the "youth." To maintain consistency of the "youth's" behavior, the graduate student was provided with specific instructions as to the particular behaviors he should display in each situation. He practiced his role in each situation several times before the pre-test was given.

Upon entering the testing situation, each person was provided with a set of written instructions that briefly described each situation (for example, "you will enter the room and greet the youth") and indicated only that the youth would be engaging in some appropriate and inappropriate behaviors. They were instructed to handle each situation as best they could. Approximately ten minutes were needed to test each person (there was a maximum of two minutes per situation). The pre-, mid-, and post-tests were recorded on videotape.

Training Procedures

The initial workshop consisted of five days and roughly fifty hours of intensive instruction and scheduled activities designed to provide the trainees with the basic knowledge and skills they need to set up and operate a Teaching-Family program.

The formal training began on Sunday evening, immediately following the pre-test, with a brief introduction to the principles of behavior modification. During the daily sessions, which began the following morning, the training staff provided detailed descriptions of the major components of the program about which the trainees would have to know in order to start their own programs: how to manage the the motivation system, how to implement the self-government system, how to teach the youths more appropriate behaviors, and how to work with parents, teachers, and community agencies. For each skill taught, the trainees viewed videotapes that showed appropriate and inappropriate teaching-parent behaviors, and they practiced the appropriate behaviors with the training staff in specially designed role-playing situations.

Teaching-parent interaction skills were taught on the second day of the workshop. On that day, the trainees learned and practiced several behaviors that teaching-parents use in their day-to-day interactions with the youths: appropriate use of praise and attention, giving a simple instruction, and delivering point consequences. The trainees were also instructed in the particular interaction skills used by teaching-parents to correct behavior problems and to teach the youths new skills. This type of teaching instruction is called a teaching interaction. For each type of interaction, the training staff described the important behavioral components and indicated when the interaction was most appropriately used. The trainees then viewed videotapes that showed at least two versions of the same interaction: one that included the important components and one that did not.

Following the descriptive presentations, taped examples, and discussions of each interaction, the trainees practiced the skills in the role-playing situations. There were three people involved in each situation: a graduate student trained to play the role of the "youth," the trainee, and an evaluator. For each type of interaction, the "youth" was instructed to display specific behaviors. The trainee was given a handout that described each interaction and indicated the specific behaviors that the "youth" would perform. The trainee was also given a list of the specific behaviors that he or she should display in the interaction. The evaluator set up and monitored the interaction, then provided the trainee with praise and feedback for his performance. The evaluator also provided additional instruction or modeled the appropriate behavior, and, if necessary, had the trainee practice again until he reached criterion performance. In providing correction feedback, the evaluators basically used the teaching-interaction components to improve the trainees' skills to criterion performance.

Each of the couples was provided with additional opportunities to observe teaching-parent behavior and to practice their own teaching skills during an evening in-home practicum at Achievement Place (at either the home for boys or the home for girls). At the practicum, the trainees watched the teaching-parents interact with the youths; they were then provided with several preplanned situations involving interactions with the youths, so that they could display their teaching skills. Following these interactions, the trainees received feedback about their performance from both the youths and the teaching-parents.

On the final day of the workshop, the trainees were introduced to the evaluation procedures that would be conducted at the end of the three-month practicum. They also filled out questionnaires that evaluated the workshop training procedures. Each person was then tested again in the same five role-playing situations as before, involving the same graduate student "youth."

Data Collection

The pre-, mid-, and post-test tapes for all subjects were randomized. The tapes were scored by two trained observers who were unaware of the purpose of the study. Each interaction was scored for the occurrence of the teaching-interaction components that were previously described. Each observer scored four behavioral components. The complete definitions and procedures for recording can be obtained from the senior author.

Reliability

For approximately one-fourth of all tapes, a third observer made independent records simultaneous with each of the primary observers. Occurrence reliability was calculated for each behavior by dividing agreements by agreements plus disagreements. With two of the original components, rationale for appropriate behavior and rationale for inappropriate behavior, occurrence reliability for the type of rationale was less than 60 percent. These two components were then combined and agreements were calculated for the occurrence of either form of rationale. With this collapsed category, occurrence reliability for rationale was 89 percent. For all other behavioral components, reliability was 80 percent or better.

RESULTS

The overall pre- and post-test results for both the trained and the untrained couples appear in Figure 3-1. Each bar represents the average number of all components of the teaching interactions for all of the situations. The mid-test data are not shown; however, for all of the couples involved, the

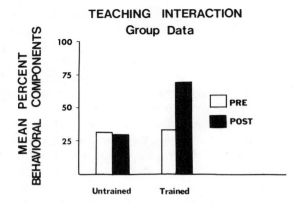

Figure 3-1 *Mean percentage of all behavioral components of the teaching interaction engaged in by the trained and untrained couples before and after the teaching-parent workshop.*

mid-test performance was very similar to the post-test performance. Prior to the workshop, the couples displayed comparable teaching skills: each engaged in about 30 percent of the teaching-interaction components in the interactions. Following the workshop, the untrained couples stayed at about this 30 percent level, but the trained couples increased to a usage of 70 percent of the components.

Figure 3-2 shows the breakdown of the teaching interaction into its

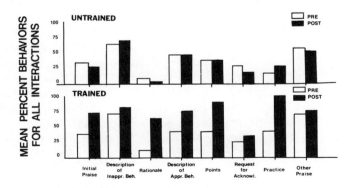

Figure 3-2 *Mean percentage of the individual behavior components of the teaching interaction engaged in by the trained and untrained couples before and after the teaching-parent workshop.*

component behaviors; again, the results were summarized for both groups. All six couples showed comparable levels of performance on each behavior in the pre-test. Most of the components were included in less than 50 percent of the interactions. For both groups, only two components—description of inappropriate behavior, and other praise—were used in more than 50 percent of the interactions. On the post-test, the changes in usage of each component by the untrained group were negligible, in contrast with the trained couples, who showed an increased use of each component. As shown in Figure 3-2, the training procedures were not equally effective in training each component behavior. Only one component, practice and feedback, achieved the 100 percent level; most increased to about 75 percent, and two components were considerably below the 75 percent level. Clearly, the procedures were least effective in training requests for acknowledgment, which was displayed in only 30 percent of the interactions, and rationale giving, which occurred in only 60 percent of all interactions.

DISCUSSION

Because it was not possible to use a random assignment to determine the trained and the untrained groups, these data permit only preliminary conclusions about the effectiveness of the training procedures. However, the results of this study suggest that workshop training procedures can be used to develop specific behaviors and that measurement procedures can be devised to detect behavioral changes over time. The couples who received workshop training nearly doubled their use of the teaching-interaction components, whereas the performance of the untrained couples remained unchanged.

The pre- and post-test data indicate that the training program was at least 75 percent effective in establishing consistent teaching-interaction skills. That is, the trainees displayed most of the component behaviors in most of the interactions. However, two component behaviors, rationale and request for acknowledgment from the youth, were consistently omitted from many of the interactions both prior to and following training. The data gathered from the mid-test largely supports the findings, and indicates that the teaching skills were learned during the first three days of the workshop and were thereafter maintained at about the same 75 percent level.

These data show that the training procedures were less than 100 percent effective. With this feedback, the training staff has subsequently modified the training procedures to improve the quality of interaction, particularly that of the component behaviors that occurred infrequently. In future workshops, similar pre- and post-tests will be conducted to measure the effects of these modifications. These data are also being used by the training staff to provide the trainees with feedback, both to remind them of the importance of using the teaching interaction and to point out the component behaviors that may not have been displayed enough or that need additional emphasis.

This research has shown that trainee behavior can be modified. Whether such changes generalize to the group home setting and how durable they are once the treatment programs are implemented remain critical yet unanswered questions. However, this research has resulted in the development of a measurement procedure that may permit such evaluations in the near future. When evaluators visit treatment settings, they will be provided with a check list of the behavioral components of the teaching interaction, much like the recording sheet used by the observers. By using the behavior definitions developed for the workshop, the evaluators will be able to evaluate the trainees' teaching skills in terms of the presence or absence of the specific component behaviors of the teaching interaction. With such a measurement system, it will be possible to compare workshop performance to treatment-setting performance to determine the generalization and durability of the training effects. Moreover, the measurement procedure will also enable the evaluator to provide for the trainee objective and detailed feedback concerning his teaching skills.

Meanwhile, research is currently being done in one teaching-family home to evaluate the effectiveness of the teaching interaction, as compared with other procedures for teaching new behavior (Ford, Ford, Christophersen, Fixsen, Phillips, and Wolf, unpublished). Preliminary results of this comparative study suggest that a teaching instruction combined with point consequences for appropriate behavior produces more immediate and durable changes in a youth's behavior than verbal and written instructions describing appropriate behavior combined with point consequences for displaying the behaviors described. In the Ford *et al.* study, the youths learned to 100 percent criterion the appropriate behaviors used to answer the phone, to greet visitors at the door, and to complete a maintenance task, only when the teaching interaction was implemented. Verbal and written instructions combined with point consequences produced some improvement over baseline performance, but behavior clearly fell well below 100 percent performance. These results strongly recommend the teaching interaction as a tool for encouraging youths to display new behaviors.

Additional available evidence suggests that the youths prefer the interaction skills that are being taught in the workshop. In a recent study by Wilner, Ayala, Fixsen, Phillips, and Wolf (unpublished), the youths at Achievement Place for Girls were asked to grade the "good" and "bad" examples of interaction shown in the workshop training tapes. The tapes were scored on an ABCDF grading scale, where A indicated an excellent interaction and F a poor interaction. The results of this study were polarized: all of the "good" interactions were rated A, and all the "bad" interactions were rated F. The youths clearly preferred interactions that contained all the components of the teaching interaction over those that did not. The girls were subsequently asked to explain why they preferred one form of interaction over another. In their comments, they most consistently mentioned their preference for interactions that contained praise and instructions about the appropriate behaviors expected.

This additional evidence suggests that the teaching-interaction skills that are presently taught in the workshop training program are relevant to the operation of treatment programs. The results of Ford *et al.* indicate that the interaction components were effective in teaching new behaviors. In addition, these types of interactions appear to be clearly preferred by the youths. This evidence provides important feedback to the training staff, feedback that underscores the importance of continuing to teach teaching-interaction skills. In future workshops similar pre- and post-test measures of trainees' performance, together with additional follow-up studies in the treatment setting, will be conducted in order to validate some of the other critical skills being taught in the worshop.

10 / Training Counselors as Researchers in the Natural Environment

Jerry W. Willis · *Tom R. Hobbs*
Dorcas G. Kirkpatrick · *Kent W. Manley*

Recent investigations have applied behavior modification techniques to group counseling with elementary school children (Hinds and Roehlke, 1970; Tosi, Upshaw, Lande, and Waldron, 1971), high school students (Krumboltz and Thoresen, 1964), college students (Ryan and Krumboltz, 1964), preadolescent boys' groups (Stedman, Peterson, and Cardarelle, 1971), high school underachievers (Andrews, 1971), child management counseling for parents (Mira, 1970; Rose, 1969) and teachers (Hall, 1971). The recent interest in applying behavioral principles to counseling is perhaps due to their demonstrated effectiveness in other situations and to the ease with which such application can be evaluated. The emphases on precise definition of measurable behavior, reliability of observa-

The authors wish to express their appreciation to Ms. Jeanne Crowder, Dr. Jim Mottin, and Dr. Doug Torney for their assistance in preparing this manuscript.

175

tion, structured change techniques, and methods for scientifically verifying behavior change all encourage the application of behavioral principles and procedures to counseling.

Traditionally, the field of counseling has assumed that behavior change occurs as the result of a warm, trusting, and accepting relationship (Fiedler, 1950) between an empathic, caring, open, and genuine counselor (Rogers, 1961) and committed clients who are willing to discuss their difficulties (Ohlson, 1970). Behavioral counselors would not take issue with the idea that counselors should be warm (that is, should provide a high rate of positive reinforcement for desirable behavior). However, traditional counseling has in recent years been criticized on several points. Vargas (1954), Lewis (1959), and Hobbs (1962) questioned the traditional and basic assumption that the acquisition and verbal expression of insight automatically results in changes in behavior. More recently, Brodsky (1967) demonstrated that changes in verbal behavior do not necessarily indicate that simultaneous extratherapeutic behavior change has occurred. Furthermore, "clients" in an applied setting, especially the school, are often referred to the counselor as a result of behavior that is defined by the referral source as objectionable. Therefore, the school counselor is frequently asked to work with youngsters who are not particularly concerned about their behavior, and who do not wish to become involved in traditional counseling sessions.

Though several writers question basic counseling assumptions, possibly the most stringent criticism of traditional counseling concerns its methods of evaluating the effectiveness of treatment. Edwards and Cronbach (1952) criticized counseling for having vague criteria for behavior change as well as for having global goals. Bergin (1963) criticized counselors for relying too heavily on subjective value judgments in assessing behavior change, and Paul (1967) noted that test instruments used to assess behavior change often have poor reliability and validity, and are frequently insensitive to change (Bereiter, 1962).

It appears, then, that a crucial problem for the field of counseling is its marked lack of adequate criteria for and measures of behavior change. This problem appears almost as serious in the behavioral counseling literature as in the reports of more traditional methods. Lack of empirical data reduces a counselor's selection of a behavior-change approach to one of personal preference. Once selected, the use of an approach is often maintained by factors unrelated to actual effect, for counselors are rarely trained or inclined to collect objective data on the effect of their work. This paper describes the operation of a graduate course for counselors in public schools that attempted to teach basic techniques of behavioral counseling and data collection methods that could be used by the typical counselor in his day-to-day work.

METHOD

Subjects and Setting

"Behavioral Approaches to Counseling" was offered as a graduate course with three semester hours of credit, at the request of a large county school system. The course was taught by the staff of the Birmingham School Consultation Project (Willis and Willis, 1972), and was one of several offered by the Center for In-Service Teacher Education and Research at the School of Education, University of Alabama in Birmingham. The Center assists school systems and university professionals in developing experimental or tailored educational programs for teachers. New courses are easily approved, and training need not follow a semester or quarter schedule. In this case, the course met for two hours a week for twenty-three weeks from October to April. Eleven junior high and high school guidance or vocational counselors enrolled in the class. The course was designed to produce counselors who could:

1. Describe the basic principles of changing behavior in school settings.
2. Identify and illustrate the appropriate use of applied research designs.
3. Design, conduct, and evaluate a behavior change project.

Goals 1 and 2 were evaluated by paper-and-pencil tests. The degree to which goal 3 has been accomplished was measured by requiring each counselor to complete at least one project during the course.

Course Structure and Material

Each class session usually consisted of three phases, with the greater amount of time being devoted to the area that most interested the counselors during a given session.

Condition 1: Lecture

This approach was used primarily in the initial stages of the course in order to teach the basic principles of behavior modification and applied behavior analysis. Students were taught how to pinpoint and precisely define behavior, how to count it, how to obtain reliability data, and how to develop an adequate research design. The authors also made use of selected articles from the research literature. However, articles on counseling that met even a majority of the criteria for acceptable scientific research were rare, and many articles from respected journals fell far short of these criteria. In addition, the authors also relied heavily on Hall's *Managing Behavior* series (1971), which briefly summarizes the applied behavior analysis approach. Three written tests concerning basic principles were given during the course, the combined results of which composed 25 percent of the student's final grade.

Condition 2: Group Reports

The class, after being divided into several subgroups, was requested to report on a research article describing a behavioral approach to a problem of interest to them. They were asked not only to summarize the article concisely but also to assess its acceptability as scientific research. The criteria used for judging the "believability" of any article discussed during the course included:

1. a precise, objective, and measurable definition of the problem behavior
2. objective baseline data on the problem behavior (or a proper control group whose behavior was objectively measured)
3. reliability data
4. systematic application of objectively defined procedures
5. objective outcome data
6. scientific verification, such as a reversal, multiple baseline, or control group
7. objective follow-up data

These criteria were adapted from several sources, including Campbell and Stanley (1963), Hall (1971), and Gelfand (1968). The class soon became adept at critically analyzing a given article and readily reaching a conclusion regarding its scientific "believability."

Condition 3: Application

Each counselor was required to develop a behavior change project in his respective school setting. Each counseling project was to be designed so as to meet the same criteria that had been used by the class in evaluating other research articles. Frequently, much of the class session was devoted to the development, maintenance, and follow-up of each counselor's ongoing project. Each week, projects were discussed in terms of recent problems and proposed changes. The counselors received points for each of the previously discussed criteria met by their study. Objective baseline data, for example, earned 20 points, reliability earned 10 points, follow-up data earned 10 points, and so forth. The counseling project composed 75 percent of the counselor's course grade. Extra points could be earned by completing extra group or individual counseling projects.

Results

The effects of the course can best be illustrated by the following examples of completed counseling projects. The first project demonstrates the counselor's role as a consultant to a teacher who was experiencing a group behavior problem. The second study illustrates a counselor's approach to an interesting, but not unique, off-campus group behavior problem. The last project exemplifies the consultative role of the counselor, involving not only a teacher but also a parent, in dealing with an individual behavior problem.

STUDY 1

Subjects and Setting

A junior high school mathematics teacher sought help from the counselor who conducted this study. The teacher reported that one 45-minute class of 27 seventh-grade students was so disruptive that learning was virtually impossible. In spite of threats and punishment, a large number of students frequently interrupted the class by making loud, irrelevant comments, moving about the room, and chatting with neighbors. The guidance counselor chose to help the teacher develop a different approach to classroom discipline, instead of establishing the weekly group discussion sessions for students that were usually suggested. The counselor made her decision from the viewpoint of operant psychology. Behavior must be viewed within the environmental context where it occurs. Thus, the question was not how to change "bad" students but how to develop an environment that would promote more appropriate learning behavior.

Behavior Measured

Talk-outs were recorded whenever students talked out in class or spoke to other students at inappropriate times during the class period. A record was also kept of the number of times students left their desks without permission. A student teacher tallied the talk-outs and out-of-seat behaviors. A ninth-grade student made an independent, simultaneous record during each of four experimental *conditions*. Agreement of the records ranged from 77 percent to 100 percent, with a mean of 90 percent.

Methods and Results

Baseline$_1$

Baseline data were recorded for 5 days. Figure 3-3 presents a record of the number of talk-outs and out-of-seat behaviors during the daily

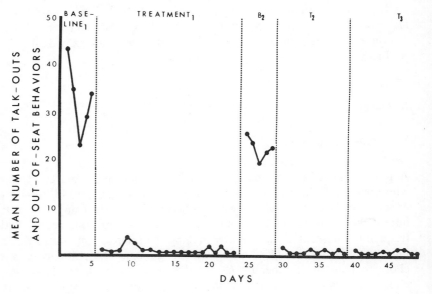

Figure 3-3 *Mean number of talk-outs and out-of-seat behaviors (combined) for 27 seventh-grade students across successive experimental conditions.*

45-minute mathematics session. Because data for the two behaviors were quite similar, the figure presents the total of the two behaviors. The mean number of inappropriate behaviors counted during baseline$_1$ was 32.8.

Treatment$_1$

On the sixth day, the students were told that if the entire class displayed no talk-outs or out-of-seat behavior during the first 15 minutes of the class, they would have 5 minutes of free time at the end of the period to talk, relax, and eat a snack provided for them if they wished. During the second week of treatment, the contingency was in effect only for the first 20 minutes of the class; the third week, 30 minutes of acceptable behavior were required; and by the fourth week, 40 minutes were covered. In all instances, 5 minutes of free time was the reward. Throughout the condition, the teacher was asked to provide praise along with the tangible and free-time reinforcers. After the contingency was imposed, the mean number of disruptive behaviors per class dropped to one. During this condition, the students failed to meet the requirement for reinforcement only once—a Monday after a three-day vacation from school.

Baseline$_2$

Snacks and free time were not provided during a five-day reversal (days 26 to 30). During this phase, the mean number of disruptive behaviors increased to 21.6.

Treatment$_2$

On day 31, the conditions during the fourth week of treatment$_1$ were reinstated. This reintroduction of the contingency resulted in a decrease in inappropriate behavior to a mean of .8.

Treatment$_3$

On day 41, students were told that they would not always receive a reward every day the criteria were met. From then on, they never knew whether a given day was a reinforcement day until the last five minutes of class. Actually, reinforcement occurred an average of once every five days. During this condition unacceptable behavior remained at a low rate, with a mean of .8.

STUDY 2

Subjects and Setting

The subjects were fifty black children in grades one through eight who rode a bus to school. The children came primarily from poor areas of Birmingham. Many had experienced several years of busing, changing schools, and community turmoil. For the most part, the children had been well accepted at the elementary school they attended. The children were usually quiet and remained in their seats during the morning trip to school, but in the afternoon they were quite noisy and disruptive. They often walked or ran through the aisle, climbed over seats, or stood in their seats and shouted.

The problem of major concern to the bus driver was the group's high frequency of out-of-seat behavior, which made the driver's job difficult and imposed safety risks to the occupants of the bus.

Behavior Measured

The bus driver, who was also a counselor at the local high school, observed and recorded the number of times students left their seats during the ten-minute trip from the school to the first stop, the period during which most of the disruptive behavior occurred. Reliability checks were made by an eighth-grade girl, who had been instructed to do so without the knowledge of the other students. The smaller count divided by the larger yielded a mean reliability of 74 percent for the 4 days that reliability checks were made.

Method and Results

Baseline$_1$

Observations were made for 6 days prior to the institution of the behavior change procedures. During baseline $_1$ the mean number of out-of-seat behaviors was 34, with a range from 22 to 43. (See Figure 3-4.)

Treatment$_1$

On the seventh day, the students were told that the bus was to be divided into two sections by the aisle, and the students on each side would receive a piece of inexpensive candy if the members of their group did not get out of their seats more than 3 times. If one side did not qualify to receive any candy, the other side could still receive their reward as they left the bus if they met the criteria. The candy was given out by an eighth-grade girl who rode the bus regularly. Praise was consistently paired with the awarding of candy. On the first day of treatment $_1$, 2 out-of-seat behaviors occurred. Both sides received their rewards as they left the bus. On day 12, 5 out-of-seat behaviors occurred on one side of the bus, and that side received no reward. On day 14, the driver was absent and no count was taken. The last day that a group exceeded the criteria was day 15, when both sides failed to receive a reinforcer. The mean number of out-of-seat behaviors during treatment $_1$ was 1.5.

Baseline$_2$

On day 21, the students were told that no more candy would be available. When the opportunity to earn rewards was removed for 4 days, the

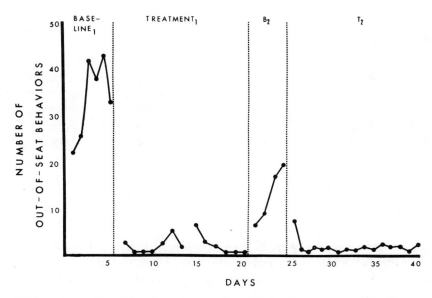

Figure 3-4   *Total number of out-of-seat behaviors on the school bus by 50 elementary and junior high school youngsters across successive experimental conditions.*

number of out-of-seat behaviors rapidly increased to 20 on the final day of the reversal, with a mean of 13.8.

Treatment$_2$

On day 25 of the study, treatment procedures were begun again. However, candy was given only every other day beginning with day 27 and, eventually, an average of every third day, with the students not knowing which day they would be rewarded. Once treatment was reintroduced, out-of-seat behavior dropped to a mean level of 1.8 per day, and both sides met the criterion every day of the period even though reinforcement was given an average of only every third day during the final week.

STUDY 3

Subject and Setting

A 13-year-old, eighth-grade boy was the subject. His classroom teachers had become irritated with his "forgetfulness" in often coming to class without the proper tools, such as pencil, paper, and books.

Behavior Measured

The teachers agreed that their main objective was to teach the student to assume responsibility for coming to class with the appropriate materials. "Irresponsible behavior" was defined as coming to class without at least a pencil, paper, and the appropriate textbook. Each teacher simply observed each day whether the subject entered class with the necessary equipment.

Method and Results

Baseline₁

Baseline data were recorded for 5 days. Figure 3-5 presents a record of the number of irresponsible behaviors recorded by the subject's teachers each day. A mean of 4.5 per day was recorded during baseline.

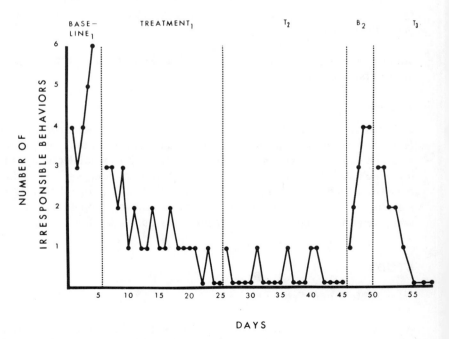

Figure 3-5 *Total number of irresponsible behaviors exhibited by an eighth-grade boy, across successive experimental conditions.*

Treatment$_1$

After consultation with the counselor, the teachers agreed to award one point to the student each time he exhibited responsible behavior (that is, each time he came to class with pencil, paper, and text). The student could, therefore, earn a maximum of 6 points per day. In addition, the counselor negotiated an agreement between the subject and his parents whereby the subject could exchange points for leisure time to listen to the radio, play records, or play his guitar. Each hour of leisure time required 4 points. During this 4-week treatment, the number of irresponsible behaviors decreased to a mean of 1.4.

Treatment$_2$

During this 4-week condition, reinforcement was provided on an intermittent basis. For the first 2 weeks, points were awarded every other day; for the second 2 weeks, points were awarded only on Friday. Thus, the accumulation of points was contingent on progressively longer periods of responsible behavior. The number of irresponsible behaviors during this phase decreased to a mean of .25.

Baseline$_2$

For 5 days, conditions were the same as during baseline$_1$. The mean number of irresponsible behaviors increased to 2.8.

Treatment$_3$

Conditions for the final two weeks of the study were the same as in treatment$_2$. The mean decreased to 1.4.

Discussion

The results of these studies indicate that typical counselors in typical public school settings can develop and implement practical intervention programs and can gather objective data on the effect of their work. For every counselor in the course, the studies described here were the first empirically based evaluations of their effectiveness on the job that they had made. Some authorities might argue that the time invested in gathering objective data is wasted—that it might be better spent in reaching more children than in research activities. This position might have some merit in other professions. An engineer who builds bridges does not usually collect precise and objective data on the longevity and durability of the bridges he builds. However, the engineer has, through training, acquired a large number of skills related to bridge building that have broad application and a considerable amount of demonstrated utility. For the engineer, new information is being produced continually, but it is added to an already large body of accumulated knowledge. Unfortunately, counseling does not have a large number of widely accepted, empirically validated tools that the practicing counselor can learn and utilize throughout his professional career. As noted previously, several writers have seriously questioned some of the fundamental tenets of counseling. In fact, there are probably not enough scientifically believable data at this point to either accept or reject most counseling procedures, (though Carkhuff [1971] and his associates appear to be making significant contributions in this area). The principles, techniques, and ideas that are passed from counseling educators to neophyte counselors are largely untested, though not invalidated.

In the absence of a coherent, well-established body of knowledge about counseling, it seems more than appropriate to teach counselors methods of gathering valid and reliable information on the effect of their work. The within-subjects designs used in this study appear to have great utility for this purpose, but are rarely taught to counselors in training. Indeed, training seems to foster in counselors the position that research is a function of university professors, and counselors are either not able or too busy to do research. However, the growth and development of the individual counselor as well as the profession would be fostered by an increased emphasis on careful study of effect, and the obvious point at which to begin such an emphasis is in university training programs.

11 / The Role of Instructions, Modeling, Verbal Feedback, and Contingencies in the Training of Classroom Teaching Skills

Hewitt B. Clark • John W. Macrae
Donna Mae Ida • N. Rebecca Smith

One aspect of education that has received a great deal of research attention over the last decade concerns the effects of teacher's behavior on the academic and social behavior of the students (for example, Allen, Hart, Buell, Harris, and Wolf, 1964; Allen, Henke, Harris, Baer, and Reynolds,

This research was supported by the North Carolina Department of Mental Health. The authors wish to thank Dr. James E. Favell and Dr. Judith E. Favell for their suggestions concerning this research. The authors are also indebted to the following persons for their cooperation and assistance: Dr. Lawrence A. Larsen, Assistant Superintendent for Education and Research at Western Carolina Center; Dr. Benjamin Brooks, Director of Special Education at Appalachian State University; and Mr. Erin Caldwell, Coordinator of Appalachian State University Intern Program at Western Carolina Center.
The senior author, Hewitt B. "Rusty" Clark, is currently the Acting Director of the Johnny Cake Child Study Center and holds an appointment as an Adjunct Assistant Professor in the Department of Human Development at the University of Kansas.

187

1967; Becker, Madsen, Arnold, and Thomas 1967; Hall and Broden 1967; Johnston, Kelley, Harris, and Wolf, 1966; McAllister, Stachowiak, Baer, and Conderman, 1969; Schutte and Hopkins, 1970; Thomas, Becker, and Armstrong, 1968; Waisk, Senn, Welch, and Cooper, 1969). More recently, several studies have isolated a variety of teacher-applied contingency programs that are effective in managing appropriate classroom behavior and/or improving academic behavior (for instance, token systems—O'Leary and Drabman, 1971; and "good-behavior game"—Barrish, Saunders, and Wolf, 1969). However, it is clear from the literature, as well as from a tour through almost any school, that only a small percentage of teachers have been trained to use the teaching skills needed to implement these programs. Thus, it would seem that if society wants to better educate its children, teachers should be trained to use the teaching skills that consistently improve students' academic and social behaviors.

Several researchers have recently begun to investigate variables that might be important in training teachers to use these teaching skills. Four variables that have been researched extensively are:

1. *Graphic feedback.* This form of feedback has typically been based upon an observer's record of the teacher's use of a particular teaching skill. For example, a graph may show the frequency of social praise given for appropriate behavior (Cooper, Thomson, and Baer, 1970). It may also include a measure of the students' behavior (Hall, Panyan, Rabon, and Broden, 1968).

2. *Teacher's self-scoring.* This variable in teacher training consists of a teacher's scoring of his or her use of a particular teaching skill. This has involved, for example, the use of videotape replays from which the teacher counted his or her use of social praise for appropriate behavior (Rule, 1972; Thomas, 1971). In a variation of this training procedure, a parent counted her use of social praise during training sessions while working with her child (Herbert and Baer, 1972).

3. *The modeling of teaching skills.* One modeling procedure that was relatively effective involved a supervisor who replaced the teacher for five minutes whenever the teacher had not used enough praise. During this five-minute period, the teacher was to observe the model of the supervisor's use of teaching skill (Rule, 1972).

4. *Instructions.* In each of the studies cited, these variables have been combined with a fourth one, instructions. In some of the studies, the instructions (oral or written) were complete descriptions of the teaching skills and their uses; in other studies, the instructions involved a definition of the teaching skill that the teacher was to employ following appropriate behavior, as well as a definition of appropriate and inappropriate student behaviors.

In general, the results of these and other studies have been convincing enough to suggest that these four variables are useful in teaching new skills to teachers. However, the results also yielded too much inter- and intra-subject variability to suggest that any one of these variables is sufficient to train all teachers.

The purpose of the present study was to find a combination of variables to compose a "training package" that would be effective in teaching a variety of teaching skills to all of the teacher trainees employed in the study. The teacher training package was composed of the following variables: (1) written instructions, (2) modeling, (3) verbal feedback, and (4) graphic feedback.

METHODS

Subjects

Four female and two male undergraduate students from Appalachian State University spent one academic quarter at Western Carolina Center in a practicum internship in classroom teaching of educable mentally retarded pupils. Although four of the interns had been exposed to classroom teaching and all six interns had received 12 to 35 hours of academic instruction in behavior modification, they had not received any formal supervision in the use of these techniques prior to their participation in this teacher training study.

Measurement of Teacher Skills

Behavioral Definitions

During each 30-minute teacher training session, an intern was observed and his use of the following four different teaching skills was recorded: verbal praise for appropriate classroom behavior; verbal praise for correct academic responses; correction procedures employed following incorrect academic responses; and fining procedures employed to minimize inappropriate classroom behavior. Each of these skills was broken into two or three different forms. These four teaching skills and their different forms were defined as follows.

Verbal praise for appropriate classroom behavior was defined as any statement(s) or comment(s) of affection, approval, or praise given by the intern to a pupil for a particular appropriate classroom behavior. An instance of this kind of praise was scored after the intern had finished praising a pupil for a particular behavior he displayed. Two forms of verbal praise for classroom behavior were scored:

1. *Specific Classroom Praise:* praise that consisted of a description of the classroom behavior for which the pupil was praised (for instance, "Good Billy, you're sitting quietly"; or "Mary, I'm proud of you for not talking until I called on you").

2. *General Classroom Praise:* praise for classroom behavior that did not describe the behavior being praised ("That's good, Bob"; "Good boy"; "Good").

Verbal praise for correct academic responses was defined as any statement(s) or comment(s) of affection, approval, or praise given by the intern to a pupil for a particular correct academic response. An instance of this was scored only after the intern had finished praising a pupil for a correct response he had made. Two forms of verbal praise for academic behavior were scored:

1. *Specific Academic Praise:* praise that consisted of a description or repetition of the academic response for which the pupil was being praised (Intern: "Joyce, what rhymes with top?" Pupil: "Mop." Intern: "That's right, Joyce! Top, mop."; Intern: "Jim, point to the biggest animal." Pupil points to the biggest of three animals. Intern: "Good, you pointed to the biggest one.").

2. *General Academic Praise:* praise for an academic response that did not describe or repeat the response being praised (Intern: "Larry, what shape is this?" Pupil: "Rectangle." Intern: "Good, that's exactly right!").

The third teaching skill was the correction procedure employed immediately after an incorrect response (or failure to respond) to an intern's question. Three forms of correction were scored:

1. *Form I Corrections* were scored whenever a pupil made an incorrect response and the intern (a) said "No," (b) modeled the correct answer, and (c) addressed the same question to a pupil other than the one who had just answered incorrectly.

2. *Form II Corrections* were scored whenever a pupil made an incorrect response and the intern (a) said "No," (b) modeled the correct answer, and (c) addressed the same question to the pupil who had just answered incorrectly.

3. *Form Other Corrections* were scored whenever an incorrect response was made and the intern used a procedure other than those defined as Form I or Form II.

Fining, the fourth teaching skill, included the procedures used by the teacher immediately following a pupil's display of inappropriate classroom behavior (A pupil could be fined, for instance, for leaving his seat without permission or for talking without permission.) Three forms of fining were scored:

1. *Form I Fining* was scored whenever the intern (a) said the pupil's name, (b) stated "This is a fine for . . .," (c) briefly described the behavior(s) being fined, and (d) recorded the fine-mark next to the pupil's name on a fine-chart ("Mary, this is a fine for not paying attention").

2. *Form II Fining* was scored whenever the intern (a) said the pupil's

name, (b) said, "No," and (c) recorded a fine-mark next to the pupil's name on a fine-chart ("Larry, no").

3. *Form Other Fining* was scored whenever the intern (a) threatened a pupil with a fine, or (b) used some statement or procedure other than Form I or Form II to fine a pupil.

Observation and Recording of Data

Continuous observation of each intern was made during each teaching session. Records were made simultaneously, but independently, by a head observer and a second observer (the supervisor of the interns). Both observers used a small panel containing ten buttons. Each button was labeled to correspond to one of the ten forms of teaching skills. The depression of a button advanced a corresponding counter by one and momentarily deflected a corresponding event pen on a 20-channel Esterline Angus recorder. The counters and Esterline Angus recorder were housed in a sound attenuating chamber in a corner of the classroom.

The data that accumulated on the counters during each intern's teaching session measured his use of each teaching skill. The charts from the Esterline Angus recorder were used to obtain an estimate of inter-observer reliability.

Interobserver Reliability

A separate reliability was made from the Esterline Angus recorder charts for each of the ten forms of teaching skills. The ten inputs from the head observer's panel were recorded on the odd-numbered channels of the recorder, and the ten corresponding inputs from the second observer's panel were recorded on the even-numbered channels. By having the head observer's input and the second observer's input for the same teaching skill recorded on adjacent channels, and by using chart paper that was printed with grid lines separated by a distance corresponding to 10 seconds, inter-observer reliability was relatively easy to determine.

The reliability estimate for a given teaching skill was obtained in the following fashion. First, the adjacent pair of channels for a given teaching skill were scored for instances of agreement and disagreement. An agreement was scored whenever both channels had been marked within 10 seconds of each other. A disagreement was scored whenever one of the channels had been marked, with no corresponding mark on the other channel within 10 seconds. Next, the estimate was calculated by dividing the sum of the agreements by the sum of all the agreements plus all the disagreements, and multiplying the result by 100. The average interobserver reliability figures for each teaching skill, computed for the two interns whose data are presented in this paper, are shown in Table 3-1.

Table 3-1 *Interobserver Reliability Estimates Averaged for Each Form of Teaching Skill Exhibited by Intern A and Intern B*

FORM OF TEACHING SKILL	INTERN A	INTERN B
Specific Classroom Praise	90%	90%
General Classroom Praise	*	**
Specific Academic Praise	95%	93%
General Academic Praise	92%	91%
Form I Corrections	91%	90%
Form II Corrections	90%	**
Form Other Corrections	65%	72%
Form I Fining	78%	92%
Form II Fining	81%	86%
Form Other Fining	**	**

* No occurrences of these forms were scored by either observer. Thus, there was 100% agreement that none had occurred.
** The observers scored five or less occurrences of these forms during the sessions covered in these figures. The authors considered this level of occurrence too low for the calculation of a meaningful reliability estimate.

Classroom Setting for Teacher Training Program

Each of the six interns participated in the teacher training program for approximately one-half hour every other day, Monday through Friday. Three interns participated one day, and the other three the next day. The training program was conducted in a self-contained, special-education classroom, which served five elementary-school-aged students who had been labeled as educable mentally retarded. Their regular teacher was a 29-year-old female who was highly skilled in the application of behavior modification techniques in classroom settings.

The regular teacher employed a token system in her classroom. The students earned tokens (plastic strips) and social praise for appropriate classroom behavior (such as sitting quietly, or attending to lesson materials) and for correct academic response to the teacher's questions. At designated times during the school day, these token earnings could be exchanged for a variety of backup reinforcers. A system of fining was also used to help minimize the frequency of inappropriate classroom behavior. For example, if a pupil, Bob, hit another pupil, the teacher would say, "Bob, that's a fine for hitting." She would then place a fine-mark next to Bob's name on the fine-chart, which was displayed on an easel in front of the class. Depending on the number of fine-marks each pupil acquired, he would lose some portion of his tokens and thus reduce the amount of backup reinforcers he could purchase.

During the teacher training sessions, three persons were in the classroom besides the regular teacher and her pupils—an intern and the two observers. The observers sat approximately four feet apart and eight feet behind the pupils, who occupied chairs on the outside perimeter of a semicircular table. From behind the pupils the observers could easily view the intern as he taught since he was seated on a swivel chair in the center of the semicircular table.

While the intern taught, the regular teacher observed from a chair located near the two observers. Occasionally, the regular teacher modeled the teaching of the intern's lesson. During the modeling, the intern observed from a chair located behind the pupils, but opposite the observers. A diagram of the classroom and the location of the persons present during the teacher training program is shown in Figure 3-6.

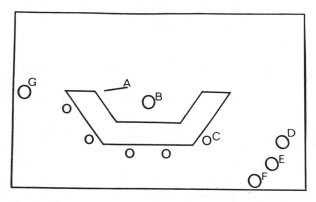

Figure 3-6   *Overhead view of the classroom and the location of persons present during the teacher training program: A = fine-chart posted on easel. B = intern taught from swivel chair. C = pupils sat at semicircular table. D = regular teacher. E = head observer collected data on intern's use of teaching skills. F = second observer (supervisor of interns). G = chair from which intern viewed the regular teacher when she modeled teaching skills.*

Procedures

For three mornings prior to the start of the teacher training sessions, and throughout the remainder of the quarter, the supervisor of interns and the regular teacher helped the interns prepare lesson plans and materials. Lesson plans were prepared before the interns went to their training sessions. Each lesson plan provided (1) a behavioral statement of what the students were to be able to do by the end of the lesson, (2) a description of the lesson materials to be used, and (3) sample questions that the students were to be asked. Also, during these first three days the interns were given a set of detailed written instructions describing the ten forms of the teaching skills. The interns studied the instructions and took a quiz based on 108 study-guide questions that had been given to them with the instructions. Quizzes covering different sets of these questions were given until each intern passed a quiz with 90 percent accuracy.

The day before the first set of three interns were to begin the training program, all of the interns were assigned the forms of teaching skills to be used during their first training session.

Teacher Training Sessions

Each morning that an intern had a session, he met with the regular teacher to review his lesson plan and materials. Her familiarity with the lesson was important because she would later model the assigned forms of teaching skills for the intern, using his lesson plan and materials. At least an hour prior to the intern's session, he was also given a list that assigned the forms of the teaching skills he was to use. He was also told which of these was the target form for which he would receive specific graphic feedback.

At a designated time, the intern began teaching. After 4 minutes the regular teacher, who was observing the intern, took over the teaching and modeled the assigned teaching skills. Meanwhile, the intern observed from a chair located behind the students. After the regular teacher modeled for 4 minutes, she signaled the intern to resume teaching. After another 4 minutes, the regular teacher again interrupted the intern, this time for a brief conference during which the regular teacher commented favorably on the assigned teaching skills that in her opinion, had been employed correctly (that is, contingently and with adequate frequency). She also pointed out to the intern instances where he had, in her opinion, employed (1) a skill on a noncontingent basis, (2) an incorrect form of a teaching skill, (3) a skill too frequently or too infrequently, or (4) inadequate presentation of the lesson materials (for example, asking questions too rapidly, or not providing clear enough instructions or models for the pupil to display the required response). The regular teacher answered any of the intern's questions concerning the topic areas listed above. This first conference was held at the intern's regular teaching location; the intern merely turned away from the pupils for 30 seconds to 1 minute. Following this conference, the intern taught for another 8 minutes.

When the intern had completed his 16 minutes of teaching, the regular teacher escorted him from the classroom into the hall, where they could have a second conference with fewer distractions. During this conference, which typically lasted from 3 to 5 minutes, the regular teacher commented, as before, on the intern's use of the various teaching skills. The supervisor joined the conference after about 2 minutes and waited for the regular teacher to finish her comments. Once through, the regular teacher returned to the classroom, and the supervisor assigned grades to the intern for several aspects of his teaching performance during the session. One session grade was either an "A" or an "F" depending on whether all of the following aspects of the session were met:

1. The intern arrived on time and was prepared to begin teaching.

2. The intern conducted the lesson in such a way that the pupils could remain seated.

3. The tasks given the pupils required only responses that were verbal, or that involved pointing to or manipulating some objects (no written responses).

4. Only one pupil at a time was called on to respond.

The average of these session grades determined one of the 17 credit hours earned at Western Carolina Center and was employed to insure that the interns attended to these four points.

Contingencies

As stated previously, at least an hour before an intern began his session, he was assigned the particular forms of the teaching skills he was to use. From among these, the target form, for which contingencies (graphic feedback, grades, and quizzes) were in effect, was also specified. Graphic feedback was a plot of the percentage of the occasions in which the teaching skill was used in the target form. If the target form occurred at a frequency of less than 90 percent, the supervisor showed the intern what criterion percentage level he was to achieve in the next session. The criterion was based on the percentage of times the particular target form occurred during the first session, and was raised by increments of ten points. The criterion was raised, however, only if the intern equalled or surpassed his criterion. Thus, if during the first session the intern utilized the particular target form on 63 percent frequency, then his criterion for the next session was set at 73 percent on the graph. If during the next session he reached or exceeded the 73 percent level, then his criterion was raised to 83 percent (that is, 73 percent plus 10 percent). If, however, the intern failed to reach the 73 percent criterion, then this criterion remained unchanged until he achieved it. The criterion was never raised above 90 percent.

A grade based upon the intern's performance of the target behavior was determined by the following rules:

1. Whenever a new target form was assigned, the intern was given a grade

of "B" for the first session unless he achieved 90 percent or greater, in which case he received an "A."

2. On all subsequent sessions, an "A" was given when the percentage achieved was greater than the criterion.

3. A "C" was given for a session in which the percentage achieved was less than the criterion, but greater than the percentage achieved in the previous session.

4. A "D" was assigned if the intern failed to meet his criterion and failed to improve upon the percentage level achieved in the previous session.

The mean of these grades represented three credit hours for the quarter.

Whenever an intern received a "C" or "D" grade for a session, he was required to pass a quiz that covered the set of instructions for using the teaching skill. These quizzes, like the previous ones, contained sample study-guide questions, but covered only the target form being taught. The intern was required to take such quizzes until he passed one with 90 percent accuracy. On the morning after having received a "C" or "D," the intern was required to take a quiz before he began that day's teaching assignment.

RESULTS

Prior to the first session of the teacher training program, the interns were tested to insure that they could describe all forms of the teaching skills. In addition, each intern was told the form of each skill he was to employ and the particular target form for which contingencies (graphic feedback, grades, and quizzes) were in effect. Initially, all six interns were instructed to use exclusively the following forms of the teaching skills: Specific Classroom Praise, General Academic Praise, Form I Corrections, and Form I Fining.

Throughout the entire experiment, instructions, modeling, and verbal feedback were in effect for *all* forms of the skills that were to be employed. The contingencies were in effect only for the one particular form of skill assigned as the target.

The effects of the teacher training program on intern A's use of the teaching skills are shown in Figure 3-7. Each of the five graphs presents the data collected on the percentage or rate of use of two forms of each teaching skill. The ordinate-scale label above each graph and the key to the far right of each graph identify how each measure of the teaching skill was plotted. The vertical dashed lines and the solid figures (circles or squares) mark the duration of the application of the complete training package to a particular form of teaching skill. The teacher training sessions are numbered along the abscissa of the bottom graph.

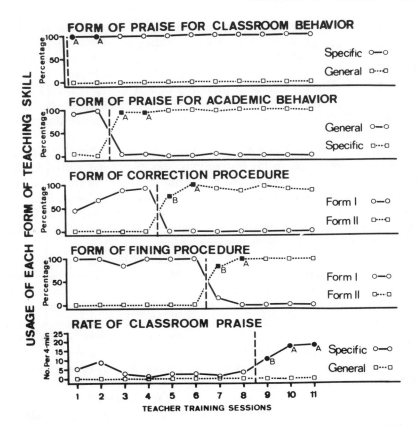

Figure 3-7 *The training of intern A across a variety of teaching skills. Each of the five graphs displays the data collected on the percentage or rate of use of two forms of each skill. An ordinate-scale label over each graph and the key to the far right of each graph identify how each measure of the teaching skill was plotted. The vertical dashed lines and the solid figures (circles or squares) mark the application of the complete training program to the target form of a teaching skill. The teacher training sessions are numbered along the abscissa of the bottom graph.*

Prior to sessions 1 and 2, intern A was assigned the use of the forms listed above, and Specific Classroom Praise was specified as the target form. As can be seen in the top graph of Figure 3-7, intern A used Specific Classroom Praise on 100 percent of the occasions that she praised pupils for appropriate classroom behavior (during sessions 1 and 2). Because each of these sessions resulted in at least a 90 percent usage of the target form, the intern earned a grade of "A" following both sessions. The letter grade she earned for each session is shown next to the plot of the target form.

Despite the fact that no contingencies were in effect for any of the other teaching skills, intern A used more of the other forms that had been assigned than their alternative forms (an average of 96 percent General Academic Praise versus 4 percent Specific Academic Praise; 59 percent Form I Corrections versus zero percent Form II Corrections; 91 percent Form I Fining versus zero percent Form II Fining). Intern A also used an average of 7 classroom praise statements per four minutes during these first two sessions.

Prior to sessions 3 and 4, intern A was told to use Specific Academic Praise as a new target form. Instructions, modeling, and verbal feedback were now applied to the use of this new form. As is evident from the second graph, intern A discontinued her use of General Academic Praise and began using 100 percent Specific Academic Praise. Again, in each of these sessions the intern earned "A" grades for achieving 90 percent frequency or better on the use of this target form.

Next, intern A was assigned Form II Corrections as the target form, and its use was acquired readily (third graph, sessions 5 & 6). Note that in session 5, the intern earned a grade of "B" because she achieved less than 90 percent frequency on the new target skill. After session 5, she was shown a graph on which 75 percent frequency was plotted, given a grade of "B," and shown her criterion percentage—85 percent—(75 percent plus 10 percent) for the next session. In session 6, intern A achieved 100 percent Form II Corrections, which surpassed her criterion percentage, and she earned an "A."

During the next two sessions, intern A was assigned Form II Fining as the target form. As was the case with each of the previous manipulations, the new form of teaching skill was used immediately and the use of the alternative form was discontinued (fourth graph, sessions 7 and 8). Intern A earned a "B" in session 7 for having achieved only 83 percent Form II Fining, but she earned an "A" in session 8 by achieving 100 percent.

Over the first eight sessions, intern A averaged only 3.3 classroom praise statements per four minutes (bottom graph), despite having received instructions, verbal feedback, and modeling for this skill. During these same sessions, the regular teacher modeled an average rate of 8.3 Specific Classroom Praise statements per four minutes. Then, prior to the ninth session, the intern was told to increase her rate of Specific Classroom Praise. She was told that she would receive a grade of "B" unless she used 16 or more Specific Classroom Praise statements per four minutes, in which case she would earn an "A."

Following this ninth session, intern A was shown her feedback graph, on which the supervisor had plotted her rate of Specific Classroom Praise statements. The supervisor then showed her the criterion rate that she was to achieve during the next session: a rate four responses above the rate she had achieved on the ninth session. Thus, the criterion rate was 14.5 per four minutes because the intern had averaged 10.5 Specific Classroom Praise statements per four minutes during Session 9. As is evident from the data in the fifth group (sessions 10 and 11), the training package resulted in an increased rate of Specific Classroom Praise.

Intern B received a sequence of training similar to that of intern A. For the first two sessions, the target form was Specific Classroom Praise. As was the case with intern A, intern B used a larger percentage and a higher rate of each assigned form than of the alternative forms (see Figure 3-8, sessions 1 and 2).

For sessions 3, 4, 5, and 6 Intern B was assigned Specific Academic Praise as the target form. In session 3, intern B used Specific Academic Praise following only 57 percent of the pupils' correct responses. He

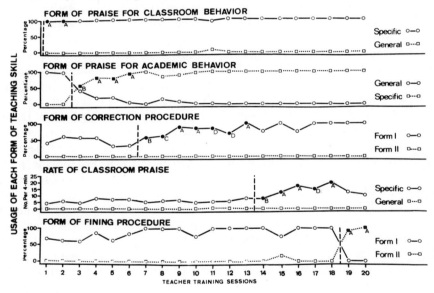

Figure 3-8   *The training of intern B across a variety of teaching skills. Each of the five graphs displays the data collected on the percentage or rate of use of two forms of each teaching skill. An ordinate-scale label over each graph and the key to the far right of each graph identify how each measure of the teaching skill was plotted. The vertical dashed lines and the solid figures (circles or squares) mark the duration of the application of the complete training program to a particular target form of a teaching skill. The teacher training sessions are numbered along the abscissa of the bottom graph.*

received a grade of "B" in this session, and his criterion for Session 4 was set at 67 percent. He achieved 81 percent frequency during session 4, and thus received an "A," increasing his criterion percentage ten points to 77 percent. In session 5 he achieved 81 percent, and in session 6, 100 percent. The intern earned an "A" in both of these sessions by exceeding his criterion percentage in session 5 and exceeding 90 percent frequency in session 6.

Over the first six sessions the intern used Form I Corrections with an average frequency of only 48 percent, even though he had received instructions, modeling, and verbal feedback concerning their use. Prior to session 7, the intern was assigned this form as the target. He achieved 56 percent Form I Corrections during session 7, received a "B," and was assigned a criterion percentage of 66 percent for the next session. During session 8, intern B achieved 60 percent, which failed to meet his criterion but which was an improvement over his previous 56 percent; thus, he received a "C" and his criterion remained at 66 percent. Because his grade was less than a "B," he had to take a quiz on correction procedures. Intern B achieved 88 percent on session 9, earning himself an "A." The criterion percentage for the next session was increased ten percentage points from the last criterion, making it 76 percent. On session 10, intern B achieved 86 percent and thus earned another "A" with the criterion percentage set at 86 percent for session 11. Intern B decreased to 84 percent and then to 73 percent on sessions 11 and 12, respectively. Following both of these sessions he received a "D" and had to take another quiz on the written instructions over correction procedures, since he had not met the 86 percent criterion and had decreased from the percentage achieved on the previous session. Form I Corrections was used following 100 percent of the incorrect academic responses emitted by the pupils during session 13.

Prior to each of the next five sessions intern B was assigned, increasing his rate of classroom praise as the target form. The intern was informed that he could earn an "A" by achieving a rate of 16 or more Specific Classroom Praise statements per 4 minutes on session 14. A "B" would be given for any rate lower than 16 per 4 minutes. During the first thirteen sessions, intern B had averaged 5.6 Specific Classroom Praise statements per 4 minutes, whereas the regular teacher had modeled a rate of 7.6.

As shown in the fourth graph in Figure 3-8, intern B averaged only 7.5 Specific Classroom Praise statements per four minutes during session 14. He earned a grade of "B" for this, and was given graphic feedback showing his performance rate for session 14 and his criterion (7.5 plus 4 equals 11.5 per four minutes) for session 15. During session 15, intern B exceeded his criterion of 11.5 classroom praises per four minutes. Thus, he earned an "A" and the criterion was increased by 4, setting it at 15.5 classroom praises per four minutes. During session 16, the intern again exceeded the criterion, averaging 17.3 classroom praises per four minutes.

The criterion was again increased, but this time only to 16 classroom praises per four minutes. In session 17, intern B decreased his rate of classroom praise to 14; he thus earned a "D" and had to take a quiz concerning the use of a high rate of Specific Classroom Praise. Intern B surpassed the criterion rate during session 18 by averaging 19.8 classroom praises per four minutes.

The use of Form II Fining was the next assigned target form. The results shown in the bottom graph of Figure 3-8 reveal that the complete training package effectively established the use of Form II Fining instead of Form I Fining, which had been used almost exclusively in the previous 18 sessions.

The findings for the remaining four interns were consistent with those shown for interns A and B.

DISCUSSION

The purpose of the present study was to evaluate the effectiveness of a teacher training package in establishing the appropriate use of a variety of classroom teaching skills. The training package was composed of written instructions describing the use of each teaching skill, the modeling of the skills, verbal feedback, and consequences, including graphic feedback. A multiple-baseline analysis across teaching skills for two interns suggests that the package is effective in establishing the use of a variety of teaching skills and in increasing the rate of praise by the interns.

Another aspect of these data suggests that the contingencies (graphic feedback, grades, and quizzes) may not be necessary to the acquisition of every skill by every intern. This was particularly evident in that both interns showed appropriate use of most skills prior to contact with the contingencies. However, there were some skills the acquisition of which occurred only after the intern had contact with some of the contingencies (intern A, rate of classroom praise; Intern B, Form I Corrections and rate of classroom praise). Though not included in this report, data from the other four interns also provide instances in which the contingencies appeared to be necessary for the acquisition of the skills.

For a teacher training package to be usable requires that it not only be effective, but also that it be acceptable to the teachers and economically feasible to the educational institution. If the teachers find a training program so aversive that they will attend only when given a mandate from their school board, it is unlikely that the program will be effective—fortunately, it will probably not survive. In an attempt to address this issue more directly, current research is being conducted to determine 1) whether teachers have consistent preferences for various training components, and 2) under what conditions teachers can choose, on a daily basis, the training components they need in order to best learn the new teaching skills.

The second aspect of a teacher training program requiring consideration is its economy, both monetary and temporal. There are three criteria which may help in evaluating a program's economic feasibility. Perhaps the most crucial of these is that the method can be initiated and maintained with few, if any, new staff additions. The second criterion is that the time required to acquire the necessary skills be minimal and preferably accomplished within the existing work schedule, with the educational services to the children continuing. The third criterion is that the overall monetary cost of the procedure, materials, and equipment be in line with current allocations of the existing budget.

Although a cost-efficiency analysis was not undertaken during the present study, several aspects of this program appear favorable with respect to its economic feasibility. Due to the requirements of an experimental analysis, the present study necessitated that three staff members attend each session. It may be, however, that this training could be conducted as effectively by a regular classroom teacher and a consultant who would supervise training of a number of persons. Also of importance is the fact that the training in the present study was accomplished during regular working hours and maintained, what the regular teacher suggested was, "excellent educational benefits for my students."

Although no definitive solution to the problem of teacher training presently exists, the cumulative efforts of applied researchers and educators across the country should bring us closer to a humane, effective, and economically feasible model for preparing teachers to provide quality education to their pupils.

12 / A Training Model That Bridges the Gap Between the Art and the Science of Teaching

Keith D. Turner • *K. Eileen Allen*

Applied behavior analysis has little appeal for teachers who believe that a successful teaching process depends upon freedom, spontaneity, and intuition on the part of teachers to meet what they see as the unpredictable variables involved in children's learning. Many behavior analysts find it difficult to communicate with these teachers—teachers who are *not* impressed with the tremendous impact applied behavior analysis has had on education. The extension of the practice from some of the early studies

The authors of this article were staff members at the Model Preschool for Handicapped Children (with professional training, research, and service components) in the Experimental Education Unit of the Child Development and Mental Retardation Center at the University of Washington. The Model Preschool was funded in part by P. L. 91–230, Title VI, Part C. Keith Turner was a Project Coordinator-Trainer, and K. Eileen Allen was an Educational Training Coordinator, Developmental Disabilities Project, for the Experimental Education Unit.

(Allen, Hart, Buell, Harris, and Wolf, 1964; Harris, Johnston, Kelley, and Wolf, 1964) using behavioral techniques with individual children to the present day where, in many cases, every teacher in a school uses the procedure with all her children (Haring and Hayden, 1972; Bushell, 1972; Hall, 1973)—is very impressive; but not impressive enough to change those teachers who believe that teaching is 99 percent art. And many of them are highly effective teachers. Therefore, it may well be that the key to solving some of our many educational problems is to motivate these teachers, who believe in the art of teaching, to begin to assess their own programs systematically.

This will not be a quick and easy conversion, for the ascientific attitude of these teachers presents a challenge, especially to the field trainer or consultant who is assigned to train these individuals. Another factor complicating the conversion is that many teachers have "heard about behavior modification" or have "tried" some version of behavior modification, and report heatedly that they are against it. These individuals view behavior modification with skepticism, even outright avoidance behavior, declaring that it is too rigorous, or too individualized, or too dehumanizing. Yet these are the teachers who must be reached—with a method designed to motivate them to begin to assess their programs systematically. In most instances, it must be a low-cost training method.

This paper describes a low-cost model of assessment, designed for those teachers who dislike behavior modification procedures and research in general. Because this procedure is designed to provide assessment and not research per se, it has been labeled a functional approach. There are three simple components in this functional assessment approach:

1. Goals should be stated in measurable terms.
2. Procedure should be agreed on by all involved in the teaching process.
3. Evaluation should be designed to be simple and meaningful to the teacher.

Hopefully, the goal can be stated in behavioral terms, but the trainer may have to use successive approximations of such terms so that the teachers will not initially be antagonized by the trainer's insistence on objective measurement. Of critical importance in the procedure is that a compromise be made so that one unified approach to solving the problem results. In designing the data system, it is better to get some information than no information; thus, in many cases it is well to avoid sophisticated recording procedures at the outset.

The trainer must be subtle in motivating and shaping the teachers to begin to use the functional approach, but this is easy as long as he does not dictate goals, procedure, or evaluation procedures. Involving the teachers from the first in designing their own assessment procedure is possible because no training or background in research is necessary. Thus, the functional approach begins on the teacher's present level and attempts to make the assessment procedure inherently reinforcing by allowing the teachers to design it to meet the "unique" characteristics of their program. As we will see, the functional approach is a natural procedure for shaping teachers to do more sophisticated research. Frequently, many of us in applied behavior analysis forget the operant principle that states that it is impossible to modify a behavior until it occurs. We all know that we should use successive approximations to achieve a terminal goal rather than attempt to shape the terminal behavior initially. We seem to remember this when working with children, but tend to forget it when working with teachers. And when we fail to train the teachers, we blame them, when the blame actually rests on our inconsistency in practicing what we preach.

So, the functional approach says, "start where the teacher is with whatever repertoire is at hand." By beginning with this approach, it is eventually much easier to shape the systematic manipulation of independent variables. In the functional approach, teachers have successful experiences with measurement and data collection, so this is no longer a problem. Hopefully, teachers learn too (as did the teacher in the second case study to be reported) that behavior occurs in a logical manner. From the functional approach they also acquire some background and interest in research because they will inevitably begin to question how the changes occurred. The motivation to do research then comes from within the teacher, which certainly facilitates the training. Thus, to mix an old metaphor, trainers can lead teachers to the principles of behavior analysis, but they can't make them swallow those principles until the teachers are ready. In order to demonstrate how this functional approach has been used to solve the routine problems of everyday classroom teachers who had little research interest and no research background, three classroom case studies are presented.

CASE 1: EVALUATING AND
MODIFYING DISRUPTIVE BEHAVIOR

The major problem for the teachers in a Head Start classroom was an overly aggressive boy of 4 years, 6 months who often hit other children without apparent reason. With only two adults to work with sixteen children, a child like this can be a source of tremendous concern, especially when the aggression seems to occur for no apparent reason. Thus, the teachers' interest was twofold: to discover what motivated the child to be disruptive, and to determine if his disruptive behavior could be controlled.

Because prediction implies control, the first approach was to attempt to discover what caused the child to be disruptive. The method chosen was an anecdotal record sheet, which the teachers designed, indicating the events prior to and subsequent to the occurrence of each disruptive behavior (see Table 3-2). After three days, there appeared to be no observable

Time	Mark	Preceded	Area	Child Involvement	Teacher Involvement
9:00-9:15	ℍℍ	J. was talking during story changing from story to rug	rug rug rug rug	Hit J - told him to be quiet; knocked down girl in orange dress	was told to stop
9:15-9:30	I	Playing together with dishes	house	knocked him down	
9:30-9:45					
9:45-10:00	IIII	J. and girl in red were fighting	bathroom	hit girl with red top; grabbed J.;	told to sit chair and think about what he had done
		girl with red top took things Michael was working with	art	got paint all over his face	
10:00-10:15	II	watching girls wash	washtub	ran out side left play-dough; went over; splashed girl in purple	told to go back to art area
10:15-10:30	II	boy with blue-striped shirt came over to watch play-dough activity	art	Michael tried to rub dough in boy's hair	
		was told it was closed; ran around room			

Table 3-2 *Anecdotal Record Sheet Designed to Find What "Caused" the Problem Behaviors*

antecedents to his hitting children, so the teachers focused on providing consequences for behavior.

The second approach required that the teachers determine which disruptive behaviors should be eliminated (goal), and what course of action they would use to do so, when those behaviors occurred. The teachers defined the disruptive behavior as having four components: (1) throwing materials, (2) hitting, (3) running away, and (4) screaming. It should be stressed that it is essential to define goals that are agreed upon by all parties concerned with a child's improvement, so that the child's progress may be facilitated by all.

The teachers in this study had no trouble writing a mutually agreeable definition, from which they quickly devised an ingenious method of counting and controlling the child's disruptive behavior. Because they felt it too time consuming to collect all the information with an anecdotal recording sheet, they decided to put round discs on a pegboard every time the child was disruptive. The teachers agreed that if there were more than three discs on the board, the child would lose free play—a most enjoyable activity for this child. In initiating their plan, they told the child at the beginning of each day exactly what would happen if he was disruptive more than three times.

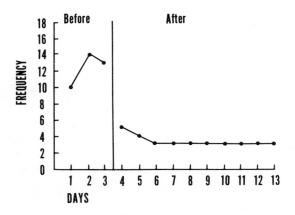

Child's Disruptive Behavior

Figure 3-9 *Number of disruptive behaviors.*

Evaluation was no problem: the number of discs on the board at the end of the day represented the number of disruptive behaviors. As Figure 3-9 indicates, the number of disruptive behaviors was controlled very easily. Such episodes dropped from an average of 12 to an average of 3 per day. Apparently, a few disruptive episodes were quite tolerable for these teachers, inasmuch as they decided to leave it at 3 per day for the rest of the year. The project was concluded because both the child and the teachers were happy.

What caused the change in the child's behavior? There is no clear-cut answer in this simplified version of classroom research. It is highly probable that the variable accounting for the change—a variable that was not recorded—was the encouragement of the child's peers for him to "be good." The teachers reported that when he started to engage in disruptive behavior, his friends would warn him so that he would not lose his outside play privileges.

Training costs were minimal in this study—a total of five hours was spent on the project. The consultant used the functional approach to organize the teachers' efforts to solve the problem, but all the solutions were the teachers' own. This approach merged the teachers' expert knowledge of the child with the consultant's scientific method of problem solving; it resulted in a very efficient and effective solution to the teachers' and the child's problems. The teachers collected the data but asked that the consultant graph the results; he did so as a reward for their data collection.

CASE 2: CONTROLLING "ON-THE-CEILING" BEHAVIOR

Of all the classroom studies conducted in the quest for a functional research approach, Case 2 was probably the most influential in demonstrating that science had not met the needs of the majority of the teachers in the field. The Director of the Seattle Public Schools Hearing Impaired program called to say that there was a seven-year-old deaf child who was driving the teacher "up the walls." The principal was also concerned—about the teacher as well as the child. The supervisor stated further that the principal and the teacher did not want any high-powered behavior modification expert telling them what to do, and quoted the principal as saying that if the teacher did not like what was proposed as an intervention strategy, the project would be finished. How could any dyed-in-the-wool behavior modifier refuse a challenge like that? It was decided that a very low-key "sell" was the approach to use in solving this disruptive child's problem.

From the first meeting with the teacher, it was apparent that this would be a difficult project because of the child's past history. For a half-hour each day in his former school, he had been on a continuous reinforcement schedule (Fruit Loops) for correct responses. The present teacher used only social reinforcement for the entire school day because she "believed" that the child could respond to such a setup. Her goal was admirable, but her convictions about the child were shaky, for she also believed that he was incapable of controlling himself and that his outburst behaviors were totally unpredictable. These outbursts were classified by both the principal and the teacher as "on-the-ceiling" behavior, which meant an uncontrollable series of fast-paced disruptive behaviors: throwing, kicking, and screaming. To this point, most of the teacher's daily records focused on events that followed the occurrence of the "on-the-ceiling" behavior. An example of one of the teacher's anecdotal records contained the statement, "My anger seems to get results in stopping some of Pete's behavior, but it is temporary and has no lasting effect." Using the familiar premise that if one can predict the occurrence of a behavior, then the probability of controlling the behavior is measurable, it was decided that the primary goal was to identify events that produced these so-called "uncontrollable" tantrums. With this new goal in mind, a system of note taking was agreed upon that focused on events prior to as well as subsequent to the behavior.

The teacher was used to keeping a running record, and in the new note-taking system she did essentially the same thing, with the slight modification of recording the information in specific categories. The evolution of the record-keeping forms was rapid and efficient. The first one recorded general prior events (antecedents), behavior ("+" for attending and "−" for nonattending or disruptive), and events following the behavior. An example of one of the first sheets is shown in Table 3-3. Within a week a considerably more elaborate recording sheet was developed (see Table 3-4). This sheet categorized the events over a period of time, making it possible to observe a sequence of events and their consequences. Prior events recorded were time of day and type of activity; behaviors recorded were "junk" verbal (JU), attending behavior (+), and negative behavior (−); and consequences recorded were praise (R. R.), ignoring (i), comments (c+ or c−), time out (T. O.), and going to the office (O).

To reduce the amount of writing required, it was necessary to code behaviors so that more accurate and efficient recording was possible. Table 3-5 shows how the behaviors were categorized as minor or major, and shows some consequences for these behaviors. The minor behaviors were those that annoyed but did not disrupt the teacher, whereas the major behaviors disrupted the teaching process. The occurrence of a rapid sequence of two or more major behaviors was called "on-the-ceiling" behavior. Generally, the consequence of a minor behavior was for the teacher to ignore the child, but a major behavior resulted in time-out in a chair or a trip to the office. All "on-the-ceiling" behaviors resulted in the child going to the office.

The final two recording forms developed were quite sophisticated, for the teacher was capable and dedicated, with a good set for scientific logic; but prior to the project, she had not found an efficient way to incorporate it into her teaching. The system in Table 3-6 required very little writing (with the exception of occasional anecdotal notes the teacher felt were necessary),

Friday, 3-17	Behavior Response	+
Accident		−
Language on the board		Behavior
Hallway	+	
Mini Concert	+	
is silly	+	
Matching bottle caps to bottle and putting them on	+ −	Got up-ran around verbalizing E. screams him − He licks caps, jumps up gets water. E. tells on him He puts sack over head. Claps for
I took one chip ————		himself screams B. thinks " − did the task, threw
don't touch the bookt		bottles into sack 2 chips "Yes"

Table 3-3   *Record Keeping Form Developed the First Week*

as it was coded. To appreciate the final recording form (Table 3-7), one must be aware that the transformation of a running record into this complex and efficient recording form occurred within the span of one month and was almost entirely teacher-initiated.

Thus far, only two aspects of this project have been discussed—the goal and the method. Certainly, the teacher was making progress, but what

March 24, 1972

Friday		- + J.V. H.S.	P.R.	O
			i	
			C ∓	T.O.

Time	Task	Behavior	After	
9:00	Coming in	J. V. grabbing turning, jumping	i	
9:07	Opening	+ Put gum in garbage	P. R.	
		ran for chips	i	
		+	P. R.	
		threw cards		
	Show me yest.	found	"No" 1	I said
		+		
	Started to tease	+ stopped	i	
		+ sat down	i C +	
9:40	Calendar	− played with		
	Changing	− colors		
		+ stopped	C+PR	
		grabbed colored paper	C −	
		cried	i	
		sitting	C +	
		J. V.	i	
	Fit #'s in	Struggled - out of sequence	j	
		E helped	+	

Table 3-4 *Record Keeping Form Developed the Second Week*

about the child? Evaluation of the child's progress was inherent in the recording system, which not only suggested possible sequences of events but also indicated the frequency of the child's inappropriate behaviors. For the data collection to have meaning, the teacher had to be able to have the

Possible Behavior

Minor

Junk Verbalization
Frowning
Not sitting in chair
Hands in desk
Chewing on pencil or something
Not attending (timed

Visu	Audio	Res.
40 S	1 m	

what is
he learning

Major

Running around
Standing and leaving the lesson
Jumping up ____ ____ ____ ____
Screaming   2:10   ignore – (1–2 min)
Feet on table   Come to me – If not T.O.
Crying   (Praise)   Command – If not T.O.
Falls on Floor   Creates 2 or more Majors
Smashing his pencil   goes to office

_____

Hitting   Respond immediately)
Kicking   goes to
Erase the black board   T.O.
Manipulates something he's not to touch
Throwing

Table 3-5 *Classifications of Possible Behaviors into a Code*

data "talk" to her in terms of how she was doing and how the child was doing. These data did that for this teacher. However, graphing the results was delayed for two weeks so that the teacher could fully appreciate that a given data point reflected a great deal of information that she herself had

Tuesday, 4-11-72

Time	Task	Major	Minor	On Ceiling
8:40	Bus ride			
9:00	Opening	I	III	
9:15	Oral language			
9:45	Frosting Reading Pouring	II III	II	I P R a task was stopped because of his behavior
10:15	Outside			
10:30	P. E.			
11:00	Math	II	III	
11:20	Washing			
11:30	Lunch			
12:00	Outside			
12:30	Written large	I	I	I placed him in nurse's offices

Table 3-6   *A More Advanced Record Keeping Form*

recorded but heretofore had not found easy to interpret. By the time graphing procedures were initiated, each data point "talked" to the teacher as clearly as had her written records.

The goals of the project were obtained, as can be seen in Figure 3-10. Within a month, "on-the-ceiling" behavior fell to a rate of zero. In effect, two goals were achieved: the reduction of "on-the-ceiling" behaviors, and the development of a method for predicting the child's behavior. The graph displayed in Figure 3-10 was not a very sensitive instrument, however, as it measured only the most severe behaviors and did not reflect major changes, such as a new student teacher. Therefore, a more sensitive measurement that reflected major changes was also used.

The results of this measurement are shown in Figure 3-11, a graph

(BEHAVIOR)   *New Student Teacher*

Date___*Monday May 8, 1972*_____

Time	Task	Major	Response	Minor	Response	ON Ceiling	Response
8:40	Bus Ride						
9:00	Opening	I *T.O.* ///	*iii*				
9:15	Oral Language	*THL* /	*ii* c	////	*ii*		
9:30	Frostig	//	*ii*	/	*i*		
	Reading	/	*i*				
	Visual Discrim.						
10:15	Outside						
10:30	P.E.						
11:00	Math	////	*iii office*				
11:20	Washing						
11:30	Lunch						
12:00	Outside						
P.M. 12:30	Written Language	//	*T.O.*	/			
1:00	Oral Reading						
1:15	Music						
	Reading						
1:30	Social Studies	////	*office*				
1:50	Outside	//					
2:00	Art or Work Activity	///	*No Pop CiRN*				
2:30	Free	//	c				
2:45	Clean-up to Go Home	*very good*					
		30		*6*			

COMMENTS:_____

Table 3-7 *The Final Record Keeping Form*

that depicts major and minor undesirable behaviors. This display reflects
such things as the effect of the new student teacher on the child's behavior.
One such effect, which was described by the teacher, was that the child
manipulated new teachers or aides and acted inappropriately for their
attention. She noted on one of her recording sheets an interaction between
the child and the new student teacher: "In the office he grabbed his stomach
and acted as if he had to go to the bathroom. When that did not work, he
lay on the floor pretending to be in pain. The nurse spoke to him. He was
fine."

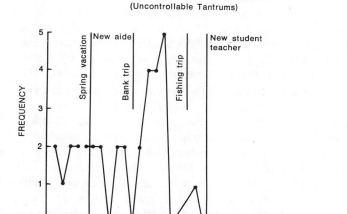

Figure 3-10   *Frequency of deaf child's "on-the-ceiling" behavior.*

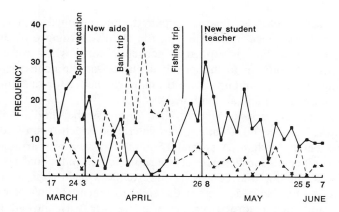

Figure 3-11   *Frequency of deaf child's major and minor disruptive behaviors.*

Probably the greatest reason for this "success story" is that the teacher, by developing sensitive recording instruments for evaluating the child's performance, found him to be highly capable of controlling his own behavior. Thus, his acting was solved as far as this teacher was concerned! She was even able to tell others how to control him. The high incidence of major inappropriate behaviors when the student teacher was present decreased markedly when the regular teacher taught her more effective ways to interact with the child. For instance, the teacher would say, "Give the majority of your attention to the child's appropriate behavior, and ignore his attempts to get attention by behaving inappropriately. "

In this case study, the total time spent training the teacher was 12 hours. The consultant met with the teacher once a week at noon, as this was the only time available to her. The functional approach was used quite differently than in the first case study. Much of the emphasis was on identifying the child's problem behaviors and attempting to specify antecedents. It would have been ridiculous to attempt a specific program to change the child's behavior immediately, because the teacher did not believe the child was capable of controlling his behavior. Because of the consultant's use of the functional approach, the teacher was able to generate a satisfactory procedure to control the child's behavior. The teacher made numerous modifications in data-collection procedures, did the graphing, and was the best public relations agent that anyone could ask for.

CASE 3: IDENTIFYING A COMMUNICATION PROBLEM

A teacher of a seven-year-old, hearing-impaired child enrolled in a class for the deaf asked assistance in determining the child's learning problems. The teacher complained that he replied in nonsense words when asked to repeat a sentence. In addition to this problem, there was the controversial question of which type of communication training was better for this child: aural or total (aural and manual combined).

A two-part project was developed: first, to assess the child's ability to repeat phrases; and, second, to attempt to determine which type of communication was better for him. A special 15-minute session was arranged, in which he was taken to another part of the room for an individual lesson that was similar to the one that he was having trouble with in class. In this tutorial session, the teacher's aide asked the child to repeat a four- or five-word sentence and then recorded his performance. He was allowed five attempts to repeat each sentence correctly. The scoring was very simple: each word in the sentence was given a number, so that as the child repeated the five-word sentence the teacher wrote, for example, "1, 3, 4, 5." This indicated that he had repeated all the words in the correct order, but had omitted the second word. Table 3-8 presents a typical day's performance, where two sentences were given both aurally and with total communication labeled "signed" on the data sheet presented. The first five days indicated that the child's classroom performance was related to communication diffi-

1 Oral The girl has a banana	2 Signed The cat sees two birds
1 2 3 4 5	1 2 3 4 5
2 3 5	1 2 5
1 2 - -	1 2 15 5
2 1 5 signed	1 2 5
2 3 5	1 2 3 4 5

___ Signs	Oral bird cat friend
1 2 5	5 2 5 signed
1 2 is 5	1 2 is 5 4
1 2 5	1 2 is 5
1 2 5 oral	2 5 2
MONEY	

1 2 5	1 2 4 5 signed

Table 3-8   *A Data Sheet Used to Record Child's Recall of Sentences*

culties, which caused his apparent "learning problem" in the classroom. Thus, his difficulty appeared to be more of a communication problem than a learning problem per se.

The purpose of the second part of the study was not to establish which type of communication was better for *all* deaf children, but only the type that was better for *this particular child.* A series of questions had been developed for the first part of the project to determine if the child had equal difficulty with two different types of questions, which were labeled descriptive (for instance, "What color is the pumpkin?"—to which the child would name the color) or repetitive (for example, the child was asked to repeat a phrase such as "Hit the ball hard"). A data sheet similar to the one shown in Table 3-9 was developed. During this phase, the child was

	3/6 Signed 1	Th Oral 2	F Oral 3	4
1. What color are the hearts?	O	/	/	
2. What color is the rabbit?	2	Rabbit is White /	/	
3. What color is the paper?	O	Wrong Color Blue /	/	
4. What color are the flowers?	Wrong Color Blue 2	Wrong Color Blue /	/	
5. 3, 8, 2	/	Signed 2	/	
6. 1, 9, 3	2	No sign /	2	
	oral	signed	signed	
7. What color is the tomato?	/	Two word answer /	/	
8. What color is the pumpkin?	/	/ "	P. is having orange 2	
9. What color is the paper?	/	/ "	red /	
10. What color are the apples?	/	/ "	apple (same) green /	
11. 9, 1, 5	2	2	No sign /	
12. 7, 3, 5	/	7- -5 0	No sign /	

Not sure
Josh watched
sign

Table 3-9 *A Data Sheet Used to Assess which Type of Communication was Best for the Child*

allowed two trials for each question. If he replied correctly the first time, he was given a "1"; if he did not reply correctly until the second trial, he was given a "2." If he failed both times, the teacher recorded a "0." It proved to be a most efficient data system, one that did not interfere with the teacher's asking of the questions.

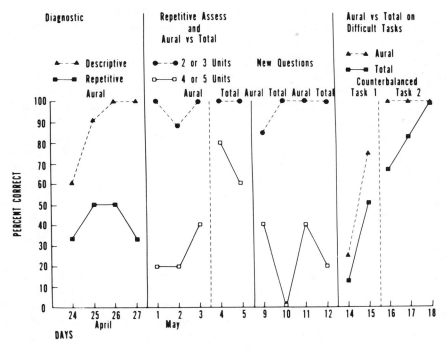

Figure 3-12 *Deaf child's communication assessment.*

The results of the first assessment (Figure 3-12) indicated that with the aural method, the child's performance on descriptive-type questions was consistently superior. As very little learning was apparent in the repetitive questions, the next phase was to assess which type of communication promoted better learning with short repetitive phrases (2 or 3 units) and long repetitive phrases (4 or 5 units). Figure 3-12 indicates that for repetitive questions, aural communication was again consistently superior to total communication. The results of the first five days of this phase were confounded because of the practice effect caused by the use of the same questions each day. After the sixth day, however, new questions were introduced each day, and it became evident that aural communication was more effective. The last condition of the study was to use questions like those in the regular program (which combined description and repetition) to determine which type of communication was more efficient. The results were again the same—aural communication was more effective than total communication.

The significance of this finding was that the child did not really fit into the model being used in this particular program—a program that advocated total communication for all children. There appeared to be no reason to suspect that this child would do better with only aural communication; he knew several signs, and it was argued that two different forms of input are better than one. But this child was an exception, and the functional model allowed him to be an individual and allowed the teacher to instruct him in an effective manner, thus increasing her success.

A total of 12 hours was spent training the teachers to use the functional approach. All of the content of the questions was supplied by the teacher; the consultant provided ideas on methods of collecting the data. The teachers collected all the data while teaching, but the consultant graphed the results. The teachers understood the results without the graphing, but appreciated having them graphed by the consultant.

DISCUSSION

The success of these three case studies indicates that there are several positive statements to be made about the functional approach. One such statement is that the success of the functional approach in motivating teachers to do research in the classroom can be attributed, mainly, to its simplicity. Immediately, at first contact, the teachers and the behavioral consultant communicate on the same level about the real concerns of the teacher. No jargon or definitions are needed to explain the approach. Instructions are simple. First, decide what you are going to do. Second, decide how you are going to do it. Third, ask whether or not you did it. Regardless of success or failure, the teacher can be optimistic because a strategy for attacking classroom problems has been developed with the assistance of a consultant whose function it is to *help* the teacher, not to *teach* the teacher. The simplicity of this low-keyed approach to behavior analysis helps establish rapport.

Training teachers without making them aware of the training must be considered another positive feature, for this approach motivates teachers to embrace the technique as their own; very rapidly, they are "carrying the ball" by themselves. As was indicated in the case studies, an average of only ten hours of consulting time was devoted to the projects, which indicates the efficiency as well as the minimal costs of this training technique. And the consultants spent half of that time merely in reinforcing the teachers for continuing the project and in sharing with them their growing enthusiasm for it!

Several other positive statements might be made. For example, the effectiveness of the functional approach in solving everyday problems probably results, in large part, from the structure it provides for consistency

—a critical need in many programs. If teachers are confused about the goals of their program and how to implement them, imagine the confusion the children must experience as they attempt to second-guess the teachers! Another positive feature of the functional approach is the ability of the teacher to realize small gains in each child. So often, this is masked by the teacher's forgetting where the child was initially. Such forgetting may lead to a dampening of optimism that should not occur, for one thing that teachers need with problem-behavior children is optimism, no matter how small the dose.

Finally, in the particular situations described in this paper, still another indication of the success of the approach taken with the teachers was a request by the supervisor to the consultant, which came after the successful completion of the two case studies involving learning-impaired children. The supervisor, who had said originally that he did not want any "high-powered behavior modifier on the premises" offered the consultant a contract for the coming year to work with all of his teaching staff, who were by then requesting assistance with problems in their own classrooms. The teachers of hearing-impaired children also requested two quarters of in-service behavior modification training, taught from the functional approach. In other words, the functional approach appeared to motivate teachers to develop an interest and background in research techniques because the teachers related them to their common goal of providing the best education for each child. Thus, still another asset of the functional approach is its potential to motivate teachers to do more sophisticated research.

There is also the possibility that additional, more rigorous research could be generated from the results of the functional approach. If a combination of procedures consistently had the same results, then skilled behavior analysts could design a study to systematically assess the variables involved. The probability of innovative solutions to traditional educational problems appears to be enhanced because of the greater flexibility given the teacher and because more teachers are willing to evaluate their teaching. All of which is grist for the experimentalists' mill.

In conclusion, comparing the traditional and the functional approaches of training teachers to use behavioral techniques may be helpful. In the traditional approach, teachers are initially presented with logic that implies that their present methods of teaching are inappropriate; therefore, it would be wise for them to change their teaching styles. It is essential, too, this approach dictates, that they have a background in operant psychology (or acquire one rapidly) so that they can be aware of antecedents and consequences of behavior. A review of the literature on how effective behavior modification has been is often recommended. Additional time is spent on research design to promote the teachers' acceptance of a need for a stable baseline from which to assess treatment effects. Also, much time is spent training teachers to manipulate only one independent variable at a time. As if this were not enough, even more time is spent on different types of data-collection procedures and on very sophisticated charting techniques that range from cumulative curves to logarithmic scales. For teachers who know that science and mathematics are not their strengths, this seems to be a very complicated approach, one that they have great difficulty in embracing or in relating to any of their background or expertise.

The functional approach, on the other hand, involves an action-oriented plan: identify a problem, decide upon a solution, and begin immediately to gather information to show whether the solution is correct. The logic of science is disguised in such a way that after the teacher uses the approach, he has acquired the ability to establish behavioral goals and measure progress toward these goals. As indicated previously, the teachers' request for in-service training suggests that they have also developed an interest in acquiring more information, which should facilitate training in more systematic procedures.

Effective training of teachers in the applied analysis of behavior will not be self-maintaining until the procedure becomes intrinsically reinforcing; until applied behavior analysts can design these systematic procedures so that the majority of teachers find them reinforcing, alternative procedures must be developed. The functional approach is one such procedure that has been successful where there was resistance to traditional behavior modification training. It is also a means, as has been amply demonstrated, of introducing teachers to a scientific approach, and certainly the time has come for the teaching profession to grow with other scientific disciplines. Hayden and Torkelson (1973) speak most succinctly:

> The measure of the maturity of a profession is the extent to which it pinpoints or identifies its *own* problems and seeks solution to these difficulties through disciplined inquiry, systematic treatment or technology, measurement, and evaluation of its performances and services.

Hopefully, the functional approach will provide another alternative for teachers to grow in their own profession by incorporating the logic of science into the art of teaching.

part 4 / Research
in Classrooms

13 / An Inexpensive Fading Procedure to Decrease Errors and Increase Retention of Number Facts

Edward J. Haupt · *Maria J. Van Kirk*
Thomas Terraciano

In two experiments, gradually covering the answer to a number fact with cellophane or tracing paper (fading) was contrasted with regular drill or study procedures. In both cases, the fading procedure produced fewer errors and better retention. Fading procedures are recommended for tutorial situations with children who have learning problems.

Terrace (1966) used the term "fading" to indicate a gradual change in the intensity or other dimensional characteristics of a stimulus when stimulus control is shifted from one dimension (such as light-dark) to another stimulus dimension (such as hue). Procedures for the use of this principle (Sidman and Stoddard, 1968) have required elaborate equipment, which has prohibited the routine use of fading procedures in classrooms.

Zuromski and Smith (1972) described a system for handwriting improvement through fading that used up to 12 carbon sheets and ordinary paper. This fading procedure consisted of gradually lightening the carbon-copied guidelines for spacing letters that were copied through successive

225

carbons. The current study presents a similar simple method of using fading in teaching number facts.

EXPERIMENT 1

Method

Subject

The subject was a nine-year-old girl who had repeated first grade. At the time of the experiment, she was in second grade but was still performing at a first-grade level in arithmetic, according to her classroom teacher. She had consistent trouble retaining number facts.

Materials

New-Math Addition Flashcards #261 and New-Math Subtraction Flashcards #262 (Copyright 1966 by Educards, Inc.) were used. The cards were 6 inches by 4 inches in size. A cover that slid horizontally along the card always covered the answer to each additional problem. The same sort of cover but with a cut-out window to expose the answer was used with each subtraction problem. Thirty-two small pieces of yellow cellophane were cut so that they fit into one cover for the subtraction problems. A Sony stereo tape recorder, Model TC-255, was used to record the child's answers.

Procedure

PRE-TEST.   To test the subject's knowledge of addition facts, 100 sums of two digits from zero to 9 were presented once each to the subject in a random order. The subject failed to solve most of the sums that totaled more than 10. The subject solved most sums by counting on her fingers, which she held in front of her. When the subject could not find the sum within 15 seconds or when she said she did not know the answer, the experimenter proceeded to the next sum. The experimenter made no response to any answer except to present the next problem. The procedure lasted about 40 minutes.

After a 15-minute break, 100 subtraction facts with subtrahends and differences ranging from zero to 9 were presented once each to the subject in a random order. The subject failed to solve most of the problems with minuends greater than 10. The same procedure for errors was used. This procedure also lasted about 40 minutes.

From the addition and subtraction facts that the subject failed to answer correctly, sets of 7 addition and 7 subtraction facts were chosen by shuffling the cards that displayed the incorrectly answered facts and by choosing 7 of each kind. The addition facts so chosen were: $8 + 3 = 11$; $9 + 3 = 12$ (the subject could solve both of these by counting, in more than 15 seconds); $5 + 8 = 13$; $7 + 6 = 13$; $9 + 5 = 14$; $7 + 8 = 15$; and $8 + 9 = 17$. The subtraction facts were: $11 - 5 = 6$; $11 - 7 = 4$; $12 - 4 = 8$; $13 - 8 = 5$; $14 - 5 = 9$; $15 - 8 = 7$; and $16 - 9 = 7$. The addition facts had undoubtedly been practiced more often, and, thus, they appeared to be an easier set than the subtraction facts. The complete pre-test took place in a 1½-hour session immediately before noon.

FADING CONDITION.   Each subtraction flashcard to be learned was presented with the cut-out window over the answer, so that the answer could be seen easily. When each of the 7 facts was correctly answered within about 2 seconds (the time taken to glance down at the experimenter's watch—which had a sweep-second hand, note the passage of 1 second, and stop the presentation), another sheet of cellophane was added to those covering the answer. There were 33 steps in the fading procedure. If the child failed to answer, or answered incorrectly more than once during one presentation of the 7 problems, the same number of cellophane sheets was used until the subject got each of the seven problems correct within the 2-second time limit. Since the answer was still visible, this was a correction procedure much like that used for the control condition. For each correct answer, the child received one point as a reinforcement. Fifteen points were equal to one nickel. The points were redeemed after the experiment was finished.

DRILL (CONTROL) CONDITION.   Each addition flashcard to be learned was presented with the answer covered. If the subject did not know the answer within the same 2-second limit after the presentation of the flashcard, the cover was removed and the correct answer was exposed. During this condition, reinforcement was given in the form of one point for each correct response.

During both the experimental and control conditions, the flashcards were presented in random order to prevent the memorization of a series of answers. The criterion for both conditions was 3 consecutive, correct answers to all 7 facts. During these conditions, the experimenter faced the subject across a table and concealed the problems behind a low pile of boxes and other flashcards. The training procedures lasted a total of 3 hours (about 2 hours for the drill and 1 hour for the fading procedure) after lunch the same day that the pre-test was given.

Results

The child performed at criterion level in 34 trials, and made 28 errors on the 7 subtraction facts that were taught by a fading procedure. When the 7 addition facts were taught by the drill procedure, in 64 trials, the child met the criterion with 149 errors. The fading procedure resulted in a reduction in time (2 hours compared with 1 hour) and errors in the learning of a series of elementary number facts.

The subtraction facts taught by the fading procedure were presented one week later. On the first presentation, the subject recalled 5 of the 7 facts. Figure 4-1 shows a comparison of errors during acquisition and facts retained. No corrections were given during this presentation. When the same flashcards were presented again, all 7 facts were answered correctly. None of the addition facts were retained when they were tested, because all were calculated by finger counting.

EXPERIMENT 2

Method

Subject

The subject was a ten-year-old boy who attended fourth grade in an elementary school. He was described by teachers as above average in intelligence and as very "artistic" and "creative." Also, his parents reported that he was doing well in school with the exception of mathematics, where he exhibited difficulty in learning one-digit multiplication facts (times tables).

Materials

Each set of multiplication facts was written on 9-by-12-inch sheets of white unlined paper with a wide-tip brown magic marker. The subject wrote his answers with a sharpened number two pencil. Genco Tracing Paper (No. 1966) was cut into 3-by-12-inch strips. These strips were arranged in multiple thicknesses (1 sheet, 2 sheets, and so on) and stapled together prior to the experimental procedure.

Procedure

The experiment was performed in two sessions. The first session lasted approximately 30 minutes, and the second session about 5 minutes.

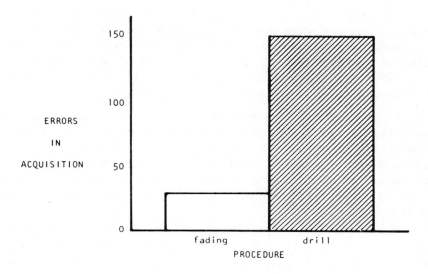

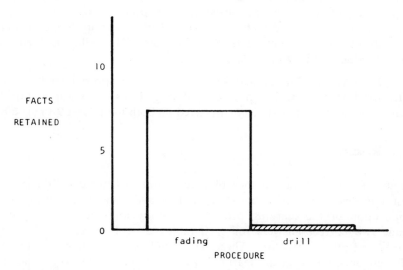

Figure 4-1   *Comparison of errors during acquisition and facts retained.*

The first session consisted of a brief pre-test (5 minutes), followed by an application of two different learning procedures (study and fading). The final session was a short post-test 2 hours later.

PRE-TEST.   At the beginning of the first session, the subject was handed 2 sheets of white paper, one at a time. The first sheet contained the 8-times table without answers. The second sheet contained the 9-times table (also without answers). The multiplication problems were written in order, beginning with 8 and 9 times 1 and ending with 8 and 9 times 12. The subject was instructed to complete these times tables.

STUDY CONDITION.   After the completion of the pre-test, the subject was presented with another sheet containing the eight times table with answers. The subject was asked to study the sheet for 10 minutes in the manner that he normally studied, which was continuous repetition to achieve memorization. After this 10-minute period, the subject was again tested on the eight times tables. The procedures were exactly the same as those for the pre-test.

FADING CONDITION.   During the second half of the first session, the subject was given another sheet of white unlined paper. Written on the paper was the 9-times table with the answer to each problem. The experimenter took one strip of tracing paper and covered the answers with it. The subject was told to write the answers on the tracing paper with a pencil. If the subject wrote the answers correctly, a 2-sheet pack of tracing paper was placed over the answers. This process continued until the answers were written correctly even though they were no longer visible to the subject. This procedure took 8 to 9 minutes. The child was then tested for retention of the 9-times table.

POST-TEST.   The second session took place approximately 2 hours after the first session. The procedure during this session was identical to that of the pre-test. The subject was tested on both the 8- and 9-times tables.

Results

Figure 4-2 shows the number of facts completed correctly during each test (pre-test, immediate post-test, and delayed post-test). Prior to the application of the learning procedures (study and fading), the subject made two correct answers for each table ($8 \times 1 = 8$; $8 \times 10 = 80$; $9 \times 1 = 9$; $9 \times 10 = 90$). These results indicated a minimum knowledge of these facts prior to the learning procedure. After the 10-minute study session, the subject correctly answered 5 of the 12 facts in the 8-times table. After the fading procedure, in which the visibility of the answers was gradually obscured through the tracing paper, the subject correctly answered 9 of the 12 facts in the 9-times table. This was an increase over the pre-test score greater than that in the study method.

The results of the post-test 2 hours later indicated that the subject

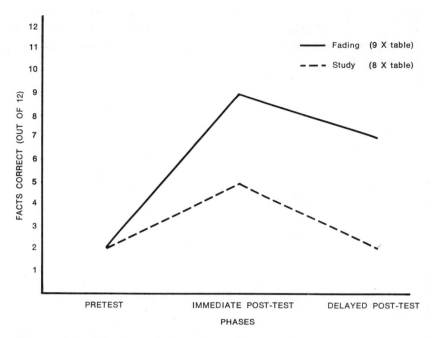

Figure 4-2 *Number of facts correctly completed during each test (pre-test, immediate post-test, and delayed post-test).*

had retained more from the fading procedure than from the study procedure. He correctly answered 7 facts from the 9-times table (fading), but only 2 from the 8-times table (study).

Discussion

The two procedures that involved a gradual reduction in the visibility of the stimulus (answer to the number-fact problems) both resulted in improvements in learning and retention over more conventional study and drill procedures. It is important that both of the children had a long history of unsuccessful use of typical drill procedures with arithmetic number facts. The subject in Experiment 1 commented during the fading procedure that it was an easy way to learn number facts.

These experiments strongly suggest that relatively simple methods of instituting fading procedures with readily available materials should be used in tutorial situations where number facts and other rote facts need to be memorized ·as an aid to more rapid performance of more complex number skills. It may also be that simple adaptations of these fading procedures are feasible for routine use with elementary arithmetic packages that make use of tachistoscopic or filmstrip projectors. Similar procedures could be instituted with cathode-ray tubes by controlling the intensity of the refreshing signal.

14 / A Comparison of Fixed-Page and Fixed-Time Reading Assignments in Elementary School Children

George Semb • *Susan Semb*

Many elementary school teachers rely heavily upon the clock in starting and stopping academic assignments. As a matter of convenience, it seems reasonable to organize a classroom so that everyone begins and ends at the same time. Other teachers, however, prefer to assign students a given amount of work to be accomplished, sometimes with, sometimes without, a time contingency. The rationale for fixed assignment lengths appears to be that both the student and the teacher can easily detect a finished project as the outcome. Though one could argue about the relative merits of each assignment schedule, there is a central research question involved: Which schedule promotes the best academic performance?

The authors wish to thank James Kent Winblad and Kristen Jolly, who served as reliablity observers. Reprints may be obtained from George Semb, Department of Human Development, University of Kansas, Lawrence, Kansas, 66044.

233

Several studies (Hopkins, Schutte, and Garton, 1971; Lovitt and Esveldt, 1970; Weis, 1971) have investigated the effects of various scheduling arrangements on academic performance by elementary school children. However, none have made direct comparisons between fixed-page and fixed-time assignments. The present study was designed to investigate the difference between these two assignment schedules.

METHOD

Subjects, Setting, and Materials

Nine elementary school children began the project. They met in groups of 3 in a small classroom as part of a six-week, summer remedial-reading program. The teacher met with one group from 9 to 10 A.M., another from 10 to 11 A.M., and the last group from 11 to 12 noon. Two children from the 11–12 group dropped out of the program before completing it, and their data are not included in the present study. Data from the third child in the 11–12 group were combined with data from the 10–11 group, inasmuch as treatment conditions were identical. Thus, for the purposes of the present study there were two groups: Group 1 (N = 3) and Group 2 (N = 4). Each child's age, class, and placement in the Sullivan Reading Series (1968) are listed in Table 4-1.

Table 4-1 *Placement in Sullivan Reading Series*

GROUP	CHILD'S CODE NUMBER	AGE	CLASS IN SCHOOL	SULLIVAN PLACEMENT TEST-BOOK
	1	9	3	6
1	2	10	4	6
	3	10	5	11
	4	8	3	4
2	5	9	4	5
	6	11	5	6
	7	13	6	6

Each child began in the Sullivan Workbook where indicated by his performance on the placement test. The answers to each frame were covered permanently with a strip of paper to prevent the child from looking at them while he was working. No feedback was given about the correctness of his answers until the end of the session.

Procedure

When the child reported to class, he went to his desk and opened his work-book to the page indicated by the teacher. As the teacher instructed the child to begin work, she noted the time on a large wall clock and wrote it on the workbook page. During the work session, the teacher moved from child to child to answer questions and give praise. Each time she interacted with a child, she recorded the time on the child's workbook. Interactions included physical contact, verbal praise, instructions, and question answering.

When the child completed his assignment, he raised his hand and the teacher recorded the time on his workbook. Next, she graded 20 frames, one or two samples from each page. If the child answered at least 18 of 20 frames correctly, he was allowed to enter free time. If he answered less than 18 frames correctly, the teacher instructed him to redo the entire assignment. As soon as the child met or exceeded criterion, he entered free time. To insure that the child's initial responses would be preserved, the child used a different color pen to make corrections when he redid an assignment.

Experimental Design

The experiment used a combination of reversal and multiple-baseline designs. Group 1 was exposed to the two treatments in ABA fashion. Group 2 was exposed to the treatments in AB order.

Fixed-Page Assignment (a)

During the fixed-page condition, the teacher assigned each child 15 pages. The child was instructed to work until he finished 15 pages (noted by a red line at the end of the fifteenth page).

Fixed-Time Assignment (b)

During the fixed-time condition, the teacher instructed the child to work until she told him to stop. To individualize the size of the time interval, the teacher calculated the mean time each child worked during the fixed-page condition. For example, Child 1 worked an average of 21.3 minutes during the fixed-page condition. Thus, he was required to work 21 minutes during the fixed-time condition. When the child completed the interval, the teacher instructed him to finish the page on which he was working at that moment.

Reliability

Work Time

During at least three sessions of every condition, a reliability observer recorded the time each child started and stopped working. An agreement was defined as two times that did not differ by more than 16 seconds. A total of 86 reliability checks were made. Agreement between the two observers was 100 percent.

Teacher Interactions

During at least three sessions of every condition, a second observer recorded the time the teacher interacted with each child. At the end of each session, the observer compared his time sheet for each child with the teacher's time marks in the child's workbook. An agreement was defined as two times that differed by no more than 16 seconds. If the time discrepancy was greater than 16 seconds, the observer checked to see if either he or the teacher had missed an interaction. If the next time corresponded to the one he was checking, it was counted as an omission (one disagreement). If, however, the next two times corresponded, the previous teacher time and observer time were both counted as disagreements. A sample reliability calculation is shown in Table 4-2. Reliability was computed by dividing the number of agreements by the number of agreements and the number of disagreements × 100. Eighty-seven reliability checks were made. Agreement ranged between 71 and 100 percent, with a mean across all children of 95 percent.

Sample Grading

The reliability observer also checked the teacher's grading sample for accuracy at least twice during each condition for each child. Agreement between the two was 100 percent in all instances.

RESULTS

The Sullivan Workbooks (1968) were graded at the end of each session. The grader computed the number of pages completed, frames done, frames done correctly, and time worked. Frames were judged correct or incorrect according to the child's initial responses, independent of any corrections he may have made when he was required to redo an assignment. A frame was

Table 4-2   *Sample Reliability Calculation of Teacher Interactions*

TEACHER TIME	OBSERVER TIME	OUTCOME
10:01:20	10:01:15	Agreement
04:10	04:10	Agreement
05:00		Disagreement *
	06:00	Disagreement *
07:25	07:15	Agreement
08:50	9:00	Agreement
10:30	10:30	Agreement
11:45	11:50	Agreement
12:30		Disagreement-omission
14:20	14:15	Agreement
16:00	15:55	Agreement

* Discrepancy between the two times was greater than 16 seconds.

Occurrences: Teacher — 10   Agreements   — 8
               Observer — 9   Disagreements — 3

Reliability: $A/A+D \times 100$ — 73 percent

defined as correct only if all characters or marks corresponded to an answer book prepared by the experimenters. If any part of the child's answer failed to match this model, the entire frame was marked as incorrect. A second grader independently scored two assignments for each child in each condition. Reliability was calculated by dividing the higher of the two numbers into the smaller. Agreement between the two graders was 100 percent regarding the number of pages done and 99 percent regarding both number of frames done and number of frames done correctly.

Data for each child in Group 1 are summarized for each condition in Table 4-3. The data for children in Group 2 are presented in Table 4-4. The mean number of pages completed decreased for 6 of the 7 children during the fixed-time condition. (On seven different occasions, children worked one page beyond the red mark in the fixed-page condition. The extra page was included in the present analysis. Thus, the mean number of pages worked was slightly greater than 15 pages for some children in the fixed-page condition.) However, the number of pages completed does not necessarily reflect differences in the effects of the two treatments because the number of frames per page differed across conditions. Another possible dependent variable that takes into account the number of frames per page is the number of frames completed. The number of frames completed decreased for all 7 subjects during the fixed-time condition. However, as Lovitt (1970) has noted, frames completed neither reflect changes in the

Table 4-3 *Group 1 Summary*

Child's Code Number	Assignment Schedule	Number of Days	Mean Pages Done	Mean Frames Done	Mean Frames per Page	Mean Time Worked	Mean Rate Correct	Mean Error Rate	Teacher Interactions per Minute
1	15 pages	10	15.1	141	9.3	21.3	6.30	0.34	0.59
	21 minutes	9	10.9	88	8.1	21.9	3.76	0.28	0.54
	15 pages	5	15.0	107	7.1	23.3	4.30	0.33	0.53
2	15 pages	10	15.3	148	9.7	25.1	5.78	0.13	0.58
	25 minutes	10	14.9	113	7.5	25.5	4.29	0.13	0.52
	15 pages	5	15.0	106	7.1	18.6	5.47	0.26	0.47
3	15 pages	10	15.1	114	7.6	21.2	5.21	0.15	0.59
	21 minutes	10	9.7	96	9.9	22.2	4.08	0.27	0.56
	15 pages	4	15.0	150	10.0	25.8	5.45	0.31	0.56

Table 4-4 *Group 2 Summary*

Child's Code Number	Assignment Schedule	Number of Days	Mean Pages Done	Mean Frames Done	Mean Frames per Page	Mean Time Worked	Mean Rate Correct	Mean Error Rate	Teacher Inter-actions per Minute
4	15 pages	16	15.0	144	10.0	35.1	4.00	0.13	0.52
	35 minutes	9	11.3	125	10.0	36.8	3.31	0.09	0.50
5	15 pages	15	15.1	140	9.3	39.1	3.51	0.11	0.48
	39 minutes	9	12.7	100	7.9	40.3	2.39	0.11	0.46
6	15 pages	16	15.1	160	10.6	44.6	3.50	0.14	0.48
	45 minutes	8	17.2	145	8.4	48.4	2.77	0.24	0.46
7	15 pages	13	15.2	135	8.9	22.6	5.90	0.09	0.50
	24 minutes	8	12.9	95	7.4	25.6	3.62	0.12	0.47

child's response accuracy, nor do they take into account the amount of time worked. Hopkins, et al. (1971) and Lovitt and Esveldt (1970) have both used correct responses per minute to reflect changes in accuracy as well as the quantity of work accomplished. The same response measures were used as the major dependent variables in the present analysis—rate correct (number of frames correct per minute) and error rate (number of frames incorrect per minute).

Rates correct and error rates for Groups 1 and 2 are presented in Figure 4-3. Mean rate correct for Group 1 decreased from 5.86 correct responses per minute during the fixed-page condition to a mean of 4.08 correct responses during the fixed-time condition. When the fixed-page condition was reinstated during session 21, mean rate correct recovered to 5.10

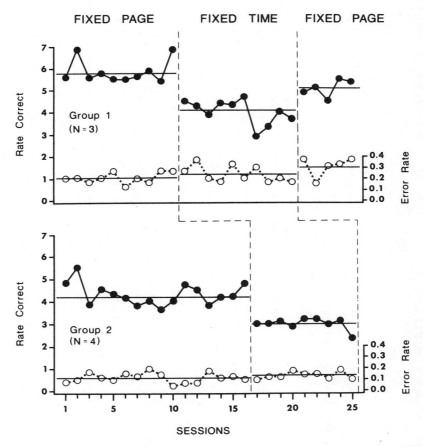

Figure 4-3 *Rate correct (closed circles) and error rate (open circles) plotted over session for Group 1 (top) and Group 2 (bottom). Horizontal lines represent means during each condition.*

responses. Error rates remained relatively constant during the fixed-page and fixed-time conditions, but increased slightly during the last fixed-page condition. Rate correct for Group 2 averaged 4.26 responses during the fixed-page condition, but decreased to 3.02 during the fixed-time condition. At the same time, error rates remained relatively constant between conditions.

Individual data for the 3 children in Group 1 are presented in Figure 4-4. In all instances, rate correct decreased during the fixed-time condition and recovered when the fixed-page condition was reintroduced during session 21. Error rates for all 3 subjects were relatively low during the 3 conditions and did not vary systematically.

Figure 4-5 shows the individual data for subjects in Group 2. Once

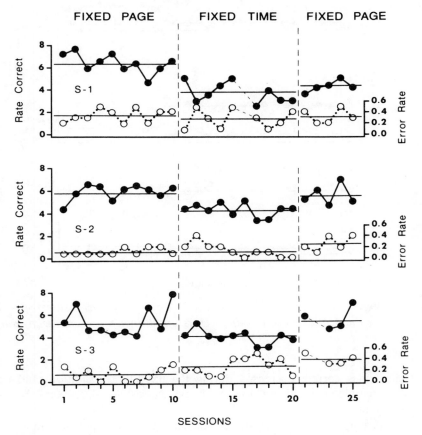

Figure 4-4   *Rate correct (closed circles) and error rate (open circles) for the 3 students in Group 1. Horizontal lines represent means during each condition.*

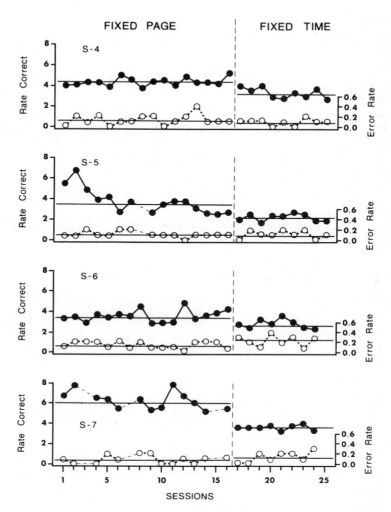

Figure 4-5 *Rate correct (closed circles) and error rate (open circles) for the 4 students in Group 2. Horizontal lines represent means during each condition.*

again, rates correct decreased during the fixed-time condition, and error rates remained relatively low with no consistent differences between conditions.

Finally, the mean number of teacher interactions per minute are presented for each child in each condition in Tables 4-3 and 4-4. Interactions remained relatively constant across conditions, suggesting that differences in rates of teacher interactions *were not* responsible for the changes observed in rates correct during the two treatments.

DISCUSSION

The results of the present study demonstrate clearly the superiority of fixed-page assignments over fixed-time assignments. On the average, the children worked correctly more than one frame faster per minute during the fixed-page condition. This represents between a 25 and 30 percent increase in efficiency, which suggests that teachers should set page or problem assignments, rather than schedule assignments solely on the basis of time.

To assess the long-term effects of a 25 percent increase in efficiency, consider the entire Sullivan Reading Series (workbooks). The 20 workbooks (Sullivan, 1968) have a total of 3,024 pages and 28,750 frames. If a child works 15 pages a day, he will complete the series in 202 days. At a rate correct of 4.0 frames per minute and an error rate of 0.2 frames per minute (comparable to the fixed-time condition in the present study), his work will be 95 percent accurate for a total of 114.4 hours. If, however, he works at a rate correct of 5.0 frames per minute and an error rate of 0.3 frames per minute (comparable to the fixed-page condition), he will complete the series in 91 hours with an average accuracy of 94 percent. The accuracy in both conditions is roughly equivalent, but the time saved in the faster condition is a little over 23 hours.

The fixed-time conditions in the present study were derived by averaging the time each child had worked during the previous fixed-page condition. One would not expect the typical classroom teacher to make such fine calculations. For the purposes of the present research, however, "individualizing" the time interval made the two conditions more comparable for each child.

The measure of teacher interactions used in the present study proved to be a reliable technique that could be applied easily in a variety of classroom settings. A clipboard carried by the teacher—to record verbal interactions when he or she is not in the child's proximity, and to record the times of each interaction on the child's worksheet—provides an easy way for a teacher to keep track of both the number of interactions and the distribution of interactions among students.

Finally, the teacher in the present study graded 20 sample problems from the child's assignment. Much more research is needed to determine the limits of grading samples. What percentage of problems should be checked? Who should do the checking, the teacher or the student? What is the relationship between grading samples and overall accuracy?

15 / An Analysis of the Effects of Lectures, Requests, Teacher Praise, and Free Time on the Creative Writing Behaviors of Third-Grade Children

Karen Blase Maloney · *Cindy R. Jacobson*
B. L. Hopkins

Very little research has employed objectively defined creative responding as a dependent variable. Perhaps the first researchers to approach the area were Pryor, Haag, and O'Reilly (1969). They reinforced only those gross motor responses of a porpoise that had never been previously observed in the training of *that* porpoise. Their procedure resulted not only in motor responses never observed in the training of that porpoise, but also in some responses that had never been observed by other trainers in other locations in the training of their porpoises. The study therefore deals with the response in terms of the past responding of a particular subject, and in terms of the past responding of the population of which the subject is a member.

A given response or product may be judged or trained as creative, relative either to the norms of the population of which the individual is a member or to the given individual's past behavior. However, recent studies dealing with human behavior in applied settings have focused on behaviors of the individual that are novel in a particular session. For example, in a study by Goetz and Baer (1971) social reinforcement, contingent upon blockbuilding forms not previously produced by a given child for a particular construction, increased form diversity. A similar procedure was employed by Goetz and Salmonson (1972) to increase the number of different painting forms produced by a given preschool child in a particular painting. In these studies creativity is in part defined as, or is in some way identified with, different behaviors not previously displayed in specific setting, session, or product.

Although there are numerous settings, sessions, and creative products that could be analyzed experimentally, the product of children's story writing seems to offer a plausible set of responses for analyzing creative behavior. Storywriting behavior offers the researcher a permanent product to analyze and numerous definable compositional variables to manipulate. However, relatively few studies have attempted to specify and manipulate compositional variables objectively. Brigham, Graubard, and Stans (1972) used a multiple-baseline design in varying the total number of words, number of different words, and number of new words in the compositions of 13 students in a fifth-grade remedial classroom. Blase and Hopkins (1973) manipulated the number of different adjectives, action verbs, and sentence beginnings in the ten-sentence stories written by fourth-, fifth-, and 6th-grade students. Both studies also indicate that higher quality or creativity ratings were obtained during contingency conditions than during baseline conditions.

The study by Blase and Hopkins (1973) employed a set of independent variables that included written examples of particular parts of speech, extra recess time, and candy. The general purposes of the present study were to evaluate some of the above-mentioned procedural aspects and to obtain further rating data on creativity. More specifically, the procedures evaluated the effects of teacher lectures and requests on the use of particular parts of speech in stories written by children. The effects of teacher praise for nonrepetitive grammatical responses and of free time contingent upon the nonrepetitive use of designated parts of speech were also measured. A paired-comparison rating procedure was employed to provide rating data on the creativity of stories written during various procedural conditions.

METHOD

Subjects and Setting

Nineteen third-grade children attending a public school classroom located in Haworth Hall at the University of Kansas, participated in the study. The research procedures were implemented by the third-grade teacher, who received written instructions from the experimenter. Observations of teacher and child behaviors were made from an observation booth behind a one-way mirror located along one wall of the classroom. Observations of verbal behaviors were facilitated by the use of two microphones suspended from the ceiling of the classroom and connected with an amplifier and speaker in the observation booth.

General Procedures

At the beginning of each session, the teacher passed out a blank sheet of paper and a pencil to each child. The classroom lights were then switched off, and the class viewed a color-slide projected on a screen. A different slide was shown each day. Slides were presented in random order from a series of photographs of color pictures taken from the Follett Educational Corporation's *The World of Language,* Books 2, 3, and 4. The slide could be viewed for the entirety of each session, though the classroom lights were switched on after 20 seconds. When the teacher had performed the procedures appropriate for the experimental condition, she noted the class's "start" time by using a continuously running time clock to clock in. The children then began writing five-sentence stories. After each child completed his five-sentence story and had it checked satisfactorily by the teacher, the child inserted his paper in the time clock, which stamped his "stop" time on his paper. After handing his completed paper to the teacher, the child was allowed a minimum of two minutes of play time in the free play area. A record player, toys, and games were available in the free play area.

Response Measures

The first five sentences of each child's story were scored for a number of compositional variables by a scorer who was not informed of the purposes or procedures of the experiment. The response definitions employed for each of the compositional variables were the number of the following:

1. Words: any group of letters, written or printed, representing a spoken word. Misspelled words were counted as words.
2. Nouns: the names of people, places, or things. Nouns appearing as objects of prepositions were counted as nouns.
3. Adjectives: words that modify nouns to denote the quality of the thing named, to indicate quantity or extent, or to specify a thing as distinct from something else. Pronouns such as this, that, these, those, its, hers, and his were not scored as adjectives.

4. Adverbs: modifiers of a verb, an adjective, another adverb, a phrase, a clause, or a sentence; expressing some relation of manner, quality, time, place, degree, number, cause, opposition, affirmation, or denial; and ending frequently with the suffix "ly."

5. Prepositions: words that are combined with a noun, pronoun, or noun equivalent to form a phrase.

6. Action verbs: words that express an act or movement, but not modes of being, thinking, feeling, tasting, seeing, or smelling.

Different sentence beginnings were counted for all sentences that began with a word different from that of any previous sentence in the same story. The number of *different* nouns, adjectives, adverbs, prepositions, and action verbs were also scored for each paper. A "different" word was defined as a word used for the first time in a given category in a given five-sentence story. Once a word was scored in a given category for a given paper, repetitions of that word could not be scored again as "different." The number of minutes each child took to complete each assignment was computed by figuring the difference between the class "start" time and each child's "stop" time. This time measure was used to compute the mean number of words written per minute. The mean number of words per sentence was also computed.

Teacher praise was also scored by an independent observer who was uninformed as to the purposes and procedures of the experiment. The observer recorded in ten-second intervals for five consecutive intervals, but did not record in any sixth ten-second interval. Recording began when the teacher checked in at the time clock and ended when the last child checked his paper out at the time clock.

General Teacher Praise

This was recorded and defined as a verbal initiation or response by the teacher to a child, contingent upon on-task behavior by the child. On-task behavior was defined as writing, orienting toward writing materials on desk, working without talking, sitting up straight, and so forth. An example of general teacher praise would be, "Sue, you're working so hard today."

Specific Teacher Praise

Specific teacher praise was recorded and defined as a verbal initiation or response by the teacher to a child, contingent upon the use of a specific part of speech or a specific sentence structure in that child's story. Examples of specific teacher praise are, " 'Blue' is a very good adjective," or " 'Run' is a great action verb, Mike." Different symbols were used when recording specific teacher praise in order to designate the part of speech praised. For example, the letter "J" was recorded if the word "adjective" was mentioned in the teacher's specific praise.

Reliability

An independent observer took reliability measures for each of the dependent variables by scoring duplicated copies of the stories. Checks were taken at least three times per condition per variable, for a total of 42 reliability checks for each compositional variable.

Overall reliability ranged from 70 to 100 percent, with an overall mean reliability of 97 percent. For the number of words used, reliability was computed by dividing the smaller number by the larger; this averaged 99 percent. For all other measures, reliability was computed by dividing the number of agreements by the number of agreements plus disagreements and multiplying by 100. Mean reliability scores were 97 percent for nouns and 96 percent for different nouns; and 96 percent for adjectives and 95 percent for different adjectives. Interobserver reliability was 95 percent for both adverbs and different adverbs. For both the number of action verbs and the number of different action verbs, mean reliability was 99 percent. For prepositions and different prepositions, agreement was 95 percent, and for different sentence beginnings, it was 99 percent. Agreement on the computing of the number of minutes from the "start" time to the "stop" time was 100 percent.

An independent observer also took reliability measures on the recording of the types of teacher praise. All reliability measures were computed by dividing the number of agreements by the number of agreements plus disagreements and multiplying by 100. A total of 40 reliability checks were made on each variable, with at least three checks per condition per variable. Reliability for general teacher praise was 94 percent. Nonoccurrence reliability was 100 percent for noun, preposition, sentence beginning, and word praise. An occurrence of any of these four types of praise was never recorded. For specific action-verb praise, reliability averaged 93 percent, and for specific adjective praise, 96 percent. Specific adverb praise reliability averaged 94 percent. Agreement that none of the defined praise behaviors, either general or specific, occurred in a given ten-second interval was 94 percent.

In addition, reliability was measured between the parts of speech praised by the teacher and those counted by the independent scorer. For example, if the teacher was praising adverb usage during a session, she would place a small red check mark above each adverb as she praised a child for using it in a story. After the session, five stories were selected randomly and copies were made. Red check marks were then placed above every word in every child's original story before the stories were given to the independent scorer. The scorer was then instructed to circle every adverb in the five selected stories and, in addition, to draw a line above every different adverb. By comparing the teacher's original check marks on the copies with the the scorer's circled words on the original papers, reliability data were obtained and measures were then computed according to the formula used for the reliability measure of the teacher's behaviors. Teacher-scorer reliability averaged 94 percent overall, with 90 percent agreement on action verbs, 93 percent for adjectives, and 100 percent for adverbs. When reliability was measured between the independent scorer and the teacher, the previously mentioned adverb definition was not used. Instead, the independent scorer was instructed to circle only those adverbs that directly modified an action verb, as these were the only types of adverb usage presented in the lecture and praised by the teacher.

Experimental Conditions

Baseline

During days 1 through 9, the general procedures were in effect. On day 1, after paper and pencil were given to each child, the teacher read the following instructions to the class:

> You're going to see a picture on the screen. I would like each of you to write a five-sentence story about what you see. Don't just tell me what is in the picture, but be sure to make up a story about the picture.

The children then viewed the slide and wrote five-sentence stories. Access to a minimum of two minutes of free time was contingent upon writing a five-sentence story. The teacher was given written instructions to praise only general work behavior, such as working quietly and writing neatly. She was instructed never to praise the usage of a specific word or part of speech in any child's story.

Lecture

On days 9 through 12, the teacher read a standard written lecture at the start of each session. The lecture defined nouns, action verbs, adjectives, and adverbs, in that order. During the lecture, the children were asked to give three different examples of a noun after it had been defined verbally in the lecture. The examples of the different nouns were written on the chalkboard by the teacher as they were verbalized by the children. After adjectives were defined in the teacher's lecture, three children were called on to give oral examples of an adjective. The children were asked to provide an example of an adjective that could be combined with each of the different nouns already written on the board. The same procedure was followed for action verbs and adverbs. At the end of the lecture three phrases were written on the chalkboard, each containing a noun, an adjective, an action verb, and an adverb. After the teacher erased the three sample phrases, the children viewed the slide and wrote their stories. The teacher continued to praise only general work behavior, and free time remained contingent upon writing a five-sentence story.

Baseline₂

Baseline conditions was reinstituted during days 13 through 16, and the procedures were the same as for days 1 through 8.

Lecture₂

During days 17 through 21, the standard lecture procedures employed on days 9 through 12 were reinstated.

Request

On day 22, following the standard lecture procedure, and after erasing the examples of parts of speech, this request was written on the chalkboard: "Please use five different action verbs." Again, general work behavior was praised by the teacher, and free time was still contingent upon writing a five-sentence story.

2 Request

The same request procedures occurred on days 26 through 29, except that a different request was written on the chalkboard: "Please use five different action verbs and five different adjectives."

Action Verb

Three changes were made in the basic procedures during days 30 through 35. First, the second request written on the chalkboard after the first lecture was changed to read as it did in the beginning: "Please use five different action verbs." Second, access to free time was now contingent upon using at least five different action verbs when writing the five-sentence stories. (That is, the teacher checked each child's paper to be sure there were five sentences and at least five different action verbs.) If the child did not include at least five different action verbs in the five-sentence story, the teacher drew a red line across the child's paper below the five sentences and instructed him to check out at the time clock, return to his seat, and write additional sentences until he had used five different action verbs. The child was instructed not to change any of his previous sentences, but to write additional sentences below the red line. Free time was available only after the child used five different action verbs, checked out with the teacher, and clocked his "stop" time on his paper. The third procedural change instituted during days 30 through 35 was the use of teacher praise contingent upon action-verb usage. That is, praise for general work behavior decreased and praise for the use of different action verbs in stories increased. For example, if Mark used the word "jump" as an action verb in his story, the teacher might say, "Wow, 'jump' is a great action verb, Mark."

Adjective

Similar procedures were followed on days 36 through 40, except that the request written on the chalkboard after the lecture was: "Please use five different adjectives." Free time was contingent upon using five different adjectives and writing a five-sentence story. Most teacher praise was contingent upon the children's use of different adjectives.

Adverb

On days 41 through 45 the children were instructed: "Please use five different adverbs." Most teacher praise was contingent upon the children's use of different adverbs, and free time was contingent upon using five different adverbs and writing a five-sentence story.

Action Verb and Adjective

During the last condition, on days 46 through 50, a double request was written: "Please use five different action verbs and five different adjectives." Most teacher praise was contingent upon the children's use of different action verbs and different adjectives, and free time was contingent upon using five different action verbs and five different adjectives, and writing a five-sentence story.

Rating Procedures

In order to obtain data on the creativity of the stories written during the various conditions, four independent raters were employed. None had any knowledge of the research. One rater was an elementary school teacher, two were journalism majors, and the fourth was an English major. Paired-comparison ratings were used. That is, one story was selected randomly from each of the seven conditions for each child. Each randomly selected story written by a given child was paired with another selected story written by the same child.

Each of the four raters was given the following written instructions:

> Third-grade children wrote five-sentence stories about pictures. The pictures were presented as color-slide presentations. Each member of each pair was written by the same child. After reading both stories in a given pair, please point to the story that you consider to be more creative. Please *don't* base your judgments of creativity on spelling, punctuation, or the topic of the story that was assigned by the presentation of the slide.

Raters 1, 2, and 3 rated stories from 7 of the subjects. Raters 1, 2, and 4 rated the stories of the remaining 12 subjects. All of the pairs of stories read by the raters were typed exactly as they had been written, with no spelling or punctuation corrections.

RESULTS

During baseline, days 1 through 8, general teacher praise averaged 65 percent of the intervals across the condition, and no praise was ever given for the use of specific parts of speech. During this first baseline period, the mean number of both total and different action verbs remained nearly constant at about 1.7 per five sentences. The mean number of total and different adjectives decreased slightly, and the mean number of total and different adverbs rose slightly across the condition. These results are plotted on the first three sets of coordinates in Figure 4-6.

Noun, sentence beginning, and preposition usage, both total and different, remained fairly constant during baseline, as graphed on the first two sets of coordinates in Figure 4-7. The bottom set of coordinates in Figure 4-7 plot the mean number of words per sentence, which decreased slightly during baseline, and the mean number of words written per minute, which remained fairly constant across the condition.

On days 9 through 12, the teacher read a standard grammar lecture and continued to praise general work behavior in about 76 percent of the intervals. With this lecture procedure, no change occurred in the mean number of total and different action verbs, adjectives, or adverbs, as plotted on the first three sets of coordinates in Figure 4-6. However, the data plotted on the first set of coordinates in Figure 4-7 indicate that the mean number of nouns, both total and different, decreased from the baseline levels of 8.7 and 6.8 to 6.9 and 5.3 per five sentences.

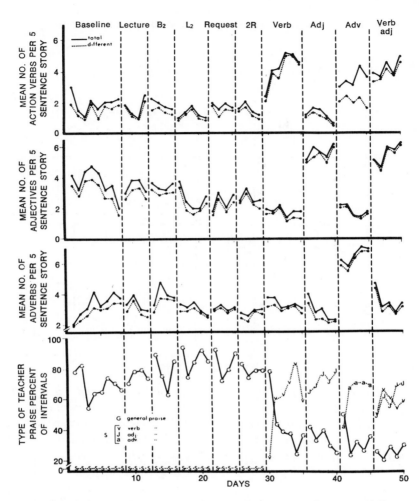

Figure 4-6 *Mean total number (solid lines) and mean different number (dashed lines) of action verbs, adjectives, and adverbs used per five-sentence story. Bottom coordinates illustrate the percentage of ten-second intervals of general teacher praise (G) and specific teacher praise (S,V,J,A).*

A return to baseline procedures on days 13 through 16 and a reinstatement of the lecture procedures on days 17 through 21 did not clearly replicate the decrease in noun usage during lecture conditions. The mean number of different and total nouns used did not recover to the baseline level on days 13 through 16, and noun usage continued to decline when

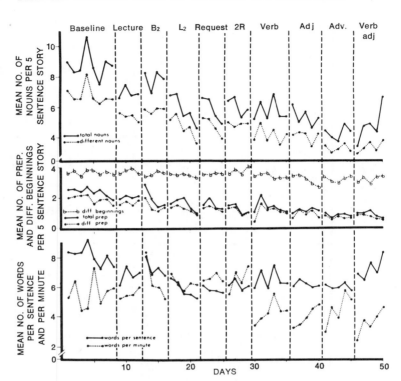

Figure 4-7 *Mean total number (solid lines) and mean different number (dashed lines) of nouns and prepositions and mean number of different sentence beginnings per five-sentence story. Bottom coordinates illustrate the total mean number of words written per sentence (solid lines) and the total mean number of words written per minute (dashed lines).*

the lecture procedures were reintroduced on days 17 through 21. These data are plotted on the first set of coordinates in Figure 4-7. Teacher praise for general work behavior occurred an average of 79 percent of the intervals during the second baseline condition (days 13 through 16), and 87 percent of the intervals during the second lecture condition (days 17 through 21).

An examination of the first set of coordinates in Figure 4-6 indicates that when a "request" to use five different action verbs was added to the procedures (days 22 through 25), there was no change in the mean number of action verbs used per five-sentence story. No changes occurred in the use of any of the other variables, as can be seen by inspecting the rest of Figures 4-6 and 4-7.

The addition of a second request—to use five different adjectives (days 26 through 29)—did not result in changes in the mean number of either action verbs or adjectives, as illustrated by the first and second sets of coordinates in Figure 4-6. Teacher praise for general work behavior was fairly constant, occurring an average of 84 percent of the intervals for both of the request conditions, as illustrated by the bottom set of coordinates in Figure 4-6.

On days 30 through 35 the following conditions were in effect: after the grammar lecture, the children received a verbal and written request to use five different action verbs; the teacher praised action-verb usage in about 59 percent of the intervals; and free time was contingent upon writing a five-sentence story that included five different action verbs. When these procedures were in effect the mean number of total and different action verbs increased from about 1.4 per five sentences in the previous request condition to a mean of 4.2, as is portrayed on the upper coordinates of Figure 1. A slight increase in the mean number of total and different adverbs also occurred from about 2.7 in the previous condition to about 3.25 during this verb condition. No increases occurred in the usage of any other parts of speech.

Total and different adjective usage increased on Days 36-40 when the request was for five different adjectives; teacher praise for different adjective usage averaged 72 percent of the intervals; and free time was contingent upon writing five sentences and using five different adjectives. The second set of coordinates of Figure 1 graphically illustrates the increase in different adjective usage from 1.2 per five sentences on Days 30-35 to a mean of 5.3 per five sentences. Action verb usage decreased from 4.1 on Days 30-35 to 1.0 per five sentences on Days 36-40. There were no other changes in any of the dependent variables, except for a slight decrease in total and different adverb usage from about 3.25 to about 2.5 per five sentences.

On days 41 through 45, the request, the free-time contingency, and teacher praise all focused on different adverb usage. Teacher praise for different adverb usage occurred in 68 percent of the intervals, and different adverb usage increased from 2.2 to 6.3 per five sentences. Total and different action verb usages also increased from 1.2 and 1.0 to 3.6 and 2.1, respectively, per five sentences. The use of total and different adjectives both decreased to 1.7 per five sentences. These results are graphed on the first three sets of coordinates in Figure 4-6.

During the last condition (days 46 through 50), the request, teacher praise, and free-time contingencies all centered in the use of different action verbs and different adjectives. Praise for different adjective usage occurred an average of about 61 percent of the intervals, and praise for different action-verb usage, about 55 percent of the intervals. The mean number of different action verbs increased from 2.1 to 3.8, and the mean number of total action verbs increased from 3.6 to 4.1. The mean number of different adjectives increased from 1.7 in the adverb condition to 5.4 in the last condition.

Figure 4-7 graphs the nontargeted, dependent variables, for which teacher praise and free-time contingencies were never in effect. The data graphed in Figure 4-7 indicate a decreasing trend throughout the study in the mean numbers of total and different nouns per five-sentence story—from 8.7 and 6.8 during baseline conditions to 4.7 and 3.3 during the last condition. The use of total and different prepositions also decreased—from means of 2.4 and 1.9 during baseline to .8 and .7 on days 46 through 50. There was a fairly stable use of about 3.4 different sentence beginnings per story throughout the study. The data plotted on the bottom set of coordinates in Figure 4-7 indicate that the mean number of words per sentence remained fairly constant across the conditions at about 6.5, decreasing slightly during baseline and increasing slightly during the last condition. The writing rate, in terms of the mean number of words written per minute, decreased from 6.5 on day 29 to 3.5 on day 30, when the request, teacher praise, and free time-contingencies were placed on action-verb usage. Thereafter, this decrease in writing rate was evident each time the use of a new part of speech was required—as on days 36 and 41—or when the requirement was increased—as on day 46. However, within each of these last four conditions, the writing rate showed evidence of recovery, as indicated by the dashed lines on the last set of coordinates in Figure 4-7.

Individual Results

In general, the mean individual results are represented accurately by the mean group results in Figures 4-6 and 4-7, with the following exceptions.

1. During the first lecture condition (days 9 through 12), mean noun usage either increased or remained the same for 4 of the 19 subjects, and decreased for the other 15 subjects.

2. Three subjects showed an increase in their mean usage of action verbs during the first request condition (days 22 through 25), and 1 of the 3 subjects clearly maintained this greater-than-baseline mean during the second request condition (days 26 through 29).

3. All 19 subjects increased their mean rates of action-verb usage on days 30 through 35, and 12 of the 19 subjects also increased their mean rate of adverb usage on those days.

4. During the adjective condition (days 36 through 40), 18 of the 19 subjects used more adjectives than in the previous condition. The one subject who did not increase his use of adjectives was the only subject who had shown a mean rate of five different adjectives per five sentences during the previous verb condition. This subject maintained this rate during the adjective condition, but did not increase it.

5. Increases in adverb usage occurred for each of the 19 subjects during the adverb condition (days 41 through 45). In addition, 17 of the 19 subjects used more action verbs than in the previous (adjective) condition.

6. During the last condition, all 19 subjects increased their mean rate of adjective usage over the previous adjective condition, and 18 of the 19 subjects increased their mean rate of action-verb usage.

7. Of the 19 subjects, 16 exhibited a decreasing trend in mean noun usage across the study. Also, 18 of the 19 subjects showed a decreasing trend in mean preposition usage.

Figure 4-8 graphically illustrates the percentage of subjects fulfilling the written request in each condition within the first five sentences of the story. During the two request conditions (days 22 through 29), from zero to 11 percent of the subjects met the requested criterion. On days 30

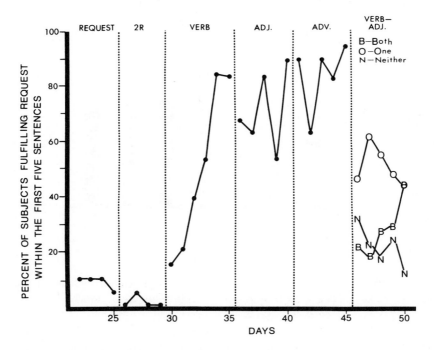

Figure 4-8 *Percentage of subjects fulfilling the written request in each condition within the first five sentences of a story.*

through 35, from 16 to 84 percent of the subjects met the criterion by using at least five different action verbs in their five-sentence stories. From 53 to 89 percent of the subjects met criterion by using at least five different adjectives on days 36 to 40. During the adverb condition (days 41 through

45), from 63 to 94 percent of the subjects used at least five different adverbs per five-sentence story. In the last condition, when both five different adjectives and five different action verbs were required, from 17 to 44 percent of the subjects met both criteria. From 44 to 61 percent met one criterion or the other, but not both; and from 12 to 32 percent met neither requirement in the first five sentences.

Rating Results

The combined results from the four raters are presented in Figure 4-9 in terms of the mean percentage of times that given stories from a given condition were chosen as more creative. According to the raters, stories from

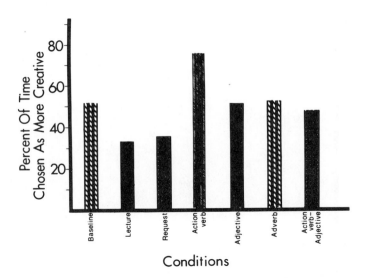

Figure 4-9 *Mean percentage of times given stories from given conditions were chosen as more creative by independent raters.*

the lecture conditions were rated more creative only 33 percent of the time. Stories from the request conditions were chosen as more creative 35 percent of the time, followed by stories from the verb-adjective condition, which were rated as more creative 47 percent of the time. Stories from the adjective condition were chosen as more creative 51 percent of the time. Stories from both the baseline and adverb conditions were rated as more creative 52 percent of the time. Stories written during the action-verb condition were rated as more creative 75 percent of the time.

Reliability among raters 1, 2, and 3 and among raters 1, 2, and 4 was computed by dividing the number of agreements by the number of agreements plus disagreements and multiplying by 100. In order for an agreement to be scored, all three of the raters had to agree in their choice of which of a given pair of stories was more creative. The probability of three raters agreeing in this fashion on a chance basis is 25 percent. Actual reliability among raters 1, 2, and 3—across 7 of the subjects—ranged from 29 percent to 76 percent and averaged 50 percent. Among raters 1, 2, and 4—across the remaining 12 subjects—actual reliability averaged 55 percent and ranged from 38 to 71 percent.

DISCUSSION

The findings of surveys confirm the fact that the teaching of grammar and word usage is accorded a large proportion of classroom time (Pooley and Williams, 1948; Farmer and Freeman, 1952; Pooley, 1957). One of the best-known general teaching methods is the lecture method (Wallen and Travers, 1963), and there are normative data that indicate that teachers give from 260 to 620 instructions per day in order to inform students of responses to be made (Lovitt and Smith, 1972). However, the results of the present study indicate that lectures and requests to use specific parts of speech were not sufficient to change the storywriting behaviors of some third-grade children. However, to what extent the lectures and instructions were a necessary part of effective training procedures cannot be determined from this study, for they were always in effect from day 22 to day 50.

These results do indicate that the regular classroom teacher successfully changed the writing behavior of her students by lecturing, by requesting and then praising the use of particular parts of speech, and by making the "natural" classroom reinforcer of free time contingent upon the use of particular parts of speech. This study also demonstrates that for this particular teacher, verbal praise comments could be altered by written instructions from the experimenter.

The slight increase in both the total number and the number of different adverbs used when action verbs were required, and the more substantial increase in action-verb usage when adverbs were required are consistent with the findings of Blase and Hopkins (1973). Those results indicated that when action-verb usage increased, adverb usage also increased. Those results and the findings of the present study may indicate the existence of a response class that subsumes adverb and action-verb usage.

Diederich, French, and Carlton (1961) reported a very low degree of agreement when they asked 53 readers to sort compositions into nine different piles in order of "general merit." The readers were instructed only to use whatever "hunches, intuitions, or preferences you normally use in deciding that one paper is better than the other." There was extreme variability in grading: every paper received at least five of the nine possible grades. In the present study, which incorporated similar instructions but used a paired-comparison rating procedure, reliability measures were greater than those that would occur by chance among three raters.

The rating results also indicate clearly that stories written during the lecture and request conditions were rated much less creative than stories written during other conditions. These lower creativity ratings might have been due to the decrease in noun usage during these conditions. Likewise, the higher creativity ratings during baseline may have been due in part to the greater numbers of nouns used in the baseline stories. Ratings similar to the baseline ratings existed for stories written during the adjective, adverb, and action-verb–adjective conditions. Perhaps this indicates that increased use of other parts of speech compensated for the decrease in noun usage. The rating results do indicate clearly that stories written during the action-verb condition were rated more creative than stories written during any other condition. This result agrees with the rating results of the Blase and Hopkins study (1973), which also showed that stories written when action verbs were required were rated as most creative stories. In general, however, it is also possible that although the raters were instructed not to base their judgments on spelling, punctuation, or topic, in fact their decisions were somehow related to these dimensions.

Future research on creativity might well concern itself with effective methods of increasing responses that differ from *all* previous responses of a particular child during the entire length of a study, rather than increasing the responses that differ merely from the other responses within a given product or session. The difficulty in establishing such contingencies lies in providing feedback to the subject and teacher or experimenter in such a manner that new and different behavior can be readily discriminated, generated, and reinforced, without spending great amounts of time reviewing current behavior and comparing it with past behavior. In addition to developing this broader base for reinforcing "different" responses, researchers should also give attention to developing procedures that maintain and reinforce "appropriate" creative behavior, as opposed to "deviant" or "bizarre" behaviors. In general, the reinforcement of "different" responses that occur in a specific setting or session is only a beginning step in the development of procedures that might increase creativity. Likewise, the use of raters to select creative responses is only a beginning step in the evaluation of creative behavior.

16 / The Use of Minimum Objectives as an Ongoing Monitoring System to Evaluate Student Progress

Judith F. LaForge • *Marybeth M. Pree*
Susan E. Hasazi

The use of operant conditioning procedures in classroom situations has become widespread in recent years. Such procedures have been applied successfully to several areas of academic behavior, including reading. For example, several studies have demonstrated that the acquistion of a reading repertoire can be facilitated by contingent reinforcement procedures (Staats and Butterfield, 1965; Staats, Finley, Minke, and Wolf, 1964a, 1964b; Whitlock, 1966; Wolf, Giles, and Hall, 1968). Such studies are clearly relevant to the design of reading instruction programs, and it has also been suggested that such programs would be further enhanced by the systematic use of instructional objectives (Gagne, 1965; Gray, Baker, and Stancyk, 1969; Popham and Baker, 1970).

According to Gagne (1965), behaviorally defined objectives are important in any instructional system because they determine the terminal sequence of the program. Additionally, Gagne points out, such objectives are important in that they can suggest the kinds of modification required throughout the program. Similar points have been made by Gray, Baker, and Stancyk (1969) and by Popham and Baker (1970); together they suggest the concept of a minimum objective, or the specification of the level at which a given student should perform throughout an instructional sequence. For example, Popham and Baker (1970) state that "student minimal levels are particularly useful in identifying individuals who may need remedial instruction." A demonstration of the utility of instructional objectives in reading instruction is provided by the Performance Determined Instruction system developed by Gray, Baker, and Stancyk (1969). This system incorporates operant conditioning procedures and instructional objectives, and has been shown to facilitate the acquisition of reading skills.

The present study investigated the effectiveness of using minimum objectives in monitoring and evaluating student progress. The experimenters in this study have implemented a minimum-objective system in their classroom for nineteen students with deficient reading skills. Specific objectives to be accomplished within a prescribed time limit were defined for a reading comprehension series. Children who did not meet the objective within the prescribed time limit were placed in a contingency program.

METHOD

Subjects and Setting

The program was implemented in the sixth-grade class at the Hinesburg Elementary School in rural Vermont. The class consisted of sixty students, grouped according to age, in one open-space classroom. Two teachers and an aide worked together as a team. The nineteen students chosen for this study all scored below the 5.8 level on the previous year's Durell Listening Reading Series test.

Procedures

In order to insure an ongoing system of evaluating pupil progress, minimum objectives were set for the nineteen students. A minimum objective, which defines the amount of work each student must complete within a specified time limit, was determined by estimating the weekly reading output of students who were reading on or above grade level. Specifically, the established minimum objective that each student read at least three stories per week in the *New Practice Reader Series* [1] and complete the corresponding comprehension test with a score of at least 80 percent accuracy.

---

[1] *New Practice Readers,* Books A through D, published by the Webster Division of McGraw-Hill.

Minimum-objective graphs were used to record student progress (see Figure 4-10). The vertical axis represents the number of stories read. The horizontal axis represents school weeks. The dotted horizontal line indicates the minimum objective. If, after one week, the student had completed three

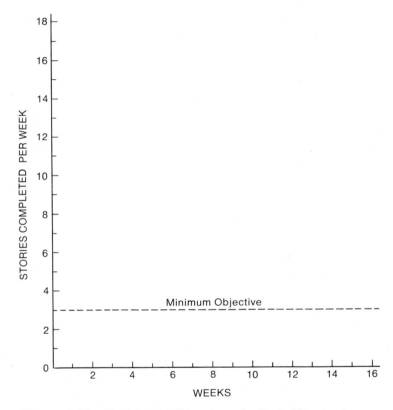

Figure 4-10   *Sample graph used to chart weekly progress.*

stories successfully, a point was placed on the dotted line. If, after one week, the student had completed six stories successfully the point was placed above the line. However, if the student had completed only one story, the point would be below the minimum-objective line. Thus, the teacher could see at a glance if extra help was needed.

An entry-level test was prepared for each book used in the program. Ten sample sentences were taken from each book, consecutively from beginning to end. The percentage of total correct responses of words in these sentences was recorded. If a student scored below 90 percent on an entry-level test he was placed in the book that corresponded to that entry-level test. Following the determination of entry level, word-list data sheets were prepared for all new vocabulary words given in each book. The words were arranged by story number. Each student was given a word list that corresponded to his book, and was assigned a peer tutor. The student then read each consecutive word orally to the peer tutor until he missed ten words. A plus was scored for each correct response made within three seconds, and a zero for each incorrect response.

After the student missed ten words on the word list, the tutor prepared flashcards of these words. He then displayed each card, pronounced the word correctly, and had the student repeat the word. Next, the tutor held up the flashcard without pronouncing the word and recorded the student's responses. A word was considered learned following six correct, consecutive, unprompted responses. The student then read the corresponding story and answered the comprehension questions in writing. The teacher corrected the answers, and if the score was 80 percent or above, the student proceeded to the next story; if the score was below 80 percent, the student reviewed the story and corrected his incorrect responses until he met criterion.

Experimental Design: Independent and Dependent Variables

An ABAB experimental design was used. The dependent variable was the number of stories completed by each student each week of the study. The independent variables of the study are described below.

During the first condition of the study (baseline 1), each student worked at his desk in the classroom. The students were instructed to complete three stories each week, but no contingencies for attaining this objective were programmed. Baseline 1 lasted six weeks.

Experimental condition 1 followed baseline 1 and lasted for a period of four weeks. During this condition students were divided into two teams of nine and ten students. The nine-member team was expected to complete twenty-seven stories per week, and the ten-member team was expected to complete thirty stories per week. If a given team met their minimum objective, a half-hour movie or an extra recess period was provided. No other contingencies were programmed during this phase of the study.

Finally, baseline 2 and experimental condition 2 followed. These conditions were replications of the previous baseline and experimental conditions, and lasted two weeks and four weeks, respectively.

RESULTS

Reliability was computed daily by two teachers. As the students' work was completed, it was corrected by one teacher and rechecked by the other teacher. Both teachers used a scoring key that was prepared by the publisher. The second scorer could not be influenced by the first scorer because each child's one-word answers either corresponded exactly to the key or did not. Reliability was always 100 percent.

During baseline condition 1, the class completed an average of .8 stories per week. During experimental condition 1, the number of stories completed increased to 5.7 per week, as shown in Figure 4-11. During baseline condition 2, the class average was zero stories per week. The overall class average during experimental condition 2 increased to six stories per week.

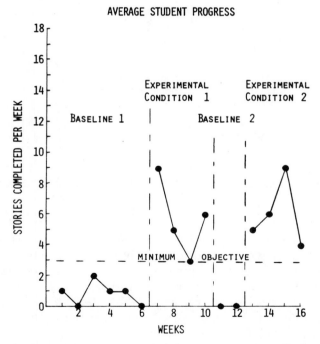

Figure 4-11 *Average number of stories completed per week by nineteen students, for all conditions.*

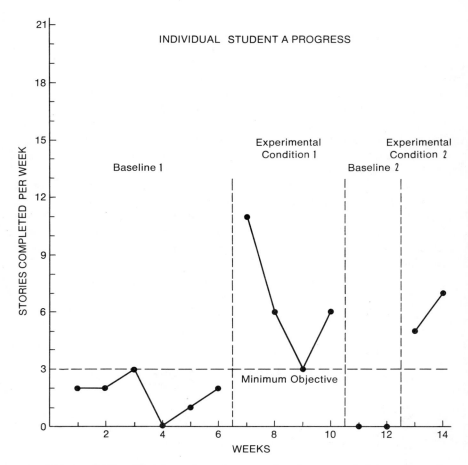

Figure 4-12   *Number of stories completed per week by student A, during all conditions.*

Figures 4-12 and 4-13 represent two sample individual case studies. During baseline conditions, both students were below the minimum objective. Student A averaged 1.6 stories per week, and student B averaged .8 stories per week. During experimental condition 1, student A (Figure 4-12) completed an average of 6.5 stories per week, which placed him above the minimum objective. Student B (Figure 4-13) completed an average of 6.25 stories per week, which placed him above the minimum objective. During baseline condition 2, both students completed zero stories per week. During experimental condition 2, student A averaged six stories per week and student B averaged five stories per week. During experimental condition 2,

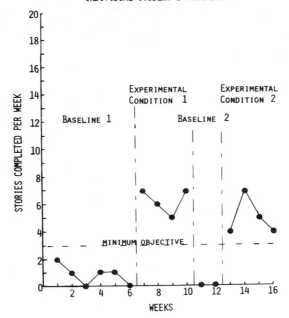

Figure 4-13   *Number of stories completed per week by student B, during all conditions.*

student A completed the entire series in week 14, and not only met but surpassed his minimum objective. Consequently, only two data points are provided for student A during this condition.

The systematic changes in reading rate across the phases of the study demonstrate clearly the control of this behavior achieved through teacher-controlled variables. However, baseline and experimental conditions differ from one another in more than one way. As such, it is impossible to determine the relative effects of each of the manipulations on student behavior. Specifically, these behavior changes could be attributed to the use of the contingency on student output, the division of pupils into groups, and the possibility of group competition, as well as to interactions of these variables.

DISCUSSION

With the popularity of large open classrooms increasing, it has become evident that an efficient system for monitoring and evaluating student progress is essential. Initially, this program was designed for nineteen students. However, as a result of its effectiveness in alerting the teachers to students who were not progressing at a specified rate, the experimenters are presently designing and implementing minimum-objective programs in reading and mathematics for all students.

17 / Modification of Disruptive Behavior in a Large Group of Elementary School Students

Adler J. Muller • *Susan E. Hasazi*
Mary M. Pierce • *Joseph E. Hasazi*

Behavior modification in school settings has typically involved reinforcement contingencies for the behavior of individual students. However, several studies have applied reinforcement contingencies on a group basis to an entire classroom of students (Barrish, Saunders, and Wolf, 1969; Herman and Tramontana, 1971; Medland and Stachnik, 1973; Packard, 1970; Schmidt and Ulrich, 1969). In such studies, a common consequence is provided contingent upon the performance of a group of students. The advantage of group contingencies is clearly that such procedures are more efficient than those that require attending to several individual contingencies (Herman and Tramontana, 1971).

Though most studies of group-contingent events have investigated specific academic or social target behaviors, the effects of group consequences upon the level of classroom noise has also been studied (Schmidt and Ulrich, 1969). In this study, it was found that the level of classroom noise decreased dramatically when group contingencies involving free time

269

were manipulated. Though classroom noise is obviously the product of some behavior and not the behavior itself, contingencies applied to noise level would have to influence student behavior to be effective. Consequently, the use of noise level in group settings may provide a convenient method of indirectly observing and modifying a wide range of student behaviors. Likewise, when contingencies are applied effectively to disruptive behaviors among large groups of students, one would expect decreases in group noise level.

Many school situations outside of the classroom, such as the cafeteria and the auditorium, often involve high rates of disruptive behavior and a high noise level. The present study was designed to investigate the modification of student behavior in these settings, as well as the changes in noise level that occurred when a variety of disruptive behaviors were brought under control. Finally, the present study was designed to investigate the role that elementary school students can play in managing contingencies for large groups of fellow students.

METHODS

Subjects and Setting

The participants in this study were 455 students in grades one through eight in a combination elementary and middle school. The school was in a rural community, and the classrooms were large open-space environments that contained between 42 and 62 students. All of the children ate lunch in the cafeteria, at various intervals, between 11:45 A.M. and 12:45 P.M. The room included 14 large tables, seating 16 children each, and the children were permitted to sit wherever they wished.

Dependent and Independent Variables

The dependent variables were all measured during lunch time in the cafeteria. The problem behaviors were defined as running, loitering, and physical aggression. Continuous measurement of the ambient sound level was also taken. Loitering was defined as any instance where students remained in the cafeteria after their scheduled lunchtime had elapsed. Physical aggression was defined as any instance of hitting, kicking, or pushing. The recorders were all Student Council members and were familiar with the grade level of all of the students; they tallied the above-mentioned behaviors.

The recorders were assigned in pairs to observe for specific time periods lasting fifteen minutes each. These periods corresponded to the class changes in the cafeteria. One student in each pair was designated the recorder, and the other, the reliability observer. Concurrently, pairs of students recorded the number of instances in which the sound-level meter exceeded 80 decibels (a noise level predetermined to be reasonable for this situation).

The independent variable was points awarded to those classes not engaging in disruptive behaviors. The points that each class had accumulated were registered in the early afternoon on a large chart in the main hall of the school, and were announced daily over the public address system. One point was awarded daily to each class for nonoccurrence of the target behaviors. When a total of 25 points was earned, an extra half-hour recess was awarded the winning class or classes.

Recorders from the seventh and eighth grades were trained by the principal to collect data. Four training sessions lasting 45 minutes each were conducted, during which the principal explained each definition and familiarized the students with the sound-level meter. The students role-played and recorded instances of the target behaviors.

During the daily 15-minute sessions, each pair of observers tallied the target behaviors on data sheets prepared by the experimenters. Each observer had his own clipboard and data sheet, which were given to the principal at the conclusion of the lunch period. At the end of the day, the experimenters computed the total number of instances of each of the target behaviors that occurred during the lunch time. Reliability between observers was determined by dividing the lower number of behaviors recorded by the higher number of behaviors recorded, and multiplying by 100.

Experimental Design

An ABAB design was used. The first baseline condition was in effect for seven days, during which measures of running, loitering, and physical aggression were obtained, as were measures of the sound level. However, in the first baseline period no instructions concerning these behaviors were given to the students, no points for appropriate behavior were provided, and no other contingencies were programmed. A seven-day experimental condition followed. Prior to the beginning of experimental condition 1, the principal visited each classroom and informed the children of the point system that would be implemented. During this period, points were given contingent upon nonoccurrence of the target behaviors. A second baseline and a second experimental condition concluded the experiment. Prior to baseline condition 2, the principal announced on the public address system that no points would be given that week because of the upcoming school vacation. Baseline condition 2 (five days) and experimental condition 2 (seven days) were replications of the previous baseline and experimental conditions, respectively.

RESULTS AND DISCUSSION

Figures 4-14, 4-15, and 4-16 show, respectively, the frequencies of occurrence of each of the three target behaviors on each day of the study. Figure 4-14 depicts the number of instances of physical aggression during each

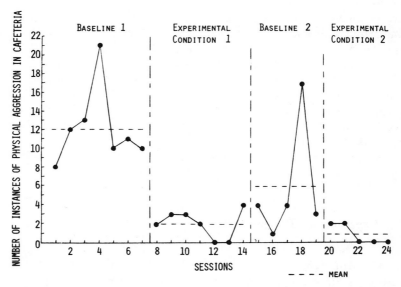

Figure 4-14 *Number of instances of physical aggression per session under baseline and experimental conditions.*

phase of the study. The horizontal dotted lines across each phase represent the average number of occurrences of the target behavior. Figure 4-15

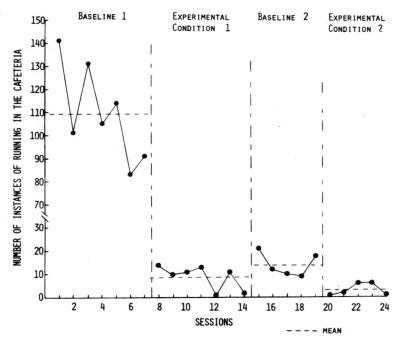

Figure 4-15   *Number of instances of running per session under baseline and experimental conditions.*

depicts the number of instances of running, and Figure 4-16 depicts the number of instances of loitering.

The baseline levels of all the target behaviors were high at the onset of the study, as seen in Figure 4-17. Likewise, it is also clear that the frequency of each target behavior was lowered dramatically by the addition of the point contingency. During the second baseline and the second experimental condition discriminable changes in response frequencies occurred. However, in no case was there a return to the previous baseline rates.

The failure to recover the baseline rate in each case is probably attributable to several factors. First, the initial baseline frequencies were extremely high and may have taken long periods to develop; the second baseline period may therefore have been too short to allow for a return to baseline. A more likely reason is that there were natural reinforcers in the students' environment, which assumed control once changes were effected.

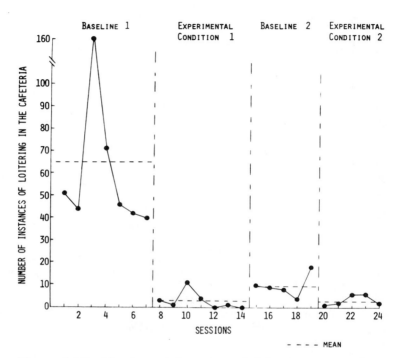

Figure 4-16 *Number of instances of loitering per session under baseline and experimental conditions.*

In addition, the occurrences of each of the target behaviors were probably interrelated. For example, running and loitering may have increased the probability of physical aggression. Such probabilities are supported by the data concerning noise levels.

The frequency of noise levels exceeding 80 decibels was graphed for each day of the study, and a mean line indicating the average number of instances the noise level exceeded 80 decibels was graphed for each condition; these data are presented in Figure 4-18. This graph demonstrates clearly that systematic changes in sound level occurred across the phases of the study, even though contingencies were never specifically arranged for sound level. Sound level can thus be considered as existing in a response-response relationship with the other target behaviors examined.

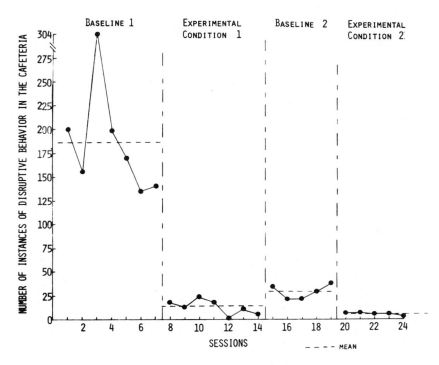

Figure 4-17   *Number of instances of disruptive behavior per session under baseline and experimental conditions.*

Such a finding is not surprising in many respects, but, nonetheless, is particularly interesting for several reasons. First, it demonstrates that an aversive feature (at least for teachers) of the environment occurs in connection with specific student behaviors that are amenable to manipulation. As the results of the study demonstrate, a procedure designed to eliminate inappropriate behavior in large groups of students may have favorable side effects for both students and teachers. More important, the finding suggests that if noise and other inappropriate behaviors exist in some response-response relationship, one might be able to manipulate large classes of such behaviors by applying contingencies directly to noise levels. Though such a procdure was not attempted in the present study, the results suggest that this is an exciting prospect for future large-group intervention in elementary schools.

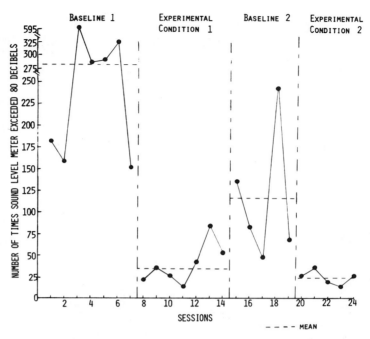

Figure 4-18 *Number of times sound-level meter exceeded 80 deci-bels under baseline and experimental conditions.*

18 / A Component Analysis of the Effects of a Classroom Game on Spelling Performance

Saul Axelrod · *Jolena Paluska*

In a frequently cited study by Barrish, Saunders, and Wolf (1969), the experimenters used a "good-behavior" game to reduce the rate of out-of-seat and talking-out behaviors exhibited by a group of fourth-grade students. The class was divided into two teams, according to the rows in which they sat. The team that committed fewer violations of the rules pertaining to out-of-seat and talking-out behaviors was declared the winner. Members of the winning teams received a variety of privileges, including the right to wear victory tags and the opportunities to line up first for lunch and to engage in extra free-play time. Whenever each of the teams violated the rules five times or less, both sides were regarded as the winners. Although the procedure successfully reduced the rate of the behaviors of concern, it is difficult to determine which aspect of the "good-behavior" game was responsible for the improvement. The experimenters did not determine whether simply winning the game accounted for the changes in behavior or whether the combination of winning the game and receiving additional privileges produced the changes. Medland and Stachnik (1972) investigated additional aspects of a "good-behavior" game that dealt with out-of-seat, talk-ing-out, disruptive, and permission behaviors. The game involved rules and consequences similar to those employed in the Barrish et al. (1969) study; in addition, the students received feedback on their performance. A green light meant that "all was well," and a red light indicated that someone had violated one of the rules of good behavior. The experimenters found that the game resulted in decreased rates of disruptive behavior, and that after association with the game, the use of rules alone, and the combination of rules plus the feedback lights were effective in maintaining the decreased rates.

The Medland and Stachnik (1972) study paralleled the Barrish et al. (1969) experiment. However, the investigators failed to separate the effects of a game alone from the effects of a game plus backup reinforcers for the winners. In the present study, the experimenters investigated the effects of simply winning a team game, with winning a team game and receiving back-up reinforcers, on the daily spelling performance of elementary school children.

METHOD

Subjects and Setting

The subjects were 22 third- and fourth-grade children in a classroom in Willimantic, Connecticut. Academically, most of the children were work-ing at grade level, compared with national norms.

Recording Procedures

The dependent variable was the number of words the children spelled cor-rectly on daily six-word spelling tests. The words were selected at random from fourth-grade reading books before the study began. Each day, the teacher graded the papers and recorded the scores in her notebook. Twice during each experimental condition, the papers were scored independently by a second observer; in each case there was 100 percent agreement.

Experimental Phases

Baseline$_1$

During the initial 5 days of the study, the teacher listed six words on the board, pronounced the words, and used them in sentences. The teacher then requested the students to copy the words, and informed them that they would be tested on the words the next morning. After the children took the test, the teacher immediately graded the papers and returned them to the children. The students had a few minutes to inspect their papers, and then returned them to the teacher.

Game$_1$

The students were divided into two groups: the "blue" team and the "red" team. The members of the two teams were matched according to their baseline$_1$ scores, and the teams were thus composed of children of approximately equal ability. During this 10-day phase, the children continued to receive six words daily and to take a test the next day. After the test, the teacher added the scores of each team to determine which side had a higher total. Whenever a student was absent, the teacher added his previous day's score to his team's total. The teacher then announced the winning team and pointed to a chart bearing the names of each of the students on the winning team. She also read aloud the names of the winners and permitted them to stand by their desks and cheer. Whenever the groups were tied, all members of the class engaged in the winners' ritual. Children in the winning group did not receive any other privileges, or backup reinforcers.

Game and Prizes

This condition was the same as the previous one, except that each child on the winning team received a prize. The prize varied from one day to the next, but consisted of an item such as a candy bar, a pencil, an eraser, or a toy car. The teacher did not inform the students what the prize was until a winning team was determined. If the teams were tied, all students received the surprise.

Game$_2$

This was a reinstatement of the game$_1$ condition. The students were divided into teams, but the winners did not receive prizes following a victory. The game$_2$ condition lasted 15 days.

Baseline$_2$

The final condition was the same as baseline$_1$. Students again received six spelling words daily, but were not divided into teams. Baseline$_2$ was conducted for 7 days.

RESULTS

Figure 4-19 depicts the daily class average during each of the experimental conditions. During baseline$_1$, the scores ranged from 2.8 to 4.6

words correct out of a total of 6.0. The class average for this condition was 3.48, which is equivalent to 58 percent accuracy. When game$_1$ was in effect, scores ranged from 2.8 to 4.8, with a mean of 3.65 (61 percent) for the 10-day period. This was an increase of 3 percent over the baseline$_1$ level. The individual means for each condition indicated that in game$_1$, 17 children in-

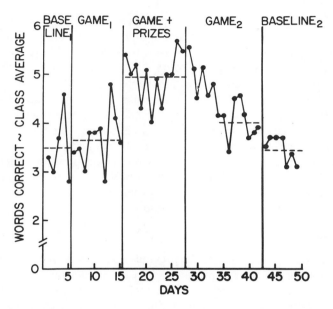

Figure 4-19   *Mean number of words spelled correctly per day for 22 third- and fourth-grade students.*

creased their accuracy over baseline$_1$. In three cases, however, the average daily difference was 0.1 word or less, and in six cases the difference was 0.3 word or less. Five children did better during baseline$_1$ than they did during game$_1$. When the winning of the game was followed by the awarding of prizes (the third condition of the experiment), scores ranged from 4.0 to 5.7 words a day, and the daily class average increased to 4.95 words, or 82.5 percent accuracy. This represented a 21.5 percent increase over the game$_1$ level. During the game-and-prizes condition, 21 of the 22 children increased their accuracy over each of the first two phases; the other child's average was lower.

During game$_2$, there was a sharp decrease in the daily class average. Figure 4-19 indicates that stability in the data was present from days 34 to 42 (the final 9 days of game$_2$). This observation was verified by calculating the slope of the line which was $b = -.02$ (Walker and Lev, 1953). Scores ranged from 3.4 to 4.55 words correct whereas the daily class mean for the final 9 days of game$_2$ was 4.03 words per day, or 67 percent accuracy. This represented a decrease of 15.5 percent from the level achieved during the game-and-prizes condition. The individual data indicated that the scores of all students during the last 9 days of game$_2$ were less than those they attained during the game-and-prizes condition.

During baseline$_2$, when the students no longer played the spelling game, scores ranged from 3.1 to 3.7 words correct, and the class average decreased to 3.46, or 57.5 percent accuracy. This level was 9.5 percent less than that achieved during the last 9 days of game$_2$, and almost identical to the 58 percent level that the students attained during baseline$_1$. A comparison of the individual scores that the students attained during the last 9 days of game$_2$ with those they achieved during baseline$_2$ indicated that 15 students increased their accuracy during game$_2$, and 7 increased their accuracy during baseline$_2$.

DISCUSSION

A comparison of the group means attained during baseline$_1$ and game$_1$ indicated that there was no more than a slight tendency for the game to improve the spelling accuracy of the youngsters. Individual data revealed that the majority of the students did better when the game was played, but for many children the improvement was small; in several cases, the students actually did better during baseline$_1$ than they did during game$_1$. A comparison of the game$_2$ and baseline$_2$ stages indicated that there was a 9.5 percent gain in the group average during game$_2$, but that almost one third of the youngsters did better during baseline$_2$ than they did during game$_2$. In summary, there was a tendency for the game conditions to produce small gains in group averages, but these gains were not found consistently among individual youngsters. A comparison of the game-plus-prizes condition with game$_1$ and game$_2$ revealed that the addition of prizes produced a large improvement in the group average, and that the effect occurred for 21 of the 22 children. One student did better during game$_1$ than he did during game-plus-prizes, but his score during game$_2$ was less than it was during the prize phase. Hence, there is some doubt about which aspect of games used in the Barrish et al. (1969) and Medland and Stachnik (1972) studies accounted for the students' improvement, for these studies confounded the game with the awarding of privileges to the winners.

Anecdotal reports from the teacher gave some indications as to why the children did better during game-plus-prizes than they did during game$_1$ and game$_2$. During all of these conditions, the students were enthusiastic about the prospect of winning the game. They ran up to the teacher's desk while she was grading the papers and cheered for themselves if they won the game. During the game-plus-prizes stage, however, the students performed additional behaviors. They often drilled each other on the words, and some youngsters studied the words frantically when the teacher announced the test. These behaviors were notably absent during $game_1$ and $game_2$. Hence, although the students seemed to be overjoyed when they won the game during the $game_1$ and $game_2$ conditions, they did not appear to perform the antecedent behaviors necessary to improve their spelling performances. The study therefore reemphasizes the importance of having teachers keep data on the academic performance of their students, for it is likely that the enthusiasm of the students during $game_1$ and $game_2$ would mislead many teachers to believe that by playing the classroom game the children were improving their scholastic behavior.

There are some differences between the Barrish et al. and Medland and Stachnik experiments that should be mentioned. Both studies were set up in such a manner that ties were common. Ties occurred on 82 percent of the sessions in the Barrish et al. study and 87 percent of the time in the Medland and Stachnik experiment. It is possible that such an arrangement decreased the competition between the teams and in some way affected the scores. In the present study, ties occurred on only 3 of the 37 sessions (8 percent) in which the game was played. This result is more likely with games played in the natural environment, and probably fosters more competition between the players. Also, Barrish et al. called their procedure a game, but it could be regarded as two separate group contingencies as long as the students performed five or fewer misbehaviors. It became a competitive game only after both teams exceeded five misbehaviors. Inasmuch as the teams performed fewer than five misbehaviors in 82 percent of the sessions, the Barrish et al. procedure was a competitive game in only 18 percent of the sessions, and even then it was competitive for only a portion of the period. Finally, Barrish et al. and Medland and Stachnik indicated that the teams were structured by dividing the children according to the rows in which they sat. With such an arrangement, it is possible that one team will be vastly superior to the other and that the members of the poorer team will eventually decrease their efforts following consistent losses. In the present experiment, the teams were matched according to their $baseline_1$ scores, and there resulted a similar number of wins for each team.

19 / The Use of Modeling Techniques to Influence the Acquisition of Computational Arithmetic Skills in Learning-Disabled Children

Deborah Deutsch Smith · *Thomas C. Lovitt*

Behavior-analysis research has been conducted in many curriculum areas. Reading (Gray, Baker, and Stancys, 1969), arithmetic (McKenzie, Egner, Knight, Perelman, Schneider, and Garvin, 1970), spelling (Lovitt, Guppy, and Blattner, 1969), and handwriting (Hopkins, Schutte, and Garton, 1971) have all been targets of behavior-analysis research.

Modeling has been used effectively in many different situations. Csapo (1972) used peer models to modify inappropriate classroom behavior. Through modeling, rather than direct reinforcement, Brigham and Sherman (1968) showed that young children can be taught to imitate Russian words. Baer, Peterson, and Sherman (1967) developed imitation of motor behavior in retarded subjects by a combination of demonstration and reinforcement procedures. Modeling techniques have also been used to reduce

This research was partly supported by a grant from the National Institute of Education, Grant Number OEG-0-70-3916 (607).

the phobic reaction of young children (Bandura, Grusec, and Menlove, 1967).

Although modeling techniques have long been used by teachers to help their pupils learn arithmetic facts, we found no research that investigated the influence of modeling on arithmetic performance. The purpose of this research was to analyze the influence of modeling procedures on arithmetic performance. The modeling technique used throughout this research was manipulated by a teacher, who computed the problems for the pupils and also explained the process.

Teachers are assigned the task of helping pupils develop competencies in many academic subjects. To develop competencies in an academic subject, the learner passes through three stages: acquisition, proficiency, and maintenance. Teachers must, therefore, help children to acquire new skills, to become proficient in using those skills, and, finally, to maintain that level of proficiency.

The focus of this study was on the acquisition of arithmetic facts. The intervention strategy was a modeling technique.

METHOD

Subjects

Seven boys, ranging in age from eight to eleven, participated in the study. All had been referred by the same local school district to the Experimental Education Unit because of academic deficiencies. All had been labeled learning-disabled at one time or another, and all were unable to perform certain arithmetic problems.

Setting

The research was conducted in the Curriculum Research Classroom at the Experimental Education Unit of the Child Development and Mental Retardation Center at the University of Washington. This classroom exists for the primary purpose of conducting educational research: to study the efficacy of curricular materials and teaching tactics. Children are assigned to this classroom for one year, and then return to their home district.

Because most of the school day (5½ hours) is devoted to educational research, student enrollment is held to a maximum of seven pupils. Two full-time teacher-researchers are responsible for classroom management and supervision, and for the implementation of the research projects. Throughout this study, the computational arithmetic curriculum for all of the students was presented by the first author of this paper.

Preintervention Procedures

Each child was given Key Math (Connolly, Nachtman, and Pritchett, 1971) and a nonstandardized, criterion-referenced computational arithmetic battery. After the administration of each battery, the results were calculated and recorded.

Key Math is a standardized, individually administered mathematics achievement test, and was used as an initial assessment of each child's arithmetic performance level. Table 4-5 shows a profile of each child: name, age, subtest scores, and overall Key Math score. This test indicated that the children had different levels of mathematics performance: their scores ranged from a 2.9 to a 4.4 grade level.

The purpose of administering the criterion-referenced arithmetic battery was to assess the exact level of each child's arithmetic performance. Through this probing system, different types of arithmetic problems were selected for each child. Many types of problems were tested in order to determine which classes of problems would be used in this research.

The types of problems used were those that the child did not know how to compute, yet had the necessary prerequisite skills for. The criterion for selecting the type of problems was a correct score of zero. If, for example, a child knew all the subtraction facts and could solve problems of several digits in length that did not require borrowing, but could not borrow, problems that required borrowing were arranged for him. Once such a type of problem was identified for a child, arithmetic sheets were constructed.

Materials

Three sets of arithmetic pages were arranged for most of the children. The first two sets for each child were drawn from the same pool of arithmetic problems. If the first set of problems was of the type that required borrowing with a zero in the units column ($280 - 128 = ?$), the second set also required subtracting from a zero in the units column, but the problems were different. Two sets of five sheets were constructed from the same pool of problems, and Sets 1a and 1b were thereby created. No problem appeared more than once on any sheet.

A third set of problems was arranged for most of the children. This set was also composed of problems that the child could not compute, but they were of a different nature. Five variations were drawn from this pool

Table 4-5 *Child Profiles*

NAME	AGE	CONTENT			OPERATIONS				Mental Computation	Numerical Reasoning	APPLICATION					Total Grade Level
		Numeration	Fractions	Geometry Symbols	Addition	Subtraction	Multiplication	Division			Word Problems	Missing Elements	Money	Measurement	Time	
Billy	9	3.5	4.7	3.4	3.4	3.1	3.9	4.1	4.4	3.8	4.3	5.3	3.4	3.0	2.9	3.7
Jon	10	5.0	6.2	3.9	4.1	2.8	3.9	4.1	4.5	3.8	3.2	3.9	4.0	3.9	3.3	4.0
Kenny	11	3.3	4.6	5.3	4.8	3.2	3.9	4.1	3.5	3.8	3.2	4.3	6.6	4.3	6.0	4.3
Richie	10	2.8	4.0	3.4	4.6	3.9	3.8	4.1	4.4	5.2	3.75	3.9	5.7	4.8	4.2	4.2
Roger	10	4.2	4.0	5.3	3.6	4.8	4.5	5.0	4.4	6.4	4.2	4.3	3.4	5.2	3.3	4.4
Scott	10	3.5	4.8	4.3	3.4	4.0	3.8	5.9	5.2	6.3	2.7	4.3	4.8	4.1	3.7	4.2
Samuel	8	3.4	2.3	3.0	2.5	1.5	2.5	2.4	3.5	2.7	2.95	3.9	2.1	3.75	3.3	2.9

of problems to form Set 2. Extending the example situation described earlier, the problems of this type required borrowing with a zero in both the units and tens columns $(700 - 468 = ?)$.

Design

This research was composed of several studies; each study comprised several experiments. Each experiment followed an A-B-A format. Because of the extensive preintervention probes, the baseline phase for each experiment lasted only three days. After this, an intervention was applied only to the Set 1a problems. No intervention was applied to either Set 1b or Set 2 problems. This was done to test for within- and across-class generalization. The intervention in each experiment lasted at least seven days. For the condition to end, the scores for three consecutive days had to be 100 percent on the Set 1a problems.

Baseline conditions were then reestablished to test for maintenance. The expectation was for the learned behavior to remain at a high level and not to return to the low performance level of the baseline period. This non-intervention phase lasted a minimum of seven days and was concluded when three consecutive 100 percent days were noted.

Set 1a problems were then measured on a post-test basis. The child's performance on this type of problem was monitored weekly to determine whether or not the behavior was maintained.

Reliability

Three types of reliability were obtained. The first concerned timing. (Both percent and rate data were taken for this research. Only percent data are included in this report.) The subjects of this research timed their performance: each child had a stopwatch, which he stopped when the experimenter said "Pencils down." The experimenter also timed the performance on every set of pages. The times recorded by experimenters and pupils were in agreement 99.7 percent of the time.

The second reliability measure assessed accurate correcting. At the end of each week, the experimenter gave a classroom teacher all the arithmetic pages the children had worked on during that week (approximately 105). The teacher randomly selected ten of these pages to recorrect. Only two problems were found to be miscorrected during these checks.

The third reliability measure assessed accurate recording. All data plots were checked against the raw data sheets. If the data were plotted incorrectly, the plots were changed accordingly.

General Procedures

At the same time every day, each child received his individually arranged arithmetic pages, which were paper-clipped together. A different variation of each set of problems was given to every boy each day. The order of presentation of the sets also varied each day. If, for example, Set 1a was on the top of the stack one day, that set of problems was not presented first the next day. As there were five variations for each set, every sixth day the children received the same page of problems.

At the beginning of each session, the children were instructed to put their names and the date at the top of each page of problems. The boys were told to work the top set of problems first. The experimenter then said, "Ready, start working." At the end of two minutes, the experimenter said, "Pencils down. Switch pages. Ready, start working." After the children had worked the problems from each set, the pages were collected.

Since all of the studies in this report focused on arithmetic skill acquisition, the children had to demonstrate during the baseline that they could not solve the problems presented to them. Therefore, the mean percentage of correct scores for the baseline conditions was zero. If this criterion had not been met by a child, a new set of problem types would have been devised for that child. Unless feedback was scheduled as an intervention, the children were not provided with feedback regarding their performance.

At the conclusion of the arithmetic period, the experimenter corrected each set of problems for each child, calculated the rate and percentage scores, entered the data on score sheets, and graphed the data.

Besides these general procedures, additional procedures were used for each set of experiments. These specific procedures are discussed under separate headings.

STUDY 1

Demonstration Plus Permanent Model

The intervention selected for this study has been used by teachers for many years. When a new arithmetic process is introduced, teachers often go to the chalkboard, give verbal directions, and demonstrate how to solve the new type of problem. Frequently, the sample problem remains on the board as the children compute similar arithmetic problems.

The purpose of this set of experiments was to study the effectiveness of this procedure. Because the children were solving different types of problems, the teacher provided the children with individual demonstrations and a sample problem, rather than giving general instructions to the whole class.

Procedures

At the beginning of this set of experiments, the children were placed at one performance level or another. Three students, Billy, Jon, and Kenny, knew how to borrow for certain types of problems but could not borrow when the problem contained a zero (470 − 249 = ?). Therefore, three-digit problems that required borrowing with a zero in the units column were presented to these children.

Roger and Richie had different needs. They could borrow, but could not perform certain types of multiplication problems. They knew the necessary multiplication facts but could not compute two-digit non-carry multiplication problems (22 × 13 = ?). This type of problem composed the set of target problems for them.

Scott did not know the multiplication facts when a zero was on the bottom (8 × 0 = ?). Therefore, one-digit multiplication problems were selected as the target problems for him.

The procedures for all children were the same during this part of the experiment, regardless of the type of problem. The general procedures, explained earlier, applied to this set of experiments. Additional procedures are discussed by condition.

Baseline

During the baseline, the children were given no instructions regarding the appropriate procedures for computing their individual problem types. No feedback or reinforcement contingencies were given to the children for their performance.

Demonstration Plus Permanent Model

During this condition, a red box was drawn around the first problem on the Set 1a page. This served as a signal to the experimenter and the child that some intervention was scheduled for that page. Before the child worked that page of problems, the experimenter came to the child's desk and demonstrated the appropriate procedure for solving the problems. As she worked the sample problem, she also verbalized the procedures that were used to compute the problem. Because the experimenter had worked the sample problem on the child's page, it served as a referent for the child to use as he computed the remaining problems.

Maintenance

During this condition, a return-to-baseline procedures was established.

Weekly Post-Test

Once a week, the child was presented one of the five variations of the Set 1a pages. No instructions, feedback, or contingencies were in effect.

Results

The results for this set of experiments are reported by condition.

Baseline

This condition lasted three days for each child. All the scores were at zero percent for three consecutive days.

Demonstration plus Permanent Model

Two of the three children who worked on the borrowing-with-a-zero problem type increased their percentage scores from zero percent during baseline to 100 percent on the first day of this condition. This 100 percent performance level continued throughout the condition. Both Billy and Kenny had median scores of 100 percent.

Jon, who worked on the same type of problems, also improved his computational skills. He did not, however, obtain a median score of 100 percent; his score was 91 percent. He did not reach the criterion of three consecutive days at 100 percent during this condition. Jon required one more condition before entering the Maintenance Condition. During this phase, Jon was still provided with the Demonstration-Plus-Permanent-Model, but was told in addition that he had been making careless subtraction errors and that he should be more careful. During this condition, Jon's median score rose to 100 percent.

The two children who worked on the two-digit multiplication problems also improved during this condition. Roger's performance was much like Jon's. He did not achieve mastery (three consecutive days of 100 percent) during the Demonstration-Plus-Permanent-Model condition; his median score was 90 percent. Therefore, additional conditions were arranged for him. Richie showed gains similar to Kenny and Billy, scoring 100 percent on the first day of this condition. He, too, had a median score of 100 percent.

Maintenance

Billy and Kenny maintained their high level of performance (median of 100 percent) during this condition, even though the instructional tactic was withdrawn. During the Maintenance Condition, Jon's performance dropped slightly to a median of 93 percent. (See Figure 4-20.)

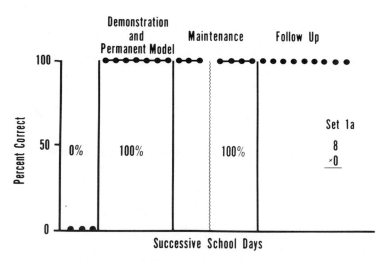

Figure 4-20   *Percentage-correct data for Scott's Set 1a problems during Study 1. Only successive data days are connected by lines. The curved line indicates a school holiday longer than two weeks.*

After three additional conditions, the Maintenance Condition was scheduled for Roger. He obtained three consecutive 100 percent days (with a median of 93 percent). Richie did not maintain his previously high median score during this condition. His percentage-correct median dropped to 84 percent. Scott maintained his mean percentage score of 100 percent during this condition.

Weekly Post-Test

All but one of the children continued to accurately compute the problems presented to them during this study. Billy maintained his performance until the four-week Christmas break. When he returned to school, he could no longer compute these problems, and these were rescheduled for a later condition. Kenny's performance also deteriorated after the Christmas break, but he brought his score back to 100 percent without additional interventions. The other children remained at 100 percent.

STUDY 2

Procedures

Once again, the children worked on different types of problems. Two of the children worked on the same types of problem. Billy and Kenny were assigned nonborrowing three-digit subtraction problems that yielded a two-digit answer. Problems of this type are constructed in the following manner: in the units column the top numeral or minuend is larger than the bottom numeral or subtrahend; in the tens column the minuend is also larger than the subtrahend; in the hundreds column both numeral are equal ($187 - 134 = ?$).

Scott worked on two-digit noncarrying multiplication problems ($23 \times 22 = ?$). After Christmas vacation, Billy could no longer correctly compute the type of problem taught in the first study. Therefore, those problems were used in this study. (This was the second time Billy participated in this study.) This type of problem consisted of problems that required the student to borrow from a zero in the units column ($780 - 267 = ?$).

As in the first study, the procedures were the same for all the children, regardless of the type of problem. These procedures are discussed by condition.

Baseline

During this condition, no instructions, feedback, or contingencies were in effect.

Correction and Error Notation (Feedback)

After the baseline period, a feedback procedure was investigated. After the child computed the Set 1a problems, the experimenter came to the child's desk and corrected that page in his presence. A "c" was placed beside each correct answer. A slash was drawn through each incorrect answer; the child was also told which answers were wrong.

None of the children raised their median percentage scores above zero during this seven- or eight-day condition; therefore, a second condition was scheduled, using the same procedures as in Study 1.

Demonstration plus Permanent Model

The procedures used in the first study were then begun. Once again, a red box was drawn around the first problem for the Set 1a problems. Before the child worked the Set 1a page, the experimenter came to the child's desk and used the first problem as the sample. After she verbalized and demonstrated the appropriate process to follow when computing these problems, the sample problem remained as a referent for the child.

Maintenance

During this condition, a return-to-baseline procedures was begun. No instructions, feedback, or contingencies were in effect.

Weekly Post-Test

Baseline procedures were still in effect, but Set 1a problems were presented to the child weekly instead of daily.

Results

Baseline

During the three days of this condition, all of the children had a mean score of zero percent. Kenny's data (Figure 4-21) are typical of the other children's.

Correction and Error Notation

This condition lasted seven days for three of the children and eight days for the fourth. The median percentage-correct scores for all four experiments was zero percent.

Demonstration plus Permanent Model

The median scores for all four children rose to 100 percent. Three of the children raised their scores from zero percent in the previous phase to 100 percent on the first day of this condition. Billy took two days to reach 100 percent.

Maintenance

The median score for all four children was 100 percent.

STUDY 2

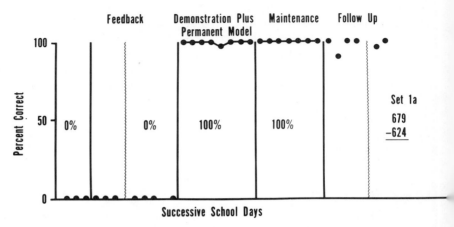

Figure 4-21   *Percentage-correct data for Kenny's Set 1a problems during Study 2.*

Weekly Post-Test

All of the children maintained the 100 percent level of performance.

STUDY 3

Component Analysis of the Demonstration and the Permanent Model Intervention

This study was conducted to investigate the Demonstration-Plus-Permanent-Model procedures in more detail. In this research, the Demonstration was presented separately from the Permanent Model in an attempt to determine which variable was the cause of the dramatic increase in the correct percentage scores in the previous two studies.

Procedures

The four children who participated in this study worked on different types of problems. Kenny was assigned two-digit multiplication problems that did not require carrying ($22 \times 23 = ?$). Jon was given subtraction problems with two zeros in the top numeral; borrowing was required (800 − 349 = ?).

Samuel was required to compute problems that had two digits in both the minuend and the subtrahend, and required borrowing (36 − 18 = ?). Scott was assigned multiplication problems that had two digits in the top figure (multiplicand) and one digit in the bottom figure (multiplier), and required carrying in both the units and tens columns (27 × 8 = ?).

Some children received the Demonstration alone in the first condition. For others, the Permanent Model alone was scheduled initially. Though not necessarily sequential, the specific details for the procedures are discussed by condition.

Baseline

Throughout this condition, no instructions, feedback, or contingencies were in effect.

Permanent Model

Before the child received his Set 1a page for the day, the experimenter worked the first problem on the page. If slash-marks or other notations (320 − 129 = 201) were required to solve the problem, they were included. The correct answer was also provided. The experimenter handed the child the stack of arithmetic pages as she had done throughout the other studies, and gave no other instructions or feedback.

Demonstration

In this condition, the experimenter came to the child's desk before he worked the Set 1a problems. A problem of the target type for that child was written on an index card. While working the sample problem for the child, the experimenter verbalized the appropriate procedures for the child to follow when computing this type of problem. Following this demonstration, the experimenter took the index card and the sample problem and left the child's desk. The child then worked on the Set 1a problems without a sample problem as a referent.

Maintenance

During this condition, no instructions or feedback were given to the child regarding his performance.

Weekly Post-Test

Baseline procedures remained in effect. Rather than being scheduled daily, the Set 1a problems were scheduled weekly.

Results

Not all of the children who participated in this study needed both intervention procedures to reach mastery—three consecutive 100 percent days.
Results are discussed by condition.

Baseline

During this condition, all of the boys exhibited a mean performance
level of zero percent.

Permanent Model

This intervention was scheduled for three children and was effective
with only one. The condition lasted eleven days for Samuel. On the seventh
day, Samuel increased his score to 50 percent. However, this was not maintained: he soon dropped back to zero percent.

Kenny's correct percentage scores rose above zero on three occasions
during this condition (see Figure 4-22). On the first day of this condition,

STUDY 3

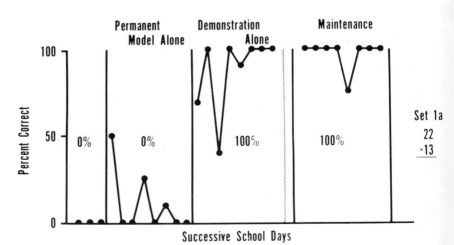

Figure 4-22 *Percentage-correct data for Kenny's Set 1a problems
during Study 3.*

he obtained a score of 50 percent. This did not maintain, and only two other scores above zero percent were noted.

Jon was the only child who attained mastery during this condition (see Figure 4-23). (Jon's second intervention was not the Permanent-

STUDY 3

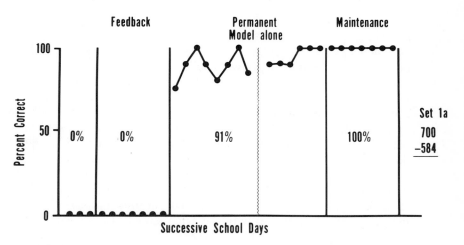

Figure 4-23   *Percentage-correct data for Set 1a problems, showing Jon's performance during Study 3.*

Model intervention. He received the feedback tactic that was used in Study 2. During this condition, he remained at zero percent. After the seven days of that phase, the Permanent-Model intervention was scheduled.) The tactic was effective on the first day. His median score for the eleven-day condition was 91 percent.

Demonstration

Both Kenny and Samuel initially received the Permanent-Model condition. The median score for each child was zero percent. The Demonstration-alone condition was then scheduled. The performance of each child improved to a median of 100 percent during this condition.

The Demonstration condition was initially scheduled for Scott. He did not improve on the first day of this condition. Soon, however, his performance on Set 1a problems rose to 100 percent.

Maintenance

All of the children maintained high percentage scores during this condition.

GENERALIZATION

As mentioned earlier, most of the children were presented other sets of arithmetic pages. Set 1b was a companion set for Set 1a problems. No intervention procedure was ever applied directly to this set. Set 1b problems were composed of the same problem type as Set 1a, the set associated with the various conditions. The purpose for giving Set 1b pages to each child was to determine whether or not generalization occurred: whether or not the learning on the first set would transfer to other problems of the same class. This is discussed in the next section, "Within-Class Generalization."

The experimenters were concerned with another type of generalization: "Across-Class Generalization." Set 2 (and occasionally Set 3) problems in each experiment were arranged for this purpose. In this case, problems that were not exactly the same as Sets 1a and 1b, but similar, were presented to each child. If, for example, Set 1a and Set 1b problems required borrowing with one zero ($270 - 138 = ?$), Set 2 problems required borrowing with two zeros ($300 - 124 = ?$). These problems were included to determine whether or not the child could expand upon this learning and apply the appropriate computational rule to a new set of problems. These two types of generalization are discussed by study.

Within-Class Generalization

Study 1: Demonstration-Plus-Permanent-Model

During this condition, the children were given a demonstration-plus-permanent-model when they computed Set 1a problems. Three children worked on the same type of problem ($470 - 249 = ?$); they all scored zero percent correct during the Baseline Condition. During this condition, Billy and Kenny obtained a median of 100 percent on both Sets 1a and 1b. They maintained that performance level for both sets during the maintenance condition. Billy and Kenny exhibited within-class generalization. Kenny's data are shown in Figure 4-24.

Jon did not reach mastery during this condition. His median score for Set 1a problems was 91 percent; he obtained a median score of 88 percent

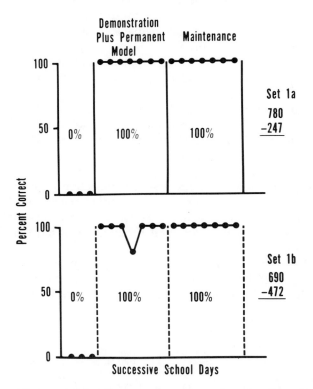

Figure 4-24 *Percentage-correct data for Sets 1a and 1b problems for Kenny. This shows within-class generalization throughout Study 1. The solid vertical lines indicate that interventions were scheduled for that set of problems. Broken lines indicate that no intervention was in effect.*

for Set 1b problems. When instructions were added regarding his careless mistakes, his scores on both Sets 1a and 1b problems rose to 100 percent. Again, within-class generalization occurred.

Richie and Roger worked on two-digit noncarrying multiplication problems ($22 \times 23 = ?$) and also demonstrated within-class generalization. During the first condition, Roger had a median score of 90 percent for Set 1a problems. His score for the Set 1b problems was slightly higher: 95 percent. For the first three days of this condition, however, Roger's Set 1b scores were lower than his Set 1a scores. Once he mastered the rule for performing this type of problem, he was able to apply it to problems on the 1a sheet and those on the 1b page.

Roger required several additional procedures to achieve mastery on the Set 1a problems. During the Demonstration-plus-Permanent-Model Condition, Roger made "careless" errors. The third condition, then, was the addition of the statement, "You are making careless mistakes. Please be more careful when you work these problems today." This caused only a slight increase in Roger's scores for Set 1a problems. His scores on the Set 1b problems dropped from a median of 95 percent to one of 80 percent.

Another procedure was begun for the Set 1a problems, and the demonstration-plus-permanent-model and instructions were discontinued. After the child computed the Set 1a problems, the experimenter corrected the page. This led to a decrease in performance for both Sets 1a and 1b problems, with median percentages of 71 and 75 percent, respectively.

Although scores were lower, within-class generalization occurred. A fourth procedure was then arranged. For every problem the child computed incorrectly on Set 1a, he lost one minute from shop time. This resulted in a rise in percentage scores for both Sets 1a and 1b problems. Again, within-class generalization occurred.

Richie generalized his learning of the problem type immediately, and received a median score of 100 percent for both sets of problems during the demonstration-plus-permanent-model condition (see Figure 4-25). After

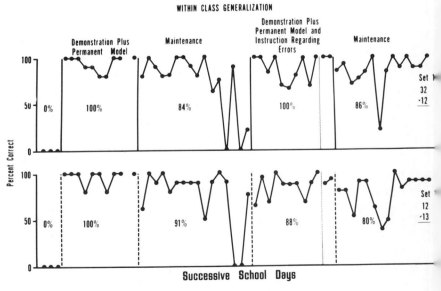

Figure 4-25 *Within-class generalization data of problems for Sets 1a and 1b. Richie's data from Study 1.*

mastery was attained, the Maintenance Condition was scheduled. During this condition, Richie's performance level dropped for both sets of problems, indicating that within-class generalization occurred again.

Because Richie did not retain the high level of performance during maintenance, another demonstration-plus-permanent-model was instituted. But, additionally, instructions were given regarding the careless errors he had made previously on Set 1a problems. Richie improved on both sets of problems, though the median level for Set 1b (89 percent) was lower than that in the prior condition (100 percent).

The Maintenance Condition was scheduled once again. The median percent-correct scores for both sets of problems dropped. Although Richie's data indicated that within-class generalization occurred, his scores were not as high as those of some of the other children.

Study 2: Replication of the Demonstration-plus-Permanent-Model

This study first investigated a type of feedback and then replicated the Demonstration-plus-Permanent-Model study. Billy exhibited perfect within-class generalization during both conditions of this study. In both experiments during the demonstration-plus-permanent-model condition, he attained 100 percent for both Sets 1a and 1b problems. This rate was maintained when the intervention was discontinued.

Kenny also demonstrated within-class generalization. He, too, obtained median scores of 100 percent for both sets during both post-baseline conditions.

Scott worked on two-digit noncarrying multiplication problems during this study. He, too, exhibited within-class generalization. During the demonstration-plus-permanent-model condition, Scott had a median score of 90 percent. During the maintenance phase, Scott continued at a high level of performance on the Set 1a page, but began to deteriorate on Set 1b, with a median score of 87 percent.

Study 3: Component Analysis of the Demonstration-and-Permanent-Model Intervention

During this set of experiments, two experimental conditions were investigated: the Demonstration Condition and the Permanent-Model Condition. During Study 3, Samuel computed subtraction problems that required borrowing. Set 1a and 1b problems were two-digit problems that required borrowing in the units column ($37 - 18 = ?$). During the permanent-model intervention, Samuel scored above zero percent on Set 1a problems only twice. On Set 1b problems, he never scored above zero. Within-class generalization did not occur for the two days that Samuel obtained scores above zero. The demonstration-alone condition was then scheduled for him. On the first day of this condition, his performance on Set 1a problems rose to 100 percent, and remained at a high level throughout the remainder of the study. On the second day of this condition, his score on the Set 1b problems rose to 100 percent. Within-class generalization occurred once again.

The Sets 1a and 1b problems for Kenny were two-digit multiplication facts that did not require carrying ($23 \times 22 = ?$). He obtained slightly better scores on Set 1b problems during the Permanent-Model Condition, and his rate of correct completion was zero during five days of Set 1a problems and three days for Set 1b problems. During the Demonstration Condition, Kenny's median score was 100 percent for Set 1a and 84.5 percent for Set 1b. Within-class generalization occurred, but not to the extent that it had in other experiments.

During this study, Scott computed multiplication problems that required carrying ($28 \times 8 = ?$). The demonstration-alone was initially scheduled for him. On the second day of this condition, his performance on Set 1a problems rose to 100 percent. By the fourth day of this condition, he obtained this level of performance on Set 1b problems also. Again, within-class generalization occurred, but not as dramatically as in the other experiments.

Jon worked on three-digit subtraction problems that had two zeros in the minuend ($700 - 376 = ?$). His performance indicated within-class generalization. During both the baseline and feedback conditions, Jon's scores were zero percent for both Sets 1a and 1b problems. During the Permanent-Model Condition, he attained and maintained mastery for both sets.

Across-Class Generalization

In addition to within-class generalization, the experimenters wished to investigate whether or not learning one type of problem would transfer to another set of similar problems. The Set 2 problems were designed for this purpose. In some cases an additional set, Set 3, was included to test for further generalizations; this set could be considered an expansion of Set 2. Again, discussion is by study.

Study 1: Demonstration-plus-Permanent-Model

Jon received an expanded version of his Set 1 problems, but this occurred midway through the experiment. During the latter part of the demonstration-plus-permanent-model, Set 2 problems were included in his daily package. At this time, Jon received scores above 70 percent on problems that required borrowing with one zero ($340 - 127 = ?$). During this condition, on the three days that he received problems that required borrowing with two zeros ($700 - 346 = ?$), he had scores of zero percent. His scores also remained at zero percent for the two additional conditions of the study; thus, no across-class generalizations occurred.

During this study, Scott worked on multiplication problems in which the bottom numeral was a zero. His Set 2 problems were two-digit multiplication problems that did not require carrying ($12 \times 21 = ?$). Throughout this study, his scores remained at zero percent for these problems. Again, no across-class generalization was noted.

Both Richie and Roger were assigned two-digit noncarrying multiplication problems. Originally, their Set 2 problems were two-digit multiplication problems that required carrying ($67 \times 89 = ?$). After the study began, the experimenters concluded that this type of problem might not be an expanded version of Set 1; therefore, three-digit multiplication problems that did not require carrying were included. The children continued to work on the two-digit problems that required carrying (Set 3). They also worked on the three-digit noncarrying multiplication problems (Set 2).

Set 2 problems were assigned to Roger three days after the first intervention tactic, the demonstration-plus-permanent-model, had been applied. At that time, he indicated that he could compute three-digit noncarrying problems. His score on that day was 100 percent; thus, across class-generalization occurred. The boy's level of performance on Set 2 problems, however, did not remain at 100 percent. His median score during this phase was 68 percent.

During the next condition, when instructions regarding careless errors were used for Set 1a, his performance on Set 2 problems did not change appreciably (median score of 67.5 percent). During the feedback condition, Roger's performance deteriorated on all of his pages; a type of across-class generalization was thereby indicated (median score of 33 percent). During the loss-of-shop-time condition, the boy's performance improved for Set 2 problems. Again, across-class generalization had occurred.

Roger remained at zero percent during the first and second conditions on the Set 3 problems. This indicated no across-class generalization. During the loss-of-shop-time condition, Roger attained three scores above zero percent. On the third and fourth days of this condition, Roger received 100 percent on these problems. He then dropped back to zero percent. On the sixth day, he attained a 50 percent score. For the remainder of the phase, however, he did not compute those problems correctly.

Richie received the Set 2 problems on the second day of the intervention phase. At this time, he could compute three-digit noncarrying multiplication problems accurately. He obtained a median score of 100 percent during this condition, which indicated across-class generalization. During the maintenance phase, his performance deteriorated, as it did for Sets 1a and 1b problems. Though not desirable in this instance, across-class generalization occurred once again. During the Demonstration-plus-Permanent-Model and Maintenance Conditions, Richie remained at zero percent for Set 3, which indicated that no across-class generalization occurred for those problems.

Study 2: Replication of the Demonstration-and-Permanent-Model

During this study, two children received the same type of problem. Their Set 1 problems were three-digit subtraction problems that had a two-digit answer ($148 - 134 = ?$). These children received two expanded versions of this type of problem. Set 2 was composed of four-digit non-borrowing problems that yielded a three-digit answer ($3,567 - 3,243 = ?$). Set 3 was also composed of four-digit nonborrowing subtraction problems, but in this case the thousands and hundreds columns had the same numerals ($3,578 - 3,522 = ?$). This type of problem, therefore, had a two-digit answer.

For Billy, Set 2 problems were scheduled during the last two days of the feedback condition (see Figure 4-26). At this time, he computed

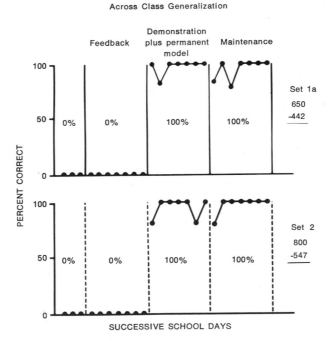

Figure 4-26 *Percentage-correct data for Sets 1 and 2 problems for Study 1. Billy's across-class generalization data.*

these problems incorrectly. When the children were shown how to compute Set 1a problems and were given a permanent model as a referent, Billy also improved his accuracy on Set 2 problems (a median of 100 percent). He maintained that level of performance throughout the study. Set 3 problems were introduced on the second day of the Demonstration-plus-Permanent-Model Condition. He attained a score of 100 percent on that day and the remaining days of the study, and, thus, across-class generalization occurred. Kenny's data were almost identical to those of Billy. Across-class generalization occurred for both Sets 2 and 3 problems. These were the same as those described for Richie and Roger. During the Demonstration-plus-Permanent-Model Condition, Scott's performance on Set 2 problems improved. He improved from zero percent in the prior condition to a median score of 50 percent during the intervention condition. During the maintenance condition, Scott continued to improve (a median of 78 percent). Though some across-class generalization was noted for the Set 2 problems, none occurred for the Set 3 problems. Scott's scores on the latter problems remained at zero percent throughout the study.

In Billy's second experiment in this study, Set 2 and 3 problems were also arranged. In this case, Billy worked on subtraction problems that required borrowing with one zero. His Set 2 problems, therefore, contained two zeros from which to borrow ($800 - 345 = ?$), and Set 3 problems contained three zeros ($5,000 - 3,467 = ?$). Across-class generalization occurred for both sets during the study.

Study 3: Component Analysis of Demonstration-and-Permanent-Model

During this study, Jon worked on subtraction problems that contained two zeros ($500 - 346 = ?$). Set 2 problems required borrowing from three zeros ($5,000 - 3,672 = ?$). Although Jon's performance improved for both Sets 1a and 1b, generalization across class was not noted. His performance on Set 2 problems remained at zero percent.

Samuel computed two-digit subtraction problems that required borrowing ($36 - 18 = ?$). His Set 2 problems were three-digit subtraction problems that required borrowing in the units column. Samuel was also given Set 3 problems. These were subtraction problems in which the minuend was a two-digit figure, the subtrahend was a single digit, the remainder was also two digits, and borrowing was required ($34 - 9 = ?$). Samuel's median baseline performance on Set 3 problems was 50 percent, rather than the zero percent of the Sets 1 and 2 problems. The permanent-model-alone proved to be an ineffective tactic for Samuel. His scores for all of the Sets 1 and 2 pages were zero percent (the median score for Set 3 was 56 percent). The Demonstration Condition was then scheduled. During this condition, Samuel achieved mastery on Set 1 problems. He did not generalize his learning to Set 2 problems. He did, however, generalize to Set 3 problems, attaining a median score of 100 percent.

Kenny did not show any across-class generalization during the course of this experiment. His Set 2 problems were three-digit noncarrying multiplication problems. Although his performance improved to mastery level for Set 1a problems, his performance on Sets 2 and 3 problems remained at zero percent.

Discussion of Within- and Across-Class Generalization

Within-class generalization was more apparent than across-class generalization. Of the fourteen experiments conducted during this research, within-class generalization was achieved in each experiment.

In Study 3, some generalization data not apparent in the percent scores should be noted. During the Permanent-Model Condition, Samuel moved progressively toward the appropriate procedures to use in order to solve Set 1a problems. These were two-digit problems that required borrowing in the units column. The permanent model included all the slash-marks, number reductions, and additions necessary to solve the problem ($\overset{21}{\cancel{3}6} - 18 = 18$). Throughout this condition, Samuel began to use these notations properly. Despite this, his answers were incorrect. When Samuel computed the Set 1b problems, he did not use these notations. In other words, he generalized the solution but not the process. Regardless, the percent data indicated that within-class generalization occurred in all fourteen experiments.

Twelve experiments were conducted which monitored across-class generalization. Of the twelve, across-class generalization occurred seven times for Set 2 problems. Only eight experiments used Set 3 problems. Of those eight, across-class generalization occurred three times. There are some important points about across-class generalization that should be mentioned. It might be that some children never generalize across classes. Jon, for example, never did so successfully: although he was taught to borrow with one zero, he had to be taught to borrow with two zeros. After that type of problem was taught, additional teaching was required for Jon to correctly solve a subtraction problem with three zeros in the minuend.

None of the children were able to generalize across classes perfectly in the multiplication problems. None of the children who received the two-digit-carry problems (to test for across-class generalization) were able to compute these problems accurately without some sort of experimental intervention. It is possible that these problems were not similar enough to Set 1 problems for this to occur.

In Set 2 three-digit noncarrying multiplication problems, across-class generalization occurred for some of the children. Scott, during Study 1, did not generalize across class when his Set 2 problems were two-digit noncarrying multiplication problems. When this type of problem later composed the Set 1 problems, he generalized to the new Set 2 (three-digit noncarry multiplication problems). Richie and Rodney, during Study 1, generalized to Set 2 problems in a manner similar to Scott. When presented with the same sets as the three children, Kenny did not generalize.

DISCUSSION

This research comprised three studies. Each study contained several experiments. In the first study, six individual experiments were conducted. The demonstration-plus-permanent-model served as the intervention tactic. This technique effected appreciable change for all of the children's arithmetic performance. When the intervention was applied, all the children's scores increased to a median level of 90 percent or better. Some of the children required additional interventions to achieve mastery (three consecutive days of 100 percent). Although additional interventions were scheduled for three of the children, the demonstration-plus-permanent-model should be considered an effective tactic.

Study 2 was a replication of the first study. In each of the experiments conducted in this study, the demonstration-plus-permanent-model influenced the children's performance positively (a median of 100 percent). The children retained this high level of performance throughout the maintenance and weekly post-test situations. Once again, the effectiveness of this technique was demonstrated.

Study 3 was a component analysis of the demonstration-plus-permanent-model technique. In this study, the demonstration was separated from the permanent model. Not all the children required the entire demonstration-plus-permanent-model technique. For one child, the permanent model alone was sufficient to achieve mastery. The others required the demonstration alone. Since the demonstration-plus-permanent-model is inexpensive in terms of teacher time (it requires less than one minute), we recommend that the complete tactic be used.

It should be remembered that the children who participated in these studies needed to acquire new computational arithmetic skills. Their accuracy in certain computational arithmetic problems was zero. In such cases, the demonstration-plus-permanent-model technique is both effective and efficient.

This tactic also influenced positive changes for problems that did not receive the demonstration-plus-permanent-model technique. When learning occurred in the set of problems taught (Set 1a), it also occurred in the set of untaught problems that were of the same type (Set 1b). Within-class generalization occurred in all the experiments conducted.

Across-class generalization did not occur as consistently as within-class generalization. In the six experiments when multiplication problems were presented, across-class generalization did not occur. It did occur in most of the experiments in which subtraction problems were used. Further research needs to be conducted to determine which factors impeded the occurrence of across-class generalization in multiplication problems.

The tactic used in this research is not new. Teachers have used chalkboards to give instruction for many years. They have used this aid to demonstrate the appropriate process to follow when computing different types of arithmetic problems. Often, they leave a permanent model on the chalkboard for the children to use as a referent. The present research demonstrated that when this traditional technique is applied in an individualized setting, children learn to compute the target type of problem.

Although modeling is a technique used often in education, most of the research on this topic has been conducted in nonacademic situations. Bandura (1965) stated that for response acquisition, modeling is exceedingly efficient and should be considered no-trial learning. This is supported by the research included in this report. In all cases when the demonstration-plus-permanent-model technique was applied, computational behavior changed immediately and remained at a high level of performance.

The demonstration-plus-permanent-model technique could easily be adapted to other curriculum areas that necessitate written responses. Handwriting and spelling, for example, might be targets for further research that investigates the efficacy of this tactic. The permanent model used as a referent for the child would be difficult to apply to curriculum areas that require a verbal response. In such cases, the demonstration alone might be a more appropriate intervention.

The long-range purpose of this research is to determine which instructional technique is most suitable for each stage of arithmetic instruction—acquisition, proficiency, maintenance. This information should benefit all arithmetic teachers; for if a teacher's repertory of arithmetic instruction techniques is varied, and if she is able to discriminate the stages of arithmetic development and subsequently arrange an appropriate technique for each, more children will be aided more efficiently to become better mathematicians.

20 / The Effects of Performance Contingencies on the Assignment Completion Behavior of Severely Delinquent Youths

V. William Harris • *Stephen R. Finfrock*
David K. Giles • *Betty M. Hart*
Phillip C. Tsosie

Modern criminology has deemphasized the threat and use of punishment as a means of controlling criminal behavior. At the same time, efforts have been made to rehabilitate the individual offender after he commits a crime. Rehabilitation for juvenile delinquents has generally taken the form of education or job-training programs. The assumption is that increasing legitimate forms of income-producing behavior may result in corresponding decrements in juvenile law breaking. Typical training schools for juveniles include a large-group, dormitory-style living arrangement and an assortment

This research was supported by Grant MH21853-02 from the National Institute of Mental Health (Center for Studies of Crime and Delinquency) to the Indian Development District of Arizona. Reprints may be obtained from V. William Harris, Director of Research, Southwest Indian Youth Center, 615 East Adams Street, Tucson, Arizona, 85705.

of schools and trade training facilities (Gibbons, 1970). Due to a concern regarding escapes from juvenile corrections facilities, training schools have been located in areas far removed from major community settings.

Recently, an interest in community-based juvenile corrections programs has developed due to the growing conviction that traditional training programs have been ineffective in altering juvenile delinquent behavior. One such community-based program is the Southwest Indian Youth Center. The Center uses small group residential homes (halfway houses) located in a large urban community, and are staffed by trained teaching-parents (Giles and Harris, 1972). Youths committed to this program have participated in community institutions such as public schools, junior college, vocational training centers, and private industry and business. Hence, the community-based corrections program for juveniles may differ notably from traditional approaches with respect to location in major urban communities, living arrangements for the youth, and training environments in which the young offender's deviant behavior is treated.

The community-based corrections program discussed above relies heavily on the principles of behavioral psychology. It is patterned after Achievement Place, an effective, well-documented, community-based program for predelinquent and dependent youths (Phillips, 1968; Bailey, Timbers, Phillips, and Wolf, 1971; Fixsen, Phillips, and Wolf, 1972; Phillips, Phillips, Fixsen, and Wolf, 1971; Wolf, Phillips, and Fixsen, 1972), and employs a token system in which points are given for appropriate behavior and removed for inappropriate behavior.

The ability of a community-based corrections program to effectively manage the behavior of the youth when the youth is not under the immediate supervision of the corrections staff is an important issue. Procedures for enhancing a behavior (assignment completion) important to a community institution (public schools) were investigated in the present study. The purpose of the present experiment was to establish a convenient, effective, home-based management technique to control public school classroom behavior of institutionalized delinquent youths.

METHOD

Subjects and Settings

Five American Indian male youths, ranging in age from 14 to 18, were the subjects. All five youths were chronic legal offenders committed by a federal, state, or tribal court to the Southwest Indian Youth Center. Each youth had recorded, on the average, four arrest convictions prior to entering the Youth Center. The offenses ranged from disorderly conduct, burglary, and theft to escape from a state penal institution. All of the youths had extensive histories of failure (for instance, poor grades, truancy, and suspension). Three of the five youths had dropped out of school programs prior to commitment at the Youth Center.

Each halfway house at the Center is staffed by two full-time houseparents who monitor four to seven youths, sixteen hours a day. During the remaining eight hours of the day, the youths attend public school, junior college, a corrections facility GED (high school) training classroom, or on-the-job training programs. A point system is an integral part of the family-style living arrangement in each halfway house. Points are earned daily for appropriate or constructive behaviors such as getting up on time, making the bus to school or work, daily and weekly house maintenance jobs, and appropriate social behavior. Points are removed for inappropriate behaviors such as not getting up on time, not completing assigned tasks, and threatening verbal statements. Points are exchanged for privileges such as use of the phone and television, snacks, recreation events, unsupervised leisure time, and bonds. The bonds are accumulated and used to advance through various program levels and, ultimately, to gain release from the corrections facility.

An important feature of the corrections program is encouraging participation in educational and vocational opportunities available to the trainees. Each trainee has the choice of enrolling in a public school or a GED educational program sponsored and staffed by the corrections program. After graduating from high school or passing the GED examination, trainees have the option of employment in private industry or enrollment in a local junior college.

The five youths involved in the present experiment all chose to enroll in public school. They were placed in a predominately white high school located in an upper-middle-class neighborhood. The five youths carried a normal course load including mathematics, history, English, art, welding, and physical education. To promote and maintain regular attendance and punctuality, the five students received a small daily monetary reward for attending all classes on time. Unexcused absences and tardiness resulted in monetary fines. In addition, youths were rewarded for superior quiz and test performances completed in the classroom.

Behavioral Measures and Reliability of Recording

Assignment completion behavior was measured daily for each of the five youths in all high school classes. Each day, teachers checked a form indicating whether or not an in-class or homework assignment had been completed. Teachers were asked to record on the forms only those assignments recorded in the teacher's grade books. Frequent checks comparing assignments recorded on the forms with assignments recorded in the grade books indicated that this request was followed. On the last day of each school week these forms were collected by the research staff, and the percentage of assignments completed for each youth in the various classes was calculated. These data were communicated to the family houseparents, who provided social consequences to the youth contingent upon assignment completion. Occasionally, the assignments completed during a week by the youth were collected from the teacher in order to check agreement between the number of written assignments scored by the teacher and the number of written assignments turned in by the student. This comparison was made at least once for each class during each condition. The number of written assignments scored by the teacher almost always agreed with the number of written assignments turned in by the student.

In order to assess the assignment completion behavior of the youth as compared with normative classroom assignment completion performance, the percentage of assignments completed by all other youths (n = 279) in each classroom was calculated weekly from assignment completion information recorded in grade books by the teachers.

Procedure

Baseline

Assignment completion percentages for each of the five subjects and 279 control students (that is, all other youths attending the same classes as the five subjects) were computed on a weekly basis for four weeks. Halfway houseparents verbally encouraged assignment completion performance by the youths.

Assignment Completion Performance Contingencies

After four weeks, point contingencies for assignment completion were initiated. Each youth was instructed that he would receive a bonus of 300 points for completing all assignments in each class during the following week, but for each incomplete assignment he would lose 100 points. As described previously, these points were redeemable for such privileges as the opportunity to watch television, use the telephone, participate in recreation events, and engage in unsupervised leisure time. To secure all available privileges, youths were required to earn a minimum of 2,100 points per week. Significant point loss resulting from incomplete assignments adversely affected the youths' leisure activities and ultimate release from the program. The contingencies for assignment completion were announced weekly to each of the youths for four weeks. The same assignment completion information was collected for all students in the classrooms attended by the subjects.

RESULTS

Figure 4-27 shows the mean percentage of assignments completed by experimental and control groups during each week of the four-week baseline and treatment conditions. During the baseline, the experimental subjects completed a mean of only 37 percent of their assignments compared with a mean of 65 percent for control subjects. The introduction of performance contingencies for assignment completion was accompanied by an immediate improvement in assignment completion performance for the five youths. In the presence of point contingencies, assignment completion

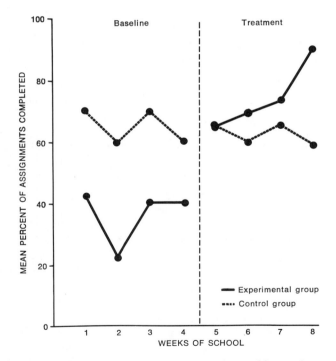

Figure 4-27 *Mean percentage of weekly assignments completed during baseline and treatment conditions for experimental and control groups.*

increased 40 percentage points to a mean of 77 percent for the five youths. In contrast, the assignment completion behavior of other youths declined from an average of 65 percent to 62 percent across the same period of time.

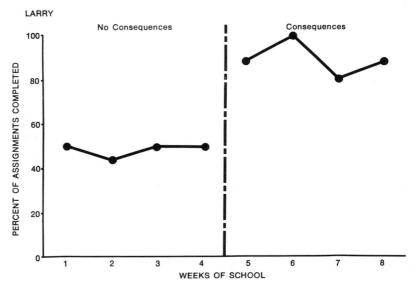

Figure 4-28 *Mean percentage of weekly assignments completed by one subject showing the median percentage point gain during baseline and treatment conditions.*

Figure 4-28 shows the percentage of assignments completed weekly by one experimental subject, who represents the median gain from baseline to treatment conditions. In the absence of point contingencies, he completed only 50 percent of all assignments; after the initiation of point contingencies, he completed 90 percent of all assignments.

Table 4-6 shows the mean percentage of assignments completed during baseline and treatment conditions in all classes for each of the five subjects. Assignment completion improved for each youth. Gains achieved by each subject ranged from 16 to 66 percentage points. During baseline, only two subjects completed at least half of their assignments, whereas four of the five youth completed at least 70 percent of their assignments after the introduction of performance contingencies.

The contingencies for assignment completion, first implemented near the beginning of the school semester, effectively maintained improved assignment completion performance for the duration of the academic semester. Figure 4-29 shows the mean grade-point averages for the five youths during the last complete semester immediately preceding contingencies for

Table 4-6 *Mean Percentage of Assignments Completed During Baseline and Treatment Conditions by Each of the Five Subjects*

SUBJECTS	MEAN PERCENT: BASELINE	MEAN PERCENT: TREATMENT	PERCENTAGE POINT GAIN
1	18.2	45.5	37.3
2	50.0	90.0	40.0
3	56.0	71.9	15.9
4	20.0	85.7	65.7
5	42.9	92.9	50.0

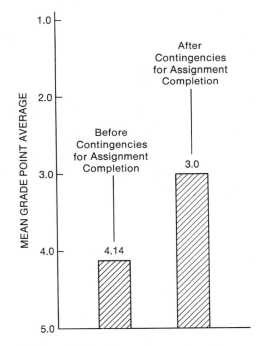

Figure 4-29 *Semester grade-point averages of experimental group prior to and following treatment; 1.0 = A, 5.0 = F.*

assignment completion and during the semester in which contingencies for assignment completion were employed. The grade-point system ranged from 1.0 = A (excellent) to 5.0 = F (failing). Before contingencies for assignment completion were initiated, students averaged 4.14 (D—) on their semester course grades, compared with a mean grade-point average of 3.00 (C) following the initiation of assignment completion contingencies. Hence, an improvement of one full letter grade was correlated with improved assignment completion for the five youths.

DISCUSSION

The present study examined the effects of performance contingencies on the assignment completion behavior of institutionalized delinquent youths in a public high school. The contingent application of points, exchangeable for a variety of reinforcers, dramatically increased the youths' performance in completing assigned classroom work. A comparison of the institutionalized youths with all other youths attending the same high school classes suggested that the enhanced assignment completion performance was a function of the performance contingencies employed.

The movement toward community-based corrections programs represents a major trend in juvenile rehabilitation practices. One advantage of such a movement is the savings realized by corrections facilities if they use existing community institutions as treatment environments. However, the extent to which corrections programs may use community environments for rehabilitation may be a function of their ability to effectively control ward behaviors that are appropriate to the various community institutions. Hence, the investigation of procedures that effectively control such behaviors becomes a major concern of community-based corrections programs utilizing community institutions as training environments.

part 5 | Research
with Children as
Behavioral Engineers

21 / Elementary School Children as Behavioral Engineers

T. F. McLaughlin · J. E. Malaby

Children in a classroom can fulfill many of the roles reserved normally for adults, such as observers, proctors, and experimenters. This experiment investigated some ways in which young children can be effective behavioral engineers. Four ways in which students offered their services in the classroom were: (1) as self-observers for routine data collection, (2) as observers of specified target behaviors such as inappropriate verbalizations or thumb sucking, (3) as proctors in a Keller-type individualized instruction

The authors wish to thank Warren C. Cook, Principal, Columbia Elementary School, for his support of this research during the past two years. They also wish to thank Joe Ferguson, who was the student experimenter, and Miss Anita Hotchkiss and Miss Theresa Foresman, student observers. Reprints may be obtained from either Thomas McLaughlin, Spokane School District #81, W825 Trent, Spokane, Washington, 99201; or John E. Malaby, Department of Psychology, Eastern Washington State College, Cheney, Washington, 99004.

program, and (4) as experimenters who actually design and conduct simple behavioral control experiments. Each of these are discussed in turn.

METHODS AND RESULTS

Pupils as Routine Data Collectors

We have reported (McLaughlin and Malaby, 1971, 1972a) a token-economy system for the control of a wide variety of classroom behaviors, with special emphasis on homework completion. The management of the token economy involves the recording of points earned for desirable behaviors and points lost for undesirable behaviors. In our system the teacher records the data for research purposes, but the pupils also keep complete records of the points that they have earned or lost. There are two reasons for having pupils do this. First, it provides the pupil with constant and immediate feedback concerning his performance, along with all the attendant reinforcement that feedback may provide. Second, the pupil may then compute all the transactions necessary in the exchange of points for the various privileges that we use as backup reinforcers, without adding to the work of the teacher.

In this experiment the contingency for inaccurate record keeping was a large point loss, and the teacher kept parallel data. As a result, we found that sixth-grade students kept accurate records. Furthermore, we have reported (McLaughlin and Malaby, 1971) that various features of the recording system may be improved by giving bonus points for correct recordkeeping.

The use of pupils was originally prompted by the need to reduce an unassisted teacher's work in the token economy. The effective performance of the peoples stimulated further ideas as to how they might be employed as behavioral engineers. We shall describe some of the other uses below.

School Children as Observers

We have reported twice (McLaughlin and Malaby, 1971, 1972b) on the use of sixth-grade pupils to record inappropriate verbalizations. On one occasion, two sixth-grade girls observed and recorded inappropriate verbalizations made by a class in the presence of two different teachers. The reliability of their observations is shown in Figure 5-1. The two girls obtained about 93 percent interobserver agreement, with a low (on only one occasion) of 85 percent agreement. The data they collected are shown in Figure 5-2.

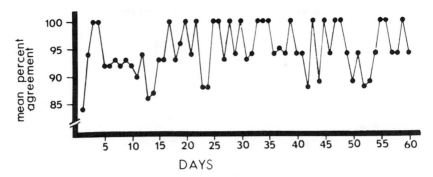

Figure 5-1   *Mean percentage of agreement between two sixth-grade pupils who were recording inappropriate verbalizations.*

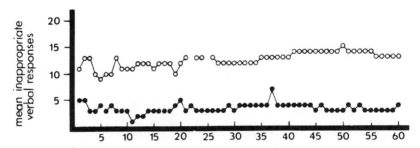

Figure 5-2   *Mean inappropriate verbalizations in the presence of a teacher who used traditional control techniques (open circles) and a teacher who managed the class with a token economy (closed circles).*

These data provided important information about classroom behavior in two different situations. In comparison with a teacher who managed the classroom with a token economy, approximately twice as many inappropriate verbalizations occurred in the presence of a teacher who used traditional classroom control techniques.

On a second occasion, three sixth-grade girls were employed to record inappropriate verbalizations while various contingencies were manipulated. Table 5-1 shows that the pupils were again capable of recording reliably. Interobserver agreement was not as high as that reported in Figure 5-1, but it was high enough to insure accurate measures. The data that the girls collected in this instance showed that when points were given to the pupils while they were studying, the number of inappropriate verbalizations decreased (see Figure 5-3). When points were not given for studying, and,

Table 5-1 *The Percentage of Observer Agreement for each Experimental Condition.*

	EXPERIMENTAL CONDITIONS		
OBSERVERS	Study Points	No Study Points	Study Points 2
O_1 x O_2	60	87	72
O_2 x O_3	64	91	67
O_1 x O_3	60	92	62

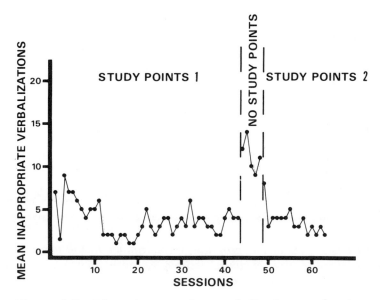

Figure 5-3 *Mean inappropriate verbalizations under two experimental conditions: bonus points for studying, and point loss for inappropriate verbalization.*

instead, fines were levied following inappropriate verbalizations, the number of inappropriate verbalizations increased.

Training

We have found that sixth-grade pupils need no more training, either qualitative or quantitative, than do college students or other adults. In both of the studies quoted above, the pupils were given the written definition of inappropriate verbalizations that was used by O'Leary and Becker (1967). After reading the definition, the pupils were shown specific examples by the

teacher. The pupils were then allowed to practice recording the target behaviors until they achieved agreement. Each pupil observed without knowledge of how the other observer was recording. In the first study, four days
of such practice were needed; in the second study, five days. Plans were
made in both cases to reexplain the definition if the observers failed to reach
agreement, but this never happened.

Sixth-grade pupils have also observed a preschool child who sucked
his thumb. The observers signaled the teacher when the preschooler was not
sucking his thumb so that the teacher could reinforce this "other" behavior.
This was the same procedure used by Hall, Lund, and Jackson (1968), who
employed specialized personnel. Using only sixth-grade pupils, however, we
obtained the same results as Hall, Lund, and Jackson. Figure 5–4 shows the

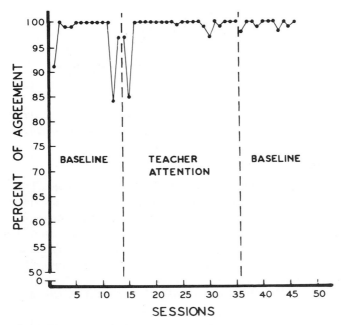

Figure 5-4 *Percentage of observer agreement for two sixth-grade
pupils who recorded thumb sucking by a preschool child.*

interobserver agreement. Again, the observers attained approximately 90
percent agreement. Figure 5-5 shows the data recorded by the pupils in this
study. Although our procedure is simple, we feel that many teachers may
fail to use behavioral techniques in their classrooms because they believe
that trained specialists are required.

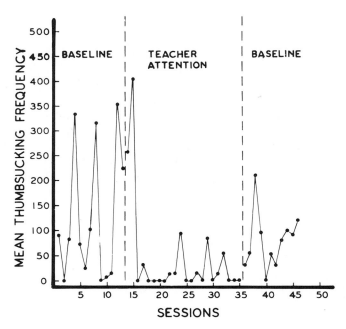

Figure 5-5 *Mean thumb-sucking in a preschool child under conditions of no teacher attention and teacher attention for thumb-sucking.*

Keller's Individualized Instruction Program

A third way that we have employed pupils is as proctors in a self-tutoring system based on Keller's (1968) procedures. In this system, pupils proctor one another; they give and score tests for one another; and they record grades in the teacher's grade book. Two of the three times that we have used this system, course material was divided into units by the teacher. On the third occasion, commercial materials already divided into units were used.

The procedure involved a pupil going to a central desk where he took an assignment sheet. This sheet assigned the source in the text book and also contained various study questions. For the first assignment, the pupil could obtain help from the teacher. For the remaining assignments, he obtained whatever help he needed from other pupils. The teacher, of course, was available, but only when student proctors could not help. The proctor always had access to an answer key that included the textbook page numbers of the answers. Occasionally, the teacher scored both study questions and quizzes to check reliability. Teacher and pupils agreed in their scoring over 90 percent of the time.

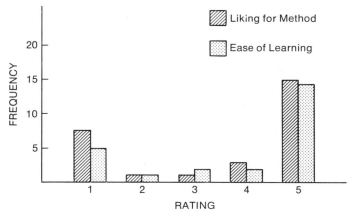

Figure 5-6 *Student rating of Keller plan on a scale ranging from 1 (poor) to 5 (good) for two selected items: "Rate the method in comparison with other methods you have encountered," and "Rate the method in terms of ease of learning."*

Figure 5-6 shows how "satisfying" the procedure was, and how easy it was to learn under such a system. The frequency distribution was bimodal, but most students liked the system and found learning easier. The procedure appears to be as effective for sixth-grade pupils as it is for college students.

The procedure of making the receipt of an assignment contingent upon completing the preceding assignment and completing a quiz with 100 percent mastery is reflected in the grade distribution (see Figure 5-7). When this contingency was in effect, there was an increase in the number of As and Bs and a decrease in the number of Cs and Ds relative to the procedure in which a pupil could receive an assignment after completing the preceding one, whether or not it was 100 percent correct. Also, one may note in Figure 5-8 that for at least some of the pupils, the rate of assignment completion increased.

Pupils as Experimenters

Sixth-grade pupils are capable of a more creative role in behavioral research than in the examples we have described thus far. We found that a pupil who knows a few behavioral principles may be able to put them to use.

The senior author of this report regularly teaches a unit in operant conditioning as a portion of the science curriculum. Pupils learn observation

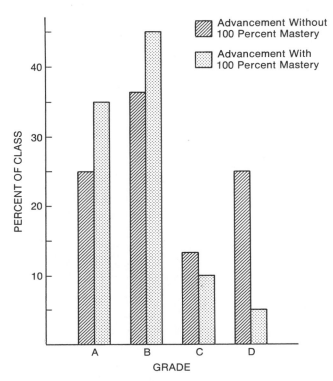

Figure 5-7 *Grade distributions obtained under conditions in which a pupil could advance to a new assignment without 100 percent mastery, and under conditions in which a pupil had to complete an assignment with 100 percent mastery before advancing.*

and data recording techniques, fundamentals of reinforcement, shaping, extinction, schedules of reinforcement, and discrimination training. In the following instance, one pupil was given the opportunity to apply these principles.

A sixth-grade boy was observed to be extremely untidy. Litter of all types could always be found around his desk. The senior author asked one of the untidy pupil's classmates to design and verify a procedure that would eliminate the littering. First, the young experimenter conducted a baseline observation to determine the rate of littering. He then awarded points for nonlittering. Next, points were given whenever litter was present. Finally, points were given again when no litter was present. The experimenter collected the data, which are shown in Figure 5-9. Reliability checks were made on thirty occasions, and agreement was found to be 100 percent.

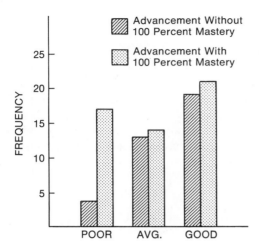

Figure 5-8   *Assignment completion for a poor student, an average student, and a good student under conditions in which a pupil could advance to a new assignment without 100 percent mastery, and under conditions in which a pupil had to complete an assignment at 100 percent mastery before advancing.*

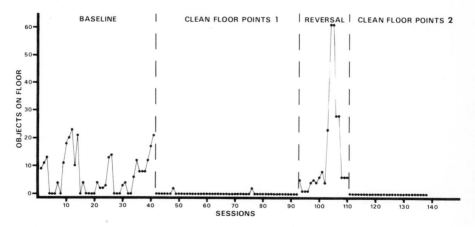

Figure 5-9   *The number of litter objects on the floor, under two experimental conditions: in one, the pupil earned points for having a clean floor; in the other, he earned points for having litter on the floor.*

DISCUSSION

Young pupils can participate in classroom modification programs in a sophisticated and effective manner. They can maintain records, observe and record reliabily, tutor one another, and, under some circumstances, design and conduct experiments. All teachers have these potential behavioral engineers at their disposal, and may readily use them to attempt behavioral studies that the teacher may previously have considered beyond his ability.

22 / The Modification of a Peer-Observer's Classroom Behavior as a Function of His Serving as a Reinforcing Agent

Lawrence J. Siegel · Warren M. Steinman

The successful application of modeling techniques to the modification of behavior has been demonstrated in several studies. One area that has attracted much research attention is "vicarious reinforcement" (cf. Flanders, 1968; Bandura, 1971; Gewirtz, 1971). "Vicarious reinforcement" refers to the increased behavior of an observer that results from his observation of a model being directly reinforced for comparable behavior (Flanders, 1968). Presumably, the observer's behavior becomes more or less probable, depending upon whether the consequences delivered to the model for performing the behavior are positive or negative.

This investigation was supported in part by United States Public Health Service Training Grant MH 05089. The authors express their appreciation to the staff at Herman N. Adler Zone Center for their assistance in the conducting of this research. We also wish to thank Kathy Bromley and Howard Mumm for serving as observers throughout the study.

Very few studies have investigated the utility of vicarious reinforcement procedures in applied settings (two that have are Carnine, Becker, Thomas, Poe, and Plager, 1968; and Broden, Bruce, Mitchell, Carter, and Hall, 1970). Carnine et al. (1968) studied the effect of reinforcing appropriate behavior in one group of children on the classroom behavior of a second group of children, who observed the behavior and consequences of the first group. Though the observing group increased their appropriate classroom behavior and decreased their disruptive behavior, the changes were weak and short-lived. A similar finding was reported by Broden et al. (1970). Vicarious reinforcement procedures produced stable, but modest, changes in classroom behavior, and were not nearly as effective as direct reinforcement for the same behaviors. The present study also investigated vicarious reinforcement procedures in a classroom setting. However, instead of examining vicarious reinforcement effects on children who simply observed a model being reinforced, we examined the effects on the behavior of a peer modifier.

Any child who observes and provides consequences for another child's behavior is involved in an essentially vicarious reinforcement procedure, since the conditions for vicarious reinforcement procedures are (1) that the observing peer sees the behavior, and (2) that he sees the consequences of the behavior. If the observing peer is effective in changing the behavior of the target peer, one should find changes in the behavior of the observing peer.

A number of studies have investigated the efficacy of using children as behavioral engineers for peers (Winnet, Richards, Krasner, and Krasner, 1971; Staats, Minke, Goodwin, and Landeen, 1967). In addition, the present study investigated the effects of having the child simply observe another child when reinforcing consequences are provided, relative to having him both observe and administer the reinforcement himself (Phillips, 1968; Surratt, Ulrich, and Hawkins, 1969). Just as it has been shown that peers can maintain inappropriate behavior in another child (Buehler, Patterson, and Furness, 1966), it has been shown that peers can be trained to function as effective behavior modifiers in the development of appropriate behavior.

Investigations of children as behavior modifiers for their peers have been concerned primarily with behavior change in the target child as a result of the consequences provided by the peer. The focus has been largely on the manpower issue—that is, the efficacy of using such agents as behavioral engineers and the efficiency and economy of using them in the natural environment. No attempt has been made to investigate possible beneficial changes in the modifier's behavior as a result of his controlling (and observing) contingencies for the target individual. It is possible that the same variables that produce change in the observer's behavior in studies of vicarious reinforcement may operate in the context of one peer acting as a reinforcing agent for a second peer. That is, by serving as a behavior modifier, the reinforcing peer is functioning in a manner that is procedurally similar to an observer in an investigation of vicarious reinforcement. If functioning as a behavior modifier produces beneficial changes in the modifier's behavior as well as in the target child's behavior, not only would the vicarious reinforcement literature be strengthened, but also the rationale for using peers as behavioral engineers in a variety of situations.

The present study investigated the changes in classroom behavior produced by having a child serve as a reinforcing agent for another child in the classroom. In addition, the study assessed the effects of having the child simply observe the second child receive reinforcing consequences, relative to having him both observe and administer the reinforcement.

METHOD

Subjects and Setting

Two ten-year-old boys in a residential treatment program for children with behavior problems participated in the study. The boys attended a special school for conduct-problem children provided by the institution. One class in their school day was used for the study. Five other children were also in the class.

The two subjects were chosen by the teacher because of the severity and similarity of their behavior problems in the classroom. Several days prior to the baseline observations, the subjects were assigned adjacent desks in the classroom. The desk change was explained as the result of the addition of a new child to the classroom.

Measurement Procedure

Subjects were observed on consecutive school days through a one-way mirror in the classroom. An intercom system permitted the observers to monitor all verbal behavior. Two undergraduate observers collected the data. Daily interobserver reliability was computed by dividing the number of intervals in which there was agreement between the observers by the total number of intervals observed, and multiplying by 100. Agreement between the observers for all three behaviors measured ranged from 84 percent to 95 percent, with a mean of 90 percent for the 35 days of observation.

Experimental sessions were scheduled during the same period of the day throughout the study (9:30–10:00 A.M.). The subjects were assigned individual seatwork. The lesson involved the use of a workbook in which reading comprehension and spelling were the main academic subjects. During the first 15 minutes (9:30–9:45) only the target child (the model) was observed. A time-sampling procedure was used in which behavior was observed for 10 seconds, followed by 5 seconds of recording. Both subjects were observed, on an alternating basis, during the final 15 minutes (9:45–10:00) of each session: one child was observed for 10 seconds, followed by 5 seconds of recording; then, during the next 15 seconds, the second child's behavior was observed and recorded. To minimize observer bias, the observers were not told the nature of the experiment until it was completed; instead, they were told that this was a study to see if a peer could accurately record and reinforce another child's behavior.

To maintain consistency in the teacher's behavior, she was instructed not to initiate contact with the children, though she did respond to the children if they initiated the contact (for instance by raising a hand). The teacher initiated no contacts with the subjects in most of the observational sessions, and did so no more than twice in any one of the several phases of the study.

Experimental Design and Behaviors Observed

A multiple-baseline procedure was used in which three classes of behavior were measured concurrently for each child. This technique involved the sequential application of experimental procedures to one behavior at a time, and continuous observation and recording of the frequencies of the manipulated and unmanipulated behaviors. The three behaviors were:

1. *On-task behavior:* The child was rated as being on-task when he was appropriately engaged in behavior relevant to the assigned academic activity— for instance, reading in the assigned book, writing on a work sheet, or looking at the teacher when she was presenting material. The child was required to be on-task for the entire 10-second interval of observation in order to be scored as being on-task for that interval.

2. *Independent behavior:* The child was rated as working independently when he was engaged in any constructive behavior in the classroom that did not involve interactions with the teacher or other children in the class. To be scored as independent behavior, these activities had to continue for the entire 10-second observation interval. It was possible for the child to be on-task but not engaged in independent behavior. For example, any assigned group activity or help from the teacher could satisfy the criteria for on-task behavior, but would not satisfy the criteria for independent behavior. Conversely, independent behavior could occur but not be scored as on-task behavior if it did not involve assigned material or classroom activities.

3. *Compliance:* To be scored as compliant, the child had to follow a request from the teacher within 15 seconds of the request. This behavior was

timed by the observers with an additional stopwatch. In each session, at least 3 and as many as 8 requests per 15 minutes were made of each child. The mean number of teacher requests was 5 per day for the 35 days of the study.

Experimental Conditions

Baseline

During the baseline condition (sessions 1–10), the frequency of the three behaviors was recorded for each child. Brad was selected to be the behavior modifier or "observer," and Jimmy was selected to be the target or "model." Jimmy was selected as the target subject because he exhibited a somewhat higher frequency of appropriate classroom behavior during the baseline condition and, therefore, would provide Brad with a greater opportunity to observe and reinforce appropriate classroom behavior.

Count Only

On the eleventh class day, the two children were told that they could participate in a project to help Jimmy with his classwork. Brad was told that his task was to record whether Jimmy was working on the lesson assigned by the teacher (that is, whether his behavior was in the "on-task" category). He was also told to record whether Jimmy was working independently on any activity (the "independence" category). The teacher helped Brad learn the criteria for the two scoring categories, and he was able to score the behaviors reliably. Jimmy was told to continue working on his classroom assignments as he had been doing previously.

Brad was provided with a small light box (5 by 4 by 3 inches) that was placed on the corner of his desk. An automatic timer in the box turned the light on for 5 seconds in each 15-second interval. Brad was given a recording sheet divided into columns representing on-task and independent behavior. When the light on the light box turned on, Brad was instructed to place an "X" in the appropriate column if Jimmy had been on-task or working independently for the entire 10 seconds preceding the light. If Jimmy had not engaged in these behaviors or had not engaged in them for a full 10 seconds, Brad placed a "O" in the appropriate column.

Brad recorded Jimmy's behavior only during the first 15 minutes of each session. At the beginning of the second 15 minutes of the class period, Brad was given his daily classroom assignments and was instructed by the teacher to begin his classwork. Jimmy continued to work on his assigned classwork during the second 15-minute period.

Brad was given points for accurately recording Jimmy's on-task and independent behavior. Points were exchanged for various backup reinforcers at the end of class. Brad's accuracy was computed by summing the number of intervals in which Brad's scoring of Jimmy's behavior agreed with the scoring of both undergraduate observers, and dividing by the number of intervals on which both undergraduate observers agreed. The accuracy with which Brad recorded Jimmy's on-task and independent behavior ranged between 74 percent and 84 percent for on-task and between 85 percent and 93 percent for independent work. Over the 23 days that Brad recorded Jimmy's on-task and independent behavior, there was no trend toward increased or decreased accuracy in Brad's agreement with the two other observers. Overall, Brad's accuracy varied around a mean of 85 percent.

Reinforcement Condition 1

The first reinforcement condition of the study began with session 16. Brad continued to record both on-task and independent behavior. He was instructed to place a plastic token in a container on Jimmy's desk each time he observed that Jimmy was on-task for a complete 10-second interval. (Independent behavior was not reinforced during this condition.) Brad continued to receive points for accuracy during this condition. Both the tokens and the points were traded for a variety of backup items after the session.

Reinforcement Condition 2

In the second reinforcement condition, Brad continued to deliver white tokens to Jimmy for his on-task behavior. In addition, he was now instructed to place a black token in a second container on Jimmy's desk each time he observed Jimmy to be working independently throughout a 10-second interval. Jimmy's compliance still was neither reinforced nor recorded by Brad.

Reinforcement Condition 3

In the third condition of the study, the teacher became a reinforcing agent. Brad continued to reinforce and record Jimmy's on-task and independent behaviors, as he had in the previous condition. However, Jimmy's third behavioral category, compliance, which never was recorded or reinforced by Brad, was now reinforced by the teacher. The teacher placed a yellow token in a third container on Jimmy's desk each time he complied with her requests within 15 seconds of the request.

Reinforcement Condition 4

In this condition, Brad and the teacher traded behaviors to reinforce. Brad continued to record and reinforce Jimmy for working independently, but instead of also recording and reinforcing his on-task behavior, Brad now recorded and reinforced Jimmy's compliance. The teacher reinforced Jimmy's on-task behavior, instead of reinforcing compliance.

Reversal of Peer Functions

In the final phase of the study, Brad and Jimmy exchanged functions. Jimmy became the reinforcing agent, and Brad became the recipient of reinforcement. Jimmy recorded Brad's on-task and independent behavior, and reinforced him with tokens for each 10-second interval in which Brad remained on-task or worked independently. Jimmy also received points for accurately recording Brad's on-task and independent behavior. Brad's compliance was neither recorded nor reinforced by Jimmy or the teacher.

RESULTS

Figure 5-10 summarizes Brad's on-task, independent, and compliant behavior for the 35 days of the study. Figure 5-11 provides a comparable summary of Jimmy's behavior. In the figures, dotted lines connect percentages observed in the first 15 minutes of each session. Solid lines connect behavior observed in the second 15 minutes.

Baseline

The number of 10-second intervals in which Brad was observed to be on-task varied around a mean of 45 percent for the 10 sessions of baseline. He was engaged in independent work during about 51 percent of the intervals, and he complied with teacher's requests on 56 percent of the opportunities to comply. Jimmy's behavior in these three categories was between 5 percent and 10 percent higher than Brad's for the same 10 sessions (with means of 50 percent, 60 percent, and 65 percent, respectively). Also, during baseline, there typically was little different in Jimmy's classroom behavior between the first and second 15 minutes of each session.

Count Only

Brad began recording Jimmy's on-task and independent behavior in session 11. During the 15 minutes in which Brad recorded these behaviors, Jimmy's on-task and independent work increased about 15 percent above the baseline means for these behaviors. However, in the second 15 minutes of each session, when Brad no longer recorded Jimmy's behavior and both

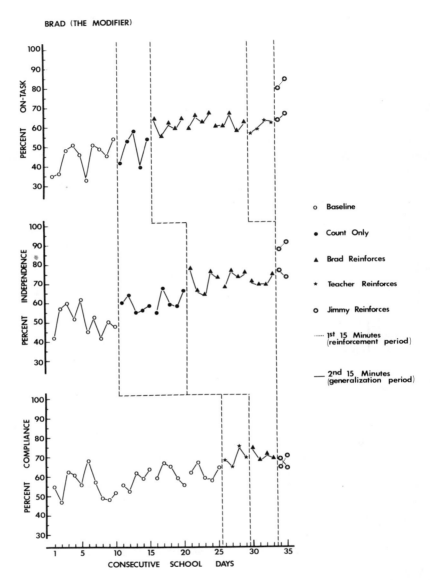

Figure 5-10 *Summary of on-task, independent, and compliant behaviors of the child serving as peer modifier (Brad).*

children worked on their classroom assignments, Jimmy's on-task and independent behaviors returned to their baseline percentages. Jimmy's compliance, which was not recorded by Brad, remained at baseline levels in both 15-minute segments.

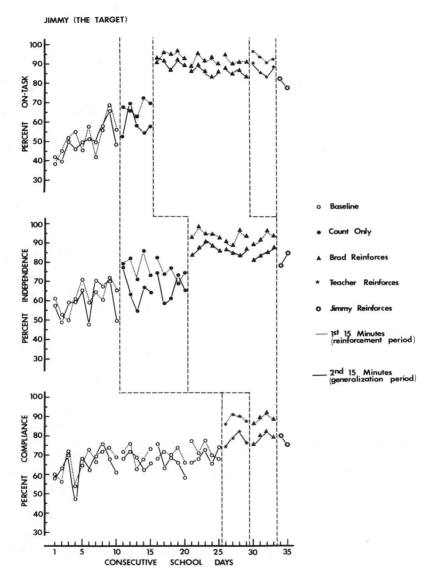

Figure 5-11   *Summary of on-task, independent, and compliant be-haviors of the target child (Jimmy).*

For Brad, the counting procedure in the first 15 minutes of each session had no noticeable effect on his on-task behavior in the second 15 minutes. However, his mean independent behavior did increase somewhat (8 percent) above his baseline mean. Brad's compliance was unaffected.

Reinforcement Condition 1

When Brad began to reinforce Jimmy's on-task behavior (starting with session 16), the number of intervals in which Jimmy remained on-task increased from a mean of 67 percent in the Count-Only condition to a mean of 94 percent. His on-task behavior was maintained at this high rate (90 percent) throughout the second 15 minutes, though it was no longer being reinforced with tokens. The recorded, but unreinforced, independent behavior remained at its previous level, as did the unmanipulated compliance behavior.

Brad's on-task behavior also was affected by this initial reinforcement procedure. When Brad delivered tokens to Jimmy for being on-task, his own on-task behavior increased from a mean of 49 percent in the Count-Only condition to a mean of 60 percent. Also, as with Jimmy, Brad's independent behavior and compliance did not change noticeably in this experimental condition.

Reinforcement Condition 2

In the second reinforcement condition (sessions 21 through 25), Brad reinforced Jimmy's independent behavior while continuing to reinforce him for being on-task. Jimmy's on-task behavior continued at its previous high rate when reinforced (91 percent), and, as before, was maintained at a slightly lower rate in the unreinforced second 15 minutes of each session (86 percent). Similarly, Jimmy's independent behavior increased immediately from a mean of 73 percent in the previous condition to a mean of 94 percent when Brad began to reinforce it, and the independent behavior was maintained at a somewhat lower rate (87 percent) in the unreinforced second 15 minutes of each session. Jimmy's compliance, which still was neither recorded nor reinforced by Brad, remained at baseline levels in both 15-minute segments of these sessions.

Brad's on-task behavior continued to show the modest increase developed in the first reinforcement condition. However, in addition, now that Brad was reinforcing Jimmy's independent behavior as well, Brad's independent behavior also increased from a mean of 61 percent in Condition 1 to a mean of 72 percent in Condition 2. Brad's compliance was unaffected.

Reinforcement Condition 3

In sessions 26 through 29, the teacher reinforced Jimmy for complying with her requests, while Brad continued to reinforce his on-task and independent behavior. Jimmy's on-task and independent behaviors continued at the rates established in the previous conditions. In addition, his compliance increased, during the 15-minute segments in which it was reinforced, from a mean of 73 percent in the preceding sessions to a mean of 88 percent. However, there was a relatively large reduction in his compliance (to a mean of 77 percent) in the second, unreinforced, 15-minute segments of these same sessions.

Brad also maintained his increased on-task and independent-work behavior. In addition, his compliance also showed a slight increase. Although Brad's increase in compliance was only about 9 percent higher than in the preceding conditions, that increase was the largest overall increase in Brad's compliance since the baseline condition. Also, the magnitude of Brad's increase in compliance was similar to the magnitude of Jimmy's increase in compliance within the same (second) 15 minutes of the session.

Reinforcement Condition 4

In the fourth reinforcement condition, Brad and the teacher traded behaviors to reinforce. Brad reinforced Jimmy's independent and complaint behavior and the teacher reinforced Jimmy's on-task behavior. These changes in reinforcing agents had little effect on Jimmy's behavior. The behaviors occurred at approximately the same rates as they had occurred previously. There also was little or no change in Brad's behavior.

Reversal of Peer Functions

In the final condition of the study, Brad became the recipient of reinforcement for his classroom behavior and Jimmy became the reinforcing agent. During the 15 minutes that Brad was reinforced for his on-task and independent behaviors, these behaviors increased markedly, but the unreinforced compliance remained unaffected. However, during the second 15 minutes of each session, when Brad's behavior was no longer recorded or reinforced, his on-task and independent behaviors dropped to the levels that had been attained in the preceding conditions, when Brad was the reinforcing agent rather than the recipient of reinforcement.

Jimmy's on-task and independent behaviors were maintained at a higher level than baseline, but occurred at a slightly lower frequency than they had in the comparable 15 minutes of the preceding conditions. His compliance was unaffected.

DISCUSSION

The results indicate that a reliable, but small, increase in appropriate classroom behavior can be achieved when a child functions as a reinforcing agent for the classroom behavior of another child. In other words, peers not only can function as effective observers and behavior modifiers of other children, they also may acquire beneficial behaviors themselves when they do so.

The data also indicate, however, that it may not be necessary for a peer to function as a reinforcing agent in order to attain the indirect gains found in the study. Although in each instance the gains attained were specific to the particular behaviors being reinforced at the time, it was not necessary for the peer himself to be the reinforcing agent for his behavior to be affected. Simply observing the teacher reinforce a particular behavior of the target child was sufficient to produce similar changes in the behavior of the observing child. These data are consistent with those of other classroom studies investigating vicarious reinforcement procedures, and they suggest that variables similar to those in operation in the vicarious reinforcement paradigm may also be operating when peer-reinforcement procedures are used. Obviously, the relationship among observational learning, vicarious reinforcement, and peer reinforcement procedures needs further clarification.

The generality of the effect is encouraging. Although the target child's classroom behavior was influenced most profoundly when the reinforcement operations were in effect, the gains achieved in the reinforcement segment of each session were maintained largely in the second segment of each session, when the reinforcement operations no longer were in effect. There was a decrease in appropriate behavior in the unreinforced segment, but the decrease stabilized at a level intermediate between the baseline level and the reinforced level. This was true both for the target child and for the peer modifier, and for all three behaviors manipulated.

The results also provide further support for the use of peers as behavior modifiers. Jimmy's appropriate classroom behavior increased markedly whenever he was directly reinforced for such behavior. It made little or no difference whether the agent dispensing the reinforcement was the teacher or his peer. Because both children were affected positively by the peer-reinforcement system, it would seem reasonable to suggest that peers might be used for this function whenever the special skills of the teacher might best be used otherwise—for example, to work with particular students on academic skills or to develop management plans. Peers could be enlisted to maintain a contingency system while the teacher is busy creating and modifying such systems.

23 | Five-Year-Olds as Behavioral Engineers for Younger Students in a Day-Care Center

Joetta Long · Charles H. Madsen, Jr.

Parents, students, and other paraprofessionals have successfully used behavioral techniques to increase appropriate behavior in young children (Zeilberger, Sampen, and Sloane, 1968; Holland, 1969). Students, both elementary and secondary, have also served as reinforcing agents for peers (Surratt, Ulrich, and Hawkins, 1969; Ulrich, Louisell, and Wolf, 1971; Wiesen, Hartley, Richardson, and Roske, 1967; and Drass and Jones, 1971). In fact peer reinforcement appears to be a major form of influence

This paper is a portion of a thesis submitted to the Florida State University in partial fulfillment of the requirements for a Masters degree in psychology. Sincere appreciation is expressed to the staff at the Early Child Care Educational Center, Tallahassee, Florida, and to the observers, Marcia Ziegler, Gary Barr, Ann Christianson, Cheryl Sudderth, Jim Whitaker, Tom Lease, Marta Cilone, and Dora Lagueruela. Of course, those who made this study possible were the reinforcing agents and those who were reinforced, whom we wish to thank for their cooperation.

on the social behavior of young children (Hartup, 1970). Peer influence appears to have maximum effects when the peer modifiers and students are of different ages (Ferguson, 1964). The results of using peers as reinforcing agents in a preschool day-care center frees teachers for important teaching functions. The object of this study was to determine whether or not preschool children could apply behavioral principles with young children in structured activities.

METHOD

Subjects

Four kindergarten children ranging in age from five years to five years, seven months served as reinforcing agents for four children ranging in age from three years, four months to three years, ten months. The children attended a private day-care center in Tallahassee, Florida, and according to teachers were performing at an average academic level. The three-year-olds were selected as subjects because they were reported by their teachers to have social repertoires below the level expected of peers whose ages were the same. The five-year-olds were chosen as behavioral engineers because they were reported by teachers to demonstrate adequate social adjustment. Three subjects were male and one was female; there were two male and two female peers.

Setting

The entire preschool class was divided into four small groups of eight to ten per group, and each group rotated from one activity to another every 15 minutes (Story, Snack, Art, and Circle periods). Subjects were observed in Story, Snack, and Art periods after their group had settled into each activity. Activities were conducted in different areas of a large room.

Observer Training

Seven adult observers (all undergraduates at Florida State University) were trained in systematic behavior observation and recording. Training involved (1) an observer's manual (Madsen and Madsen, 1974) covering appropriate observer conduct and operational definitions of sample behaviors to be observed (two hours), (2) lectures and discussions on observation techniques (eight hours), (3) practice in observing videotapes (two hours), and (4) actual observations of children at the day-care center (six hours). Throughout the training, feedback on techniques and results of observations were provided to the observers. Rehearsal observations were practiced until all observers achieved 80 percent reliability.

Observational Definitions

Specific inappropriate social behaviors were defined for each of the three observational periods:

1. *Inappropriate behaviors during story period:* included attending to stimuli other than the story for more than five seconds, gross motor movements (turning 90 degrees from the original position, touching another child or the storyteller, crawling, walking, extending arms straight out from body), inappropriate talking out, touching the book, and not responding to the teacher's questions.

2. *Inappropriate behaviors at snacktime:* included throwing, spilling, or stealing food, not eating, standing up, not putting wrappers in the proper place, not keeping hands under the table while food was served, having hands unfolded during grace, and putting food in hair or on clothing.

3. *Inappropriate behaviors during art:* included abusing art materials (throwing, spilling, or eating them), attending to stimuli other than the art project for more than five consecutive seconds, removing hands from lap during instructions, failing to scrape paintbrush before applying paint to paper, and failing to wash hands when finished.

In addition to the behaviors described above, the aggressive disturbance of others, tantrums, thumb and/or finger sucking, leaving the activity area, tipping benches, and screaming were considered inappropriate behaviors in any of the three periods.

Peer Approval

This consisted of (1) words (praise), (2) proximity of peer to subject, including touching affectionately, patting, taking hand, or kissing, (3) expressions such as smiling, and (4) things (M & M chocolate candies). Social reinforcement could occur at any time. However, M & M dispensing was restricted to one per bell interval (recorded on a cassette) for each child.

Peer Disapproval

This included (1) withholding things (M & Ms), (2) expressions (such as grimaces), or (3) words, including statements such as "You're not a responsible person," or "That's bad."

Recording

Observations were made for 10 consecutive minutes during storytime, snacktime, and art. Symbols representing each behavior were recorded if the behavior occurred in any 10-second interval. No symbol was recorded more than once per interval. Data recording sheets differed for the baseline and treatment conditions. During baseline, only the inappropriate behaviors of the subjects were recorded. During treatment, the observers recorded inappropriate behaviors, peer approvals or disapprovals of the child's behavior, and whether or not each such approval or disapproval was appropriate or inappropriate (that is, whether it was a mistake of reinforcement).

Each observer was equipped with a clipboard and pencil, sunglasses, and an earphone. An electronic timing device emitted a beep that observers received through earphones every 10 seconds as a cue for recording a behavior. A cassette tape recorder was used as a signal (bell) for the peer to record his subject's behavior. The recorder emitted the bell signal randomly at 20-, 40-, and 60-second intervals.

Experimental Conditions

Elements of both reversal and multiple-baseline designs were incorporated into the present experiment. A reversal design was replicated for each subject in each of the three periods. Baseline 1 was followed by Peer Reward 1 condition, and this was repeated, producing an ABAB design. Conditions were changed simultaneously for all subjects in the same activity period. These conditions, however, were not altered simultaneously in all periods. Peer Reward 1 condition was instituted in Story period on day 10, in Snack period on day 20, and in Art period on day 25. A reversal to baseline (Baseline 2) was begun in Story on day 25, in Snack on day 30, and in Art on day 35. Peer Reward 2 was instituted in Story on day 30, in Snack on day 35, and in Art on day 40. The staggering of conditions across activity periods (multiple baseline) was implemented in an attempt to assess generalization effects across activities (see Figure 5-12).

Training Peer Observers

Peer observers were trained in simple techniques of behavioral engineering during the Baseline 1 condition in Story (10 days). Informal discussions with peer observers emphasized appropriate and inappropriate school be-

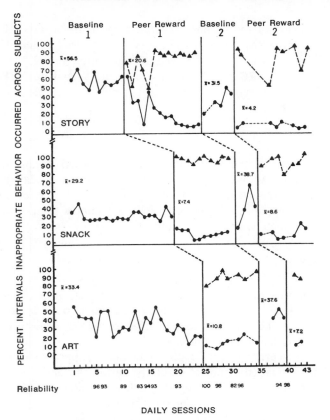

Figure 5-12 *Percentage of intervals in which inappropriate behavior occurred across four subjects, including peer reinforcement percentages (coefficients of consistency are indicated by triangles).*

haviors for three-year-olds. The children were asked questions such as "What should children be doing during storytime?" and were intermittently praised and given M & Ms for correct responses. The peer observers were also asked to observe a model and decide if the behavior modeled was appropriate or inappropriate. Pairs of children role-played classroom situations while peers observed and judged behaviors. Correct peer responses were reinforced. Ignoring inappropriate behavior and delivering reinforcers promptly were stressed throughout the training sessions, as were appropriate observing behaviors, following instructions, and volunteering for learning tasks.

After four days of training, peer observers were given modified data sheets and began recording like the "big" people. The data sheet was a large, simplified version of the baseline recording sheet. Each interval was large enough for a large "X" to be marked with a preschool pencil. Upon a verbal cue to "watch," each peer observed a child until a verbal "record" signal was given (usually 20 to 40 seconds after the verbal cue). Peers learned definitions through active involvement, prompting, and role playing.

Baseline 1

Inappropriate behaviors of the four subjects were recorded during Story, Snack, and Art periods. Additionally, a very short baseline (two days) was obtained on the peer observers to measure their average rate of social approval and disapproval as they interacted with a group of three-year-old children that did not include any of the subjects.

Peer Reward 1

Each peer observer was assigned a three-year-old subject. Peer observers were situated behind and to the side of their respective subjects so that they could plainly see their actions and facial expressions. However, the subjects could not see the observers directly.

The young observers, equipped with an adequate supply of M & Ms, were instructed to observe the subject carefully during the entire interval. When the bell rang, peer observers judged whether or not the subject had earned a reward for that interval. One occurrence of an inappropriate behavior during the interval constituted an "inappropriate" interval and no reward was given. If the interval was scored "appropriate," the peer observer placed an M & M directly in the child's mouth. Initially, peer observers were given occasional prompts as to when they should reward the subjects. This was done by the experimenter or an adult observer, and consisted of verbal cues. Each time the peer observer correctly rewarded or ignored the subject's behavior, he was in turn given feedback (reinforced) with a pat on the back by the adult observer.

Peer observers were also given one point for each interval in which they appropriately ignored or rewarded the subject. At the end of each experimental session, the points for each peer observer were totaled and recorded in a notebook; this provided a visual record of his performance. Each point was worth one M & M, distributed to the peers at the end of the daily session. If the peer consistently rewarded the appropriate student behavior, he could receive an average of 15 M & Ms per activity.

For each peer observer, a coefficient of consistency was calculated that indicated how closely the young behavioral engineer agreed with a highly trained adult observer. The coefficient of consistency was obtained by dividing the number of intervals in which the peer modifier appropriately rewarded or withheld reinforcement by the total number of reinforcement intervals available to the three-year-olds in the specific activity (usually about 15 to 20, depending on the activity and its length). When the co-efficient was 80 percent or better for five consecutive days, the peer modifier was taken shopping and could buy a small toy with his points.

Baseline 2

Peer rewards were removed and observations were continued under the same conditions as Baseline 1. Adult observers recorded subjects' inappropriate behavior.

Peer Reward 2

Peer observations and rewarding were consecutively reinstated within each activity. (The coefficient of consistency was again tabulated.)

Reliability

Reliability between two adult observers was calculated by dividing the number of agreements by the total number of agreements plus disagreements and multiplying by 100, when two observers recorded the same behavior simultaneously. An agreement was scored when both observers counted either an inappropriate or an appropriate interaction in the same 10-second interval. A disagreement was scored when both observers did not agree that the interval was either appropriate or inappropriate. Reliability averaged 93 percent, with a range of 82 percent to 100 percent across 14 days (see Figure 5-12).

A reward reliability was also measured by two adults who observed whether or not the peer gave or withheld his reward appropriately. This reliability was calculated on intervals that were defined as the total number of seconds from one bell to another (an average of 40 seconds) during which peer rewards were possible. This calculation was made by dividing the number of agreements by the total number of intervals and multiplying by 100. An agreement was scored if both observers agreed that the peer observer reacted to the subject's behavior in the same way. This reliability averaged 94 percent, with a range of 75 percent to 100 percent across 18

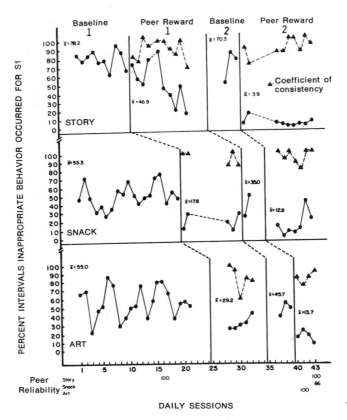

Figure 5-13 *Percentage of intervals in which inappropriate behavior occurred across three activities for subject 1, and percentage of contingent reinforcement by peer modifier 1 (coefficients of consistency).*

days. Daily percentages of reliability are shown on the bottom of individual subject's graphs (see Figures 5-13, 5-14, 5-15, and 5-16).

RESULTS

Group Results

Results indicate that peer rewards were effective in reducing inappropriate behavior in three-year-olds in three separate morning activities (see Figure 5-12).

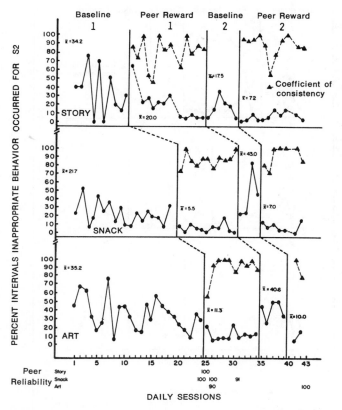

Figure 5-14 *Percentage of intervals in which inappropriate behavior occurred across three activities for subject 2, and percentage of contingent reinforcement by peer modifier 2 (coefficients of consistency).*

Baseline Inappropriate Behavior

Baseline performance across children was stable in both Story (an average of 56.5 percent inappropriate behaviors during 10 days) and Snack (average of 29.2 percent, 19 days) periods. In Art, however, the rate of inappropriate behavior trended downward beginning on day 18, when rewards were introduced during Storytime (average of 33.4 percent, 24 days).

Peer Reward 1

Rewards administered by peers decreased inappropriate behavior (Story average of 20.6 percent; Snack average of 7.4 percent; Art average of

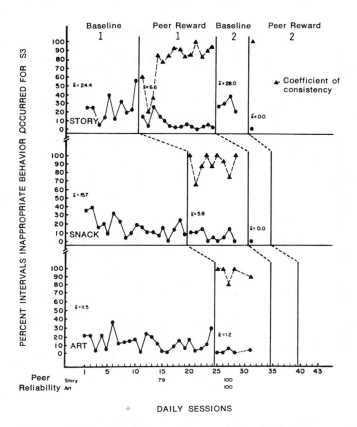

Figure 5-15 *Percentage of intervals in which inappropriate behavior occurred across three activities for subject 3, including percentage of contingent reinforcement by peer modifier 3 (coefficients of consistency).*

10.8 percent). The largest effect was demonstrated in Story, where behavior decreased from 62 percent on day 10 of Baseline 1 to 7 percent on the last day of Reward 1, though performance varied greatly the first week of Peer Reward 1 (see Table 5-2 and Figure 5-12).

Baseline 2

Average inappropriate behavior during Baseline 2 increased the first day in Story (13 percent) and continued to rise (average of 31.5 percent). The increase was not as high as the original level (47 percent at the end of Baseline 2, compared with 62 percent at the end of Baseline 1). Inappropriate behaviors also increased during Snack (average of 38.7 per-

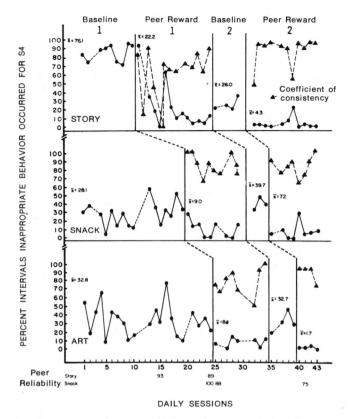

Figure 5-16 *Percentage of intervals in which inappropriate behavior occurred across three activities for subject 4, including percentage of contingent reinforcement by peer modifier 4 (also peer modifiers 1 and 3, since peer modifier 4 was dismissed).*

cent) and Art (average of 37.6 percent). In fact, behavior increased in Snack during Baseline 2 to 66 percent on day 33, 25 percent higher than in Baseline 1. Similarly, the group's behavior rose to its pre-experimental level in Art, beginning on day 35.

Peer Reward 2

With the reinstatement of peer rewards, inappropriate behavior decreased during all three activities (Story average of 4.2 percent; Snack average of 8.6 percent; Art average of 7.2 percent). There was also an apparent stability in this condition, compared with baselines. During Story, inappro-

Table 5-2 *Mean Percentages of Inappropriate Behavior Across Conditions*

| | CONDITION | | | |
SUBJECT	Baseline 1	Reward 1	Baseline 2	Reward 2
	STORY			
S1	78.2	46.9	70.3	3.9
S2	34.2	20.0	17.5	7.2
S3	24.4	6.6	28.0	0.0
S4	76.1	22.2	26.0	4.3
Group	56.5	20.6	31.5	4.2
	SNACK			
S1	53.3	17.8	35.0	12.9
S2	21.7	5.5	43.0	7.0
S3	15.7	5.8	0.0	—
S4	28.1	9.0	39.7	7.2
Group	29.2	7.4	38.7	8.6
	ART			
S1	55.0	29.2	45.7	13.7
S2	35.2	11.3	40.6	10.0
S3	11.5	1.2	—	—
S4	32.8	8.4	32.7	1.7
Group	33.4	10.8	37.6	7.2

priate behavior ranged from zero to 9 percent (13 days). During Snack, inappropriate behavior decreased from 40 percent (day 34) to 8 percent (day 35). Similarly, behavior decreased from 40 percent (day 39) to 7 percent (day 40) in art.

Generalization Across Activities

One aspect of generalization is an observed change in one activity corresponding to behavior manipulated experimentally in another. Inappropriate behavior gradually decreased in Art during Baseline 1 (day 21). Peer rewards had previously been introduced in Story, and were then introduced during Snack. Therefore, children were receiving contingent rewards in the two activities immediately preceding, and inappropriate behavior decreased in Art. However, inappropriate behavior trended slightly upward (beginning in Snack on day 25, and in Art on day 29) when rewards were removed in Storytime.

Peer Consistency

The degree to which peers were consistent in their reinforcement is represented by a daily coefficient of consistency that was calculated for each peer by using the following formula:

$$\frac{\text{number of appropriate peer responses}}{\text{total number of peer responses}} \times 100$$

Average consistency coefficents demonstrate an aspect of experimental control critical to the present study (triangles in Figures 5-12 through 5-16 represent average coefficients of consistency across activities). The mean accuracy ratio for peer I (the peer for S1 and occasionally for S4) was 86.24; 87.13 for peer 2 (peer for S2); 85.86 for peer 3 (peer for S3, and eventually S4); and 53.75 for peer 4 (peer for S4 across the first eight sessions).

Consistency coefficients indicate that there was a relationship between peer modifiers' degree of consistency and percentage of inappropriate student behavior. Similar trends in performance were evident for all four subjects, but there are individual differences.

Subject 1

Baseline performance in Story was fairly stable (78.2 percent average). Behavior was not affected by Peer Reward 1 until it dropped on day 17 (average of 46.9 percent). A 70 percent difference is evident comparing day 1 with day 21. Behavior increased during Baseline 2 (only three data points are due to S1's surgery; average of 70.3 percent). Reinstatement of rewards decreased behavior 70 percent, with an ultimate average of approximately 3 percent inappropriate behavior.

A fairly stable baseline in Snack (average of 53.3 percent) preceded an immediate drop in inappropriate behavior in Reward 1 (average of 17.8 percent; the six-day gap is due to illness). Following an increase across two days, there was an abrupt decrease upon return to school during Reward 2 (average of 12.9 percent). A sharp increase in inappropriate behavior appeared on day 42, when a change in schedule necessitated Snack being eaten in a different setting; this increase also indicated the relationship between the coefficient of consistency and inappropriate behavior. Results during Art follow a similar pattern (see Figure 5-13).

Subject 2

During storytime, a downward trend and high variability in inappropriate behavior was evident (a Baseline 1 average of 34.2 percent). Inappropriate behavior decreased on day 20, the tenth day of Reward 1 (average of 20 percent). A return to baseline level was not demonstrated with S2 during Story (average of 17.5 percent), although the variability in behavior decreased during contingency conditions. The mean percentage of inappropriate behavior was 34.2 percent in Baseline 1 and 7.2 percent during Reward 2.

There was a downward trend in behavior during both Snack and Story baselines. A decrease in inappropriate behavior was observed at the beginning of Reward 1, as well as decreased variability. The mean percentage of intervals in which inappropriate behavior occurred in Baseline 2 was twice that of Baseline 1.

Subject 2's behavior was quite variable during Art baseline (average of 35.2 percent), much like baseline performance in Story. The experimental effect was obtained in Reward 1 (average of 11.3 percent), and behavior increased to Baseline 1 level during Baseline 2 (average of 10 percent).

Subject 3

An upward trend was observed in S3's baseline inappropriate behavior during Story (average of 24.4 percent); and behavior decreased to nearly the zero level in Peer Reward 1, beginning on day 16 (average of 6.6 percent). A pre-treatment level of behavior was established during Baseline 2 (average of 28 percent), but behavior returned to zero the first day of Reward 2 (the single data point in Reward 2 was due to withdrawal from school following frequent absences).

There was a slight downtrend in Snack Baseline 1 (15.7 percent average), which continued into Reward 1 where behavior became more stable (average of 5.8 percent). The single data point in Baseline 2 of zero indicates that she did not attain her pre-treatment level in Snack.

Art produced the most stable baseline, which lasted 24 days (average of 11.5 percent). An abrupt decrease to zero percent on the first day of Reward 1 and the sustained low level (average of 1.2 percent) indicate the effectiveness of peer rewards in reducing inappropriate behavior. A decrease in variability characterized S3's performance during Reward conditions across all activities.

Subject 4

Baseline performance was very stable during Story (average of 76.1 percent). A decrease in inappropriate behavior was observed beginning the second day of Reward 1. Performance was variable following initiation of rewards, but stabilized on Day 17, remaining at a low level in Reward 1 (average of 22.2 percent). Although behavior did not return to Baseline 1 level, increases were evident in Baseline 2 (average of 26 percent). At the beginning of Reward 2, behavior during Story decreased nearly to zero (average of 4.2 percent), a level that was maintained throughout the study except for day 39 (an increase of about 15 percent).

Following a fairly stable baseline in Snack (average of 28.1 percent), behavior decreased about 15 percent during Reward 1 (average of 9 percent). Behavior during Baseline 2 attained its Baseline 1 average level of 39.7 percent, based on three data points (due to absences). During Reward 2, behavior remained at a low level (average of 7.2 percent) except for day 40 (the consistency of rewards by the peer was also low that day).

During Art, baseline behavior was variable with no evident trends (average of 32.8 percent). There was a decrease in frequency and variability during Reward 1 (average of 8.4 percent). A pre-treatment level of performance was attained during Baseline 2 (32.7 percent), followed by a decrease to near zero (7.2 percent average) during Reward 2.

DISCUSSION

Results of this study suggest that five-year-olds can be effectively trained in a short period of time to consistently reinforce the appropriate behavior of younger students. The effectiveness of the procedure was demonstrated by increases in appropriate behavior during three different preschool activities. The inappropriate behaviors did not immediately decrease when reinforcement was instituted for the first time. The more immediate changes during Snack and Art, contrasted with initial applications during Story, substantiate this contention. Similarly, inappropriate behavior decreased rapidly when rewards were again initiated following a return to baseline in all activities. Conversely, when contingent reinforcement was removed, the inappropriate behaviors increased during each activity. Consequently, it is likely that the experimental manipulation directly affected target behaviors in the desired direction.

The contingencies that resulted in the receiving of rewards by the peer observers were probably crucial in teaching and maintaining the chain of behaviors involved in monitoring the younger children. Required peer behaviors included visual attention to the subject for long periods of time, retention of specific definitions of a long list of rule violations, immediate discrimination between appropriate and inappropriate behaviors, the rapid motor response of placing a reward in the child's mouth, and finally, many responses to an auditory cue. An anecdotal demonstration of the importance of contingencies for the peer observers occurred when the mother of one observer forced her to throw away her weekly toy (a nail polish kit). Performance decreased the following day.

This study indicates that knowledge of behavioral principles generalized across activities and settings. For example, it was reported that one peer observer spontaneously shaped her dog to do certain tricks by using M & Ms, and subsequently attempted to teach her younger brother to work for rewards. Another peer observer, who was reported by teachers and observers to be shy at the beginning of the study, became more outgoing as the study progressed (that is, he talked and interacted more frequently).

One major conclusion to be drawn from the present study involves the relationship between the consistency of peer modifiers' reinforcement and the behavior of the children being reinforced. It is apparent from the data that the inappropriate behavior of the younger children was almost directly related to the behavior of the peer observers. When the consistency of the reinforcement became stable, the inappropriate behavior of the children stabilized. It is also evident from the data that whenever the consistency dropped (except on the first few days of reinforcement, when the rewards could help maintain the behavior), the inappropriate behavior of the younger students increased. This finding may lead to practical applications in both preschool and regular school classrooms.

Results indicate that very young children can be trained successfully in the use of reinforcement techniques such as observing, recording, and reinforcing appropriately. This knowledge could be used to teach children of all ages to become efficient in increasing desired social or academic behaviors in their peers. This extra source of manpower might help alleviate the problem of unbalanced teacher-pupil ratios. Additional advantages might include quicker socialization of isolated children, and increased sensitivity and self-awareness, which would be based on understanding functional relationships between the behaviors of interacting human beings.

part 6 / Research
Methodology

24 / Reliability Scores That Delude: An Alice in Wonderland Trip Through the Misleading Characteristics of Interobserver Agreement Scores in Interval Recording

Robert P. Hawkins • Victor A. Dotson

Bijou, Peterson, and Ault (1968), in describing methods for recording data in the natural environment, give considerable emphasis to the interval method of recording. In this method, the experimental session is divided into equal time intervals for recording purposes—usually 10-second or 20-second intervals, but the size can be adjusted to suit the frequency or duration of the behavior or to make recording more convenient. For each time interval during the session, the observer records whether the response did or did not occur at any time during the interval (or, occasionally, during a certain portion of an interval). Though this method has certain limitations, it also offers some outstanding advantages. It allows an observer to easily measure several responses concurrently (Hart, Reynolds, Baer, Brawley, and Harris, 1968; Madsen, Becker, and Thomas, 1968), it shows changes in either the frequency or the duration of a behavior, and it circumvents the sometimes difficult task of defining and detecting single units of behavior (as in the case where the experimenter wishes to record talking, cooperative play, or attending to a task).

Bijou et al. (1968) also point out the necessity of measuring the inter-observer reliability of data recorded by observers (as opposed to data recorded automatically by mechanical, electromechanical, or electronic apparatus). The method they describe for calculating the agreement between the data recorded by two independent observers employs the following formula:

$$\frac{\text{agreements}}{\text{agreement} + \text{disagreements}} \times 100 = \text{percentage of agreement}$$

An agreement is any interval in which both observers recorded that the response occurred during the interval, or in which both observers recorded that the response did not occur during the interval. Disagreements are intervals in which only one observer reported that the response occurred. Thus, every interval of recording is used in the calculation of interobserver agreement by this method. We shall call this method of calculation the I-I (interval-by-interval) method.

Of approximately 97 studies involving behavior analysis in education that were reported in the first five volumes of the *Journal of Applied Behavior Analysis* (1968–72), approximately 40 percent used interval recording for at least a portion of the data. Of these studies that used interval recording, 70 percent, or 26, appear to have calculated interobserver agreement by the above formula. (Approximately 6 studies reported in the *Journal of Applied Behavior Analysis* utilized interval recording but were not conducted in educational settings. Four of them calculated interobserver agreement by the I-I method. Some researchers do not describe their calculation of reliability scores clearly enough that a reader can determine which method was employed.) Clearly, it is the most popular method of calculating agreement (three other methods will be discussed below). But how well does it serve our purposes as scientists?

In general, the purpose of checking the reliability of observer-recorded data is to assess the accuracy and objectivity of the data. But this is an insufficient analysis. First, there are at least three somewhat independent sources of error in obtaining accurate and objective data:

1. *The definition* of behavior given to the observer by the experimenter may be vague, subjective or incomplete.
2. *The observer* may be poorly trained, unmotivated, or otherwise incompetent.
3. *The behavior* may be difficult to detect because of its subtlety or complexity, because of distractions, or because of other factors obstructing the observing process.

Second, it is not simply the accuracy and objectivity of the data themselves that need to be assessed, but also the "believability" or validity of the experimental effect reported (referred to by Campbell and Stanley, 1966, as internal validity). Of course, when the data are perfectly accurate the validity of experimental effect is also perfect; but the validity of experimental effect declines more rapidly than does the validity of any particular datum when the validity of that datum is less than perfect, as will be shown later in this paper.

The purpose of the present research is to assess the degree to which the most popular method of calculating the reliability of interval data, the I-I method, serves our scientific purposes. We collected data and performed other analyses to assess the adequacy of I-I reliability scores in serving three functions: (1) as an index of how precise, clear, objective, and complete the *definition* is; (2) as an index of how competently the *observer* is recording; and (3) as an index of the *believability of the experimental effect* reported. The analyses of these three functions of reliability scores will be presented in that order.

THE ADEQUACY-OF-DEFINITION FUNCTION

Test 1

In order to test the ability of I-I reliability scores to reflect the adequacy of response definitions, we first wrote a few definitions that we felt were obviously absurd (that is, their face validity was low) in terms of completeness, precision, objectivity, and unambiguousness. These definitions were as follows:

1. *Positive affect:* any time the subject shows such feelings as pleasure, happiness, joy, affection, admiration, or excited animation
2. *Negative affect:* any time the subject exhibits such feelings as displeasure, anger, embarrassment, hate, disillusionment, discomfort, disappointment, fear, anxiety, or sorrow
3. *Neutral affect:* any time the subject is exhibiting neither negative nor positive affect, as defined above

(The personal and social significance of these behaviors is in no way being questioned; in fact, the behaviors were selected because they are significant. But anyone experienced at precise, objective measurement will quickly recognize how insufficient and overinclusive the definitions are, and how much subjective judgment is required by the observer employing them.) The observers were also instructed that at least one of these affective states would necessarily be recorded in each interval, but also that more than one could occur within the same interval.

Two trained, experienced, graduate student observers were given written copies of the definitions and asked to study them for 5 minutes. Then, they independently recorded the affect of a school child for 20 minutes, employing 10-second interval recording. Independence of recording was assured by erecting a cardboard barrier between the observers to prevent them from seeing when or what the other observer recorded. Attentiveness to the task was assured by instructing the observers as to the importance of the data and by seating one of the authors where he could watch both observers. The observers were given no hint as to the authors' hypothesis or even that the authors considered the definitions inadequate. The I-I agreement between the observers on the first and only session was 95 percent, 92 percent, and 100 percent, respectively, for these behaviors.

Using the same method, the same two observers recorded each of the following behaviors for 20-minute sessions, employing these definitions:

1. *Thinking:* Any time the child appears to be considering something, weighing opposing impulses, arriving at the solution to a problem, and so on.

2. *Excessive movement:* Any time the subject shows more bodily motion than the situation calls for. The motion may be in his whole body, as in jumping up and down, or in just a small portion of his body, as in finger tapping.

3. *Interest:* Any time the subject shows by what he says, the expression on his face, the vigor of his movement, the intonation of his voice, or other aspects of his behavior that he is interested in a particular thing. He may show that he is interested in what someone is saying or doing, in his work, in some play activity in which he is engaged, or anything else.

4. *Acting silly:* Score an interval "S" any time that the child is acting below his age.

The I-I agreement scores on these four behaviors were 83 percent, 57 percent, 84 percent, and 99 percent, respectively. Only the score on "excessive" movement falls below acceptable levels. The reason for such high agreement scores despite the obvious inadequacy of the definitions will be discussed later in this paper.

Test 2

What if a definition were so ambiguous that two different observers presented with it drew completely different meanings from it? We obtained a test of this question by accident. Two independent observers were recording several behaviors in a classroom, and one of them was writing the wrong symbols for two of the behaviors; he had reversed the symbols for writing and hand raising on four successive sessions before the error was corrected. This situation can be considered a test of the degree to which I-I scores reflect definition adequacy. It is the same problem that might have occurred if two observers were simply told by an experimenter, "Now I'd like you to record this student's hand-raising behavior," without having the behavior defined at all (except for its name), or if one of the observers thought the experimenter had said "handwriting" instead of "hand raising." These behaviors, as defined, were topographically incompatible; the only way they could both occur at the same time would be for a person to write with one hand and raise his other hand, a highly unlikely combination of responses in a junior high school classroom (perhaps somewhat more likely in a college class, where notes might be taken while waiting to contribute to discussion).

On those four sessions, in which one observer's data on writing were checked against the other observer's data on hand raising, the observers attained agreement scores of 77 percent, 80 percent, 89 percent, and 92 percent. That is, even though they were recording different responses that would rarely (in fact, rarely did) occur in the same interval, they obtained high I-I reliability scores!

Clearly, I-I reliability scores must be considered highly insensitive as an index of the adequacy of response definitions. This is a scientifically significant limitation because the definition of a response is a very important aspect of the measurement process, and measurement is the first requirement of a science. If the adequacy of a definition cannot be assessed, it is difficult for one scientist to know whether or not another scientist's definition will be useful in his work, or even what behavior is really measured by that definition. In addition, observer biases are likely to be more influential when explicit definitions are inadequate. The reasons for the insensitivity of I-I reliability as an index of the adequacy of a definition will be discussed later.

THE OBSERVER-COMPETENCY FUNCTION

Perhaps the most extreme form of observer incompetence would be to fall asleep. This is not unheard of, and is most likely to occur when a low-rate behavior is being recorded over a long session (say 45 minutes or more). To test I-I reliability as an index of observer competence, we simulated the condition where an observer falls asleep. We took the classroom data recorded by a single observer in another experiment on three behaviors over four consecutive sessions. The behaviors were teacher talking, student writing, and student hand raising. These four data sheets (each with data on three behaviors) were compared with a blank sheet representing the data of a sleeping observer (who, of course, never saw the behavior occur during the session), and I-I reliability scores were calculated between each real data sheet and the blank one. (It is common practice—though not universal —to actively record only the occurrence of a response, recording nothing for the nonoccurrence of that response. Thus, a blank data sheet might be that of an alert observer who noticed that the behavior never occurred, or it might be that of an observer who fell asleep early in the session. Although active recording of the nonoccurrence of a response is probably desirable, the present analysis and argument do not hinge on the passive "recording" of nonoccurrences. The sleeping observer could also be simulated by arbitrarily marking a data sheet to indicate 100 percent nonoccurrence—or any other pattern of occurrence.) The agreement scores on teacher talking ranged from 2 percent to 54 percent (with a mean of 17 percent). These would have been reassuring scores except that the scores on hand raising ranged from 86 percent to 98 percent (mean, 93 percent), and those on writing ranged from 77 percent to 100 percent (mean, 91 percent), despite the fact that one "observer" was asleep! Apparently, I-I reliability scores provide a less adequate measure of observer competence than one might hope for.

THE BELIEVABILITY-OF-EXPERIMENTAL-EFFECT FUNCTION

If the experimental effects reported in the behavior analysis (or any other scientific) literature cannot be relied on to represent real phenomena, many of our research and programming activities could be wasted effort. To what extent do I-I reliability scores provide a safeguard against the reporting of effects that are not real or the failure to see effects that did occur? This question will be examined first by an analysis of a fictional behavior-change study.

Suppose a child was a social recluse and spent a relatively small amount of time interacting with peers during times when such interaction was considered desirable. A behavior analyst comes to the rescue, and recommends that the teacher apply some particular technique, perhaps one that happens to have been invented by this behavior analyst. An observer, perhaps the teacher, records baseline data daily by a 10-second interval method, finding that the behavior consistently fails to occur at all. The special technique is then applied and the data show an increase until the behavior is reported to occur in approximately 30 percent of the intervals, which might be well within the norms in this group of children. Perhaps the effect is even replicated in a reversal design. These fictitious results are shown in Figure 6-1. There appears to be a very significant effect from the intervention.

But suppose that, unknown to the first observer, a second observer

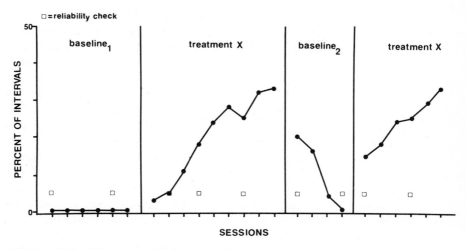

□ = reliability check

Figure 6-1 *Hypothetical data resulting from a study employing a reversal design. Hypothetical data obtained by a second, objective observer are shown as open squares.*

independently records that same behavior on several occasions, and that the second observer is totally objective and accurate, perhaps because he or she was naive as to the nature of the experiment or the behavior analyst's personal interest in the success of the technique. And suppose, further, that this objective observer saw the behavior in exactly 5 percent of the intervals on every reliability check; that is, the behavior showed no change whatever during the study (represented by the squares in Figure 6-1). If the second observer happened to record on sessions 1, 5, 8, 10, 13, 16, 19, 20, and 23, the I-I agreement scores could have had a range as high as from 80 percent to 100 percent, with a mean of 90 percent and the *lowest possible* range of I-I agreement scores would have been from 70 percent to 95 percent, with a mean of 83 percent! Thus, even though reliability was checked relatively frequently, I-I reliability scores could not warn the experimenter (or the reader of this report) that the data were grossly biased toward finding an experimental effect. (Had the second observer been given cues as to the expected effects, as is probably more typical in applied behavior analysis to date, the agreement scores might well have been even higher.)

This raises a serious question as to the ability of I-I scores to protect against significant distortion of experimental effects. However, examination of some published data would provide a more adequate impression of the practical implications of this potential distortion. We selected a classic study to examine: the first study in the first paper in the first issue of the *Journal of Applied Behavior Analysis,* a study reported in the frequently-cited paper by Hall, Lund, and Jackson (1968).[1] The data from this study, which dealt with the studying behavior of a child named Robbie, were obtained by interval recording; and the interval-by-interval method was employed to calculate interobserver agreement. The paper does not report how many reliability checks were made, but simply that there were several and that they included at least one in each experimental condition. We redrew the figure, estimating the precise values of the data represented on it. Employing the reported agreement scores, we could then calculate the data the second observer could have obtained on any particular session.

The agreement scores ranged from 89 percent to 93 percent (no mean was reported). With an 89 percent I-I agreement score, the second observer's data would have deviated 11 percentage points from the data reported by the primary observer. We arbitrarily selected sessions on which the reliability checks "occurred"; and we assumed two reliability checks per experimental phase, though we knew that only one was actually conducted in some phases. We then plotted fictional data that a second observer could have obtained, spacing the reliability checks a few sessions apart as would be typical in such research. We assumed that agreement was 93 percent on three of the ten reliability checks, and 89 percent on the other seven checks. These fictional, but possible, data from a second observer are plotted in Figure 6-2 (the square data points), which is basically a redrawing of the Hall, Lund, and Jackson (1968) figure. What appeared to be a clear effect of the experimental manipulation becomes highly questionable when one inspects the fictional data of the second observer. (The reader may note that if certain other sessions had been selected as the reliability sessions, and if it had been assumed that nine of the ten reliability checks had produced 93 percent agreement, the second observer's data would also show a clear experimental effect. However, it should be remembered that if the primary observer is biased, he would most likely show his minimal bias on days when his reliability is being checked, and, therefore, the selection of sessions on which the primary observer's data were nearer the median of all the data is probably justified. In addition, even if there were a real experimental effect, behavior analysts need to know the approximate magnitude of that effect, not simply that it was present; and only by the selection of the most extreme data points of each condition could one force the second observer's data to show a magnitude of effect comparable to that reported by the primary observer. Other criticisms of the present method of analysis can also be raised, but the point remains that I-I scores alone cannot be confi-

---

[1] Copyright 1968 by the Society for the Experimental Analysis of Behavior, Inc. The authors are indebted to Vance Hall, Diane Lund, Deloris Jackson, and to the *Journal of Applied Behavior Analysis* for permission to use the figure presented. This analysis in no way constitutes a criticism of this particular study. Many other studies with less frequent reliability checks, lower agreement scores, or smaller-magnitude changes in behavior could be criticized more readily.

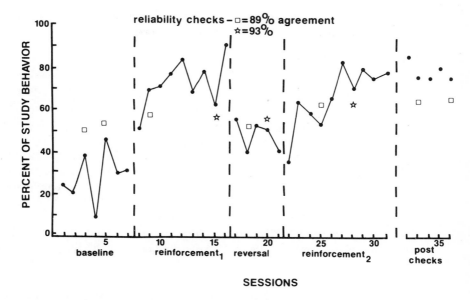

Figure 6-2 *Redrawing of Hall, Lund, Jackson (1968) data, with hypothetical data from reliability checks added. Open squares indicate possible scores obtained by a second observer.*

dently relied upon to assess the believability of the experimental effect.) Again, I-I reliability scores fail to serve an important scientific function, and here the problems of I-I scores are magnified due to the fact that errors of overestimation of behavior can sum with errors of underestimation. That is, if there is a bias toward finding an experimental effect, the primary observer's data (and perhaps even the secondary observer's data) may show the behavior to be less frequent (or shorter in duration) than it really is during one condition and more frequent than it really is during another condition; and the degree to which I-I scores fail to reflect the disagreement between observers (the invalidity of I-I scores) under the one condition is, in a sense, added to their failure to reflect disagreement in the opposite direction under the other condition (see Figure 6-2). (Thus, in Figure 6-1, the invalidity of I-I scores to detect an error of measurement during baseline$_1$ is reflected in their insensitivity to the primary observer's data being lower than the real behavior. The same invalidity during the first treatment condition is reflected in their insensitivity to the primary observer's data being higher than the real behavior.) The insensitivity of I-I scores to disagreements between observers is thus doubled when I-I scores are intended or assumed to detect biases toward finding an experimental effect. Let us now consider the nature of the basic problem with I-I reliability scores.

THE BASIC PROBLEM

The gross unreliability of I-I scores as an index of definition adequacy, observer competence, or believability of experimental effects is a result of the fact that I-I scores are highly subject to influence by the rate (or duration) of the behavior being recorded (a problem pointed out by Bijou, Peterson, Harris, Allen, and Johnston, 1969). When a behavior occurs so infrequently as to occupy very few intervals, the two observers are both virtually certain to record it in few intervals, even if they are employing a grossly inadequate definition of which the two have very different interpretations. This is exactly what produced agreement scores in the 90s for the observers recording "positive affect," "negative affect," and "acting silly." It is also the reason why two observers recording completely different, incompatible behaviors—"writing" and "hand raising"—obtained agreement scores from 77 percent to 92 percent.

Likewise, low frequency behaviors will produce high I-I agreement scores almost regardless of the incompetency of the observers. This is what occurred in the test of observer competency, where a fictitious sleeping observer agreed with an alert observer 86 percent to 98 percent on hand raising and 77 percent to 100 percent on writing.

When a behavior is so frequent (of long duration) as to occur in nearly all intervals (this is more likely to occur as one increases the size of the interval), both observers are likely to record it in a high percentage of the intervals, even if the definition is grossly inadequate. This occurred in the case of "neutral affect," "thinking," and "interest." Similarly, if an observer knows that a behavior will occur with a high frequency, he can even be so incompetent as to mark it in all of the intervals before or after the session, yet the I-I scores will fail to detect this incompetence.

The relationship of I-I reliability scores to rate (or duration) of behavior is represented graphically in Figure 6-3. The area above the heavy line represents the range of I-I scores that are most likely, given a particular rate of behavior (actually, the percentage of intervals in which the behavior occurs). If one assumes that the two observers recorded the behavior in the same total number of intervals, though not necessarily in the same intervals, the heavy line separating the shaded from the unshaded portion of the figure represents the lowest *possible* I-I score for each rate of behavior. According to this analysis, the only point at which I-I reliability scores represent an index that could be very sensitive to variables other than the rate of the behavior is when the rate of the behavior is such as to occur in approxi-

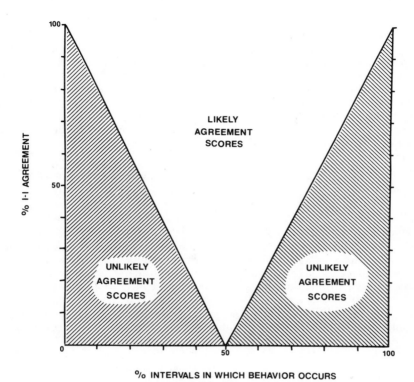

Figure 6-3 *Constraints on interval-by-interval scores at high and low response frequencies.*

mately half of the intervals. The I-I score would be of little value in serving any of the scientific functions outlined earlier, if the behavior is occurring in either a small percentage or a large percentage of the intervals. (See Figure 6-3.)

To test whether or not this analysis represents a real constraint on I-I agreement scores, a series of real agreement scores were obtained. The data were obtained by two naive observers independently recording six student and teacher behaviors in a public school classroom.[2] Three of the definitions were taken from Madsen, Becker, and Thomas (1968), and were as follows:

1. *On task:* For instance, answers questions, listens, raises hand, works

[2] We owe a debt of thanks to Robert Dobes for allowing us to use some of his data.

on assignment; must include whole 10-second interval except for turning-around responses of less than 4 seconds' duration.

2. *Turning around:* Turning head or head and body to look at another person, showing objects to another child, attending to another child; must be of 4 seconds' duration, or more than 90 degrees, using desk as a reference; not rated unless seated. If this response overlaps two time intervals and cannot be rated in the first because it is less than 4 seconds in duration, then rate in the interval in which the end of the response occurs.

3. *Academic recognition from teacher:* Calling on a child for an answer; giving "feed back" for academic correctness.

The other three definitions were written by the authors and were as follows:

4. *Hand raising:* Any time the hand raises above the elbow in an apparent attempt to gain the teacher's attention or to answer a question and is free of contact with any surface such as a desk, a book, or the subject's head.

5. *Writing:* Any time the subject, holding a writing utensil (pen, pencil, crayon), makes contact between the writing end of the utensil and writing material (paper, notebook, workbook, and so forth). Exclude writing on the desk. Include writing on a book or something of that nature even though you think it inappropriate.

6. *Teacher talking:* Any oral sound involving the vocal cords. Include simple sounds like "oh," "huh?" "uh," and laughing aloud. It is not necessary to be able to understand the words, but merely to hear the sound of the subject's voice. Whispering is excluded by the definition because it does not involve the vocal cords. Also exclude coughing, belching, sneezing, and clearing the throat, even though they involve the vocal cords.

The reliability scores from 55 of the 76 pairs of observations are presented graphically in Figure 6-4. Each letter represents one I-I agreement score; its location on the ordinate represents the value of that score, and on the abscissa, the frequency of the behavior on that session as determined by the mean number of intervals that the two observers recorded the behavior as occurring. The 21 scores not presented were all clustered tightly in the upper left corner of the figure, above the diagonal line, and are not presented because they would constitute a solid black area in the figure. Most of these omitted data were on the academic recognition response, and a few were on writing.

From the distribution of these scores, it would appear that the present analysis represents a valid concern about the scientific usefulness of I-I reliability scores. All of the scores remained within the bounds suggested in Figure 6-2, and only toward the middle range of rates did the scores fall in the 50s, 60s, and 70s. Apparently, the rate of the behavior being recorded does restrict I-I reliability scores, making them unlikely to be sensitive as an index of such variables as definition adequacy, observer competency, and observer bias.

TENTATIVE RECOMMENDATIONS

Quite possibly the ultimate solution to the problems raised in this paper will be a complex mathematical one. For example, a table or set of tables

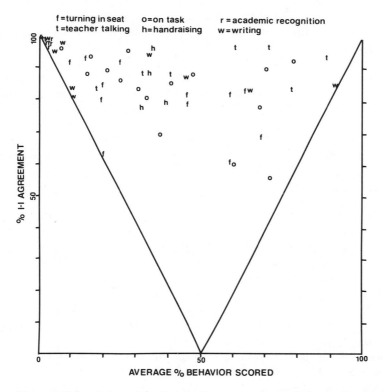

Figure 6-4 *Interval-by-interval scores obtained in a classroom observation of six behaviors.*

could be constructed from which the experimenter could assess the probability of an obtained difference between two observers' data, given a particular frequency of the behavior (perhaps the mean number of intervals, or perhaps two separate assessments based on the two observers' separate totals). However, the solution we wish to propose for the present is simpler. It is twofold, one aspect being aimed at solving the general problem of I-I reliability scores being affected by the rate of behavior, and the other aspect being aimed only at the problem of the believability of experimental effect.

It appears to us that the best simple solution is to shift to a different type of agreement score or a combination of two such agreement scores. One of these scores has seen occasional use in the applied behavior analysis literature (apparently Madsen, Becker, and Thomas, 1968, used it). We call it scored-interval (S-I) agreement. In S-I agreement, all intervals in which neither observer scored the behavior as occurring (or both observers recorded the absence of the behavior, a method used by Hall, Lund, and Jackson, 1968, with part of their data, and one that may improve recording somewhat) are ignored in calculating agreement scores. Only an interval in which both observers recorded the presence of the behavior is counted as an agreement. In effect, this would remove the diagonal line from the left half of Figure 6-2, leaving reliability scores free to vary from zero to 100, even at lower response frequencies. When the data on negative affect are treated this way, the agreement changes from an I-I score of 92 percent to an S-I score of 33 percent (four agreements, eight disagreements). Likewise, the 95 percent I-I agreement on positive affect becomes an S-I agreement of zero percent (one observer never saw it, the other saw it five times); and the 99 percent I-I agreement on acting silly becomes an S-I agreement of 50 percent (both observers saw it in one interval, and one saw it again in another interval).

But S-I reliability scores also have some serious limitations. First, S-I scores constitute a very stringent test of observer agreement, and new standards would clearly have to be established as to the levels of agreement our science should expect of interval data. Second, at extremely low frequencies of behavior, S-I scores become highly variable. For example, if one observer recorded a response as occurring in one interval and the other recorded it as occurring in no intervals, their agreement is zero percent, whereas a change of just one interval on the second observer's data sheet would make this 100 percent. Third, with extremely high frequencies of behavior, S-I reliability scores would appear to have a liability like that of I-I scores: they inevitably become high.

Perhaps a suggestion by Bijou et al. (1969) provides a method to counteract the above three limitations of S-I scores. These authors suggest that two reliability scores might be calculated, one for the occurrence of the behavior (S-I scores) and the other for the nonoccurrence of the behavior. In this second type of score, an agreement is counted only when both observers recorded that the behavior did not occur. A disagreement is counted when one observer recorded the presence of the behavior and the other recorded its absence. Intervals in which both observers scored the behavior are ignored. This kind of agreement ratio might be called unscored-interval (U-I) reliability.

The characteristics of U-I agreement scores are such that they complement those of S-I scores. When the frequency of behavior is above 50 percent of the session, U-I scores can vary from zero percent to 100 percent; but with lower frequencies of behavior, U-I scores have the same lower limits as those shown on the left side of Figure 6-2. (At first impression, it might appear that U-I scores and S-I scores on the same data would always add up to 100 percent; but this proves not to be true, generally, because of the fact that any interval in which one observer scored the behavior as present and the other scored it as absent is included in the calculation of both S-I and U-I. Thus, though the numerators of the two ratios always sum to the total number of intervals in the session, the denominators add up to more than that total—except in the case where either U-I or S-I is 100 percent.)

Although U-I scores by themselves would have the same three kinds of limitations indicated above for S-I scores, when U-I and S-I scores are presented in combination these limitations should be eliminated or greatly ameliorated. Whether or not the combination of U-I and S-I should be in the form of simply presenting both scores, presenting the mean of the two scores, or some other method of combination, is uncertain. If both scores are presented, the researcher still suffers from the high variability of one score or the other at extremely high or low behavior frequencies, whereas averaging the two scores reduces this problem.

To further understand properties of S-I scores, U-I scores, and the mean of these two, it may be instructive to inspect these scores when derived from some of the same data on which I-I scores were reported earlier in this paper. Table 6-1 presents several such comparisons. As the scores in Table 6-1 suggest, I-I scores are always equal to or larger than S-I scores, U-I scores, or the mean of S-I and U-I.

In general, it appears that the mean of S-I and U-I is a promising statistic with which to represent the degree to which two independent observers agree on the occurrence of behavior, as measured by interval recording. However, it should be noted that the mean is not free of influence by the frequency of the behavior, it has characteristics similar to those represented in Figure 6-2, except that the curve's high points are 50 percent agreement rather than 100 percent. That is, if the observers agree perfectly on the total number of intervals in which the behavior occurred, the lowest possible agreement score (mean of S-I and U-I) is zero percent, and that is possible only if the observers both saw the behavior in 50 percent of the intervals. As the agreed-upon frequency approaches either zero percent of the session or 100 percent of the session, the lower limit of agreement scores rises toward 50 percent. These lower limits appear to be much more tolerable than those on I-I scores (represented in Figure 6-2), and of course they decline as the two observers' agreement on total frequency decreases.

An additional comparison between the characteristics of I-I scores

Table 6-1 *Illustrate Comparisons of Four Different Reliability Scores Derived from the Same Data*

	INTEROBSERVER AGREEMENT SCORES			
BEHAVIOR	I — I	S — I	U — 1	$\overline{X}$ of S — I and U — I
From Adequacy-of-Definition Function:				
positive affect	95%	0%	95%	47.5%
negative affect	92	41	92	67
neutral affect	100	100	(no interval unscored)	100 (no $\overline{X}$ possible)
thinking	83	78	41	59.5
excessive movement	57	14	37	25.5
interest	84	80	32	56
acting silly	99	50	99	74.5
From Observer-Competency Function:				
teacher talking				
session 1	4	0	4	2
session 2	7	0	7	3.5
session 3	2	0	2	1
session 4	54	0	54	27
hand raising				
session 1	88	0	88	44
session 2	98	0	98	49
session 3	86	0	86	43
session 4	98	0	98	49

and those of the mean of S-I and U-I should be pointed out. It is evidenced in the lower portion of Table 6-1, in which agreement scores from "the sleeping-observer test" are presented. When one observer is asleep (fails to see the behavior in any interval), the lower limit of I-I scores is a straight line ranging from a low of zero percent (when the behavior is seen in every interval by the awake observer) to a high of 100 percent (when the behavior is seen in no interval by the awake observer), and the lower limit for the mean of S-I and U-I ranges from a low of 25 percent (when the awake observer sees the behavior in half of the intervals) to a high of 50 percent (when the awake observer sees the behavior in every interval or in no interval). (Actually, instead of reaching 50 percent agreement, the curve falls off to zero suddenly at the two extremes. This is due to the fact that an S-I score cannot be calculated—and therefore cannot be averaged with the other score—if the behavior was never recorded by either observer, and a U-I score cannot be calculated if the behavior was recorded in every interval by both observers.) Because agreement scores of 50 percent and less are unlikely to ever be acceptable in applied behavior analysis, the lower limits of the mean of S-I and U-I seem more tolerable than those of I-I.

We wish to make two further suggestions that deal specifically with the issue of believability of the experimental effect. First, when reliability checks are made, it appears essential that researchers make a practice of presenting the actual *data* obtained by the second observer, rather than merely a derived agreement score. (A fourth kind of reliability score, total-interval agreement [T-I] also serves as a safeguard against the reporting of grossly exaggerated experimental effects, but it is less effective than the simple plotting of the second observer's data. In calculating T-I agreement, the researcher simply divides the total number of intervals in which one observer saw the behavior into the number in which the other observer saw the behavior, always dividing the larger into the smaller, and multiplies by 100. This provides a much better assessment of the believability of the experimental effect than do other agreement scores, because it employs the same statistic as that used in presenting the experimental effect: the number—or percent—of intervals in which the behavior was seen. The other three reliability scores are all based on when rather than how often the behavior was seen.) The best means of presenting these data is to plot them in the figures, along with the data of the primary observer, as is done with the fictional data in Figure 6-1. Some researchers have begun such a practice already. It allows the reader of a research paper to interpret more adequately the agreement scores presented and to inspect the relationship between the two observers' scores across conditions in order to evaluate the possibility of observer bias (actually, the possibility of differential bias between observers, for either or both could be biased to find a particular effect). For example, a reader may then note that on sessions where reliability was assessed, the primary observer's data tended to show a weaker experimental effect than they showed on other sessions, as is evidenced on sessions 13 and 23 of Figure 6-1 (but not on other sessions where reliability was checked). Frequent occurrence of this phenomenon would suggest that the primary observer is biased to exaggerate the effect. Or a reader may note the primary phenomenon being illustrated in Figure 6-1: the second observer's data show considerably less experimental effect than do the primary observer's data.

Second, it seems imperative that researchers obtain frequent reliability checks, probably a minimum of two per experimental condition (thus providing an estimate of the stability of the relative biases of the observers) and a minimum of approximately one every six sessions. In addition, reliability should be assessed during sessions when the primary observer is reporting maximal experimental effect, such as sessions 13, 14, 15, 24, and 25 in Figure 6-1. These precautions should provide a reasonable safe-guard against the reporting of effects that are grossly distorted by observer (or similar) biases, provided the second observer does not have the same biases as the first.

CONCLUSION

If behavior analysts wish to continue the use of interval recording, better methods of assessing the reliability of interval data are sorely needed. Because I-I reliability scores are clearly inadequate for many of our scientific purposes, it is already likely that a significant body of applied behavior analysis has seriously misrepresented to us the relationships between certain environmental factors and certain significant human behaviors. Further, it is likely that we are making important programming decisions on the basis of such false information, decisions that affect the lives of thousands of people. Finally, it is likely that we are teaching this same false information to others, thus perpetuating and magnifying our mistakes. Though a change to S-I and U-I reliability scores may not truly solve the problem, it is an easy change to make and one that appears to offer much more accurate representation of the objectivity and accuracy of interval data. When combined with additional safeguards aimed specifically at assessing the believability of the experimental effect, these reliability measures should improve the methodology of a significant portion of applied behavior analysis in education.

25 / Multielement Baseline Design in Educational Research

Jerome D. Ulman · Beth Sulzer-Azaroff

As expressed by Wesley Becker (1972) last year, the basic question in educational research is "which instructional procedures are more effective under given conditions, given a criterion of utility." The traditional approach to this question has been by means of correlational investigations or statistical comparisons of pre- and post-test performance measures among various experimental control groups. Though correlational studies may have heuristic value and experimental vs. control-group experiments may be indispensible for seeking answers to actuarial questions (Baer, 1971; O'Leary and Kent, 1973), these two methodologies do not provide

The authors are indebted to Dr. Donald Hake for sharing his ideas regarding the use of the design in educational research, as well as for his subsequent advice and encouragement. We also wish to thank the members of the Operant Research Group of Indianapolis for their helpful criticism, Mr. Jeffrey Walker for the graphics, and Mrs. Jean G. Ulman for typing the manuscript.

useful knowledge concerning the behavior of individuals. Behavior analysis has emphasized a quite different approach: the same subjects are exposed to all conditions of the experimental variable, each serving as his own control. Behavior analysis can thereby demonstrate causal relationships, which the correlational study cannot, and eliminate intersubject variability, which the experimental control-group experiment cannot.

As in all fields of science, experiments in the field of behavior analysis are designed to determine whether an observed effect is due to manipulated variables rather than to chance or extraneous variables. In behavior analysis a variety of experimental designs have been used (Sidman, 1960), the essential characteristic of which is the repeated measures of behavior under each condition of the independent variable. In applied behavior analysis, however, experimental designs have, with few exceptions, been limited to two types: the reversal design and the multiple-baseline design (Baer, Wolf, and Risley, 1968), singly or occasionally in combination (e.g., Kazdin, 1973; Patterson and Teigen, 1973; Pinkston, Reese, LeBlanc, and Baer, 1973.)

"A *reversal design* is one in which experimental procedures are discontinued briefly so that baseline conditions are again in effect. If the behavior reverts to its former level, experimental conditions are reinstated. If this again results in a change, a cause-and-effect relationship has been demonstrated (Hall, 1971, p. 7)." The baseline period is reintroduced, therefore, to determine whether the relationship observed during the experimental phase was in fact related to the experimental condition. Many variations of the reversal design have been used. Among these variations, reversal designs differ according to the number of independent variables being manipulated, the number of sessions under each condition of an independent variable, the order in which the conditions are presented, and the number of dependent and independent variables being measured. Reversal designs may also vary in the manner by which the experimental conditions are discontinued (Bijou, Peterson, Harris, Allen, and Johnston, 1969)—by reversing the contingency; by introducing a random, noncontingent schedule (such as a DRO procedure); or by removing the contingency altogether.

"A *multiple-baseline design* is one in which two or more behaviors are measured simultaneously, prior to instituting experimental procedures. An experimental procedure is then introduced for one of the behaviors. At subsequent points, the procedure is instituted for the second, then for the third, and so on. If there are successive changes in the behaviors at the points where the experimental procedures were instituted, a cause-and-effect relationship between the behavior and the condition has been demonstrated (Hall, 1971, p. 8)." There are three basic types of multiple-baseline designs: across situations, across individuals, and across behaviors (Hall, Cristler, Cranston, and Tucker, 1970).

Although the multiple-baseline design avoids the problem of reversing a performance, it has certain drawbacks. For instance, it is necessary to record simultaneously two or more behaviors throughout the entire course of the experiment. This may not be practical in some applied situations. Moreover, Baer and Risley (1968) state that the multiple baseline is a somewhat weaker design than the reversal design, since it involves an additional assumption: that all the measured behaviors are susceptible to the same variables.

The purpose of this paper is to point out the utility of another behavior analysis design, a design that shows promise of becoming a powerful tool for educational research: *the multielement baseline design*. First, the design will be described; second, some of its possible advantages will be cited; and finally, an example of its application will be outlined.

DESCRIPTION OF THE MULTIELEMENT BASELINE DESIGN

Sidman (1960) has used the term "multielement baseline design," but equally descriptive would be the term "alternating conditions design." The former term emphasizes behavioral effects, whereas the latter emphasizes experimental manipulations. The multielement baseline involves the repeated measurement of a behavior under alternating conditions of the independent variable. In contrast with multiple-baseline and reversal designs, the multielement baseline design does not consist of experimental phases where one behavior modification procedure is applied during several consecutive sessions until stability is achieved within that condition. Rather, experimental and baseline conditions are presented in alternation—on either a consistent or an unpredictable schedule—within sessions and/or from one session to the next. As is the case with the components of a multiple schedule (Ferster and Skinner, 1957), the experimental conditions of a multielement baseline procedure are alternated independent of changes in the behavior. A distinctive (potentially discriminative) stimulus is correlated with each condition and the effects of the treatment procedure(s) can be observed by comparing differential performances. Thus, if different patterns of responding develop, and each pattern is observed to be unique to a particular experimental condition—that is, if "the subject's behavior is fractionated by stimulus control over each separate element" (Sidman, 1960)—then experimental control has been demonstrated.

To date, the use of the multielement baseline design has been confined primarily to basic research with multiple schedules of reinforcement. There are, however, some examples of its use in applied research. In a laboratory study of reading acquisition in kindergarten children, Staats, Finley, Minke, and Wolf (1964) used tokens to reinforce reading on a two-component multiple schedule. Browning (1967) evaluated the relative effects of three forms of staff attention on inappropriate verbal behavior of a patient by having the staff members respond differentially to the patient in one mode at a time, according to a counterbalanced, rotating schedule. O'Brien, Azrin, and Henson (1969) employed a multielement baseline design to study the relationship between the frequency of suggestions offered by mental patients during group meetings and the percentage of patients' suggestions followed by the group leader. Steinman (1970) investigated the social control of generalized imitation by comparing the imitative behaviors of children under two conditions that alternated several times within each session. Corte, Wolf, and Locke (1971) arranged a multielement baseline design consisting of four components—two levels of deprivation and two reinforcement procedures. In one phase of their day-care study, Doke and Risley (1972—Experiment 1) used a multielement baseline technique to compare individual and group-contingent dismissal procedures. Zimmerman and his associates (Hunt and Zimmerman, 1969; Zimmerman, Overpeck, Eisenberg, and Garlick, 1969, Figure 7; Zimmerman, Stuckey, Garlick, and Miller, 1969) utilized multielement baseline logic to compare reinforcement and control conditions in sheltered workshop settings. As a final example of the multielement baseline design in applied research, a recent study by Ulman and Sulzer-Azaroff (unpublished) will be described later in this paper.

SOME POSSIBLE ADVANTAGES OF THE MULTIELEMENT BASELINE DESIGN

Nonreversibility

When the reversal design is employed, the baseline condition is reinstated by discontinuing the treatment procedure. If the meaured level of behavior during the subsequent baseline phase does not, to some measurable degree, return toward the initial baseline level, one cannot be confident that the procedure modified the behavior. If the baseline performance is not recovered, it can be argued that uncontrolled confounding variables were responsible for the change in behavior, not the experimental manipulation. Bandura (1969) has gone so far as to state, "Intrasubject replication . . .

cannot be employed in studying learning phenomena in which certain experiences produce a more or less irreversible change in the behavior of an organism." (p. 243)

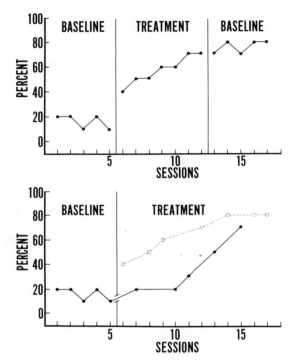

Figure 6-5 *Graphic illustration of two experimental designs (fictitious data). The top graph represents a reversal design in which the behavior did not reverse in the second baseline phase. The bottom graph is a multielement baseline design showing a session-by-session plot of behavior under baseline (closed circles) and treatment (open circles) conditions. The baseline plotted through the break in the line separating the panels indicates that the same condition was in effect during all baseline sessions. (Note: locations of treatment condition data points in the two graphs are identical, yet only the bottom graph demonstrates experimental control.)*

The fictitious data in the top graph of Figure 6-5 illustrate the problem of nonreversibility. In this hypothetical experiment the behavioral measure is the percent of work completed during daily work periods and the treatment consists of monetary reinforcement. Notice that the performance in the second baseline phase did not return to the pretreatment level.

The failure of the behavior to return toward the first baseline following the removal of the experimental procedure might have been due to any of several variables. If the multielement baseline design had been employed instead, it may have been possible to determine whether or not the behavior was functionally related to monetary reinforcement. The vertical distance between the two curves in the treatment phase is a direct reflection of the degree of experimental control produced by the treatment procedure. The decreasing separation of the curves across sessions (sessions 10 through 15 in the bottom graph) indicates that the performance in the absence of extrinsic reinforcement approached the performance maintained by monetary reinforcement. In other words, even though the location of the treatment condition data points in the two graphs of Figure 6-5 correspond exactly, only the bottom graph reflects a causal relationship. It is impossible to determine what caused the change in behavior in the top graph. On the other hand, the bottom graph—the multielement baseline design—constitutes convincing evidence of a functional relationship between the performance and the treatment procedure.

Now suppose the treatment was not effective. Then, performance under the treatment condition would not differ much from baseline performance. Consequently, the two curves plotted in the bottom graph of Figure 6-5 would overlap, and the amount of overlap would indicate the degree to which experimental control had not been demonstrated.

When a multielement baseline design is employed, overlapping data do not necessarily rule out the possible efficacy of an experimental procedure. The session-by-session alternation of conditions might obscure effects that could be observed if the same condition was presented during several consecutive sessions. It is therefore possible that a given treatment may prove to be effective with a reversal or multiple-baseline design, but not with a multielement baseline design.

Termination

Another advantage of the multielement baseline design is that the experiment can be terminated as soon as the experimenter judges that experimental control has been reliably demonstrated. Such is obviously not the case with the reversal or multiple-baseline techniques. The reversal technique requires that each phase consist of the measurement of behavior for several sessions before the experimenter can proceed to the next phase. The multiple baseline requires that at least one behavior be monitored concurrent with another behavior. Even then, once the experimental procedure is applied to one behavior, it is still necessary to continue with the monitoring of the other behavior(s) under baseline conditions. Hence, if situational exigencies arise that force the experimenter to terminate his study prematurely, the multielement baseline design may preclude the necessity of discarding the data and beginning again. Because the experimenter has several repeated measures under each condition, his data may stand by itself at an early stage of the study; or, at least, provide valuable information as a pilot study. To illustrate this advantage, refer to Figure 6-5 and imagine that it was necessary to terminate the hypothetical experiment after session 12, and then compare the two graphs.

Unstable Baseline

Unstable baselines present formidable design problems in operant research. In applied behavior analysis, unstable baselines are frequently encountered when attempting to teach new behaviors. Typically, as an individual practices a skill, there occurs a continuous acceleration of performance, which in turn produces an ascending baseline. Ascending baselines are commonly observed in investigations of academic behavior. The study of academic behavior poses additional problems for the applied researcher. Not only must he contend with the problem of long-term trends that involve ascending baselines, he must also deal with cyclic or irregular variability of performance due to changes in task difficulty. Problems associated with shifting baselines have been held responsible for the fact that educational investigators have shown more interest in classroom control than in skill acquisition (Salzberg, Wheeler, Devar, and Hopkins, 1971.) The multielement baseline design has been found to be quite useful in dealing with unstable baselines. In animal research, Sidman (1960) has observed that the multielement baseline design permits comparisons to be made between experimental conditions, even though a baseline may be changing. Powell and Hake (1971) faced a similar problem with humans. They found that matching-to-sample performance continued to improve under all experimental conditions. To avoid the problem of exposing the behavior to one condition for a prolonged period of time, they employed a multielement baseline design. Consequently, even though the matching-to-sample performance showed constant improvement, experimental control was demonstrated. Similarly, notwithstanding irregularities in performance and changes in task difficulty, Ulman and Sulzer-Azaroff (unpublished) were able to demonstrate experimental control of an academic behavior. Academic performance is an appropriate illustration, for either mastery of a skill or changes in the level of task difficulty may affect baseline performance. The authors recommend that anyone interested in studying academic behavior, or, for that matter, anyone who must otherwise contend with unstable baselines, consider the multielement baseline technique as an alternative experimental design.

Complex Behavior Analysis

Four years ago Baer et al. (1968) remarked, "At this stage in the development of applied behavior analysis, primary concern is usually with reliability, rather than with parametric analysis or component analysis." A great deal of progress has been made since then. There is a growing interest in complex behavior analyses—component analyses of multiple treatment procedures, comparative analyses of different intervention techniques, and parametric analyses of single independent variables. Many of these experiments are further complicated by the inclusion of more than one dependent variable. With few exceptions, researchers who have conducted complex behavior analyses have relied on some form of the reversal design (two notable exceptions are the complex multiple-baseline designs by Christophersen, Arnold, Hill, and Quilitch, 1972, Family Two; and Rule, 1972.) However, with the trend toward more complex behavior analyses, it is anticipated that there will be an increasing demand for more efficient research strategies.

The multielement baseline design seems to be well suited for conducting complex behavior analyses, and particularly for isolating the effects of interrelated controlling variables. Changes in performance that occur consistently with changes in experimental conditions, irrespective of the order in which the conditions are presented, lend credence to the hypothesis that the behavior is functionally related to the manipulated variables. Especially with complex behavior analyses, the more often the independent variables are manipulated, the more believable is the demonstration of experimental control. Thus, when conducting a complex behavior analysis, it is better to manipulate the independent variables repeatedly rather than only once, and it is better to vary the order of their presentation than not to do so.

A major disadvantage of using either the reversal or multiple-baseline design in a complex behavior analysis is that several sessions of one condition must be presented prior to the introduction of the next condition. Moreover, the behavior should meet some type of stability criterion before initiating the change (Sidman, 1960). Yet in practice, rarely do researchers formally specify a stability criterion (Rule, 1972, is an exception). In contrast with the reversal and multiple-baseline designs, the multielement baseline consists, not of phases, but of a succession of probes for distinctive but brief time segments (for example, a series of one-session probes). Within a given time period, the multielement baseline design therefore provides a greater number of experimental manipulations than the reversal or multiple-baseline designs. In their basic operant research with both animals and humans, Hake and his co-workers (Hake and Laws, 1967;

to the introduction of contingent praise, all subjects were exposed to conditions involving rules and ignoring. One must therefore remain in the dark as to the possible sequence effects. Praise may have produced quite different results had the subjects not been given the prior history of rules and ignoring.

One method of controlling sequence effects is to measure two behaviors concurrently, but counterbalance the order of the treatments. For example, Elam and Sulzer (unpublished) applied a group contingency to one behavior while they applied an individual contingency to another. In a subsequent condition, the contingencies were switched so that both treatments were applied to both behaviors, but in the opposite order. According to the logic of this design, if sequence effects are present, the magnitude of behavior change would be a function of the order in which the treatments were applied rather than the treatments per se. However, this design assumes that the behaviors are comparably sensitive to the experimental operations, an assumption that has not yet been verified empirically.

A second method of controlling sequence effects also involves counterbalancing the order of conditions, but measures only one behavior. This procedure requires that a condition precede and follow every other condition at least once. If three conditions (ABC) were being manipulated, for example, they might be presented in the following order: ABCACBA. With this design, also, certain unverified assumptions are made.

According to Bandura (1969), it is probably untenable to assume "that repetitive control does not alter the modifiability of the behavior in question, that behavior at different levels is equally modifiable, and that reinforcement operations are unaffected by contrast in incentive conditions." Bandura believes that the "intrasubject replication design precludes accurate assessment of the relative effects of different treatment variables," and that the effectiveness of different controlling variables can best be evaluated through the use of matched-group experimental designs. Bandura's recommendation creates as many research difficulties as it resolves. To the degree that groups are not appropriately equated through matching procedures, individual differences may introduce uncontrolled intersubject variability into the results. Moreover, group comparisons may provide useful information regarding group trends, but unless the effects are very large, such comparisons will be of little value in predicting and controlling the behavior of individuals.

The multielement baseline design may solve this dilemma. First, this design minimizes possible sequence effects by presenting each condition only briefly (for no more than two consecutive sessions), rather than for a prolonged period of time. There is evidence that suggests that the greater the prior exposure to one condition, the greater the carry-over of effects during a subsequent condition (O'Brien, 1968). Second, sequence effects may be minimized by presenting the conditions in a counterbalanced order according to the second method just described. Because conditions change from session to session rather than from phase to phase, the multielement baseline design does not require an excessive number of sessions for counterbalancing. Hence, the experimenter can arrange the conditions to precede and follow one another many times, while keeping the total number of sessions within practical limits.

Contrast Effects

The term "contrast" is usually associated with interactions among components of a multiple schedule. When behavioral contrast occurs, the behavior in the two components changes in opposite directions. Generalization or induction is a similar phenomenon, except that the change is in the same direction. "Contrast," like generalization, "furnishes an example of changes in behavior under one set of circumstances, which are caused by changes in the consequences of the behavior under a different set of circumstances" (Reynolds, 1968, pp. 45–46). For the sake of simplicity, however, we will consider contrast effects only, though the discussion may also apply to induction.

The extent to which the multielement baseline design is useful depends upon the degree of absence of contrast effects. Despite the lack of knowledge concerning contrast (see reviews by Dunham, 1968; and Freeman, 1971), it may be possible to control such effects when using a multielement baseline design. First, as was discussed regarding sequence effects, one may counterbalance the order of conditions so that each condition is followed equally often by every other condition.

Second, contrast effects may be minimized by programming only one condition per session. Powell and Hake (1971), in a study comparing the relative effects of positive and negative reinforcement on children's matching-to-sample performance, were able to minimize interactions between the two reinforcement conditions by presenting only one condition per session.

Third, a more direct method of controlling contrast effects is to assess the extent to which such effects are present. Contrast effects may be assessed by conducting control experiments in which each component appears separately. "A comparison can then be made between a given element when programmed by itself and when programmed as a component" (Sidman, 1960, p. 335) of a multielement baseline. A more precise approach would be to conduct a functional analysis by making a "quantitative alteration in a parameter of the components" (Sidman, 1960, p. 336). O'Brien's (1968) investigation of contrast effects in humans provides an example of this latter technique.

Behavioral contrast research (Dunham, 1968; Freeman, 1971) suggests that the effects are reliable, but relatively small. If similar results are found with the multielement baseline design in applied settings—if it is found that condition-change interactions are small—there would apparently be few disadvantages to its use in educational research. In the absence of a systematic investigation, however, such interactions remain unspecified, and any generalizations based on this design should be qualified accordingly.

AN EXAMPLE OF THE USE OF THE MULTIELEMENT BASELINE DESIGN

In a recent experiment, Ulman and Sulzer-Azaroff (unpublished) employed a multielement baseline design to compare the effects of group and individual reinforcement contingencies on the academic behaviors of six retarded adults in a special education classroom.

Experimental Procedures and Results

During each daily class period, the students earned money on the basis of the number of arithmetic problems they answered correctly. Under the group-contingency condition, referred to as collective reinforcement, students earned money in the same manner as they would under the individual contingency. However, at the end of the period the earnings were pooled so that each student received an equal share of the money instead of the amount he had actually earned. To provide a baseline against which to compare the two reinforcement conditions, a no-reinforcement condition was also investigated.

Students were informed of the condition that was in effect during a given session by instructions from the teacher and by a large sign: "Earn for Yourself Today" for individual reinforcement, "Earn for Your Class Today" for collective reinforcement, or "No Pay Today" for no reinforcement. The conditions were presented in a mixed series, one condition per period (session). Within every triad, or set of three sessions, beginning with the first session, a student was exposed to all three conditions. Each triad, enclosed by vertical lines in Figure 6-6, was composed of a different permutation of the conditions. Type and/or difficulty level of problems assigned to a student changed when he had met a performance criterion, and only then at the start of a session that marked the beginning of a triad—that is, sessions 1, 4, 7, and so on. As keyed in Figure 6-6, the three experimental conditions are indicated by different data-point symbols.

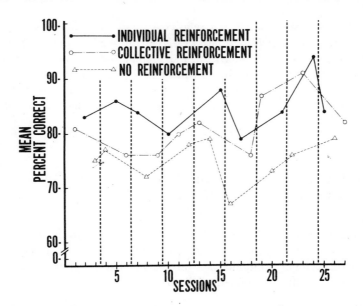

Figure 6-6   *Each data point represents the mean percentage of arithmetic problems completed correctly by the class in each session. Type and difficulty level of problems remained constant during sessions enclosed by adjacent vertical lines (panels). Data-point symbols indicate the experimental condition for a session.*

When viewed across all 27 sessions, the pattern of mean accuracy scores indicated that the experimental manipulations produced different effects. Although intersubject variability was considerable, arithmetic accuracy was generally highest under the individual reinforcement condition and lowest under the no-reinforcement condition.

Discussion

The multielement baseline design served three major purposes. First, it permitted a complex behavior analysis within a minimal number of sessions. Second, by means of a mixed-series technique, it served as a control for sequence effects. Third, it dealt successfully with an unstable baseline. Note that the difficulty level of problems could change from one triad to the next (Figure 6-6), but remained unchanged within a given panel. This procedure (a) allowed students to progress through sequenced instructional material at their own rates, and (b) allowed performances under all three conditions to be meaningfully compared within panels, despite the instability of the baseline (no-reinforcement) performance. This tactic alone would appear to give the multielement baseline design a decided advantage over the other behavior analysis designs, especially in educational research.

CONCLUSION

This paper has discussed several potential advantages of the multielement baseline design: its ability to deal with nonreversible behavior, to provide a safeguard against premature termination of an experiment, to contend with unstable baselines, to facilitate complex behavior analyses, to be acceptable to school personnel, to assess stimulus generalization across situations, and to minimize conditioning-change interactions. Considering the importance of studying academic behaviors and the growing interest in complex behavior analyses, there is an urgent need to develop new approaches to the design of experiments. Risley (1969, p. 116) has stated, "The 'ideal' experimental design would allow simultaneous measurement and comparison of the behavior of a single individual in both the presence and absence of the experimental procedures." The authors offer the multielement baseline design as an alternative to the reversal and multiple-baseline designs, but it remains for future research to determine how closely it will approximate the "ideal."

References

ALLEN, K. E., HART, B., BUELL, J. S., HARRIS, F. R., and WOLF, M. M., "Effects of Social Reinforcement on Isolate Behavior of a Nursery School Child," *Child Development,* 35 (1964), 511–18.

ALLEN, K. E., HENKE, L. B., HARRIS, F. R., BAER, D. M., and REYNOLDS, N. J., "Control of Hyperactivity by Social Reinforcement of Attending Behavior," *Journal of Educational Psychology,* 4 (1967), 231–37.

ALLYON, R. and AZRIN, N. H., *The Token Economy: A Motivational System for Therapy and Rehabilitation.* New York: Appleton-Century-Crofts, 1968.

ANDREWS, W. R., "Behavioral and Client-Centered Counseling of High School Underachievers," *Journal of Counseling Psychology,* 18 (1971), 93–96.

AZRIN, N. H. and HOLZ, W. C., "Punishment." Chapter 5 in W. K. HONIG, ed., *Operant Behavior: Areas of Research and Application.* New York: Appleton-Century-Crofts, 1966.

BADGER, E., "A Mother's Training Program: The Road to a Purposeful Existence," *Children,* 18 (1971) 168–73.

BAER, D. M., "Behavior Modification: You Shouldn't," in E. A. Ramp and

B. L. Hopkins, eds., *A New Direction for Education: Behavior Analysis, 1971,* pp. 358–67. Lawrence, Kansas: Support and Development Center for Follow Through, Department of Human Development, University of Kansas, 1972.

BAER, D. M., PETERSON, R. F., and SHERMAN, J. A., "The Development of Imitation by Reinforcing Behavioral Similarity to a Model," *Journal of the Experimental Analysis of Behavior,* 10 (1967), 405–16.

BAER, D. M., WOLF, M. M., and RISLEY, T. R., "Some Current Dimensions of Applied Behavior Analysis," *Journal of Applied Behavior Analysis,* 1 (1968), 91–94.

BAILEY, J. S., PHILLIPS, E. L., and WOLF, M. M., "Home-Based Reinforcement and the Modification of Pre-Delinquents' Classroom Behavior," *Journal of Applied Behavior Analysis,* 3 (1970), 223–33.

BAILEY, J. S., TIMBERS, G. D., PHILLIPS, E. L., and WOLF, M. M., "Modification of Articulation Errors of Pre-Delinquents by Their Peers," *Journal of Applied Behavior Analysis,* 4 (1971), 47–63.

BANDURA, A., "Behavioral modifications through modeling procedures," in L. Krasner and L. P. Ullmann, eds., *Research in Behavior Modification,* pp. 310–40. New York: Holt, Rinehart & Winston, 1967.

———, *Principles of Behavior Modification.* New York: Holt, Rinehart & Winston, 1969.

———, "Vicarious and Self-Reinforcement Processes," in R. Glaser, ed., *The Nature of Reinforcement.* Columbus, Ohio: Merrill, 1971.

BANDURA, A., GRUSEC, J. E., and MENLOVE, F. L., "Vicarious Extinction of Avoidance Behavior," *Journal of Personality and Social Psychology,* 5 (1967), 16–23.

BARBERO, G. J. and SHAHEEN, E., "Environmental Failure to Thrive: A Clinical View," *The Journal of Pediatrics,* 71 (1967), 639–44.

BARON, A., KAUFMAN, A., and STAUBER, K. A., "Effects of Instructions on Human Operant Behavior Maintained by Fixed-Interval Reinforcement," *Journal of the Experimental Analysis of Behavior,* 12 (1969), 701–12.

BARRISH, H. H., SAUNDERS, M., and WOLF, M. M., "Good Behavior Game: Effects of Individual Contingencies for Group Consequences on Disruptive Behavior in a Classroom," *Journal of Applied Behavior Analysis,* 2 (1969), 119–24.

BECKER, W. C., "Behavior Analysis and Education—1972," in G. Semb et al., eds., *Behavior Analysis and Education—1972,* pp. 11–24. Lawrence, Kansas: Support and Development Center for Follow Through, Department of Human Development, 1972.

BECKER, W. C., MADSEN, C. H., ARNOLD, C. R., and THOMAS, D. R., "The Contingent Use of Teacher Attention and Praise in Reducing Classroom Behavior Problems. *The Journal of Special Education,* 1 (1967), 287–307.

BEREITER, C., "Use of Tests to Measure Change," *Personnel and Guidance Journal,* 41 (1962), 6–11.

BERGIN, A. E., "The Effects of Psychotherapy: Negative Results Revisited," *Journal of Counseling Psychology,* 10 (1963), 244–49.

BIJOU, S. W., BIRNBRAUER, J. S., KIDDER, J. D., and TAGUE, C., "Programmed

Instruction as an Approach to Teaching of Reading, Writing, and Arithmetic to Retarded Children," *Psychological Record,* 16 (1966), 505–22.

BIJOU, S. W., PETERSON, R. F., and AULT, M., "A Method to Integrate Descriptive and Experimental Field Studies at the Level of Data and Empirical Concepts," *Journal of Applied Behavior Analysis,* 1 (1968), 175–91.

BIJOU, S. W., PETERSON, R. F., HARRIS, F. R., ALLEN, K. E., and JOHNSTON, M. S., "Methodology for Experimental Studies of Young Children in Natural Settings," *Psychological Record,* 19 (1969), 177–210.

BIRNBRAUER, J. S., BIJOU, S. W., WOLF, M. M., and KIDDER, J. D., "Programmed Instruction in the Classroom, in L. P. Ullmann, and L. Krasner, eds., *Case Studies in Behavior Modification,* pp. 358–63. New York: Holt, Rinehart & Winston, 1965.

BIRNBRAUER, J. S., WOLF, M. M., KIDDER, J. D., and TAGUE, C., "Classroom Behavior of Retarded Pupils with Token Reinforcement," *Journal of Experimental Child Psychology,* 2 (1965), 219–35.

BLASE, K., and HOPKINS, B. L., "The Modification of Sentence Structure and its Relationship to Subjective Judgments of Creativity in Writing," *Journal of Applied Behavior Analysis,* 6 (1973), (in press).

BLOOMFIELD, L. and BARNHART, C., *Let's Read.* Detroit: Wayne State University Press, 1961.

BORN, D. G., GLEDHILL, S. M., and DAVIS, M. L., "Examination Performance in Lecture-Discussion and Personalized Instruction Courses," *Journal of Applied Behavior Analysis,* 5 (1972), 33–43.

BRAY, STEVE, *The Last Whole Earth Catalogue.* New York: Random House, 1971.

BRIGHAM, T. A., GRAUBARD, P. S., and STANS, A., "Analysis of the Effects of Sequential Reinforcement Contingencies on Aspects of Composition," *Journal of Applied Behavior Analysis,* 5 (1972), 421–29.

BRIGHAM, T. A. and SHERMAN, J. A., "An Experimental Analysis of Verbal Imitation in Preschool Children," *Journal of Applied Behavior Analysis,* 1 (1968), 151–58.

BRODEN, M., BRUCE, C., MITCHELL, M. A., CARTER, V., and HALL, R. V., "Effects of Teacher Attention on Attending Behavior of Two Boys at Adjacent Desks," *Journal of Applied Behavior Analysis,* 3 (1970), 199–204.

BRODSKY, G., "The Relationship Between Verbal and Non-Verbal Behavior Change," *Behavior Research and Therapy,* 5 (1967), 183–91.

BUEHLER, R., PATTERSON, G. R., and FURNESS, J., "The Reinforcement of Behavior in Institutional Settings," *Behavior Research and Therapy,* 4 (1966), 157–67.

BUSHELL, D., JR., "Intervention and Behavior Management in the Preschool and Early Elementary Years," paper presented at the National Association for the Education of Young Children, Atlanta, (-a., November, 1972.

CAMPBELL, D. T. and STANLEY, J. C., *Experimental and Quasi-Experimental Designs for Research.* Chicago: Rand McNally, 1963.

CARNINE, D., BECKER, W. C., THOMAS, D. R., POE, M., and PLAGER, E., "The Effects of Direct and 'Vicarious' Reinforcement on the Behavior of Problem Boys in an Elementary School Classroom," unpublished manuscript, University of Illinois, 1968.

CATALDO, M. F. and RISLEY, T. R., "Design of a Model for Group Infant Day Care," Third Annual Kansas Conference on Behavior Analysis in Education, Lawrence, Kansas, 1972a.

————, "Infant Day Care," in R. E. Ulrich, T. Stachnik, and J. Mabry, eds., *Control of Human Behavior*, Vol. III: "Behavior Modification in Education." Glenview, Ill.: Scott Foresman, 1974.

————, "The Organization of Group Care Environments: The Infant Day Care Center," Annual Meeting of the American Psychological Association, Honolulu, Hawaii, 1972b.

CHRISTOPHERSON, E. R., ARNOLD, C. M., HILL, D. W., and QUILITCH, H. R., "The Home Point System: Token Reinforcement Procedures for Application by Parents of Children with Behavior Poblems," *Journal of Applied Behavior Analysis*, 5, (1972), 485–97.

CLARK, F. W., EVANS, D. R., and HAMERLYNCK, L. A., eds., *Implementing Behavioral Programs for Schools and Clinics, 1971*. Champaign, Ill.: Research Press, 1972.

CONNOLLY, A. J., NACHTMAN, W., and PRITCHETT, E. M., *Key Math: Diagnostic Arithmetic Test*. Circle Pines, Minn.: American Guidance Service, 1971.

COOPER, M. L., THOMPSON, C. L., and BAER, D. M., "The Experimental Modification of Teacher Attending Behavior," *Journal of Applied Behavior Analysis*, 3 (1970), 153–57.

CORKHUFF, R., "Training as a Preferred Mode of Treatment," *Journal of Counseling Psychology*, 18 (1971), 129.

CORTE, H. E., WOLF, M. M., and LOCKE, B. J., "A Comparison of Procedures for Eliminating Self-Injurious Behavior of Retarded Adolescents," *Journal of Applied Behavior Analysis*, 4 (1971), 201–13.

CSAPO, M., "Peer Models Reverse the 'One Bad Apple Spoils the Barrel' theory," *Teaching Exceptional Children*, 4 (1972), 20–24

DIEDERICH, P. B., FRENCH, J. W., and CARLTON, S. T., "Factors in Judgments of Writing Ability," Research Bulletin Series RB-61-15. Princeton, N.J.: Educational Testing Service, 1961.

DOKE, L. A. and RISLEY, T. R., "The Organization of Day-Care Environments: Required *vs* Optional Activities," *Journal of Applied Behavior Analysis*, 5 (1972), 405–20.

————, "The PLA-Check Evaluation of Group Care," paper read at Annual Meeting of the Kansas Psychological Association, Overland Park, Kansas, April, 1971.

DRASS, S. D. and JONES, R. L., "Learning Disabled Children as Behavior Modifiers," *Journal of Learning Disabilities*, 4 (1971), 418–25.

DUNHAM, P. J., "Contrasted Conditions of Reinforcement: A Selective Critique," *Psychological Bulletin*, 69 (1968), 295–315.

EDUCARDS, INC., *New Math Addition Flashcards #261*.

————, *New Math Subtraction Flashcards #262*.

EDWARDS, A. L. and CRONBACH, L. J., "Experimental Design for Research in Psychotherapy," *Journal of Clinical Psychology*, 8 (1952), 51–59.

ELAM, D. and SULZER, B., "Group Versus Individual Reinforcement in Modifying Problem Behaviors in a Trainable Mentally Handicapped Classroom," unpublished paper, Southern Illinois University, 1972.

ELMER, E., "Failure to Thrive," *Pediatrics,* 25 (1960), 717–25.

ESTES, W. K., "An Experimental Study of Punishment," *Psychological Monographs,* No. 263, 57 (1944), entire issue.

ETZEL, B. C. and GEWIRTZ, J. L., "Experimental Modification of Caretaker-Maintained High-Rate Crying in a 6- and a 20-week-old Infant (Infant Tyrannotearus): Extinction of Crying with Reinforcement of Eye Contact and Smiling," *Journal of Experimental Child Psychology,* 5 (1967), 303–17.

FARMER, P. and FREEMAN, B., *The Teaching of English in Georgia.* Atlanta: Georgia Council of Teachers of English, 1952.

FERGUSON, N., "Peers as Social Agents," unpublished Master's thesis, University of Minnesota, 1964.

FERSTER, C. B. and SKINNER, B. F., *Schedules of Reinforcement.* New York: Appleton-Century-Crofts, 1957.

FIEDLER, F. E., "The Concept of an Ideal Therapeutic Relationship," *Journal of Consulting Psychology,* 14 (1950), 239–45.

FIXSEN, D. L., PHILLIPS, E. L., and WOLF, M. M., "Achievement Place: Experiments in Self-Government with Pre-Delinquents," *Journal of Applied Behavior Analysis,* 6 (1973), 31–47.

————, "Achievement Place: The Reliability of Self-Reporting and Peer-reporting and their Effects on Behavior," *Journal of Applied Behavior Analysis,* 5 (1972), 19–30.

FLANDERS, J. P., "A Review of Research on Imitative Behavior," *Psychological Bulletin,* 69 (1968), 316–37.

FOLLETT EDUCATIONAL CORPORATION, *The World of Language,* Books 2–4.

FORD, D., FORD, M. E., CHRISTOPHERSEN, E. R., FIXSEN, D. L., PHILLIPS, E. L., and WOLF, M. M., "An Analysis of Effects of Teaching Skills in a Token Economy for Pre-Delinquent Youth," unpublished manuscript, 1973.

FOX, R., "The Coding Manual for the Responsive Teaching Computer Retrieval Program," unpublished manuscript, University of Kansas, 1972.

FREEMAN, B. J., "Behavioral Contrast: Reinforcement Frequency or Response Suppression," *Psychological Bulletin,* 75 (1971), 347–56.

GAGNE, R. M., "The Analysis of Instructional Objectives for the Design of Instruction in Reading," in R. Glaser, ed., *Teaching Machines and Programmed Learning II: Data and Directions,* pp. 21–65. Washington, D.C.: National Education Association, 1965.

GELFAND, D. M. and HARTMAN, D. P., "Behavior Therapy with Children: A Review and Evaluation of Research Methodology," *Psychological Bulletin,* 69, (1968), 204–15.

GEWIRTZ, J. L., "The Role of Overt Responding and Extrinsic Reinforcement in 'Self-' and Vicarious Reinforcement Phenomena and in 'Observational Learning' and Imitation," in R. Glaser, ed., *The Nature of Reinforcement,* pp. 280–309. New York: Academic, 1971.

GIBBONS, D. C., *Delinquent Behavior.* Englewood Cliffs, N.J.: Prentice-Hall, 1970.

GILES, D. K. and HARRIS, V. W., "Behavior Modification Tactics in a Twenty-

Four-Hour Residential Rehabilitation Center for Juvenile Offenders," paper presented at 80th Annual Convention, American Psychological Association, Honolulu, Hawaii, September 2–9, 1972.

GOETZ, E. M. and BAER, D. M., "Descriptive Social Reinforcement of 'Creative' Blockbuilding by Young Children, in E. Ramp and B. L. Hopkins, eds., *A New Direction for Education: Behavior Analysis, 1971,* pp. 72–79. Lawrence, Kansas: Support and Development Center for Follow Through, Department of Human Development, University of Kansas, 1971.

GOETZ, E. M. and SALMONSON, M., "The Effects of General and Descriptive Reinforcement on 'Creativity' in Easel Painting," in G. Semb et al., eds., *Behavior Analysis and Education—1972,* pp. 53–61. Lawrence, Kansas: Support and Development Center for Follow Through, Department of Human Development, University of Kansas, 1972.

GOLDIAMOND, I., "Coping and Adaptive Behaviors of the Disabled," paper read at Conference on Socialization in the Disability Process, Chicago, Ill., March 5–6, 1973.

GOODALL, K., "Shapers at Work," *Psychology Today,* 6 (1972), 53.

————, " 'This Little Girl Won't Interact with Other Little Girls and She Crawls Around a Lot,' A Conversation with Montrose M. Wolf," *Psychology Today, June, 1973,* 64–72.

GRAY, B. B., BAKER, R. D. and STANCYK, S. E., "Performance Determined Instruction for Training Remedial Reading," *Journal of Applied Behavior Analysis,* 2 (1969), 255–63.

GREENE, F. M., "Programmed Instruction Techniques for the Mentally Retarded," in N. R. Ellis, ed., *International Review of Research in Mental Retardation,* 2 (1966), 228.

GROVER, C. and STONE, C., eds., *New Practice Readers.* New York: McGraw-Hill, 1962.

HAKE, D. F. and LAWS, D. R., "Social Facilitation of Responses During a Stimulus Paired with Electric Shock," *Journal of the Experimental Analysis of Behavior,* 10 (1967), 387–92.

HAKE, D. F., POWELL, J., and OLSEN, R., "Conditioned Suppression as a Sensitive Baseline for Social Facilitation," *Journal of the Experimental Analysis of Behavior,* 12 (1969), 807–16.

HALL, R. V., *Behavior Management Series: Part I—The Measurement of Behavior; Part II—Basic Principles; Part III—Application in School and Home.* Lawrence, Kansas: H & H Enterprises, 1971.

————, "Retrieval System for the Responsive Teaching Model and its Applications," paper presented at the Fourth Annual Conference on Behavior Analysis in Education, Lawrence, Kansas, April, 1973.

HALL, R. V., AXELROD, S., FOUNDOPOLOUS, M., SHELLMAN, J., CAMPBELL, R. A., and CRANSTON, S. S., "The Effective Use of Punishment in the Classroom," *Educational Technology,* 4, (1971), 24–26.

HALL, R. V., AXELROD, S., TYLER, L., GRIEF, E., JONES, F., and ROBERTSON, R., "Modification of Behavior Problems in the Home with a Parent as Observer and Experimenter," *Journal of Applied Behavior Analysis,* 5 (1972), 53–64.

HALL, R. V., AYALA, H., COPELAND, R., COSSAIRT, A., FREEMAN, J., and HARRIS, J., "Responsive Teaching: An Approach for Training Teachers in

Applied Behavior Analysis Techniques, in E. A. Ramp and B. L. Hopkins, eds., *A New Direction for Education: Behavior Analysis, 1971*, pp. 125–57. Lawrence, Kansas: Support and Development Center for Follow Through, Department of Human Development, University of Kansas, 1971.

HALL, R. V. and BRODEN, M., "Behavior Changes in Brain-Injured Children Through Social Reinforcement. *Journal of Experimental Child Psychology*, 5 (1967), 463–79.

HALL, R. V. and COPELAND, R. E., "The Responsive Teaching Model: A First Step in Shaping School Personnel as Behavior Modification Specialists, in *Proceedings of the Third Banff International Conference on Behavior Modification*, University of Calgary, Calgary, Canada, 1971.

HALL, R. V., FOX, R., WILLARD, D., GOLDSMITH, L., EMERSON, M., OWENS, M., DAVIS, F., and PORCHIA, E., "The Teacher as Observer and Experimenter in the Modification of Disputing and Talking-out Behaviors," *Journal of Applied Behavior Analysis*, 4 (1971), 141–49.

HALL, R. V., LUND, D., and JACKSON, D., "Effects of Teacher Attention on Study Behavior," *Journal of Applied Behavior Analysis*, 1 (1968), 1–12.

HALL, R. V., PANYAN, M., RABON, D., and BRODEN, M., "Instructing Beginning Teachers in Reinforcement Procedures Which Improve Classroom Control," *Journal of Applied Behavior Analysis*, 1 (1968), 315–22.

HANLEY, E. M., "Review of Research Involving Applied Behavior Analysis in the Classroom," *Review of Educational Research*, 40 (1971), 597–625.

HARING, N. G and HAYDEN, A. H., "What is Instructional Improvement?" In N. G. Haring and A. H. Hayden, eds., *The Improvement of Instruction*. Seattle: Special Child Publications, 1972.

HARRIS, F. R., JOHNSTON, M. S., KELLEY, C. S., and WOLF, M. M., "Effects of Positive Social Reinforcement on Regressed Crawling of a Preschool Child," *Journal of Educational Psychology*, 55 (1964), 35–41.

HARRIS, M. S., "Effects of Home-Based Contingencies on Assignment Completion," unpublished Master's thesis, University of Kansas, 1971.

HART, B. M., REYNOLDS, N. J., BAER, D. M., BRAWLEY, E. R., and HARRIS, F. R., "Effect of Contingent and Non-Contingent Social Reinforcement on the Cooperative Play of a Preschool Child," *Journal of Applied Behavior Analysis*, 1 (1968), 73–76.

HARTUP, W. W., "Peer Interaction and Social Organization," in G. Mussen, ed., *Carmichael's Handbook of Child Psychology* (3d ed.), 170–76. New York: John Wiley, 1970.

HAYDEN, A. H. and TORKELSON, G. M., *Systematic Thinking about Education*. Bloomington, Ind.: Phi Delta Kappa Educational Foundation, Fast Back No. 17, 1973.

HERBERT, E. W. and BAER, D. M., "Training Parents as Behavior Modifiers: Self-Recording of Contingent Attention," *Journal of Applied Behavior Analysis*, 5 (1972), 139–49.

HERMAN, S. H. and TRAMONTANA, J., "Instructions and Group versus Individual Reinforcement in Modifying Disruptive Group Behavior," *Journal of Applied Behavior Analysis*, 4 (1971), 113–19.

HESS, R. D., BLOCH, M., COSTELLO, J., KNOWLES, R. T., and LARGAY, D., "Parent Involvement in· Early Education," in E. H. Grotberg, ed., *Day-*

care: Resources for Decisions, pp. 265–98. Washington, D.C.: Office of Economic Opportunity, n.d.

HINDS, W. C. and ROEHLKE, H. J., "A Learning Theory Approach to Group Counseling with Elementary School Children," *Journal of Counseling Psychology,* 4 (1970).

HIRSCHI, T. and SELVIN, H. C., *Delinquency Research.* New York: Free Press, 1967.

HOBBS, N., "Sources of Gain in Psychotherapy," *American Psychologist,* 17 (1962), 741–47.

HOLLAND, C. J., "Elimination by the Parents of Fire Setting Behavior in a Seven Year Old Boy. *Behavior Research and Therapy,* 7 (1969), 135–37.

HOLLAND, J. G., "Political Implications of Applying Behavioral Psychology," In R. E. Ulrich, T. Stachnik, and J. Mabry, eds., *Control of Human Behavior.* Vol. III: "Behavior Modification in Education." Glenview, Ill.: Scott, Foresman, 1974.

HOLLAND, J. G. and SKINNER, B. F., *The Analysis of Behavior.* New York: McGraw-Hill, 1961.

HOPKINS, B. L., SCHUTTE, R. C., and GARTON, K. L., "The Effects of Access to a Playroom on the Rate and Quality of Printing and Writing of First and Second-Grade Students," *Journal of Applied Behavior Analysis,* 4, (1971), 77–87.

HUNT, J. G. and ZIMMERMAN, J., "Stimulating Productivity in a Simulated Sheltered Workshop Setting," *American Journal of Mental Deficiency,* 74 (1969), 43–49.

JEFFERY, C. R., *Crime Prevention Through Environmental Design.* Beverly Hills, London: Sage Publications, 1971.

JOHNSTON, M. K., KELLEY, S. C., HARRIS, F. R., and WOLF, M. M., "An Application of Reinforcement Principles to Development of Motor Skills of a Young Child," *Child Development,* 37 (1966), 101–9.

KARNES, M. B., TESKA, J. A., HODGINS, A. S., and BADGER, E. D., "Educational Intervention at Home by Mothers of Disadvantaged Infants," *Child Development,* 41 (1970), 925–35.

KARNES, M. B. and ZEHRBACH, R. R., "Flexibility in Getting Parents Involved in the School," *Teaching Exceptional Children,* 5 (1972), 6–19.

KAZDIN, A. E., "The Effects of Vicarious Reinforcement on Attentive Behavior in the Classroom," *Journal of Applied Behavior Analysis,* 6 (1973), 71–78.

KELLER, F. S., "Goodbye, teacher," *Journal of Applied Behavior Analysis,* 1, (1968), 79–89.

KELLER, F. S. and SCHOENFELD, W. N., *Principles of Psychology.* New York: Appleton-Century-Crofts, 1950.

KNOWLTON, P., "Treatment and Management of the Autistic Child," in M. Hammer and A. Kaplan, eds. *The Practice of Psychotherapy with Children,* pp. 215–53. Homewood, Ill.: Dorsey Press, 1967.

KRUMBOLTZ, J. D. and THORESEN, C. E., "The Effect of Behavioral Counseling in Group and Individual Settings on Information-Seeking Behavior," *Journal of Counseling Psychology,* 11 (1964), 324–33.

KUYPERS, D. S., BECKER, W. C., and O'LEARY, K. D., "How to Make a Token System Fail," *Exceptional Children,* 35 (1968), 101–9.

LANG, P. and MALAMED, B., "Avoidance Conditioning Therapy of an Infant with Chronic Ruminative Vomiting," *Journal of Abnormal Psychology,* 74 (1969), 1–8.

LELAURIN, K. and RISLEY, T. R., "The Organization of Daycare Environments: 'Zone' versus 'Man-to-Man' Staff Assignments," *Journal of Applied Behavior Analysis,* 5 (1972), 225–32.

LEVITT, E. E., "Psychotherapy with Children: A Further Evaluation," *Behavior Research and Therapy,* 1 (1963), 45–52.

LEWIS, W. A., "Emotional Adjustment and Need Satisfaction of Hospital Patients," *Journal of Counseling Psychology,* 6 (1959), 127–31.

LOVITT, T. C., "Rate as an Academic Response Measure," unpublished manuscript, University of Washington, 1970.

LOVITT, T. C. and ESVELDT, K. A., "The Relative Effects on Math Performance of Single- versus Multiple-Ratio Schedules: A Case Study," *Journal of Applied Behavior Analysis,* 3 (1970), 261–70.

LOVITT, T. C., GUPPY, T. E., and BLATTNER, J. E., "The Use of a Free-Time Contingency with Fourth Graders to Increase Spelling Accuracy. *Behavior Research and Therapy,* 1 (1969), 151–56.

LOVITT, T. C. and SMITH, J. O., "Effects of Instructions on an Individual's Verbal Behavior," *Exceptional Children* (May, 1972), 685–93.

MADSEN, C. H., JR., BECKER, W. C., and THOMAS, D., "Rules, Praise, and Ignoring: Elements of Elementary Classroom Control," *Journal of Applied Behavior Analysis,* 1 (1968), 139–50.

MADSEN, C. H., JR. and MADSEN, C. R., *Learning and Observational Manual* (for *Teaching/Discipline: Behavioral Principles Toward A Positive Approach*). Boston: Allyn & Bacon, 1974.

MANN, R. A., "The Behavior-Therapeutic use of Contingency Contracting to Control an Adult Behavior Problem: Weight Control," *Journal of Applied Behavior Analysis,* 5 (1972), 99–109.

MCALLISTER, L. W., STACHOWIAK, J. G., BAER, D. M., and CONDERMAN, L., "The Application of Operant Conditioning Techniques in a Secondary School Classrocm," *Journal of Applied Behavior Analysis,* 2 (1969), 277–85.

MCKENZIE, H. S., EGNER, H. A., KNIGHT, M., PERELMAN, P. F., SCHNEIDER, B. M., and GARVIN, J. S., "Training Consulting Teachers to Assist Elementary Teachers in the Management and Education of Handicapped Children," *Exceptional Children,* 37 (1970), 137–43.

MCLAUGHLIN, T. F. and MALABY, J. E., "Development of Procedures for Classroom Token Economies," in E. A. Ramp and B. L. Hopkins, eds., *A New Direction for Education: Behavior Analysis, 1971,* Lawrence Kansas: Support and Development Center for Follow Through, Department of Human Development, University of Kansas, 1971.

————, "Intrinsic Reinforcers in a Classroom Token Economy," *Journal of Applied Behavior Analysis,* 5 (1972), 263–70.

————, "Reducing and Measuring Inappropriate Verbalizations in a Token Economy," *Journal of Applied Behavior Analysis,* 5 (1972), 329–33.

MEDLAND, M. B. and STACHNIK, T. J., "Good-Behavior Game: A Replication and Systematic Analysis," *Journal of Applied Behavior Analysis,* 5 (1972), 45–51.

MENDELSOHN, E., SWAZEY, J. P., and TAVISS, I., eds., *Human Aspects of Biomedical Innovation.* Cambridge: Harvard University Press, 1971.

MESTHENE, E. G., in E. Mendelsohn, J. P. Swazey, and I. Taviss, eds., *Human Aspects of Biomedical Innovation.* Cambridge: Harvard University Press, 1971.

MILLER, L. K., *Introduction to Everyday Behavior Analysis.* Lawrence, Kansas: privately printed, 1973.

MILLER, L. K. and WEAVER, H. F., "The use of Generalization Programming to Teach Concepts to University Students," paper read at the American Psychological Association convention, Montreal, August 27–31, 1973.

MINUCHIN, S., "Discussion of the Present Day Scope of Clinical Services in American Child Psychiatry," in P. L. Adams, H. H. Work, and J. B. Cramer, eds., *Academic Child Psychiatry,* pp. 30–31. Gainesville, Fla.: Shorter Printing Co., 1969.

MIRA, M., "Results of a Behavior Modification Training Program for Parents and Teachers," *Behavior Research and Therapy,* 8 (1970), 309–11.

NORDHOFF, C., *Communistic Societies of the United States.* New York: Harper and Brothers, 1875.

O'BRIEN, F., "Sequential Contrast Effects with Human Subjects," *Journal of the Experimental Analysis of Behavior,* 11 (1968), 537–42.

O'BRIEN, F., AZRIN, N. H., and HENSON, K., "Increased Communications of Chronic Mental Patients by Reinforcement and by Response Priming," *Journal of Applied Behavior Analysis,* 2 (1969), 23–29.

OHLSON, M. M., *Group Counseling.* New York: Holt, Rinehart & Winston, 1970.

O'LEARY, K. D. and BECKER, W. C., "Behavior Modification of an Adjustment Class: A Token Reinforcement Program," *Exceptional Children,* 33 (1967), 637–42.

O'LEARY, K. D., BECKER, W. C., EVANS, M. B., and SAUDARGAS, R. A., "A Token Reinforcement Program in a Public School: A Replication and Systematic Analysis," *Journal of Applied Behavior Analysis,* 2 (1969), 3–13.

O'LEARY, K. D. and DRABMAN, R., "Token Reinforcement Programs in the Classroom: A Review," *Psychological Bulletin,* 75 (1971), 379–98.

O'LEARY, K. D. and KENT, R., "Behavior Modification for Social Action: Research Tactics and Problems," in L. A. Hamerlynck, L. C. Handy, and E. J. Mash, eds., *Behavior Change: Methodology, Concepts, and Practice.* Champaign, Ill.: Research Press, 1973.

PACKARD, R. G., "The Control of 'Classroom attention': A Group Contingency for Complex Behavior," *Journal of Applied Behavior Analysis,* 3 (1970), 13–28.

PATTERSON, R. L. and TEIGEN, J. R., Conditioning and Post-Hospital Generalization of Nondelusional Responses in a Chronic Psychotic Patient," *Journal of Applied Behavior Analysis,* 6 (1973), 65–70.

PAUL, G. L., *Insight Vs. Desensitization in Psychotherapy.* Stanford, Calif.: Stanford University Press, 1966.

PHILLIPS, E. L., "Achievement Place: Token Reinforcement Procedures in a Home-Style Rehabilitation Setting for 'Pre-Delinquent' Boys," *Journal of Applied Behavior Analysis,* 1 (1968), 213–23.

PHILLIPS, E. L., PHILLIPS, E. A., FIXSEN, D. L., and WOLF, M. M., "Achievement Place: Modification of the Behaviors of Pre-Delinquent Boys within a Token Economy," *Journal of Applied Behavior Analysis,* 4 (1971) 45–59.

———, *The Teaching-Family Handbook.* Champaign, Ill.: Research Press, 1974.

PINKSTON, E. M., REESE, N. M., LeBLANC, J. M., and BAER, D. M., "Independent Control of a Pre-School Child's Aggression and Peer Interaction by Contingent Teacher Attention," *Journal of Applied Behavior Analysis,* 6 (1973), 115–24.

POOLEY, R. C., *Teaching English Grammar.* New York: Appleton-Century-Crofts, 1957.

POOLEY, R. C. and WILLIAMS, R. D., *The Teaching of English in Wisconsin.* Madison, Wisc.: University of Wisconsin Press, 1948.

POPHAM, W. J. and BAKER, E. I., *Systematic Instruction.* Englewood Cliffs, N.J.: Prentice-Hall, 1970.

POWELL, J. and HAKE, D. F., Positive *vs* Negative Reinforcement: A Direct Comparison of Effects on a Complex Human Response," *Psychological Record,* 21 (1971), 191–205.

PRYOR, K. W., HAAG, R., and O'REILLY, J., "The Creative Porpoise: Training for Novel Behavior," *Journal of the Experimental Analysis of Behavior,* 12 (1969), 653–62.

QUAY, H. C. and PETERSON, D. R., *Behavior Problem Checklist.* Champaign, Ill.: Children's Research Center, University of Illinois, 1967.

RAMP, E. and HOPKINS, B., eds., *A New Direction for Education: Behavior Analysis—1971.* Lawrence, Kansas: Support and Development Center for Follow Through, Department of Human Development, University of Kansas, 1971.

REDD, W. H. and BIRNBRAUER, J. S., "Adults as Discriminative Stimuli for Different Reinforcement Contingencies with Retarded Children," *Journal of Experimental Child Psychology,* 7 (1969), 440–47.

REYNOLDS. G. S., *A Primer of Operant Conditioning.* Glenview, Ill.: Scott, Foresman, 1968.

RICHMOND, J., EDDY, E., and GREEN, M., "Rumination: A Psychosomatic Syndrome of Infancy," *Pediatrics,* 22 (1958), 49–54.

RISLEY, T. R., "Behavior Modification: An Experimental-Therapeutic Endeavor," in L. A. Hamerlynck, P. O. Davidson, and L. E. Acker, eds., *Behavior Modification and Ideal Mental Health Services.* Alberta: University of Calgary, 1969.

———, "Learning and Lollipops," *Psychology Today* (January, 1968).

RISLEY, T. R. and CATALDO, M. F., "Evaluation of Planned Activities: The PLA-Check Measure of Classroom Participation," in P. O. Davidson, Clark, and L. A. Hamerlynck, eds., *Evaluation of Social _ rograms in*

Community, Residential and School Settings. Champaign, Ill.: Research Press, in press.

ROGERS, C. R., *On Becoming A Person.* Boston: Houghton Mifflin, 1961.

ROMANCZYK, R. G., KENT, R. N., DIAMENT, C., and O'LEARY, K. D., "Measuring the Reliability of Observational Data: A Reactive Process," *Journal of Applied Behavior Analysis,* 6 (1973), 175–84.

ROSE, S. D., "A Behavioral Approach to the Group Treatment of Parents," *Social Work,* 1969.

RULE, S., "A Comparison of Three Different Types of Feedback on Teachers' Performance," in G. Semb, et al. eds., *Behavior Analysis and Education— 1972,* pp. 278–89. Lawrence, Kansas: Support and Development Center for Follow Through, Department of Human Development, University of Kansas, 1972.

RYAN, T. A. and KRUMBOLTZ, J. D., "Effect of Planned Reinforcement Counseling on Client Decision-Making Behavior," *Journal of Counseling Psychology,* 11 (1964), 315–23.

SAJWAJ, T., "Difficulties in the Use of Behavioral Techniques by Parents to Change Child Behavior," *Journal of Nervous and Mental Disease,* in press.

SALZBERG, B. H., WHEELER, A. J., DEVAR, L. T., and HOPKINS, B. L., "The Effect of Intermittent Feedback and Intermittent Contingent Access to Play on Printing of Kindergarten Children," *Journal of Applied Behavior Analysis,* 4 (1971), 163–71.

SALZINGER, K., FELDMAN, R., and PORTNOY, S., "Training Parents of Brain-Injured Children in the Use of Operant Conditioning Procedures," *Behavior Therapy,* 1 (1970), 4–32.

SCHMIDT, G. W. and ULRICH, R. E., "Effects of Group Contingent Events upon Classroom Noise," *Journal of Applied Behavior Analysis,* 2 (1969), 171–79.

SCHUTTE, R. C. and HOPKINS, B. L., "The Effects of Teacher Attention on Following Instruction in a Kindergarten Class," *Journal of Applied Behavior Analysis,* 3 (1970), 117–22.

SEMB, G., ed., *Behavior Analysis and Education—1972.* Lawrence, Kansas: Support and Development Center for Follow Through, Department of Human Development, University of Kansas, 1972.

SIDMAN, M., *Tactics of Scientific Research.* New York: Basic Books, 1960.

SIDMAN, M. and STODDARD, L. T., "Programming Perception and Learning for Retarded Children," in N. R. Ellis, ed., *International Review of Mental Retardation Research,* Vol. II. New York: Academic, 1967.

SILBERSTEIN, R. M., "Priority Services for Children," in L. Bellak and H. H. Barten, eds., *Progress in Community Mental Health,* pp. 179–200. New York: Grune & Stratton, 1969.

SKINNER, B. F., *The Behavior of Organisms.* New York: Appleton-Century-Crofts, 1938.

———, *Science and Human Behavior.* New York: Macmillan, 1953.

———, "Some relations between behavior modification and basic research," in S. W. Bijou and E. Ribes-Inesta, eds., *Behavior Modification: Issues & Extensions,* pp. 1–6. New York: Academic, 1972.

———, *Walden Two.* New York: Macmillan, 1948.

SPITZ, R. A. and WOLF, K. M., "Anaclitic Depression: An Inquiry into the

Genesis of Psychiatric Conditions in Early Childhood," *Psychoanalytic Studies of the Child,* 2 (1946), 313–42.

STAATS, A. W. and BUTTERFIELD, W. H., "Treatment of Non-Reading in a Culturally Deprived Juvenile Delinquent: an Application of Reinforcement Principles," *Child Development,* 36 (1965), 925–42.

STAATS, A. W., FINLEY, J. R., MINKE, K. A., and WOLF, M., "Reinforcement Variables in the Control of Unit Reading Responses," *Journal of the Experimental Analysis of Behavior,* 7 (1964), 139–49.

STAATS, A. W., MINKE, K. A., FINLEY, J. R., WOLF, M., and BROOKS, L. O., "A Reinforcer System and Experimental Procedure for the Laboratory Study of Reading Acquisition," *Child Development,* 35 (1964), 209–321. (b)

STEDMAN, J. M., PETERSON, T. L., and CARDARELLE, J., "Application of a Token System in a Pre-adolescent Boys' Group," *Journal of Behavior Research and Experimental Psychiatry,* 2 (1971), 23–29.

STEINMAN, W. M., "The Social Control of Generalized Imitation," *Journal of Applied Behavior Analysis,* 3 (1970), 159–67.

STEVEN and FRIENDS, "So You Think Twin Oaks is a Behaviorist Community," *Leaves of Twin Oaks,* 2, no. 22 (1973), 10–11. First published in *Communities* 1, no. 1 (1972).

STUART, R. B., "Behavioral Contracting within the Families of Delinquents," paper delivered at the American Psychological Association convention, Miami Beach, 1970.

SULLIVAN ASSOCIATES, *Programmed Reading (Rev. ed.).* Webster, Mo.: McGraw-Hill, 1968.

SURRATT, P. E., ULRICH, R., and HAWKINS, R., "An Elementary Student as a Behavioral Engineer," *Journal of Applied Behavior Analysis,* 2 (1969), 85–92.

TALBOT, N. B. and HOWELL, M. C., "Social and Behavioral Causes and Consequences of Disease among Children," in N. B. Talbot, J. Kagan, and L. Eisenberg, eds., *Behavioral Science in Pediatric Medicine,* pp. 1–89. Philadelphia: Saunders, 1971.

TERRACE, H. S., "Stimulus Control," in W. K. Honig, ed., *Operant Behavior: Areas of Research and Application,* pp. 271–344. New York: Appleton-Century-Crofts, 1966.

THARP, R. G. and WETZEL, R. J., *Behavior Modification in the Natural Environment.* New York: Academic, 1969.

THOMAS, D. R., "Preliminary Finding on Self-Monitoring for Modifying Teacher Behavior," in E. A. Ramp and B. L. Hopkins, eds., *A New Direction for Education: Behavior Analysis—1971.* Lawrence, Kansas: Support and Development Center for Follow Through, Department of Human Development, University of Kansas, 1971.

THOMAS, D. R., BECKER, W. C., and ARMSTRONG, M., "Production and Elimination of Disruptive Classroom Behavior by Systematically Varying Teacher's Behavior," *Journal of Applied Behavior Analysis,* 1 (1968), 35–45.

TOSI, D. J., UPSHAW, K., LANDE, A., and WALDRON, M. A., "Group Counseling with a Non-Verbalizing Elementary Student: Differential Effects of Premack and Social Reinforcement Techniques," *Journal of Counseling*

Psychology, 18 (1971), 437–40.

ULMAN, J. D. and SULZER-AZAROFF, B., "Collective versus Individual Reinforcement of Academic Performance in Retarded Adults," unpublished paper, Southern Illinois University, 1972.

ULRICH, R. E., "Behavior Modification and the Role of the University in Effecting Social Change," paper read at the Second Symposium on Behavior Modification: Behavior Analysis Applied to Education, Mexico City, January, 1972.

————, "The Experimental Analysis of Behavior as a Systematic Approach to Teaching Psychology," paper read at American Psychological Association Convention, New York, September, 1966. Portions subsequently published with N. Kent as "Suggested Tactics for the Training of Psychologists," in R. E. Ulrich, T. Stachnik, and J. Mabry, eds., *Control of Human Behavior.* Vol. II: " From Cure to Prevention," pp. 288–98. Glenview, Ill.: Scott, Foresman, 1970.

ULRICH, R. E., ALESSI, G. J., and WOLF, M. M., "The Learning Village: An Alternate Approach to Traditional Education," in D. Packham, A. Cleary, and T. Mayes, eds., *Aspects of Educational Technology,* Vol. 5, pp.13–26. London: Putnam, 1971.

ULRICH, R. E., LOUISELL, S. E., and WOLF, M. M., "The Learning Village: A Behavioral Approach to Early Education," *Educational Technology.* 11 (1971), 32–48.

ULRICH, R. E., WOLF, M. M., and BLUHM, M., "Operant Conditioning in the Public Schools," *Behavior Modification Monographs,* 1 (1968).

VARGAS, M. J., "Changes in Self-Awareness During Client-Centered Therapy," in C. R. Rogers and R. F. Dymond, eds., *Psychotherapy and Personality Change.* Chicago: University of Chicago Press, 1954.

WAHLER, R. G., "Infant Social Development: Some Experimental Analyses of an Infant-Mother Interaction During the First Year of Life," *Journal of Experimental Child Psychology,* 7 (1969), 101–13.

————, "Setting Generality: Some Specific and General Effects on Child Behavior Therapy," *Journal of Applied Behavior Analysis,* 2 (1969), 239–46.

WAHLER, R. G., WINKEL, G. H., PETERSON, R. F., and MORRISON, D. C., "Mothers as Behavior Therapists for Their own Children," *Behavior Research and Therapy,* 3 (1965), 113–34.

WALKER, H. M. and BUCKLEY, N. K., "The Use of Positive Reinforcement in Conditioning Attending Behavior," *Journal of Applied Behavior Analysis,* 1 (1968), 245–50.

WALKER, H. M. and LEV, J., *Statistical Inference.* New York: Holt, Rinehart & Winston, 1953.

WALKER, H. M., MATTSON, R. H., and BUCKLEY, N. K., "Special Class Placement as a Treatment Alternative for Deviant Behavior in Children," in F. A. M. Benson, ed., *Modifying Deviant Social Behaviors in Various Classroom Settings.* Eugene, Ore.: University of Oregon, 1969.

WALLEN, N. E. and TRAVERS, R. M. W., "Analysis and Investigation of Teaching Methods," in N. L. Gage, ed., *Handbook of Research on Teaching,* p. 480. Chicago: Rand McNally, 1963.

WASIK, B. H., SENN, K., WELCH, R. H., and COOPER, B. R., "Behavior Modification with Culturally Deprived School Children: Two Case Studies," *Journal of Applied Behavior Analysis,* 2 (1969), 181–94.

WEINER, H., "Conditioning History and Human Fixed-Interval Performance," *Journal of the Experimental Analysis of Behavior,* 7 (1964), 383–85.

WEIS, L., "The Effects of Various Ratios of Teacher Contacts on the Response Rates of Kindergarten Children in a Programmed Reading Curriculum," unpublished Master's thesis, University of Kansas, 1971.

WHITE, G. D., NIELSEN, G., and JOHNSON, S. M., "Timeout Duration and the Suppression of Deviant Behavior in Children," *Journal of Applied Behavior Analysis,* 1973, in press.

WHITLOCK, C., "Note on Reading Acquisition: An Extension of Laboratory Principles," *Journal of Experimental Child Psychology,* 3 (1966), 83–85.

WIESEN, A. E., HARTLEY, G., RICHARDSON, C., and ROSKE, A., "The Retarded Child as a Reinforcing Agent," *Journal of Experimental Child Psychology,* 5 (1967), 109–13.

WILLIS, J. W. and WILLIS, J. S., "The Mental Health Worker as a Systems Behavioral Engineer," in Rosemary Sarri and Frank Maple, eds., *Schools in the Community,* pp. 211–32. Washington, D.C.: National Association of Social Workers, 1972.

WILNER, A. B., AYALA, H. E., FIXSEN, D. L., PHILLIPS, E. L. and WOLF, M. M., "Adolescent Preferences for Teaching-Parent Social Interactions," unpublished manuscript, University of Kansas, 1973.

WINCZE, J. P., LEITENBERG, H., and AGRAS, W. S., "The Effects of Token Reinforcement and Feedback on the Delusional Verbal Behavior of Chronic Paranoid Schizophrenics," *Journal of Applied Behavior Analysis,* 5 (1972), 247–62.

WOLF, M. M., GILES, D. K., and HALL, R. V., "Experiments with Token Reinforcement in a Remedial Classroom," *Behavior Research and Therapy,* 5 (1968), 51–64.

WOLF, M. M., PHILLIPS, E. L., and FIXSEN, D. L., "The Teaching-Family: A New Model for the Treatment of Deviant Child Behavior in the Community," in S. W. Bijou and E. L. Ribes-Inesta, eds., *Behavior Modification: Issues and Extensions.* New York: Academic, 1972.

ZEILBERGER, J., SAMPEN, L. E., and SLOANE, H. N., JR., "Modification of a Child's Problem Behaviors in the Home with the Mother as Therapist," *Journal of Applied Behavior Analysis,* 1 (1968), 47–53.

ZIMMERMAN, J., OVERPECK, C., EISENBERG, H., and GARLICK, B., "Operant Conditioning in a Sheltered Workshop." *Rehabilitation Literature,* 30 (1969), 326–34.

ZIMMERMAN, J., STUCKY, T. E., GARLICK, B. J., and MILLER, M., "Effects of Token Reinforcement on Productivity in Multiply Handicapped Clients in a Sheltered Workshop," *Rehabilitation Literature,* 30 (1969), 34–41.

ZUROMSKI, E. S. and SMITH, N. F., "A Simple Method for Visual Fading and Its Use in Correcting a Handwriting Deficiency," unpublished paper presented at Eastern Psychological Association, Boston, April, 1972.

Contributors

Stewart Agras, Stanford University School of Medicine

K. Eileen Allen, University of Kansas

Saul Axelrod, Temple University

Hector E. Ayala, University of Houston

Donald M. Baer, University of Kansas

Willie G. Brown, University of Kansas

Hewitt B. Clark, Johnny Cake Child Study Center, Mansfield, Arkansas

Rodney E. Copeland, University of Kansas and Juniper Gardens

Larry Doke, Moccasin Bend Psychiatric Hospital, Chattanooga, Tennessee

Victor A. Dotson, Western Michigan University

Richard Feallock, MacKinnon Phillip Hospital, Owen Sound, Ontario, Canada

Stephen R. Finfrock, Southwest Indian Youth Center, Tucson, Arizona

Dean L. Fixsen, University of Kansas

Richard G. Foxx, Anna State Hospital, Anna, Illinois

David K. Giles, Intermountain Youth Center, Tucson, Arizona

R. Vance Hall, University of Kansas and Juniper Gardens

Jasper W. Harris, University of Kansas and Juniper Gardens

V. William Harris, Southwest Indian Youth Center, Tucson, Arizona

Betty M. Hart, Juniper Gardens, Kansas City, Kansas

Joseph E. Hasazi, University of Vermont

Susan E. Hasazi, University of Vermont and Chittenden South School District

Edward J. Haupt, Montclair State College and Manhattan Children's Treatment Center, Montclair, N.J.

Robert P. Hawkins, West Virginia University

Tom R. Hobbs, Jefferson County Department of Public Health, Birmingham, Alabama

B. L. Hopkins, University of Kansas

Frances Degen Horowitz, University of Kansas

Donna Mae Ida, Appalachian State University and Western Carolina Center

Cindy R. Jacobson, University of Kansas

John D. Kidder, Rainier School, White River School District, Seattle, Wa.

Kathryn A. Kirigin, University of Kansas

Dorcas G. Kirkpatrick, Jefferson County School System, Birmingham, Ala.

Judith F. LaForge, University of Vermont and Chittenden South School District

Joetta Long, Florida State University

Thomas C. Lovitt, University of Washington

John W. Macrae, University of Kansas

Charles H. Madsen, Jr., Florida State University

J. E. Malaby, Eastern Washington State College

Karen Blase Maloney, Western Carolina Center, Morganton, N.C.

Kent W. Manley, Jefferson County School System, Birmingham, Ala.

T. F. McLaughlin, University of Kansas

Jack Michael, Western Michigan University

L. Keith Miller, University of Kansas

Adler J. Muller, Chittenden South School District, Hinesburg, Vermont

Jolena Paluska, Eastern Connecticut State College

Elery L. Phillips, University of Kansas

Mary M. Pierce, Chittenden South School District, Hinesburg, Vermont

Marybeth M. Pree, University of Vermont and Chittenden South School District

Herbert J. Rieth, University of Kansas and Juniper Gardens

Todd Risley, University of Kansas

Thomas Sajwaj, North Mississippi Retardation Center, Oxford, Mississippi

George Semb, University of Kansas

Susan Semb, Lawrence Unified School District #497, Lawrence, Kansas

Lawrence J. Siegal, University of Illinois at Urbana-Champaign

Deborah Deutsch Smith, George Peabody College for Teachers, Nashville, Tennessee

N. Rebecca Smith, Appalachian State University and Western Carolina Center

Warren M. Steinman, University of Illinois at Urbana-Champaign
Stephen I. Sulzbacher, University of Washington
Beth Sulzer-Azaroff, University of Connecticut
Thomas Terraciano, Montclair State College and Manhattan Children's Treatment Center, Montclair, N.J.
Philip C. Tsosie, Southwest Indian Youth Center, Tucson, Arizona
Keith D. Turner, Temple University
Jerome D. Ulman, Indianapolis Public Schools
Roger Ulrich, Western Michigan University
Maria J. Van Kirk, Montclair State College and Manhattan Children's Treatment Center, Montclair, N.J.
Jerry Willis, University of Western Ontario, London, Ontario, Canada
Montrose M. Wolf, University of Kansas

Index

Believability-of-experimental-effect function of reliability scores, 364-67
Bergman, Pat, 144-46
Beyond Freedom and Dignity (Skinner), 7
Birmingham School Consultation Project, 177
Brake, Jill, 139-41
Braukmann, Curtis J. 161-74
Brown, Willie G., 161-74

Capitalism, 5, 8-9, 10
Center for In-Service Teacher Education and Research, University of Alabama, 177
Child guidance model, 121-22
Children's Program, The, 101-11
Clark, Hewitt B., 187-202
Clark, Marilyn, 156-58
Classrooms, research in, 225-316
  assignment completion behavior, 309-18
  creative writing behaviors, 244-60
  disruptive behavior, modification of, 269-76
  facing procedure and arithmetic, 225-32
  minimum objectives and student progress, 261-68
  modeling techniques and arithmetic, 283-308
  reading assignments, 233-43
  spelling performance, 277-82
Cleaning system, in experimental living, 79-81
Collins, Mary, 134-37
Community-based juvenile correction programs, 310, 316
Competing-response theory, 42, 43
Complex behavior analysis, 384-85
Computerized system, responsive teaching and, 124-58
Condition-change interactions, minimizing, 386-89
Conditioned stimulus, 33
Contrast effects, 388-89
Control, 5, 7-8, 10, 56
Copeland, Rodney E., 124, 125
Cossairt, Ace, 147-49
Counseling, training program for, 175-86
Creative writing, effects on, 244-60
Credit system, in experimental living, 78-79
Crowder, Jeane, 139-41
Curriculum Research Classroom, University of Washington, 284

Day care
  behavioral engineers, children as, 341-56
  community-based, for older preschoolers, 100-11
  infants and, 111-21
  as psychiatric outpatient service, 96-123
  as strategy in social intervention, 98-99
Delgado, Jose, 56
Democracy, 7
Development, conceptualization of, 13-14
Discriminative stimuli, 17
Disruptive behaviors, modification of, 269-76
Dixon, Colleen, 144-46
Doke, Larry, 98, 100-121
Dotson, Victor A., 359-76
Drill procedure, number facts and, 225, 227-31
Drugs, 54-55

Edmark programs, 68
Educational research, multielement baseline design in, 377-91
Educational system, in experimental living, 91-93
Electric shock, 33, 35, 36, 40, 42, 43
Elementary school children
  as behavioral engineers, 319-28
  creative writing behaviors, 244-60
  modification of disruptive behavior, 269-76
  reading assignments, 233-43
Environmental changes, 39-42, 44
Estes, W. K., 34, 35, 42, 43
Experimental designs, 17, 18, 264, 271-72, 378
Experimental living, 46-61, 72-96
  self-government, 85-93
  worksharing, 75-85
Experimental Living Project, 75-95
Extinction, 33-35

Fading procedure, 225-32
Feallock, Richard, 72-96
Federal funding agency, 23
Finance system, in experimental living, 89-91
Finfrock, Stephen R., 309-18
Fining, 190-91, 192
Fixed-page assignments, 233-43
Fixed-time assignments, 233-43
Fixsen, Dean L., 29, 75, 161-74
Food program, in experimental living, 81-82

DATE DUE			
DE 6 '77			
MAY 9 '78			
May 27			
OC 31 78			
DE 5 78			
DE 19 78			
AP 15			
MY 6			
FE 15			